Proliferation of the Internet Economy:
E-Commerce for Global Adoption, Resistance, and Cultural Evolution

Mahmud Akhter Shareef
Carleton University, Ottawa, Canada

Yogesh Kumar Dwivedi
Swansea University, UK

Michael D. Williams
Swansea University, UK

Nitish Singh
Boeing Institute of Internatonal Business, St. Louis University, USA

T0336178

Information Science
REFERENCE

INFORMATION SCIENCE REFERENCE

Hershey · New York

Director of Editorial Content:	Kristin Klinger
Senior Managing Editor:	Jamie Snavely
Managing Editor:	Jeff Ash
Assistant Managing Editor:	Carole Coulson
Typesetter:	Jeff Ash
Cover Design:	Lisa Tosheff
Printed at:	Yurchak Printing Inc.

Published in the United States of America by
Information Science Reference (an imprint of IGI Global)
701 E. Chocolate Avenue, Suite 200
Hershey PA 17033
Tel: 717-533-8845
Fax: 717-533-8661
E-mail: cust@igi-global.com
Web site: http://www.igi-global.com/reference

and in the United Kingdom by
Information Science Reference (an imprint of IGI Global)
3 Henrietta Street
Covent Garden
London WC2E 8LU
Tel: 44 20 7240 0856
Fax: 44 20 7379 0609
Web site: http://www.eurospanbookstore.com

Library of Congress Cataloging-in-Publication Data

Proliferation of the Internet economy: e-commerce for global adoption, resistance and cultural evolution / by Mahmud Akhter Shareef .ı. [et al.].
    p. cm.
Includes bibliographical references and index. Summary: "This book specifically develops theories to understand service quality and quality management practice of EC which is completely a new and innovative effort to formulate perceptions of global consumers"--Provided by publisher.

ISBN 978-1-60566-412-5 (hardcover) -- ISBN 978-1-60566-413-2 (ebook) 1. Electronic commerce. 2. Electronic commerce--Technological innovations. 3. Information technology. 4. Internet--Economic aspects. I. Shareef, Mahmud Akhter, 1966-

HF5548.32.P78 2009
 658.8'72--dc22

                            2008047732

British Cataloguing in Publication Data
A Cataloguing in Publication record for this book is available from the British Library.

Dedication

To my parents for their love and eternal blessings
Mahmud A. Shareef

To my brother, Dr. Dinesh Dwivedi, for his blessings, support and ever lasting
motivation
Yogesh K. Dwivedi

To my sons, Jonathan, David, and Peter, the best any father could wish for
Michael D. Williams

Table of Contents

Foreword... ix

Preface.. xi

Acknowledgment.. xviii

Division I
E-Commerce: A Global Phenomenon

Chapter I
Introduction to E-Commerce... 1
Abstract 1
Introduction... 1
Background 3
E-Commerce: A Global Phenomenon.. 5
References.. 7

Chapter II
E-Commerce Background.. 9
Abstract 9
Introduction... 9
Evolution of the Internet 11
Electronic-Commerce 15
References 33

Division II
Service Quality for Global Consumers

Chapter III
Service Quality of E-Commerce for Global Consumers 40
Abstract 40
Introduction 40
Electronic-Commerce Service Quality 41
Models of EC Service Quality 44
Service Quality, Cultural Diversity, and EC Adoption and Proliferation 55
Related Issues 56
References 57

Chapter IV
Global Quality Management Practice for E-Commerce 65
Abstract 65
Introduction 65
Quality and Quality Management Practice 67
Quality Concepts for EC 68
Quality Management Practice 71
Conclusion 72
References 74

Division III
Adoption, Proliferation, and Resistance:
Impact and Globalization

Chapter V
E-Commerce Diffusion: Critical Factors Affecting Diffusion of
E-Commerce 79
Abstract 79
Introduction 80
Diffusion of E-Commerce 82
Impacts of Diffusion 84
Prime Stakeholders of Diffusion of E-Commerce 87
Critical Factors Affecting Diffusion of E-Commerce 90
Conclusion and Future Research Direction 98
References 100

Chapter VI
Diffusion of E-Commerce in Developed and Developing Countries:
Comparative Studies... **107**
Abstract 107
Case Studies 107
Comparative Statement 133
References 136

Chapter VII
E-Commerce Adoption in Developing Countries... **140**
Abstract 140
Introduction 140
Literature Review on EC Adoption 143
Perspectives and Process of Adoption 146
Theoretical Framework for EC Adoption 148
Conclusion and Future Research Direction 157
References 159

Chapter VIII
Influencing Factors and the Acceptance of Internet and E-Business
Technologies in Maritime Canada's SMEs: An Analysis **168**
Abstract 168
Introduction 169
Background Information 170
Research Methodology 174
Data Analysis and Results 175
Findings and Discussions 178
Conclusion 180
Acknowledgment 182
References 182
Appendix 184

Chapter IX
Effect of Proliferation and Resistance of Internet Economy:
Understanding Impact of Information and Communication Technology
in Developing Countries **186**
Abstract 186
Introduction 187
Purposes of Promoting Internet Economy 189
Barriers Against Proliferation of Internet Economy 195
Readiness, Digital Divide, and Capability 201

Impact of ICT and Conceptual Framework 203
Conclusion and Future Research Direction 211
References 213

Division IV
Globalization of E-Commerce: Cultural Adaptation

Chapter X
Globalization and Relevant Strategy for E-Commerce **222**
Abstract 222
Introduction 222
Definition of Related Concepts 227
Functional Characteristics and Issues of EC for Globalization 229
Literature Review: Globalization Strategy 230
Theoretical Framework for Strategy 232
Conclusion 240
References 242

Chapter XI
Culturally Customizing International Web Sites **251**
Abstract 251
Introduction 251
Localization 254
Importance of Web Site Cultural Customization 256
Depiction of Culture on International Web Sites 258
Impact of Web Site Cultural Customization 262
Conclusion 263
References 264

Chapter XII
A Cultural Perspective on Web Site Localization **269**
Abstract 269
Introduction 270
The Localization Model 272
A Brief Literature Review of Web Site Localization 274
Examples of Good and Bad Practices in Web Site Localization 276
The Localization Model: Why and How Useful? 277
Conclusion and Implications 277
References 279

Chapter XIII
Conclusion, Implications, and Future Trends

Conclusion, Implications, and Future Trends 281
Abstract...281
Introduction 281
Conclusion..282
Managerial Implications 288
Future Trends..291

About the Authors.. **293**

Index.. **297**

Foreword

In the last decade Electronic Commerce has grown from basic trading models and the supply chain to more sophisticated applications focussing on customers, business partners, governments, virtual communities, standards, redress and reverse logistics. The principles of E-Commerce have been adopted and extended to other sectors such as E-Government, E-Research, E-Management, E-Health, E-Tourism, E-Banking, and E-Learning using the ubiquitous and universally accepted technology, the Internet. E-Commerce applications in the private sector has seen an era of rapid development and adoption, the crash and a renewed expansion due to the demands and benefits of the digital world, cost savings, mobility, ubiquity and extensive use of technology as well as globalisation.

A unique characteristic of E-Commerce is a 24/7 shop front to the global community. This feature has not only extended business worldwide, it is resulting in an appreciation of cultural and language issues in different parts of the world, universal payment methods and the need for international standards in disparate jurisdictions. E-Commerce has not only revolutionised the trading trends of the world it has transformed the back-end processes supporting businesses, modes of communication with partners and stakeholders, marketing techniques, information and records management methods and information and knowledge sharing within and outside organisations.

The increased adoption of E-Commerce worldwide is clear evidence of its diffusion in both developed and developing countries. However, E-Commerce entails technology-based transactions because of which a large percentage of the world's population is unable to take advantage of the benefits of E-Commerce. The digital divide due to access and ownership, income and education, rural population, developing nations, culture and age is even today, a barrier to E-Commerce.

This book, "Proliferation of the Internet Economy: E-Commerce for the Global Adoption, Resistance and Cultural Evolution", includes chapters addressing pertinent issues of E-Commerce development, adoption, proliferation in the global markets and the implications of digital divide supported with theories, frameworks, methodologies and implications for managers. It is definitely a valuable resource with rich information on issues on the evolution of E-Commerce, adoption patterns, issues for further expansion and strategies for overcoming barriers. The first part of the book provides a general introduction to E-Commerce concepts and its global nature, the second part of the book is related to diffusion and adoption of E-Commerce depicting its proliferation in global markets and the third part of the book includes theoretical explanations of issues related to E-Commerce in developed and developing countries highlighting future implications for overcoming cultural and digital divide barriers.

I am honoured to have been asked to write the *Forward* to this book and am very pleased to recommend this book to readers who require an understanding of the developments in E-Commerce, its adoption and diffusion patterns, its adaptation in terms of the global context and barriers of the digital divide. It is high quality learning and reference resource on the proliferation of E-Commerce since its inception.

Professor Mohini Singh
RMIT University
Australia
August 2008

Preface

The rapid expansion and adoption of the Internet throughout the entire world, increased purchasing power and huge market of developing countries, and recent extensive movement of globalization create enormous opportunities for E-Commerce (EC) to diffuse throughout the whole world. From this perspective, it is a challenging and burning issue for market researchers to conceptualize the proliferation and globalization of Information and communication Technology (ICT) and EC, for both consumers and countries, and also from a global perspective. Diffusion of the Internet has made a revolutionary change in the methodology of operating business. Therefore, it is both an interesting and challenging issue to address, explore, and conceptualize proliferation of EC and also adoption, cultural resistance, and evolution for global consumers. This book is designed to conceptualize the functions, proliferation, diffusion, cultural resistance, and impact of EC on the global economy. The book is engaged in addressing the adoption of and cultural resistance to Business-to-Consumer (B2C) EC of global consumers. Therefore, mentioning E-Commerce (EC) will signify and mean B2C E-Commerce in this book unless it is mentioned otherwise. However, some significant relevance of Business-to-Business (B2B) E-Commerce and E-government (EG) will also be investigated and revealed in a comparative and comprehensive manner in this book. The overall mission of this book reflects the contemporary issues of EC in a comprehensive manner and is engaged in providing basic paradigms, concepts and understandings of EC proliferation and globalization, plausible resistances and barriers due to socio-economical and cultural differences, religious beliefs, availability of resources, education and training, and government controls between developed and developing countries, and their impact on the future international market economy. By nature, practice, and method of proliferation, EC is inherently global. Nevertheless, its present adoption, operation, and proliferation are basically limited in developed countries to highly technology-oriented people. Therefore, for true globalization of EC, its adoption, usage, proliferation, and barriers in economically, culturally, and technologically diverged countries need clear understanding. We aim to address these issues and develop sequentially the paradigms and theoretical framework of scope and barriers of diffusion of Internet-based economy in different segmented markets, especially in the developing countries. We also provide an integrated view of EC diffusion from developed to developing countries and comprehensive concepts of the standardized market of globalized EC in this book. The book also organizes inference to understand differences in the adoption and usage criteria of EC between developed and developing countries in organizational, financial, market, and consumer aspects. To conceptualize the aforementioned concepts and ideas, the book shall fulfill the following objectives:

1. To address and discuss concepts and theories relevant to consumers' behavioral intentions, trust disposition attitude, purchase behavior, cultural differences, technology acceptance attitude, and adoption and proliferation of ICT
2. To provide an understanding of the necessity for EC proliferation from a globalization perspective
3. To identify the present condition, intentions, and fundamental capabilities of different segmented countries to adopt EC, possible barriers and resistance from socio-economical and cultural aspects, and its impact on the globalization of EC and the international market economy
4. To conceptualize multilevel factors affecting adoption, usage, and proliferation of EC among consumers of different segmented countries and to provide inference to understand the differences between developed and developing countries from this perspective
5. To explore, identify, and organize global issues and policies related to the diffusion of ICT and public and private organizational and market implications on both a macro and micro level for diffusion of ICT throughout the world through the emerging movement of globalization

These objectives are explored using ICT, marketing, service quality, organizational reformation, and globalization theories and related discourses. Addressing culture and its impact on certain apparently non-stoppable technology diffusion trends is always a challenging issue. This challenge imports more vulnerable debates when it is associated with international market economy, digital divide, and the burning issue of globalization. We, therefore, very much careful to address the debates, bypass them, and raise the debates in pertaining proliferation of EC and its semantic effect on pragmatic market economy.

The proliferation and globalization of EC throughout the world, the barriers due to socio-economical, cultural, and political factors, and the impact on future international market economy are recent areas for practitioners, researchers, and policymakers to address, investigate, and conceptualize. Only recently a few practitioners and researchers have started to explore this issue of EC diffusion in different segmented countries which is anticipated to provide enormous opportunities for the 21st Century. National and international policymakers are also starting to analyze different aspects of this issue through different globalization paradigms. As a result, only a few conference and journal papers as well as technical and policy recommendation reports have been published in this area. As far as it is known, there are no books yet published specifically related to this burning issue of the contemporary international market. As a result, at present, practitioners, academics, and policymakers who are searching for information in this issue, have to spend a lot of time and effort identifying, gathering, and synthesizing literature from different fields. Therefore, this book will have significant implications and will contribute potential advantages to the existing literature. We organize the book to impart to readers the necessary background information, concepts, and strategies to build the paradigms and fundamental discourses of globalization of EC. Then we discuss the principal issues of Internet economy related to scope and barriers for proliferation of EC globally and develop theoretical concepts of the pertaining effects of these diverged phenomena on the international market economy.

The book contains four divisions to provide, address, and explore four broad fields of issues of EC proliferation. The first division discusses background and general concepts related to EC as a global phenomenon. The second division explains perceived service qualities and the strategic quality management practice of EC for globalization. The third division conceptualizes EC adoption criteria, the effect of diffusion and resistance, and the impact of ICT proliferation with particular attention to developing countries. In this connection, this division also provides a precise description of E-Government to conceptualize one of the major applications of online systems in the public sector to encapsulate the digital divide as the irresistible and undeniable force of ICT proliferation in developing countries. The fourth division illustrates explicit paradigms of EC globalization and cultural adaptation in developed and developing countries. This division also includes conclusion, future trends, and detailed implications of the revealed paradigms. The four divisions are again divided into 13 independent but sequential parts, called chapters. Each chapter consists of a few sections and sub-sections. Excluding these regular sections and sub-sections, abstract and a list of references are also included in each chapter. In this book, we sequentially address the main issues and concepts of technology diffusion, E-Commerce present status in developed countries and proliferation in developing countries, socio-economic and cultural aspects as scope and barriers for this proliferation and its impact on the international market economy and globalization. This book intertwines different issues, as mentioned before, as a comprehensive concept to present a holistic perspective of the future Internet market economy. A brief description of each division, chapter, and section is provided below.

To conceptualize functions, proliferation, diffusion, cultural resistance, and impact on the global economy of EC, we would like to address and explain some related issues, concepts, and paradigms of EC as a global phenomenon at the beginning. The first division of this book presents a general introduction and the related concepts of E-Commerce. This division has two chapters to integrate those issues.

The first chapter is the general introduction part of this book. It addresses the background of the topic, its origin and global aspects. It has three sections to deal with the above-mentioned ideas.

Chapter II deals with the concepts of EC and its related issues in a global context. This chapter consists of three sections with sub-sections. It includes an introduction to EC and describes the evolution of one of its basic components, that is, the Internet. Then this chapter sheds light on the definition, classification, distinct characteristics, proliferation, adoption, globalization, and management issues related to EC. This chapter also briefly explains the concepts of M-Commerce, an emerging issue of the present market which is a subset of EC and E-Government (EG) which is conceptually very close to EC.

The second division explains the distinct characteristics of EC to conceptualize service quality of EC for global consumers and expands its scope to illustrate strategic quality management practice. This division has two chapters.

When we conjecture that EC is inherently global, global consumers' perception of service quality, grounded on cultural and social diversity, is a potential criterion to be addressed and analyzed. Chapter III of the book is designed to impart some general ideas about expectation and performance of different service quality attributes for B2C EC, as revealed by different researchers. This chapter is divided into five sections with Section II further split into subsections.

Implementation of quality management practice in EC is a relatively new and challenging area to researchers and management authorities. The proliferation of EC provides an opportunity for quality management practitioners to conceptualize quality dimensions suitable for globalization of EC. Chapter IV focuses on the quality dimensions required for launching a successful global EC. Implementation of quality management principles and practice in an EC context is a new theme which needs extensive research in the future. This chapter is divided into five sections with Section III divided into subsections.

The success of technology acceptance and successive diffusion is heavily dependent on the adoption capability, the way it is diffused in private and public sectors, and how it is adopted by the adopters. Diffusion of EC has multi-dimensional aspects, and the process of diffusion is controlled by cultural diversity. Division III is concentrated on the issues related to diffusion and adoption of EC and the impact and resistance of proliferation globally. This division has five chapters.

Chapter V addresses, reveals, and reshapes different aspects of diffusion of EC. The whole chapter is divided into six sections. Our fundamental efforts in this chapter are designated to developing epistemological and ontological paradigms of diffusion of EC which would contribute to form the desired framework of critical factors of EC diffusion.

Drawing inference from the proposed EC diffusion framework in Chapter V, we aim to investigate, identify, and illustrate the overall condition of some developed and developing countries in terms of diffusion of EC in Chapter VI. In this chapter, we have viewed some cases of diffusion of EC in the light of the theoretical framework as revealed in Chapter V. We have divided this chapter into two sections with Section II further divided into subsections.

Chapter VII is aimed at providing a fundamental conceptual framework for adoption of EC by the consumers of developing countries. This chapter is divided into five sections. After the introduction section, Chapter VII addresses and discusses the existing literature to get a deep insight into the adoption criteria of EC. Then it explains the adoption process and develops a theoretical framework for factors enabling adoption of EC among consumers of developing countries. Finally, a conclusion is drawn.

Chapter VIII is also designed to reveal adoption factors of Internet and EC technologies. However, it is focused on Maritime Canada's SMEs (small- and medium-sized enterprises). This study intends to examine the impact of relevant factors on the acceptance of Internet and E-business technologies in SMEs based in a region of the country with relatively poor indicators. The study draws upon a theoretical framework in the information system (IS) literature and other relevant insights in discussing the topic. Based on the research hypotheses, an empirical study is conducted. Then through proper statistical analysis, the discussions and conclusion of the study are presented with managerial implications. The chapter has six sections with subsections.

Chapter IX of the book explores and illustrates the overall impact of the Internet economy among developing countries. We have not focused on developed countries, because the positive effect of ICT on developed countries is quite obvious, and developed countries have already utilized and are also capitalizing on full features of ICT in the Internet economy by launching E-Government (EG) in the public sector and also guiding EC in the private sector. However, developing countries are at the preliminary stage in this context, so it is a challenging issue to address and evaluate the impact of proliferation of the Internet economy on the developing countries for the sake of globalization. This chapter is divided into six sections to conceptualize the purpose of proliferation of the Internet economy, possible barriers, different outcomes of the effect of this proliferation and barriers, and theoretical paradigms of the impact of the Internet economy.

Division IV is designed to provide detailed theoretical explanations of issues related to globalization of EC both for developed and developing countries by shedding in-depth light on cultural adaptation capability. Evidences of findings are also provided by some case studies. This division has four chapters including a conclusive chapter which precisely comprehends the theoretical light of this book with anticipating future trends and implications of the findings.

As one of the most topical issues, proliferation of EC and globalization has substantially captured the attention of practitioners, academicians, policy makers, and readers, and this has led to the development of a new theoretical framework to encompass the globalization strategies of EC. In Chapter IX, we provide a theoretical framework as the globalization strategy for EC. This chapter is divided into six sections to explain the related concepts of EC globalization, issues of globalization, existing literature of globalization of Internet economy, and globalization framework with a conclusion.

The continuing growth in global online markets necessitates companies to attract international consumers and motivate online transactions. Marketers are faced with the question of whether to culturally adapt their web sites or launch standardized global web sites. To conceptualize this issue, Chapter XI provides an insight as to whether the Web is a culturally neutral medium of communication or a medium impregnated with cultural values. Most marketers equate their ability to tap into the global online market by simply creating multilingual international Web sites. This chapter shows that effective international web presence is not just about translating a Web site into a local language. A truly localized Web site is one that is linguistically, technically and, most importantly, culturally customized to locale-specific requirements. This chapter has six sections which sequentially describe localization and cultural customization of Web sites with conclusive remarks.

The aim of Chapter XII is to provide deep insights into the cultural adaptation of EC Web sites. This chapter deals with the same issues as Chapter XI; however, it includes a more rigorous view of the cultural impact on globalization of EC. This chapter has six sections with sub-sections to discuss the introduction to the issue, literature review, and development of a theoretical framework, examples of good and bad practices in Web site localization, conclusion, and marketing implications.

Chapter XIII is designed to comprehend and integrate the epistemological and ontological paradigms of EC developed in this book through an extensive literature review, case studies, and the theoretical concepts of psychology, sociology, service, organization, marketing, international business, culture, and information technology as the conclusion. Then this chapter explains the implications of the findings of this book and anticipates future trends of EC as a global phenomenon. This chapter is divided into four sections to present the introduction, conclusion, implications, and future trends with a research direction.

This book provides exhaustive coverage on EC proliferation and globalization issues as well as cultural adoption and barriers in this connection. The authors hope that this will provide a significant contribution to the area of online systems proliferation in general and, specifically, to the adoption, diffusion, and cultural resistance of EC amongst global consumers.

However, in order to make further research progress and improvements in the area of adoption, diffusion, resistance, and cultural evolution of EC, we would like to welcome feedback and comments about this book from the readers. Comments and constructive suggestions can be sent to us care of IGI Global at the address provided at the beginning of the book.

Acknowledgment

The ideas presented in this book have been developed as a result of advice and assistance offered by a number of people. It is by the grace of God and the will of the Almighty that we take this opportunity to convey our regards and thanks to those who have helped and supported us at different stages in the completion of the book.

This book would not have been possible without the co-operation and assistance of the staff at IGI Global. We would like to thank our associates at IGI Global, namely Jan Travers for managing the contract and Heather Probst for managing this project and especially for answering queries and helping to keep this project on schedule.

Division I
E–Commerce: A Global Phenomenon

Chapter I
Introduction to E-Commerce

ABSTRACT

The growth, integration, and sophistication of ICT are changing our society and economy. The emergence of the Internet as a general communication channel has opened the opportunity for E-Commerce (EC) to expand worldwide. EC is now viewed by researchers and practitioners as providing the future direction in which organizations must move. Diffusion of the Internet has led to significant shifts in the methodology of operating business globally. Therefore, it is both an interesting and challenging issue to address, explore, and conceptualize proliferation of EC and also adoption and cultural resistance and evolution for global consumers.

1.1. INTRODUCTION

John Chambers, CEO, Cisco Systems believes that:

"Over the next two decades, the Internet economy will bring about more dramatic changes in the way we work, live, play, and learn than we witnessed during the last

200 years of the industrial revolution." (Hancock, 2002, quoted from 2000 Cisco Systems Annual Report).

Software guru Bill Gates, in his famous book Business @ the Speed of Thought (1999), powered this argument by saying "The fundamental rule of Business is: Internet Changes everything".

11th century Europe observed the evolution of credit-based banking systems. These concepts are still running with their modified forms (Chown, 1994). They underpin all modern forms of financial transactions. The adoption of information technology has raised the prospect of radical change to this traditional model. For the last fifteen years, information technology has gained a revolutionary strength, which ensures the transformation of the basic mechanisms of business. This transformation is accelerated and supported by computer-based applications to business processes (Miers, 1996). The emergence of the Internet as a general communication channel has opened the opportunity for Electronic-commerce (EC) to expand worldwide. The proliferation of the Internet and Internet based economy, extensive use and adoption of information and communication technology (ICT), and the changing consumer process brought about through electronic communities are likely to lead to a new wave of reengineering, reformations, mergers, and acquisitions. This proliferation of EC also significantly affects traditional marketing concepts. Once the CEO of Kodak concluded that he could not tell if the Kodak website can create money. However, he recognized it was important because it was the acceptable way of selling products since door-to-door salespersons, now the consumers are knocking on Kodak's door.

Following industrial revolution in Europe, whatever definitions are used for the electronic revolution, it is recognized that these changes take place globally. For example, global competition, interest rates, laws and regulations, social concerns, industry traditions, consumer preferences, market segmentation, globalization, cultural impact, shift of central global economy from the west to   Asian giants, like Singapore, China, South Korea, Malaysia, Thailand, Taiwan, Hong Kong, Philippine, India are all part of the broader market economy which can affect all business activities.

Two contemporary social, cultural, and economic trends are globalization, and the widespread proliferation of EC and ICT. EC is now viewed by researchers and practitioners as providing the future direction in which organizations must move to facilitate the conducting of both business-to-business (B2B) transactions and business-to-customer (B2C) transactions. Diffusion of the Internet has led to significant shifts in the methodology of operating business globally. Therefore, it is both an interesting and challenging issue to address, explore, and conceptualize proliferation of EC and also adoption and cultural resistance and evolution for global consumers. This chapter is the general introduction part of this book. It addresses background of the topic, its origin and global aspects. It has three sections to deal with the above-mentioned ideas.

1.2. BACKGROUND

The growth, integration, and sophistication of ICT are changing our society and economy. Now computers all over the world are connected via the Internet. Consumers now can use the Internet through computers and other mobile devices to interact with sellers and transact within no time. Businesses use networks even more extensively to conduct and re-engineer production processes and streamline procurement processes, reach new customers, and manage internal operations. This electronic revolution in global economy is spurring additional investments in facilities, hardware, software, services, and human capital. This advent and proliferation of ICT has changed the structure and performance of the global market, consumers' perception, and purchasing behavior.

The Internet potentially offers individuals, institutions, small and large businesses, all communities, and all levels of government with new opportunities for learning, interacting, transacting business, and developing their social and economic potential. However, availability, adoption, usage, and proliferation of the Internet, the most emerging technology of the 21st century is very insignificant in developing countries in respect to developed countries. The adoption and extension of ICT is now a major concern in developing countries. Accoring to Lanvin (1995), the development of global technology infrastructure is imperative for both the developed and developing countries to focus the image of business organizations and to exploit the global market (Wilson, 2001). It plays a significant role in the present information and knowledge based market by planning, generating, managing, and transmitting information in the most effective way through the modern information technology to provide easy access and availability across the countries and to invite potential customers by providing necessary information through the Internet.

History of EC dates back to the invention of the very old notion of sell and buy, electricity, cables, computers, modems, and the Internet. EC became reality in 1991 when the Internet was opened to commercial use. Since then, millions of businesses have been operated through web sites. EC has a great deal of advantages over traditional brick and mortar stores and mail order catalogs. Consumers can view prices, create their orders, and buy these from anywhere in the world. Web retailers also get explicit benefits from this method of electronic business. Now web retailers can reach customers globally without expensive advertising campaign. Web technology allows vendors to identify potential customers and satisfy them through customization.

"E-commerce use and applications in all aspects of work and life are expected to flourish exponentially as the Internet becomes even more ubiquitous and secure throughout the developed world," said BSA President and CEO Robert Holleyman. "And while 2001 has presented both economic challenges and global tragedies, long-term confidence remains uniquely strong in the software and information technology industries." Despite the shakeout in Internet retailing, online shopping continues to grow. EC has demonstrated promise as the channel of choice for consumers. EC based on information technology can provide many advantages: time and cost saving, instant information transfer, as well as global communication without time and space constraints.

The systematic strategy of globalization opens new barriers, scopes, and opportunities for global corporations. Internet and electronic transaction have created this wide spread scope for the firms. The opportunities include access to new markets that were previously closed due to cost, regulation, or indirect barriers, the ability to tap resources such as labor, capital, and knowledge on a worldwide basis, and the opportunity to participate in global production networks that are becoming prevalent in many industries. The adoption of online shopping channel makes it cheaper and easier for firms to extend their markets, manage their operations, and coordinate value chains across borders (Globerman *et al.,* 2001; Williams *et al.,* 2001; Cavusgil, 2002). Adoption of EC fosters globalization by reducing transaction and coordination costs and creating new and expanded markets with economies of scale (Steinfield *et al.,* 1999; Mann *et al.,* 2000). Firm globalization is heralded as a key driver of EC diffusion (Steinfield *et al.,* 1999). Due to worldwide proliferation of the Internet, the main vehicle of EC, EC is also spreading exponentially throughout the whole world among the consumers of both developed and developing countries. Adoption, usage, and proliferation of EC by the customers are enhanced for the distinctive characteristics of EC, like speed, time, location, cost, and availability of alternatives.

However, certain characteristics of services create problems for their globalization. Examples of such characteristics are the nature of the output or performance, customer involvement, human interaction during the service experience, quality control problems, perception of service quality by the customers, lack of inventory, importance of the time factor, cultural differences, religious beliefs, behavioral attitude, availability of electronic channels of distribution, and government controls (Lovelock *et al.,* 1996). Nevertheless, not every service is equally affected by these characteristics. Services that require limited or no physical contact are easier to standardize globally (Chase et al., 1978; Lovelock et al., 1996). Therefore, EC, characterized by virtual environment is a compatible industry for globalization. According to Yip (2000), "the general effect [of the Internet] is to strengthen the drivers of globalization and weaken or bypass the barriers. However, cultural differences, religious beliefs, availability of resources, unfamiliarity with modern ICT, level of education, income disparity, behavioral and trust dispositional attitudes, and government controls still play significant constraints for EC to globalize.

1.3. E-COMMERCE: A GLOBAL PHENOMENON

Globalization of EC is contingent on several factors, and consequently demands the understanding of governments' censoring role on adoption of ICT and proliferation of EC inside countries and also customers' characteristics and behavioral intention, and the fundamental attributes which make these characteristics significantly different for different nations/states or cultures. Especially, developed countries are not strict in controlling proliferation of EC inside their business periphery, and their customers are not very much reluctant in responding to EC transaction, because:

For governments of developed countries:

1. Proliferation of EC in developed countries is going too fast to control.
2. Basically principal EC organizations are the companies of developed countries.
3. Public policies of these countries are not restrictive and rules and regulation to conduct business are very much flexible.
4. Freedom of rights and justice is much more proclaimed.
5. Governments are democratic and supportive to flourish private sector.
6. EC particularly is enhancing their competitive advantage in global market, i.e. at present, developed countries are the beneficiaries of the proliferation of the Internet.

For citizens of developed countries:

1. Internet penetration rate is very high.
2. Digital divide is lower than developing countries.
3. Resources like the Internet, telecommunication, and PCs are available.
4. Skill and familiarity with modern ICT is very high.
5. Technology adoption and diffusion criteria are better.
6. Culture is more adaptive.
7. Financially more people are solvent.
8. They have more trust disposition attitudes towards states laws and policies of business organizations, because freedom of rights is protected by governments.

Consequently, a major percentage of on-line purchase is contributed by the developed countries like the USA, Canada, Japan, UK, France, Germany, Denmark, Sweden, Norway, Spain, Italy, Australia, New Zealand etc. But advanced developing countries like China, India, Mexico, Brazil, Malaysia, South Korea, Taiwan, Singapore, Thailand, South Africa etc. and other developing countries are gradually entering in Internet based markets with significant reflection of promise (GVU's www User Survey Team, 1998). With the on-going efforts to build global information infrastructure as well as world wide internet, developing countries are at the enthusiastic pace of turbulent shifts to firmly embrace information age (Lee *et al.,* 1999). Although the percentage of E-purchase from developing countries is still very low, it is growing and shows enough criteria to forecast about its steady growing in the foreseeable future. In this context, to expand business arena and to gain advance competitiveness globally, EC organizations should be capable to differentiate as well as to capture and identify adoption criteria of the customers of both developed and developing countries. Because it is strongly argued that there are some valid factors to explain the differences between the acceptance of EC in developed countries and developing countries (Lee *et al.,* 1999). Diffusion of EC, i.e., global adoption, usage, and proliferation of EC depends on some critical factors like, proliferation of and familiarity with ICT, availability of resources, customers' adoption capability, behavioral intention, quality perception, external facilities, internal arrangement, socio-economical issues, cultural and religious aspects, state of democracy, rules and regulations, trade policy, and globalization strategy. Diffusion and globalization of traditional brick and mortar business organizations has been investigated for more than two decades; especially it was fueled when Levitt (1983) announced his authoritarian doctrine about standardized approach of globalization in his seminal study. However, hardly any scholarly articles addressed proliferation and globalization of Electronic-commerce (EC), especially B2C EC and its plausible impact on socio-economic and cultural issues.

EC is inherently global whereas its present application is limited within developed countries. Since the Internet, the media of EC has been extended globally; Electronic-retailers are enthusiastically very keen and eager to expand their EC operation globally, which, in future, might reflect major share of international business. Under this perspective, practitioners are very interested to learn about diffusion of EC in developing countries. Future extension of EC and globalization strategy of Electronic-retailers significantly depends on the findings of this type of research. For the last one decade, national and international policymakers are investigating international technology diffusion and technology failure with special priority on developing countries, globalization strategy to capture huge market of developing countries, and adoption and extension of EC in developing countries. To capitalize the prospects of EC proliferation under proper globalization strategy and to interconnect less advanced countries with global information technology and international business, policymakers of both developed and developing countries are prioritizing the aforementioned issues with extensive efforts. Therefore, understanding proliferation and globalization of ICT and EC and exploring possible barriers and resistances for such proliferation due to socio-economical and cultural differences and government controls have significant implications both for information technology and international business literature, electronic business organizations, and policymakers of developed and developing countries.

REFERENCES

Cavusgil, S. T. (2002). Extending the Reach of E-Business. *Marketing Management, 11*(2), 24-29.

Chase, R. B., & Tansik, D. A. (1978). The Customer Contact Model for Organization Design. *Management Science, 29*(9), 673-687.

Chown, J. F. (1994). *A History ofMmoney from AD 800.* London: Routledge.

Globerman, S., Roehl, T. W., & Standifird, S. (2001). Globalization and Electronic Commerce: Inferences from Retail Brokering. *Journal of International Business Studies, 32*(4), 749-768.

GVU's WWW User Survey Team (1998). *GVU's 10th WWW User Surveys,* Geographic, Visualization, and Usability (GVU) Center.

Hancock, R. (2002). *Act II of the Internet Economy: Embracing E-business to Drive Real Economic Value.* IBM Institute for Business Value, http://www.ibmweblectureservices.ihost.com/ibm/online/1tt0636e/ActII.pdf.

Lanvin, B. (1995). Why the Global Village Cannot Afford Information Slums. In Drake (Ed.), *The New Information Infrastructure,* (pp. 205-222).

Lee, D., & Ahn, J. (1999). An Exploratory Study on the Different Factors in Customer Satisfaction with E-Commerce between in the United States and in Korea, *Proceedings of the 2nd International conference on Telecommunication and Electronic Commerce.*

Levitt, T. (1983). The Globalization of Markets. *Harvard Business Review,* May/ June, (pp. 92-103).

Mann, C. L., Eckert, S. E., & Knight, S. C. (2000). *Global Electronic Commerce: A Policy Primer.* Washington, DC: Institute for International Economics.

Miers, D. (1996). The Strategic Challenges of Electronic Commerce, *Electronic Commerce, Enix Consulting Limited,* (pp. 1-19).

Steinfield, C., & Whitten, P. (1999). Community Level Socio-Economic Impacts of Electronic Commerce. *Journal of Computer Mediated Communication, 5*(2), http://www.ascusc.org/jcmc/vol5/issue2/steinfield.html.

Wilson, C. (2001). On the Scale of Global Demographic Convergence 1950–2000. *Population and Development Review, 27*(1), 155-171.

Winsted, K. F. (1997). The Service Experience in Two Cultures: A Behavioral Perspective. *Journal of Retailing, 73*(3), 337-360.

Yip, G. (2000). Global Strategy in the Internet Era. *Business Strategy Review, 11*(4), 1-14.

Chapter II
E–Commerce Background

ABSTRACT

Electricity, telecommunication, integrated circuits, networking, and the Internet fostered a revolution by delivering distinctive services. The power of the net lies in restructuring the global economy to benefit consumers, businesses, society, and civilization. In general sense, electronic economy is considered to have three primary components--supporting infrastructure, electronic processes (how it is conducted), and electronic commerce transactions (buying and selling). This chapter deals with the introductory concepts of B2C EC and its related issues in the global context. It describes introduction to EC and evolution of one of the basic components of EC, that is, the Internet. Then this chapter sheds light on definition, proliferation, adoption, globalization, and management issues related to B2C EC. This chapter also explains the basic concepts of M-Commerce and E-Government (EG) as the related issues.

2.1. INTRODUCTION

EC is emerging as a global phenomenon. Internet is embraced by most of the countries in the world, and it seems its proliferation is unstoppable. Globalization of EC has enormous effects on organizational structure, economical behavior, technological adoption, social and cultural adaptability, behavioral change, marketing management, and political strategy. On one side, developed countries are pursuing globalization of EC through the Internet. World Trade Organization (WTO) is enthusiastic enough to exploit the benefits and characteristics of the Internet to expedite globalization and create uniformity in global market. Nevertheless, so many developing countries are feared enough of loosing control on domestic market, society, and political strategy due to invasion of multi-dimensional aspects from foreign countries through the Internet. Digital divide is a popular issue of proliferation of Internet economy. Proponents of Internet economy demand alleviation of digital divide through equal empowerment of all citizens across countries in accessing Internet. But, the opposite saying cannot simply be denied.

However, to conceptualize functions, proliferation, diffusion, cultural resistance, and impact on global economy of EC, we would like to address and explain some related issues, concepts, and paradigms of EC as a global phenomenon at the beginning. This chapter is designed to fulfill that idea. It deals with the introductory concepts of EC and its related issues in global context. This chapter consists of three sections with sub-sections. It describes introduction to EC and evolution of one of the basic components of EC, i.e., the Internet. Then this chapter sheds light on definition, classification, distinct characteristics, proliferation, adoption, globalization, and management issues related to EC.

After the advent of the Internet, electronic revolutions have been occurred globally. For example, global competition, interest rates, laws and regulations, social concerns, industry traditions, consumer preferences, market segmentation, globalization, cultural impact, shift of central global economy from the west to Asian giants, like Singapore, China, South Korea, Malaysia, Thailand, India are all part of the broader market economy which can affect all business activities.

The widespread diffusion of information and communication technology is changing methods of conducting business. Both consumers and businesses retailers are getting the unprecedented opportunities provided by the proliferation of the Internet and thus EC. Through online consumers can easily identify different offers, compare them, and buy the best one within no time. Business organizations use online systems even more extensively to operate their business functions, conduct procurement processes, reach new customers globally, and manage organizational relations. This electronic revolution in the global economy requires additional investments in facilities, hardware, software, services, and human capital. This advent and proliferation of information technology has changed the structure and performance of the global market, consumers' perceptions, and purchasing behavior.

2.2. EVOLUTION OF THE INTERNET

We can get insight of the evolution of the Internet from different WWW websites. Summarizing this history, we can say that in 1957, the ex-Soviet Union launched the first satellite, Sputnik I. It expedited U.S. military to create the DARPA agency to regain the technological lead. Information Processing Techniques Office (IPTO) funded the research that led to the development of the ARPANET - Advanced Research Projects Agency. Some people in the IPTO considered the potential benefits of a countrywide communications network and launched the network architecture, and based it on the new idea of packet switching. The ARPANET was initiated first in October 1969, with communications between the University of California at Los Angeles and the Stanford Research Institute. ARPANET adopted the Network Control Program as the network protocol. From 1983, TCP/IP protocol was adopted instead of the previous one, which is still now used for networking. In 1990, the National Science Foundation took over management of what was then called the NSFNet and significantly expanded its periphery by connecting it to the CSNET in Universities throughout North America, and later to the EUnet throughout research facilities in Europe. Observing the extensive use and prospective future of the Internet, the U.S. Government prompted to take initiatives to privatize it starting in 1995. Before that, in 1992, WWW (World Wide Web) started its revolutionary inception in the world market. This is the precise evolution history of the Internet.

The Internet potentially offers individuals, institutions, small and large businesses, all communities, and all levels of government with new opportunities for learning, interacting, transacting business, and developing their social and economic potential. Proliferation and usage of Internet over the last one decade is tremendous. Figures 2.1 and 2.2 show how the Internet has been extended, accepted, and grown throughout the whole world. From the Figure 2.1, we can observe that Internet connection and communication has been extended from North America to South America, Europe, Asia, Australia, and Africa.

Population use the Internet was just 50 million in 1996 and now it is increased to nearly one billion. Approximately 56% of all United States adults use the Internet. This is a six hundred percent increase since 1995, and makes the Internet the fastest growing technology in the history of the world, surpassing even the computer. Figure 2.2 shows the seamless growth of the Internet over time. The graph in Figure 2.2 demonstrates almost steady and steep rise of the Internet usages over the last one decade.

The absolute number of users, present percentage of population using the Internet, and the growth of adoption rate of the Internet throughout the world in respect to different continents (since Middle East has some significant differences in terms of culture, religious background, government policy, and information flow barriers, it

Figure 2.1. Diffusion of the Internet (Source: internet World Stats, 2006)

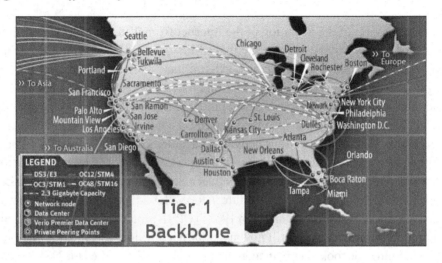

Figure 2.2. Current Internet users (Data source: internet World Stats, 2007)

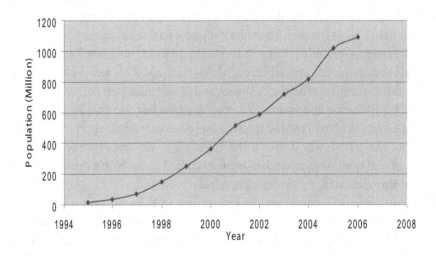

has shown separately from Asia) can be shown in Figure 2.3, Figure 2.4, and Figure 2.5 (data source Internet World Stats, 2007).

Figures 2.3, 2.4, and 2.5 demonstrate that Asia, Europe, and North America are the three leading continents in the world in terms of Internet usage. 37% world Internet users live in Asia, 27% in Europe, and 20% in North America. Again, if we look at the Figure 2.5, it is obviously visible that Internet usage growth rate is

Figure 2.3. World Internet usage among different continents (Million) (Data source: Internet World Stats, 2007)

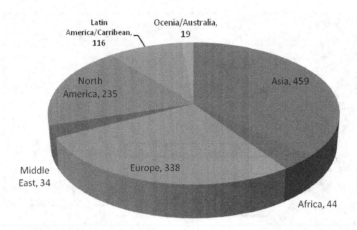

tremendous in Middle East (920.20%), Africa (874.60%), Latin America (540.70%), and Asia (302.0%) in respect to North America (117.20%), and Europe (221.50%). However, if we look at Figure 2.6 and Figure 2.7, it will be obvious that though Internet usage rate in Asia and Africa is growing, still these two continents are located far behind than North America and Europe. 37% of world Internet users live in Asia; however, 56% of world population lives in Asia. Asian Internet penetration rate is 12.40%, in Africa it is 4.70%, where as North American penetration rate is 70.20%, Australian penetration rate is 56.20%, and European penetration rate is 41.70%. Number of Internet penetration or percentage of Internet penetration as shown in Figures 2.3 and 2.4 basically do not reflect the actual picture of Internet usage rate in terms of total population (as shown in Figure 2.7), especially how alarming it is for Asia and Africa.

Figure 2.4. World Internet usage among different continents (percentage) (Data source: Internet World Stats, 2007)

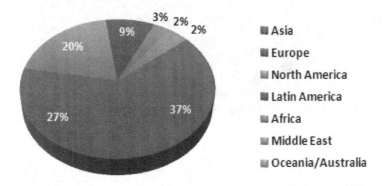

Figure 2.5. Growth of the Internet adoption rate among different continents (percentage) (Data source: Internet World Stats, 2007)

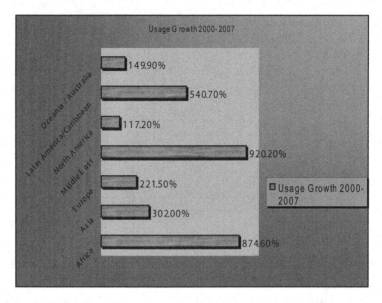

Figure 2.6. World population among different continents (percentage) (Data source: Internet World Stats, 2007)

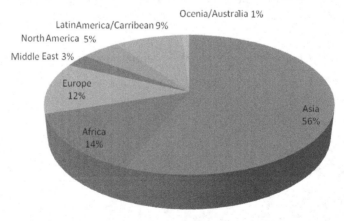

Figure 2.7. Internet penetration rate among different continents (percentage) (Data source: Internet World Stats, 2007)

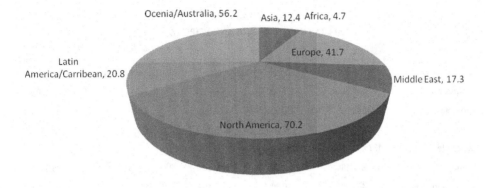

However, the most alarming issue in this aspect which should be accentuated for the readers is the significant disparities regarding Internet penetration rate among different countries in Asia. Although the overall Internet penetration rate in Asia is 12.4o%, it does not actually reflect the distribution of Internet penetration rate among different countries in Asia. While some economically developed countries have significantly higher Internet penetration rate, most of the less developed countries (LDC) in Asia have significantly less, to some extent negligible Internet penetration rate. As a result, average Internet penetration rate cannot capture the status quo of Asian Internet market. This picture is explicitly obvious in the following Table 2.1. This picture is quite similar and above comments are applicable to African countries too.

2.3. ELECTRONIC-COMMERCE

Electricity, telecommunication, integrated circuits, networking, and the Internet combined launched a revolution by delivering services in a completely new way. The scope of the Internet lies in disrupting the old methodologies of conducting business from the global economy to benefit consumers, businesses, society, and civilization. In general sense, electronic economy is considered to have four primary components--technology infrastructure, processes (how it is conducted), transactions (buying and selling), and global trading policy. Primarily the use and communication of computer networks creates the bottom line difference between electronic and other kinds of business.

Technology infrastructure is the establishment of total economic infrastructure used to support electronic transaction processes and conduct electronic commerce

Table 2.1. Country-wise Internet penetration rate in Asia (Source: Internet World Stats, 2007)

ASIA INTERNET USAGE AND POPULATION						
ASIA	Population (2007 Est.)	Internet Users, (Year 2000)	Internet Users, Latest Data	Penetration (%Population)	(%) Users in Asia	Use Growth (2000-2007)
Afganistan	27,089,593	1,000	535,000	2.0 %	0.1 %	53,400.0 %
Armenia	2,950,060	30,000	172,800	5.9 %	0.0 %	476.0 %
Azerbaijan	8,448,260	12,000	829,100	9.8 %	0.2 %	6,809.2 %
Bangladesh	137,493,990	100,000	450,000	0.3 %	0.1 %	350.0 %
Bhutan	812,184	500	30,000	3.7 %	0.0 %	5,900.0 %
BruneiDarussalem	403,500	30,000	165,600	41.0 %	0.0 %	452.0 %
Cambodia	15,507,538	6,000	44,000	0.3 %	0.0 %	633.3 %
China *	1,317,431,495	22,500,000	162,000,000	12.3 %	35.3 %	620.0 %
East Timor	958,662	-	1,000	0.1 %	0.0 %	0.0 %
Georgia	4,389,004	20,000	332,000	7.6 %	0.1 %	1,560.0 %
Hong Kong *	7,150,254	2,283,000	4,878,713	68.2 %	1.1 %	113.7 %
India	1,129,667,528	5,000,000	60,000,000	5.3 %	13.1 %	1,100.0 %
Indonesia	224,481,720	2,000,000	20,000,000	8.9 %	4.4 %	900.0 %
Japan	128,646,345	47,080,000	87,540,000	68.0 %	19.1 %	85.9 %
Kazakhstan	14,653,998	70,000	1,247,000	8.5 %	0.3 %	1,681.4 %
Korea, North	23,510,379	--	--	--	--	0.0 %
Korea, South	51,300,989	19,040,000	34,120,000	66.5 %	7.4 %	79.2 %
Kyrgystan	5,436,608	51,600	298,100	5.5 %	0.1 %	477.7 %
Laos	5,826,271	6,000	25,000	0.4 %	0.0 %	316.7 %
Macao *	500,631	60,000	201,000	40.1 %	0.0 %	235.0 %
Malaysia	28,294,120	3,700,000	14,904,000	52.7 %	3.2 %	302.8 %
Maldives	303,732	6,000	20,100	6.6 %	0.0 %	235.0 %
Mongolia	2,601,641	30,000	268,300	10.3 %	0.1 %	794.3 %
Myanmar	54,821,470	1,000	300,000	0.5 %	0.1 %	29,900.0 %
Nepal	25,874,519	50,000	249,400	1.0 %	0.1 %	398.8 %
Pakistan	167,806,831	133,900	12,000,000	7.2 %	2.6 %	8,861.9 %
Philippines	87,236,532	2,000,000	14,000,000	16.0 %	3.0 %	600.0 %
Singapore	3,654,103	1,200,000	2,421,800	66.3 %	0.5 %	101.8 %
Sri Lanka	19,796,874	121,500	428,000	2.2 %	0.1 %	252.3 %
Taiwan	23,001,442	6,260,000	14,500,000	63.0 %	3.2 %	131.6 %

continued on following page

Table 2.1. continued

Tajikistan	6,702,382	2,000	19,500	0.3 %	0.0 %	875.0 %
Thailand	67,249,456	2,300,000	8,465,800	12.6 %	1.8 %	268.1 %
Turkmenistan	6,886,825	2,000	64,800	0.9 %	0.0 %	3,140.0 %
Uzbekistan	26,607,252	7,500	1,745,000	6.6 %	0.4 %	23,166.7 %
Vietnam	85,031,436	200,000	17,220,812	20.3 %	3.7 %	8,510.4 %
TOTAL ASIA	3,712,527,624	114,303,000	459,476,825	12.4 %	100.0 %	302.0 %

transactions. It includes hardware, software, electricity, telecommunication systems, support services, and human capital used in electronic business and commerce. Examples of supporting infrastructure and associated systems are:

- Electricity
- Telecommunication networks and satellite channels
- Computers, networks, and other hardware
- Cell phones, personal digital assistants (PDAs), smart phones, and other handheld devices
- System and applications software
- Support services, such as website development, chat rooms, online payment, and encryption
- Security systems
- Privacy
- Policy statements
- Human capital resources.

Process is a networking system that governments and business organizations conduct over computer-mediated channels. It includes communication, supply chain, procurement, production, distribution, and management.

Transaction is any interactional transfer of ownership or rights to use goods or services completed over a computer-mediated network and also any functions for supply chain management. Transactions occur within selected transaction processes and are completed when agreement is reached between buyers and sellers to transfer the ownership or rights to use goods or services.

Global trading policy includes regulations of market economy and globalization specific to Internet economy particularly imposed by WTO for supervision of global Inter-based trade. However, Global policy for Internet economy has not been sought for long years and it is still under construction.

Computer-mediated networks are networking through computers. Now the World Wide Web has interconnected the whole world. Different types of networking systems including local area networking (LAN) are available to interconnect computers and even, handheld mobile devices.

The fundamental characteristics of electronic economy, generally termed as Electronic-commerce (EC), are comprised of technology, information, speed, accessibility, and globalization. These key dimensions of EC set apart the ways individuals, businesses, organizations, and governments conduct their operations from those in pre EC periods (Leinbach & Brunn, 2001). Leinbach and Brunn (2001) advocates, " globalization implies a broader geographical set of linkages and independent components, whether the objects are corporations, cities, or states" and "information is the final distinguishing feature of the post industrial era". EC is not some futuristic dream; it is the reality and distinctive characteristics of the present era.

2.3.1 Definition

The "Electronic" or "E" in front of the word "commerce" means that there is an association of electronic systems with the traditional commerce paradigms. It can be over the Internet or any VAN (Value Added Network) like the ones traditionally used to carry electronic data interchange (EDI) messages. Human intervention is only required to enter or retrieve information from the device that is being used. The computers handle the transaction. The term Electronic-commerce (EC) is widely used across many disciplines. Different perspectives arising from different disciplines make it difficult to agree to a precise definition. The Electronic Commerce Resource Center (1996) conceptualizes the objective of EC as "to mould the vast network of small businesses, government agencies, large corporations, and independent contractors into a single community with the ability to communicate with one another seamlessly across any computer platform" (Baldwin & Currie, 2000). Kalakota and Whinston (1996) suggested three distinct stages of EC based on business process. These are:

1.   Inter-organizational that represents business-to-business (B2B) transactions between organizations.
2.   Intra-organizational, which reflects the integration of internal business process.
3.   Business customer interaction, B2C, which refers to the interaction of end-users with the business in terms of product and service exchange.

The advent of EC is creating a new category of economic activity. As such, corporations have much to gain through establishing a stronghold in this new channel. Economic growth is at stake. As a result, major players in this industry are bringing their own definition of EC, driven by marketing imperatives. EC descriptions vary wildly depending on their origin. Canadian Electronic Commerce Strategy (CECS) defines EC as "any kind of transaction that is made using digital technology, including open networks (the Internet), closed networks such as electronic data interchange (EDI), and debit and credit cards". Statistics Canada defined EC as "Transaction carried over computer mediated channels that comprise the transfer of ownership or the entitlement to use tangible or intangible assets". Generally, it is defined as the sharing of business information, maintaining business relationships, and conducting business transactions by means of the Internet (Zwass, 1996; Barnes *et al.*, 2003). Boyer *et al.* (2002) defined EC as "all interactive services that are delivered on the Internet using advanced telecommunications, information, and multi-media technologies". EC is the conduct of business among electronic enterprises and consumers with the capability to exchange value (money, goods, services, and information) electronically (Anderson Consulting, 1999). Statistical Indicators Benchmarking the Information Society (2003) defined EC as "implementation of electronic transactions by placing or receiving orders over electronic networks (broad definition) or the Internet (narrow definition)." All these definitions have functionally very adherence meanings and indicates mostly intensive characteristic of technology in EC. However, EC has also political, social, and cultural aspects which should not be ignored. We, here take the scope to define EC as:

EC is comprised of all business functions related to either external information communication, product, and/or service exchange in tangible or intangible format or internal management conducted through the Internet in acceptance of governments, partners, and consumers.

2.3.2. Classification

Electronic-commerce or E-commerce (EC) transactions can be conducted between business-to-consumer, business-to-business, and business-to-government or vice versa of all these transactions. Depending on associated parties in the transactions, EC is classified or categorized with different names and functions by several researchers and practitioners. Summarizing from literature and the Internet, these are:

1. **Business-to-consumer (B2C) EC:** It corresponds to "electronic retailing", i.e. any electronic trading transaction where the purchaser is the end user of the products and services procured. Here customers interact, contact, and/or

purchase goods from electronic retailers. In B2C EC, the retailers are traditionally selling goods and/or services to unknown, un-trusted customers. Therefore trust, security, and privacy perceptions play a very potential role in B2C EC transactions.

2.   **Business-to-business (B2B) EC:** Business-to-business (B2B) Electronic-commerce (EC) refers to the implementation of electronic transactions between business organizations. B2B EC is the exchange and/or procurement of products, services, or information and between businesses rather than between businesses and consumers. It is one kind of supply chain among business organizations globally through the Internet. The term B2B is however also used very often to refer to online interactions between firms in a broader sense (Electronic-business) including the management of various business processes (from planning and marketing to inventory control to ordering).

3.   **Business-to-government (B2G) EC:** Here the two parties are government and businesses. It refers to transactions, purchase, and/or procurement between businesses and governments. Governments can purchase or procure from business organizations through this online channel.

4.   **Government-to-consumer (G2C) and Government-to-business (G2B) EC:** It is the presentation and delivery of all type of government information and services to citizens and business organizations. Electronic-government (EG) is a broader term for G2C, G2B, and B2G facilities.

5.   **Consumer-to-business (C2B) and Consumer-to-consumer (C2C) EC:** These refer to exchange between consumers and businesses or among consumers. Consumers can post their projects, goods, services and businesses or consumers can procure and/or transact to offer and/or buy.

However, based on the mission and strategic paradigms of this book, our enthusiasm will mostly be concentrated on B2C EC, though sometimes the scope of this book will be extended to review B2B EC and EG. The boundaries between Electronic-commerce and Electronic-business in reality are not so clearly defined and many of the considerations presented here are valid for Electronic-business as well as for Electronic-commerce. EC also includes electronic transactions between citizens, businesses and governments (B2G, G2C). The operations of B2C EC can be summarized in the flowing steps:

1.   Consumers search for opportunities, information, and objective
2.   Browse for selection
3.   Compare different criteria, policies, and statements
4.   Select goods / services
5.   Consumers' purchase (commit to buying)

6. The seller accepts the transaction
7. The seller delivers the goods / services
8. The buyer receives the goods / services
9. The seller supports / maintains/ provides after sale-service.

2.3.2.1. M-Commerce: A Subset of EC

In this sub-section under the section of classification of EC, we would like to provide a brief idea about the concepts and characteristics of M-commerce, a subset of EC, as an emerging topical issue. As we have already defined B2C EC in the previous section that it comprises any type of transaction between sellers and end users via electronic media. This general definition does not provide any restrictions about the use of any kind of device to gain access to the Internet. The device which is used to gain access to the Internet might be wire line, i.e., computers as end user devices or wireless, i.e., mobile phones. In M-commerce or mobile commerce, the device is mobile phone or any handheld mobile device. Therefore, M-commerce is a dynamic sub-classification of EC. It is a new trend in EC which is now widely used by consumers. It is simply defined as any kind of EC occurring over any kind of mobile device (i.e. an Internet enabled mobile phone). So, basically in M-commerce mobile technology is used in commerce. In an academic definition it is characterized in the following terms, "Mobile Commerce is any transaction, involving the transfer of ownership or rights to use goods and services, which is initiated and/or completed by using mobile access to computer-mediated networks with the help of an electronic device" (Tiwari and Buse, 2007). We can view M-commerce as: any kind of EC where buying and selling of goods and services are conducted through any wireless mobile devices such as cellular telephones, personal digital assistants (PDAs), smart phones, and/or other handheld devices. However, since in M-commerce, consumers do not need to plug in the computer with any definite location, it is more dynamic. For its inherent characteristics like ubiquity, personalization, flexibility, and dissemination, it can be anticipated as the next-generation of B2C EC (Siau *et al.*, 2001; Barnett *et al.*, 2000).

2.3.2.1.1. Characteristics and Trend

The emerging technology behind M-commerce, which is based on the Wireless Application Protocol (WAP), has made far greater strides in overall Europe and some Asian countries which are very advanced in diffusing information and communication technology (ICT) based services like, Singapore, Hong Kong, Taiwan, China, South Korea, India, Bangladesh where mobile devices equipped with web-ready micro-browsers are much more common than in the United States and

Canada. As content delivery over wireless devices becomes faster, more accessible, readily available, secure, and more compatible, this specific EC is becoming very popular especially in those countries where the use of mobile phones is extensive. The industries affected by M-commerce include:

1. Marketing and advertisement of Products, like receiving sales promotions via the hand held device is a common example. Retailers can send text messages to the subscribed customers that promote new product offerings, free trials on additional services, or other types of promotional campaigns.
2. Mobile banking is also a widely used service where customers can use their handheld devices to access their accounts and perform their personal banking.
3. Utility bill payments through handheld mobile devices are a popular example of M-commerce.
4. Information communication, i.e., getting information about current affairs like, weather forecast, financial news, sports, current traffic status is very common.
5. Auctions and mobile brokerage are familiar examples of M-commerce.

In 2000 and 2001 hundreds of billions of dollars in licensing fees were conducted by European telecommunications companies for Universal Mobile Telecommunications System (UMTS) and other 3G (third generation of mobile phone standards) licenses. This was happened, because from that time, applications of M-commerce was anticipated to be very profitable. Mobile phones, PDAs, and other handheld mobile devices have become so popular that many E-retailers are beginning to use M-commerce as a more dynamic, effective, and efficient method of reaching and communicating with their prospective customers. In order to capitalize the huge prospects of the M-commerce market, global handset manufacturers such as Nokia, Ericsson, Samsung, Philips, and Motorola are collaborating with carriers such as AT&T Wireless and Sprint to develop WAP-enabled smart phones and ways to reach them. Using Bluetooth technology, smart phones offer fax, e-mail, text messages, and phone capabilities. Therefore, educating end users about doing M-commerce on a cell phone, smart phone or personal digital assistants (PDAs) is the crucial factor for the technology to become adopted extensively.

The key stakeholders of M-commerce are consumers, mobile operators, infrastructure companies, handset & mobile applications and security vendors, as well as banks & credit card companies (Barnes, 2002). Relating to the stakeholders, Eisner (2008) has identified 11 key factors for the proliferation of M-commerce. These are:

1. User-friendly Software
2. Suitable Hardware
3. Data communication speed
4. GPS (Global positioning system) and LBS (Location-Based Services)
5. Mobile payment options with security and ease of use
6. Diffusion and marketing of mobile phones
7. Price and plan of phones
8. Branding of M-commerce
9. Mobile retail sites
10. Consumer preference for use
11. Time

Wu and Wang (2005) conducted an extensive empirical study based on the revised technology acceptance model (TAM) in Taiwan about the acceptance of M-commerce. They revealed that adoption of M-commerce can be predicted from the users' behavioral intentions, which are affected significantly by perceived risk, cost, compatibility, and perceived usefulness. Perceived ease of use does not directly influence behavioral intention to adopt M-commerce but indirectly affects behavioral intention to use through perceived usefulness.

2.3.2.2. E-Government

It is a matter of debate whether E-government (EG) is a subset of EC or EC is a subset of EG. However, both are closely related concepts emerged to focus customers/citizens needs through electronic media. When the two parties in the interaction through electronic media are businesses and consumers or businesses, we generally termed it as EC. However, when one party is a government, we call it in general term as EG. The concept of EG was worked out at the beginning of the 1990s in the USA. President Clinton took office at a time when extensive public management reforms and rebuilding were being implemented in other jurisdictions, as well as within U.S. federal and state governments. These changes were either because of pressures from global competition or as the result of local financial crises. One of the biggest pressures was the increasing public distrust in the ability of the federal government to do things right. Having promised to reinvent and reform the federal government and to make it work more effectively and efficiently with less cost, President Clinton created the National Performance Review (NPR) in 1993. The review was staffed by about 250 civil servants. In addition, some interns, state and local government employees, and consultants were involved in the workforce. Two sets of teams were organized: one would review the individual agencies and the other would focus on government systems—procurement, budget, personnel, etc.

Agencies were also encouraged to create their own internal "reinvention" teams to work with the NPR teams. The Review started with a clear set of principles and an inspiring vision with four key principles:

- Cutting red tape,
- Putting customers first,
- Empowering employees to get results, and
- Cutting back to basics: producing better government for less.

Following the principles was the action plan, which included the following key elements:

- Create a clear sense of mission,
- Steer more, row less,
- Delegate authority and responsibility,
- Replace regulations with incentives,
- Develop budgets based on outcomes,
- Expose federal operations to competition,
- Search for market, not administrative, solutions, and
- Measure success by customer satisfaction.

This was the first phase of implementation of this revolutionary government system: EG. After this first phase, national, state, and local governments from many developed countries – like Canada, Finland, Singapore, and the United Kingdom – started to reform their administrative structure, processes, and regulatory frameworks by using modern ICT and thus set the preliminary phase of EG. Therefore, EG can be seen as a powerful, dynamic, and revolutionary approach for government administration, policy, strategy, and objective reform. The dynamics and evolution of EG are a complex process resulting from strategic behavior, development of rules and standards, and appropriation of those rules and standards by the international community (Gil-Garcia & Martinez-Moyano, 2007).

The U.S. government has defined the service of EG in four quadrants of stakeholders. These are service to Government-to-citizen (G2C), Government-to-business (G2B), Government to-government (G2G), and Intra-government (IEE) (Evans and Yen, 2006).

In this sense, the sphere of the scope of EG is much wider than EC. Alternatively, EC is only a fragmented part of EG. EG is about complete relationships with civic institutions and the foundation of our next-generation states and communities. Understanding what citizens and businesses want and how government, private sectors, and other institutions will be integrated is the vital function of EG. Benchmarking the revolution requires new discourses about policy issues and political realities and their impact on the satisfaction of different stakeholders (Shareef *et al.,* 2008). The EG model should also comprehend the evolution of ICT, the reformation of public administration, and the integration of stakeholders. Therefore, EG is a much wider, more extensive, and more exhaustive application of services compared to EC, due to:

1. Presence of several stakeholders
2. Inability to target certain customer groups as does EC
3. Wider opportunity of scope of service, not only selling product or service like EC
4. Different stakeholders have so many perspectives of rendering services
5. Integrated system that is not an individual entity
6. Assurance of good governance as the prime motto
7. Presence of political commitment
8. Presence of legal system, rules, and regulations which do not embody only one transaction; rather comprises functions that are vital and mandatory as the responsibility of citizen and the whole state
9. Unlike private entities, the ultimate target is not profit but to serve better
10. Since government service is a monopoly, unlike a private entity, for EG the number of customers are huge
11. Unlike private organizations, more bureaucratic and complex relations exist.

EG service refers to the use of electronic delivery for government information, programs, strategies, and services to stakeholders. These are available from respective websites 24 hours a day and 7 days a week. It assumes a modernized front office but not necessarily a redesigned back office capacity (Evans and Yen, 2006). At the same time, EG services emphasize innovative forms of citizen involvement in decision making, and offer services that demonstrate an evaluation of citizens as customer. The strategic challenge is to deliver services to stakeholders along with dimensions such as quality, convenience, cost, availability, and transparency. EG operated by World Wide Web (WWW) has a definite global character. Interacting with foreign governments and attracting foreign investment, tourism, and business are also part of transforming traditional government systems to the electronic version. Therefore, keeping in mind the global impact, solidarity in setting the missions and objectives of implementing EG systems is an important managerial issue. The ultimate success of EG in the long run depends on the adoption intentions of different stakeholders. However, lack of consensus in setting similar explicit objectives makes the adoption criteria of EG diversified. Therefore, a number of factors have significant implications for progressive successful development in setting the course, and identifying and establishing the explicit missions and objectives of transforming the traditional government structure into the electronic version. These factors include reaching unanimous consensus on EG development; determining the state of readiness through policy making; addressing key issues; strategizing leadership, boundaries, structures, and activities; revealing technology infrastructure; and defining governance structures and policies. Identifying clear objectives of implementing EG is also important to capitalize on the full opportunities that lie behind the EG system so that different stakeholders are interested in adopting the EG system under the globalization context.

The semantic needs of EG and gradual demand are rising through public organizations and public administration across the world. More and more governments are importing technology, developing fundamental capabilities and infrastructure, and using ICT – especially Internet or web-based networks – to provide high quality and competitive services to citizens, businesses, employees, and other nongovernmental agencies. Across the world, different governments are exploring the scope and opportunities of EG by publishing static information on websites and establishing an online presence. They are striving to achieve better efficiency, effectiveness, and organizational performance that will make them competitive in the present global market (Melitski, 2001).

Reviewing existing literature on EG adoption by citizens and business organizations, we can infer that the adoption models offered so far in the academic literature are mainly conceptual (Heeks & Bailur, 2007). Extensive empirical studies among the actual users to validate and generalize the models are absent. Those, who have attempted to validate their models, mostly did not rigorously review literature and integrate discourses from technical, social, organizational, political, and cultural perspectives to develop their ontological and epistemological paradigms of model validation doctrine. The cultural aspect in exploring constructs of adoption is especially ignored, though in organizational and behavioral literature, the cultural aspect has a great impact. An empirical study conducted by Shareef *et al.* (Forthcoming) to identify the critical factors that contribute to the intention by citizens of developing countries to adopt an EG system revealed that relative advantage, perceived ease of use, perceived security, perceived reliability, and perceived privacy are the significant factors for adoption. However, from a theoretical perspective and literature review, there are evidences that the adoption criteria of EG have some potential differences in many areas for consumers of developed and developing countries; some examples are perception of quality, behavioral attitude, disclosure of information, intention to avoid physical interaction, and security feelings (Shareef *et al.,* Forthcoming).

2.3.3. Distinct Characteristics of B2C Electronic-Commerce

The formation, operation, functionality, and presentation of EC are quite different from traditional business. In EC, the interaction between a customer and a business takes place with the Internet as the interface. Generally, there is no human interaction. Another point is that customers do not buy goods or services in the traditional sense. They buy an offering, and the value may consist of many components, some of them being activities (service) and some being things (goods) (Gummesson, 1994). The two fundamental differences described here are the key factors in arguing that business process of traditional commerce may not be directly transferable and applicable to the EC environment. With the advent of the Internet, adoption paradigms is still of major importance but the question is whether the discourses developed in traditional business can be applied equally to this business medium, where the main difference is the lack of human interaction.

Based on the literature review (Bauer *et al.,* 2006; Collier & Bienstock, 2006; Kumar *et al.,* 2006), the distinctive nature of EC operations, different from the manufacturing and service systems of traditional business, lie in the fact that:

- Physically, customers do not buy goods or services in the traditional sense. They apparently buy a proposal offered in the website (Gummesson, 1994).
- It is dominated by communication and information technology interaction services in lieu of people delivered services.
- Acceptance and usage of technologies across customers depend on their technology beliefs and similar differences might exist in the evaluative process (Cowels & Crosby, 1990).
- There is high component of self-service (customer uses the website) and even in case of manufactured goods, the service component of the total offering is increasing.
- Globalization is a major aspect of EC, since in EC traditionally any consumer can purchase goods or services from any where in the world.
- Proliferation and outsourcing of EC greatly depends on cultural and social aspects and possible barriers due to cultural resistance to adopt EC.
- Digital divide is a profound concept derived from the birth of ICT. A huge number of populations cannot penetrate and get the advantage of Internet economy due to non-existence of capability (Nussbaum & Sen, Capability Theory, 1993).
- Trust, Security, and Privacy play a very distinctive role in internet-based purchase (Gefen *et al.,* 2003).

2.3.4. Proliferation

Traditional brick and mortar commerce consists of customers buying products/services from suppliers. The EC model is no different, other than the customer uses electronic signals, usually through the Internet, as the means of purchasing the same. In general, customers see a product they are interested in on a website and then have the opportunity to buy it over the web. EC began before personal computers were prevalent and has grown now into a multi-billion dollar industry. The skeleton of EC is based on information technology. Internet, the main media of EC was developed in 1969 by U.S. Department of Defense as an alternate communication strategy. Over the years, EC has expanded all over the world. The beginning step of electronic transaction era came from the development of the EDI. EDI is a set of standards developed in the 1960s used to exchange business information and do electronic transactions. At first, business could use several different EDI formats and companies could not interact with each other. However, in 1984 the ASCX12 standards became stable and reliable in transferring large amounts of transactions (Hiser *et al.,* 2001). The second major step occurred in 1992 when the Mosaic web-browser was made available. In 1994, Netscape arrived, providing users a simple browser to surf the Internet and a safe online transaction technology called Secure Sockets Layer. In 1995, two of the biggest names in EC were launched: Amazon.com and eBay.com. In 1998, DSL (Digital Subscriber Line), allowed quicker access and a persistent connection to the Internet. This prompted people to spend more time and money in online.

The meaning of the term EC has changed over time. Originally, EC meant the facilitation of commercial transactions electronically, usually using technology like Electronic Data Interchange (EDI) to send commercial documents like purchase orders or invoices electronically. Today it includes activities like purchase of goods and services over the World Wide Web via secure servers. According to a study by the Pew Internet and American Life Project, the Internet has gone from novelty to utility for many, and an increasing number of customers are spending more time shopping electronically (Horrigan & Rainie, 2002). This argument is supported by a U.S. Census Bureau report (2007). According to their reports from 1999 to the third quarter of 2007, every year Electronic-sales are increasing in USA by almost 20%. Although, still Electronic-sales present a small portion of total retail sales in USA, its proliferation rate is unbelievable. It is shown by the following graph presented in Figure 2.8.

In Canada, the European Union, and Japan, the same trend is observed. All the developed countries are experiencing almost 20-30% increase in Electronic-sales every year (U.S. Census Bureau Report, 2007). Even in developing countries, like China, South Korea, Taiwan, Singapore, India, Brazil, during the last decade, B2C

Figure 2.8. U.S. quarterly retail EC sales (Source: U.S. Census Bureau, 2007)

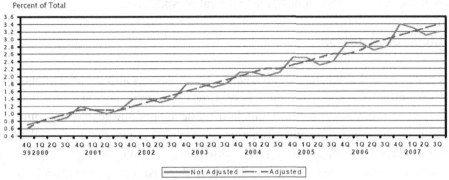

EC customers have been increased tremendously and in 2006, in an average, EC customers is now almost 200% in those countries in respect to 1999 (Information Economy Report 2006,UNCTAD).

2.3.5. Adoption

The process of globalization creates new challenges and opportunities for business organizations. The Internet and electronic transactions have created this widespread scope for the firms. The opportunities include access to new markets that were previously closed due to cost, regulation, or indirect barriers, the ability to tap resources such as labor, capital, and knowledge on a worldwide basis, and the opportunity to participate in global production networks that are becoming prevalent in many industries. The adoption of online shopping channel makes it cheaper and easier for firms to extend their markets, manage their operations, and coordinate value chains across borders (Globerman *et al.*, 2001; Williams *et al.*, 2001; Cavusgil, 2002). Adoption of EC fosters globalization by reducing transaction and coordination costs and creating new and expanded markets with economies of scale (Steinfield & Whitten, 1999; Mann *et al.*, 2000). Firm globalization is heralded as a key driver of EC diffusion (Steinfield & Whitten, 1999).

Due to worldwide proliferation of the Internet, the main vehicle of B2C EC, EC is also spreading exponentially throughout the whole world among the consumers of both developed and developing countries. Adoption of B2C EC by the customers is enhanced for the distinctive characteristics of EC, like speed, time, location, cost, and availability of alternatives. Adoption of B2C EC by the global customers depends fundamentally on several aspects like availability to use, attitude to use, ability to use, reasoning to use, and satisfaction to use. Later on, we will address the issue of adoption in details and explain that all those aspects have strong theoretical correlation with behavioral or attitudinal, organizational, technological, social, marketing, cultural, economical, and political perspectives.

2.3.6. Globalization

The adoption and extension of information technology is now a major concern in many countries. Accoring to Lanvin (1995), the development of electronic markets has created enormous opportunities for both the developed and developing countries to focus on the internal business functions and exploit the global market (Wilson, 2001). It plays a significant role in the present information and knowledge based market by planning, generating, managing, and transmitting information in the most effective way through the modern information technology to provide easy access and availability across the countries and to invite potential customers by providing necessary information through the Internet. Therefore, proliferation of global technology is the backbone of global B2C EC.

The transformation of business structure through global communication systems has redefined the basis of participation in development and modernity by creating new levels of entry into the global economy. Today, strong association and participation in the information economy has become the revised standard and fundamental precondition for sustainability. The technological inability to adopt information technology is now the latest barrier for developing countries to capitalize global resources. At the same time, universal Internet access holds great promise for:

1. Global access to ICT and appropriate content and applications
2. Gaining global market competitiveness
3. Extending markets across countries
4. Developing reputation
5. Attracting universal customers from a single location
6. Decreasing poverty around the world through the linkage of access to ICT
7. Opening up global markets through Internet commerce to any individual or entity
8. Collecting and disclosing competitive information globally and enabling of transparency in governance
9. Increasing the spread of democratization through increasing civic discourse and citizen involvement in government

Therefore, the Internet, unlike other media, represents a new collective mental space. Diffusion of the Internet has created substantial scopes for countries and individuals to come together to form collaboration, regional markets, and globalization which were never possible at this pace. The worldwide spread of information technology, telecommunication systems, and the Internet has created a homogeneous clustered market globally. Moreover, development, proliferation, and adoption of this information and communication technology by the customers across the continents are potential base of success for launching global B2C EC.

Market researchers defined international market segmentation as the division of the global market into different locations signified by some specific characteristics of those areas (Beckmen *et al.,* 1982). Market segmentation derives from the paradigms that certain locations have some similarities or convergence to be localized, and also have dissimilarities to be separated from other regions to form a single market. The specific characteristics which initiate market segmentation are basically four types namely, demographic segmentation, geographic segmentation, psychographic segmentation, and benefit segmentation (Keegan & Seringhaus, 1996; Smith & Merchant, 2001). There are actually so many ways of dividing the world into different regional markets. Consequently, forming regional markets is a way to cluster countries where, within cluster similarities and between cluster differences exist significantly (Keegan & Seringhaus, 1996). There are different paradigms regarding the strategies of globalization, like standardization, adaptation or customization, such as marketing mix (Levitt, 1983; Kustin, 1994; Yip, 2000). Though some scholarly articles advocate standardization as a means of better business performance and as a certain trend in international business, it is still a plausible and debatable paradox. There are also several researchers who believe that due to significant variations between countries in such dimensions as consumer needs, standards, consumer tastes, values, purchasing power, commercial infrastructure, culture and traditions, laws and regulations, and technological development, homogenous and standardized business strategy is not feasible. They advocate that country oriented or at least segmented market oriented business strategy is more viable and critical, especially as a measure of better business performance. However, the debate regarding which strategy is better for international business and globalization is beyond the scope of this book and therefore it is not discussed in details here. Due to proliferation of information technology, business organizations are now extending their services across countries. Globalization of service is one of the major concerns of this technology-dominated era. We argue that outsourcing and globalization through the adoption of the Internet become paradigms of success.

2.3.7. Management Issues

Diffusion and proliferation of the Internet has created revolutionary changes in the conducting of business. EC has created substantial opportunities for business organizations and consumers. Therefore, exploring adoption aspects of EC and its possible impact on customers' behavioral intention is a wide area to investigate and understand. Some scholarly researchers have explored, identified, and evaluated effects of quality factors in EC transactions and adoption (Lee & Ahn, 1999; Gefen & Straub, 2000; George, 2000; Lee *et al.*, 2001a, 2001b; May & Sculli, 2002; Tsikriktsis, 2002; Balasubramanian *et al.*, 2003; Chen & Dubinsky, 2003; Chiu *et al.*, 2005; Schaupp & Bélanger, 2005) which vigorously influence the fragile and complex behavior of consumers.

Consumers' shopping behavior is a very complex and robust subject. Consumers' purchase intentions are greatly affected and diversified by their attitudes, behavioral intent, and local environmental security perception. Therefore, understanding and estimating the effect of customers' intrinsic social and cultural characteristics which lead to customers' EC adoption, purchase intention, satisfaction and loyalty, would have important managerial implications (Tsikriktsis, 2002). If the relative importance of EC quality factors to customers is likely to vary depending on their attitudes and social and cultural behavior, EC should be contingent on these issues of customers (Furrer *et al.*, 2000), and consequently globalization strategy would be settled.

Though many companies are still just beginning to grasp the potential uses and impacts of B2C EC, advances in technologies and their applications continue. Observing the proliferation of B2C EC, companies are increasingly turning to the Internet to market products and services to gain competitive advantage. However, the effectiveness and efficiency of such online commerce systems largely depend on the degree of comfort that customers feel with the technology-based interactions. These advances often present various managerial and technological issues for customers, companies, governments, and other entities. Because of the expansion and increasing reliance on corporate websites, researchers and practitioners are equally concerned with the issues of understanding and managing B2C EC. According to Baldwin *et al.* (2000), "EC offers promises to business; it also imposes considerable challenges to government, industry, and individuals in the form of building trust, confidence, and security". Since in B2C EC, customers interact in a virtual space with a technical interface instead of interacting with employees in a physical space, it raises issues of self-service technologies (SSTs) (Meuter *et al.*, 2001). Moreover, online consumers are keenly aware of their need for privacy and security (Culnan & Armstrong, 1999; Grewal *et al.*, 2003), an issue only rarely of importance in offline retailing. In addition, many writers and scholars have suggested the unique capabilities of the online medium to provide interactivity, personalized experiences, community, content, increased product selection, and information, which again suggest that existing concepts of service and retailing quality may be inadequate in an online context. Identity theft is one of the major concerns in B2C

EC (Davis, 2003). The relationship between culture and website quality is also an increasingly important issue in the management of services and specifically EC services (Tsikriktsis, 2002). Personal behavior and trust disposition attitude create differences in trusting EC, thus purchase intention (Winsted, 1997; Donthu & Boonghee, 1998; Mattila, 1999; Furrer *et al.*, 2000). Therefore, behavioral attitude is also a managerial issue in B2C EC. Several scholarly articles dealing adoption of B2C EC by both the companies and customers revealed that perceived ease of use, perceived usefulness, relative advantage, cost, reliability, website availability, company statements and policies, reputation, third party quality certification, website design, up-to-date and accurate information, possible and related linkage, speed, time, and price constraints are the plausible managerial issues for EC to sustain, expand, and to gain competitive advantage in the fierce competitive market. Since the issues discussed so far, are all related to specific characteristics of EC, viz., customers versatile attitudinal differences especially for online, viz., virtual transaction, and diffusion and adoption of B2C EC, therefore, depending on the above findings, suggestions, and arguments, we can assume that the relation of proliferation of Internet economy and globalization with possible cultural barriers and its impact on global market demands potential priority to be addressed, investigated, and explained in details by its own merit.

REFERENCES

Anderson Consulting. (1999). E-commerce: What's All the Fuss. Presentation. *Anderson Consulting, 5*(Section 1).

Balasubramanian, S., Konana, P., & Menon, N. M. (2003). Customer, Satisfaction in Virtual Environments: A Study of Online Investing. *Management Science, 7*, 871–889.

Baldwin, L. P., & Currie, W. L. (2000). Key Issues in Electronic Commerce in Today's Global Information Infrastructure. Cognition, *Technology & Work, 2*(1), 27-34.

Barnes, S. J. (2002). The Mobile Commerce Value Chain: Analysis and Future Developments. *International Journal of Information Management, 22*(2), 91–108.

Barnes, S. J., & Vidgen R. (2001). Assessing the Quality of Auction Websites. *Hawaii International Conference on Systems Sciences.*

Barnett, N., Hodges, S., & Wilshire, M. J. (2000). M-Commerce: An Operator's Manual. *McKinsey Quarterly, 3*, 162–173.

Bauer, H. H., Falk, T., & Hammerschmidt, M. (2006). eTransQual: A Transaction Process-Based Approach for Capturing Service Quality in Online Shopping. *Journal of Business Research, 59*, 866-875.

Beckman, M. D., Kurtz, D. L., & Boone, L. E. (1982). *Foundations of Marketing.* 3rd Edition, Holt, Rinehart and Winston of Canada, Ltd, Toronto.

Boyer, K. K., Hallowell, R., & Roth, A. V. (2002). E-services: Operations Strategy—A Case Study and a Method for Analyzing Operational Benefits. *Journal of Operations Management, 20*(2), 175–188.

Cavusgil, S. T. (2002). Extending the Reach of E-Business. *Marketing Management, 11*(2), 24-29.

Chase, R. B., & Tansik, D. A. (1978). The Customer Contact Model for Organization Design. *Management Science, 29*(9), 673-687.

Chen, Z., & Dubinsky A. J. (2003). A Conceptual Model of Perceived Customer Value in E-Commerce: A Preliminary Investigation. *Psychology and Marketing, 20*(4), 323–347.

Chiu, H. C., Hsieh, Y. C., & Kao, C. Y. (2005). Website Quality and Customer's Behavioral Intention: An Exploratory Study of the Role of Information Asymmetry. *Total Quality Management and Business Excellence, 16*(2), 185 – 197.

Collier, J. E., & Bienstock, C.C. (2006). Measuring Service Quality in E-Retailing. *Journal of Service Research, 8*(3), 260-275.

Cowles, D. L., & Crosby, L. A. (1990). Consumer Acceptance of Interactive Media in Service Marketing Encounters. *The Service Industries, 10*(July), 521-40.

Culnan, M. J., & Armstrong, P. K. (1999). Information Privacy Concerns, Procedural Fairness, and Impersonal Trust: An Empirical Investigation. *Organization Science, 10*(1), 104–115.

Donthu, N., & Boonghee, Y. (1998). Cultural Influences on Service Quality Expectations. *Journal of Service Research, 1*(2), 178-186.

Eisner, K. (2008). 10 Requirements to Reach Mobile Commerce Critical Mass because of Apple iPhone (and why the Nielsen report is dangerous). *Arstechnica. com.* Available on http://www.glgroup.com/News/10-Requirements-to-Reach-Mobile-Commerce-Critical-Mass-because-of-Apple-iPhone-(and-why-the-Nielsen-report-is-dangerous-26630.html.

Electronic Commerce Resource Center. (1996). http://www.sbpm.gwu.edu/ research /centers/CASB/electronic.htm.

Evans, D., & Yen, D. C. (2006). E-Government: Evolving Relationship of Citizens and Government, Domestic, and International Development. *Government Information Quarterly, 23*(2), 207–235.

Furrer, O., Liu, B. S-C., & Sudharshan, D. (2000). The Relationships between Culture and Service Quality Perceptions: Basis for Cross-Cultural Market Segmentation and Resource Allocation. *Journal of Service Research, 2*(4), 355-371.

Gates, B. (1999). *Business @ the Speed of Thought: Using a Digital Nervous System.* New York, NY: Warner Books, Inc.

Gefen, D., & Straub, D. (2000). The Relative Importance of Perceived Ease of Use in IS Adoption: A study of E-Commerce Adoption. *Journal of the Association for Information Systems, 1*(8), 1-28.

Gefen, D., Karahanna, E., & Straub, D. W. (2003). Trust and TAM in Online Shopping: An Integrated Model. *MIS Quarterly, 27*, 51-90.

George, J. F. (2000). The Effects of Internet Experience and Attitudes toward Privacy and Security on Internet Purchasing. *Proceedings of the 8th European Conference in Information Systems (ECIS),* Vienna: Vienna University of Economics and Business Administration, (pp. 1053–8).

Gil-Garcia, J. R., & Martinez-Moyano, I. J. (2007). Understanding the Evolution of E-Government: The Influence of Systems of Rules on Public Sector Dynamics. *Government Information Quarterly, 24*(2), 266–290.

Globerman, S., Roehl, T. W., & Standifird., S. (2001). Globalization and Electronic Commerce: Inferences from Retail Brokering. *Journal of International Business Studies, 32*(4), 749-768.

Grewal, G., Munger, J. L., Iyer, G. R. & Levy, J. (2003). The Influence of Internet Retailing Factors on Price Expectations. *Psychology and Marketing, 20*(6), 477–493.

Gummesson, E. (1994). Making Relationship Marketing Operational. *International Journal of Service Industry Management, 5*(5), 5-20.

Heeks, R. B., & Bailur, S. (2007). Analyzing E-Government Research: Perspectives, Philosophies, Theories, Methods, and Practice. *Government Information Quarterly, 24*(2), 243–265.

Hiser, E., Lanka, B., & Li, W. (2001). *History of E-Commerce.* http://newmedia. medill.northwestern.edu/courses/nmpspring01/brown/Revstream/history.htm.

Horrigan, J. B., & Rainie, L. (2002). Getting Serious Online. *Pew Internet & American Life Project.* Washington, DC.

Information Economy Report. (2006). UNCTAD. http://blogs.uct.ac.za/blog/ ce-lias/2006/12/04/information_economy_report_2006_unctad.

Internet World Stats. (2006). http://www.allaboutmarketresearch.com/internet. htm.

Internet World Stats. (2007). http://www.allaboutmarketresearch.com/internet. htm.

Kalakota, R., & Whinston, A. B. (1996). *Frontiers of Electronic Commerce.* Addison-Wesley. Reading. MA.

Keegan, W. J., & Seringhaus, F. H. R. (1996). *Global Marketing Management.* Canadian edition Prentice Hall Canada Inc., Scarborough, Canada.

Kumar, V., Kumar, U., & Shareef, M. A. (2006). Implementation of Quality Management Practice in EC. *Proceedings of the Administrative Sciences Association of Canada Conference, 27,* 146-163. Banff, Calgary, Canada.

Kustin, R. A. (1994). A Special Theory of Globalization: A Review and Critical Evaluation of the Theoretical and Empirical Evidence. *Journal of Global Marketing, 7*(3), 79-102.

Lanvin, B. (1995). Why the Global Village Cannot Afford Information Slums, in Drake. *The New Information Infrastructure*, (pp. 205-222).

Lee, D., & Ahn, J. (1999). An Exploratory Study on the Different Factors in Customer Satisfaction with E-Commerce between in the United States and in Korea. *Proceedings of the 2nd International conference on Telecommunication and Electronic Commerce.*

Lee, D., Park, J., & Ahn, J. (2001a). On the Explanation of Factors affecting E-commerce Adoption. *Proceedings of the Twenty-Second International Conference in Information Systems*, (pp. 109-120). New Orleans, USA.

Lee, M. K. O., & Turban, E. (2001b). A Trust Model for Internet Shopping. *International Journal of Electronic Commerce, 6*(1), 75-91.

Leinbach, T. R., & Brunn, S. D. (2001). *Worlds of E-Commerce: Economic, Geographical, and Social Dimensions.* New York: Wiley.

Levitt, T. (1983). The Globalization of Markets. *Harvard Business Review*, May_June, 92-103.

Mattila, A. S. (1999). The Role of Culture in the Service Evaluation Processes. *Journal of Service Research*, *1*(3), 250-261.

May W. C. S., & Sculli, D. (2002). The Role of Trust, Value and Risk in Conducting E-Business. *Industrial Management & data Systems, 102*(9), 503-512.

Melitski, J. (2001). The World of E-government and E-governance, http://www. aspanet.org/solutions/TheWorld of E-government and E-governance.htm.

Meuter, M. L., Bitner, M. J., Ostrom, A. L., & Brown, S. W. (2001). Choosing among Alternative Service Delivery Modes: An Investigation of Customer Trial of Self-Service Technologies. *Journal of Marketing, 69*(2), 61-83.

Nussbaum, M., & Sen, A. (Eds.) (1993). *The Quality of Life*. Oxford: Clarendon Press.

Schaupp, L. C., & Bélanger, F. (2005). A Conjoint Analysis of Online Consumer Satisfaction. *Journal of Electronic Commerce Research*, *6*(2), 95-111.

Shareef, M. A., Kumar, U., & Kumar, V. (2008). The E-government and E-governance: Conceptual Alignment or Subtle Difference. *International Journal of Knowledge, Culture and Change Management, 8*(1), 129-136.

Shareef, M. A., Kumar, U., Kumar, V., & Dwivedi, Y. K. (Forthcoming). Identifying Critical Factors for Adoption of E-Government. *Electronic Government: An International Journal.*

Siau, K., Lim, E.-P., & Shen, Z. (2001). Mobile Commerce: Promises, Challenges, and Research Agenda (Technology Information). *Journal of Database Management, 12*(3), 4-13.

Smith, B. A., & Merchant, E. J. (2001). Designing an Attractive Website: Variables of Importance. *Proceedings of the 32nd Annual Conference of the Decision Sciences Institute*, San Francisco, CA.

Statistical Indicators Benchmarking the Information Society. (2003). http://www. sibis-eu.org.

Steinfield, C., & Whitten, P. (1999). Community Level Socio-Economic Impacts of Electronic Commerce. *Journal of Computer Mediated Communication, 5*(2), http://www.ascusc.org/jcmc/vol5/issue2/steinfield.html.

Tiwari, R., & Buse, S. (2007). *The Mobile Commerce Prospects: A Strategic Analysis of Opportunities in the Banking Sector*, Hamburg: Hamburg University Press.

Tsikriktsis, N. (2002). Does Culture Influence Web Site Quality Expectations? An Empirical Study. *Journal of Service Research*, *5*(2), 101-112.

U.S. Census Bureau Report. (2007). USA. http://www.census.gov.

Williams, A. R. T., Dale, B. G., Visser, R. L., & Wiele, T. V. (2001). B2B, Old Economy Businesses and the Role of Quality: Part 1 – The Simple Alternative. *Measuring Business Excellence, 5*(2), 39-44.

Wilson, C. (2001). On the Scale of Global Demographic Convergence 1950–2000. *Population and Development Review, 27*(1), 155-171.

Winsted, K. F. (1997). The Service Experience in Two Cultures: A Behavioral Perspective. *Journal of Retailing, 73*(3), 337-360.

Wu, J.-H., & Wang, S.-C. (2005). What Drives Mobile Commerce? An Empirical Evaluation of the Revised Technology Acceptance Model. *Information & Management, 42*, 719–729.

Yip, G. (2000). Global Strategy in the Internet Era. *Business Strategy Review, 11*(4), 1-14.

Division II
Service Quality for Global Consumers

Chapter III
Service Quality of E–Commerce for Global Consumers

ABSTRACT

Customers' perception and expectation of service quality dimensions for any field, whereas it is traditional commerce or EC, has a close relation with adoption of that system, and is significantly depend on cultural diversity of the customers. Service quality of a business, in the present competitive market, plays a very sensitive role in positive perception of that business and thus acceptance, use, and adoption. Since EC is inherently global, global consumers' perception of service quality, grounded on cultural and social diversity, is a potential criterion to be addressed and analyzed. This chapter of the book is designed to conceptualize some general idea about expectation and performance of different service quality attributes for B2C EC as revealed by different researchers.

3.1. INTRODUCTION

Diffusion of the Internet has changed the methodology of operating business. EC presents several advantages for business, consumers, and employees. Sustainability and expansion of EC depends on several factors. In absence of physical cues, service quality plays a significant role in EC. Therefore, exploring service quality factors of EC and its possible impact on customers' behavioral intention in a global context is a wide area to investigate and understand. This led to reviewing the relevant scholarly articles engaged in identifying service quality attributes and developing quality framework, summarizing and comparing the primary models in this field, and finding out the determining factors of service quality in EC. Finally, this paper is engaged in revealing the relevance with and impact of perception of service quality on cultural diversity and proliferation of EC among global consumers.

Globalization of EC is certainly a function of global consumers' acceptance, use, and adoption of this phenomenon. Very rationally, consumers' perception of EC is a determining factor in this context. Marketing literature has long been sought that service quality of a business, in the present competitive market, plays a very sensitive role in positive perception of that business and thus acceptance, use, and adoption. Especially, when we conjecture that EC is inherently global, global consumers' perception of service quality, grounded on cultural and social diversity, is a potential criterion to be addressed and analyzed. This chapter of the book is designed to impart some general idea about expectation and performance of different service quality attributes for B2C EC as revealed by different researchers. Therefore, we will look primarily on existing profound literature addressing and investigating service quality models of B2C EC. We have divided this chapter into 5 sections with section 2 into subsections. We will first provide the readers some details of concepts of service quality of B2C EC. Then, we will explore significant contributions of some researchers and compare those to get generic meanings of different attributes of service quality. Finally, we will figure out the relevance of this issue with the fundamental objectives of this book.

3.2. ELECTRONIC-COMMERCE SERVICE QUALITY

Practitioners and academics experience growing interest in the service sector's operations and in service quality in particular. The service sector has become an important part of core business strategy. The service management literature of the 1990s (both marketing and operations) supports a view that excellent service and prescriptions for improving service quality is an important way to enhance customer satisfaction and loyalty leading to increased competitiveness and profitability, both in manufacturing and in service industries. Service is an act or combination of acts to assist others. It can be measured by performance. It is intangible and may or may not be associated with product transactions (Kotler, 1973). Therefore, service is characterized by the fact that it is intangible, simultaneous, and heterogeneous.

Generally, service marketing defines service in three dimensions: Core service, Facilitating service, and Supporting or Supplementary service. The core service is the main reason for the company to be on the market. Facilitating service is mandatory for presenting the service accessible. Supporting or supplementary service is value adding component that is used to distinguish the service from the competitors' offerings (Gronroos, 1990). Business service is under different labels like, business-to business service, professional service, and industrial service in the literature. It is a process for providing significant value-added benefits to the supply chain in a cost-effective way. At present, service like, pre-sale service, on-sale service, after-sale service, and delivery service, starts to play a crucial role in business and are considered a success factor for better performance (Davis *et al.,* 1992).

The emergence of virtual channels has led to the advancement of conceptualizing the definition of EC service. EC service can be defined as "all interactive services that are delivered on the internet using advanced telecommunications, information, and multimedia technologies" (Boyer *et al.,* 2002). This definition is further extended as "The EC service encounter is the initial landing on the home page until the requested service has been completed or the final product has been delivered, and is fit for use." Gronroos *et al.* (2000) adds a new dimension, user interface service in the traditional service concept, consisting of core service, facilitating service, and supporting service. Fassnacht *et al.* (2006) defined EC service as "Services delivered via information and communication technology where the customer interacts solely with an appropriate user interface (e.g., automated teller machine or website) in order to retrieve desired benefits." Gartner (2001) defined EC service as including the processes, policies, procedures, people, tools, and technologies that enable enterprises to provide assisted and unassisted customer service using the Internet as its platform. To survive, EC must realize the importance of service quality factors (Janda *et al.,* 2002). Research pertaining to service quality has focused on developing and assessing not only models of general service quality (Parasuraman *et al.,* 1988; Bolton & Drew, 1991; Babakus & Boller, 1992; Cronin & Taylor, 1992; Zeithaml *et al.,* 1996; Cronin *et al.,* 2000), but also industry-specific service quality. The emergence of EC has drastically changed perspective, pattern, and procedure of delivery of service. Therefore, researchers, engaged in identifying quality factors of EC needed to satisfy customers, are searching for new dimensions of service quality. They are accomplishing different literature from service marketing, psychological behavior, quality management, information technology, and service quality models suitable for traditional business. Edvardsson *et al.* (1989) summarized four aspects of service quality that affect customers' perceptions:

1.   Technical quality
2.   Integrative quality

3. Functional quality
4. Outcome quality

3.2.1. Traditional Service Quality

Traditional service quality has been studied extensively over the past two decades and has become a major area of attention to practitioners, managers, and researchers due to its strong impact on business performance, lower costs, customer satisfaction, customer loyalty, profitability, and gaining overall competitive advantage in today's fierce competition (Cronin & Taylor, 1992; Gummesson, 1994; Sirdeshmukh *et al.,* 2002). Application of quality principles in different aspects of manufacturing and service systems of traditional business has a very long and successful history (Parasuraman & Zinkhan, 2002). There has been a continued research on the definition, modeling, measurement, data collection procedure, data analysis, etc., and issues of service quality, leading to development of sound base for the researchers. For manufacturing and service systems of traditional business, improvement of quality dimensions with quality principles has been well-supported (Parasuraman *et al.,* 1985; Albrecht & Bradford, 1990). Implementation of quality principles in traditional business refers to the quality of all non-internet based customer interactions and experiences with companies. This is mainly based on direct people delivered services. In this context, developing service quality models gains specific importance as it does not only help in learning the factors associated with it but also provides a direction for improvements. Different authors engaged in research of service quality presented different models (Juran, 1962; Deming 1975; Grönroos, 1984; Taguchi, 1986; Parasuraman *et al.,* 1985; Cronin & Taylor, 1992) to conceptualize service quality as an antecedent of service performance, customer satisfaction, purchase intention, and loyalty. The main ingredients for the improvement of service quality reflected in these models are:

*   Explicit vision, mission, and objective of achievement
*   Involvement, empowerment, and motivation of staff
*   Clear understanding of concepts of service quality and factors affecting the same
*   Strong involvement of top management
*   Effective measurement and feedback system
*   Effective implementation system
*   Efficient customer care system
*   Long-term social commitment

3.3. MODELS OF EC SERVICE QUALITY

Since EC is a comparatively new area to investigate, many researchers are very enthusiastic in addressing service quality dimensions of B2C EC. In this chapter, we have reviewed scholarly articles addressing service quality dimensions of EC. Then we summarize and compare the primary models in this field and postulate the determining factors of service quality in EC in general and especially in global context in Table 3.1. Many researchers addressing issues related to service quality are now putting their enthusiasm on identifying, evaluating, defining, and modeling EC service quality. However, they are not following the same procedure to conduct these researches. The most commonly followed methodologies to model EC service quality dimensions are based on the following procedures:

1.   Literature reviews concerning service quality of brick and mortar business
2.   Revision of present traditional service quality models
3.   Exploratory study among B2C EC consumers, especially students
4.   Survey among different focus groups
5.   Synthesizing existing B2C EC service quality models
6.   Extension of different technology acceptance models

In the following paragraphs, we have attempted to examine and critically analyze a few existing frameworks selected from Table 3.1, which are specifically dealing with B2C EC service quality dimensions, and have significant implications in this context. The objectives of analyzing these models are to evaluate and character-ize the critical factors of service quality which lead customers to adopt EC and consequently investigate and reveal cultural connection of these factors. We have set some selection criteria to choose the fundamental scholarly articles in this field from Table 3.1 to conceptualize the central concepts and theories of those papers. These criteria are the followings:

1.   The study should focus on B2C EC service quality attributes from the custom-ers' perspective.
2.   The study should have empirical and/or theoretical support.
3.   The study should attempt rigorously to identify and measure a specific set of service quality dimensions of B2C EC and develop a primary model in the sense that it should not be a simple extension, modification, or renaming of constructs with just addition of some scale items of existing models.

Table 3.1. Reviewed articles on B2C EC service quality

Sl. No	Study	Domain of the Measurement	Dependent Variable	Independent Variable related to Quality Dimensions
1	Alpar (2001)	Website quality	Satisfaction with website	Ease of use, info content, entertainment, interactivity.
2	Balasubramanian *et al.* (2003)	Service quality	Satisfaction	Price, Trust disposition, perceived environmental security, perceived operational competence, and perceived trustworthiness.
3	Bauer *et al.* (2006)	Service Quality	Quality	Functionality/design, enjoyment, process, reliability, and responsiveness.
4	Cai *et al.* (2003)	Service quality	Quality	Website design/content, trustworthiness, prompt/reliable service, and communication.
5	Cao *et al.* (2005)	Website quality	Intention to revisit a website	Multimedia capability, search facility, responsiveness, information accuracy, information relevance, empathy, trust, and attractiveness /playfulness.
6	Chen *et al.* (2003)	Website quality	Attitude toward the site	Entertainment, informativeness, organization.
7	Childers *et al.* (2001)	Website quality	Online shopping attitudes	Navigation, convenience, sustainability of personal examination.
8	Chiu *et al.* (2005)	Website quality	Behavioral intention	Connectivity, information quality, interactivity, playfulness, and learning.
9	Collier *et al.* (2006)	Service quality	Satisfaction	Process quality: privacy, design, information accuracy, ease of use, and functionality. Outcome quality: timeliness, order accuracy, and order condition. Recovery quality: interactive fairness, procedural fairness, and outcome fairness.
10	Dabholkar (1996)	Website quality	Intention to use	Speed of delivery, ease of use, reliability, enjoyment, control.
11	Devaraj *et al.* (2002)	Service quality	Channel satisfaction	Usefulness, asset specifity, uncertainty, price savings, time, ease of use, and assurance.

continued on following page

Table 3.1. continued

12	Fassnacht *et al.* (2006)	Service quality	Quality	Environmental quality: graphic quality, clarity of lay out. Delivery quality: attractiveness of selection, information quality, ease of use, technical quality. Outcome quality: reliability, functional benefit, and emotional benefit.
13	Gounaris *et al.* (2003)	Website quality	Internet use	Customer care and risk reduction benefit, information benefit, interaction facilitation benefit.
14	Gummerus *et al.* (2004)	Service quality	Loyalty, Satisfaction, Trust	User interface, responsiveness, need fulfillment, security.
15	Janda *et al.* (2002)	Service quality	Satisfaction	Performance, access, security, sensation, and information.
16	Kim *et al.* (2004)	Website quality	Quality	Informational fit-to-task, tailored communication, online completeness, relative advantage, visual appeal, innovativeness, emotional appeal, consistent image, ease of understanding, intuitive operations, response time, and trust.
17	Kim *et al.* (2006)	Service quality	Quality	Efficiency, fulfillment, system availability, privacy, responsiveness, contact, personalization, information, and graphic style.
18	Lee *et al.* (2000)	Website quality	Purchase behavior	Perceived usefulness, perceived use, perceived transactional risk, and perceived product/service risk.
19	Liljander *et al.* (2002)	Service quality	Satisfaction	Site design and content, trust, empathy, security/privacy.
20	Liu *et al.* (2000)	Service quality	Website success	Info and service quality; system use; playfulness; system design quality.

continued on following page

Table 3.1. continued

21	Loiacono *et al.* (2002)	Website/ Service quality	Intention to purchase; Intention to revisit	Usefulness: informational fit-to-task, tailored communications, trust, and response time. Ease of Use: ease of understanding and intuitive operations. Entertainment: visual appeal, innovativeness, and emotional appeal. Complimentary Relationship: consistent image, on-line completeness, and relative advantage.
22	Parasuraman *et al.* (2005)	Service quality	Quality	E-S-QUAL: efficiency, system availability, fulfillment, privacy. E-RecS-QUAL: responsiveness, compensation, contact.
23	Rice (2002)	Website quality	Intent to return	Design/technical evaluation, emotional experience.
24	Santos (2003)	Service quality	Quality	Incubative: ease of use, appearance, linkage, structure and layout, and content. Active: reliability, efficiency, support, communication, security, and incentives.
25	Schaupp *et al.* (2005)	Service quality	Satisfaction	Privacy, merchandising, convenience, trust, delivery, usability, product customization, product quality, and security.
26	Sebastianelli *et al.* (2006)	Service quality	Quality	Reliability, accessibility, ordering services, convenience, product content, assurance, and credibility.
27	Srinivasan *et al.* (2002)	Service quality	Customer loyalty	Customization, contact interactivity, care, community, cultivation, choice, character.
28	Szymanski *et al.* (2000)	Service quality	Satisfaction	Convenience, merchandising, site design, financial security.
29	Van Riel (2001)	Service quality	Quality	User interface, reliability, security, customization, responsiveness.
30	Wolfinbarger *et al.* (2003)	Service quality	Quality	Web site design, fulfillment /reliability, privacy /security, and customer service.

continued on following page

Table 3.1. continued

31	Yoo *et al.* (2001)	Website/ Service quality	Overall site quality; attitude toward site; online purchase intention; site loyalty; site equity	Ease of use, aesthetic design, processing speed, and security.
32	Zeithamal *et al.* (2002)	Service quality	Quality	Efficiency, reliability, fulfillment, privacy, customer service, responsiveness, compensation, contact.
33	Zhang *et al.* (2002)	Website/ Service quality	Quality	Navigation, security/privacy, product and service concerns, readability/comprehension/clarity, and site technical features.

Yoo & Donthu (2001)

Yoo and Donthu (2001) worked on service quality factors of B2C EC and presented their findings in "Developing a Scale to Measure the Perceived Quality of an Internet Shopping Site (SITEQUAL)". They developed a fundamental model for shopping website named SITEQUAL. The authors argue that high quality sites are more effective to attract browsers and shoppers because quality builds sustainable competitive assets.

Devaraj et al. (2002)

EC has gained rapid expansion in the last decade. This unprecedented proliferation of B2C EC has attracted the market and service researchers to conceptualize the service quality issues in terms of information system, website design, transaction, and customer service. Conceptualizing consumer interaction with the online shopping channel enhances the understanding of consumer behavior, which is an important factor for future expansion and sustainability. Devaraj *et al.* (2002), in the study " Antecedents of B2C Channel Satisfaction and Preference: Validating e-Commerce Metrics", explored service quality aspects of B2C EC that lead to customer satisfaction.

Janda et al. (2002)

Studies have shown that the Internet is primarily used as a tool for information search rather than as a channel for purchasing products. In fact, less than two percent of customers visiting website buy any product electronically (Bellman *et al.,* 1999). Many consumers prefer to search for product information online and then go to traditional stores to purchase (Bellman *et al.,* 1999; Dobie *et al.,* 2001; Porter, 2001; Straub & Watson, 2001). In order to attract more customers not only for information searching but also for real purchase, online retailers must be devoted to find out the service quality attributes demanded by the customers. A study revealed that poor service quality prevented 80 percent customers' not to go for online purchase (Dobie *et al.,* 2001). Studies have also suggested that companies who offer superior service quality can attain competitive advantage because they are able to create stronger loyalty among customers (Bell & Zemke, 1992; Zeithaml *et al.,* 1996). Under this perspective, Janda *et al.* (2002) directed to define and measure online retail service quality in the study "Consumer perceptions of Internet retail service quality" to improve better online offer to attract more customers for real purchase.

Loiacono et al. (2002)

In B2C EC, customers first interact with websites for either gathering information or purchasing product. Websites facilitate direct selling activities, present related materials to consumers, define a corporate image, and provide basic company information to customers. Therefore, design and deployment of quality attributes in a website from customers' perspective is considered a critical issue. Loiacono *et al.* (2002) in the study, "WebQual™: A Measure of Web Site Quality", developed an instrument to measure website quality by exploring service quality attributes of shopping website.

Zhang & von Dran (2002)

For web-based general information domains and B2B EC, ultimate users are the customers. Understanding their expectations and perceptions about the websites is a very important concern. Customers of traditional services usually experience service quality during transaction with the organizations. However, for online, users experience the service quality first and then decide whether to transact. Therefore, quality assessment for website is a challenging and important job for both the researchers and managers. Zhang & von Dran (2002) argue that the nature of certain quality factors changes over time and importance of quality is also dependent on time. They examined a quality framework for a specific site based on the Kano et al.'s model (1984) and extended this work to distinguish quality dimensions for different domains in their study "User Expectations and Rankings of Quality Factors in Different Web Site Domains".

Cai & Jun (2003)

Service quality greatly influences customers' satisfaction and intention to shop online in the future. However, expected service quality dimensions do not bear the same significance for online buyers and information searchers (Kaynama & Black, 2000). Customers, who purchase through online, perceive the Internet to have higher utilities in communication, distribution, and accessibility than those who use it for information searching. In the paper "Internet users' perceptions of online service quality: a comparison of online buyers and information searchers" Cai & Jun (2003) examined the service quality dimensions perceived by the customers and verified whether there is any difference between online buyers and information searchers in terms of online quality perception.

Santos (2003)

Service quality has been recognized as one of the key determinants of success of any business (Zeithaml *et al.,* 1996). Researchers are now using traditional service quality dimensions in B2C EC to identify and evaluate the plausible differences in quality dimensions for traditional commerce and EC. Due to significant difference of B2C EC from traditional commerce in terms of service, customer interaction, presentation, transaction, and mode of business, scholarly researchers have agreed that service quality dimensions for B2C EC must be identified in a web-based context. Santos (2003) in the research paper "E-service quality: a model of virtual service quality dimensions" attempted to conceptually develop a service quality framework suitable for B2C EC.

Wolfinbarger & Gilly (2003)

Quality is the single most important thing for customers to be satisfied with the web-based vendors. It is important to define and measure overall online e-tail quality (eTailQ) beginning from information search, website navigation, ordering, customer service interactions, and delivery to satisfaction for the ordered product. Therefore, researchers are trying to understand, explain, and measure online quality according to customers' perceptions and expectations. Wolfinbarger & Gilly (2003) in their research work "eTailQ: dimensionalizing, measuring and predicting etail quality" attempted to measure online shopping quality attributes and their relative importance.

Parasuraman et al. (2005)

Parasuraman *et al.* (1985) developed a fundamental model to capture service quality attributes for traditional service. They have been working on this topic for long years. The authors extended their efforts to develop a service quality model suitable for B2C EC service context in the present study "E-S-QUAL A Multiple-Item Scale for Assessing Electronic Service Quality".

Bauer et al. (2006)

The rapid proliferation of information and communication technology in daily business activities is the most important long-term trend in the business world (Rust, 2001). It enables companies to open virtual channels as an alternative to traditional business channels. Operation and service of B2C EC is now a challenging issue for market researchers. Sustainability and future expansion of these web-based retailers mostly depend on their ability to meet customers' expectations in the virtual shopping environment (Zeithaml *et al.*, 2002). In this regard, Bauer *et al.* (2006) expanded their research to conceptualize online shopping service quality in the study "eTransQual: A transaction process-based approach for capturing service quality in online shopping."

Collier & Bienstock (2006)

Service quality inclusion in service design has been considered as an important strategy for marketers who are trying to differentiate their service offerings by establishing customer value and satisfying customer needs. The issue of service quality is being recognized as strategically more important for B2C EC. Service quality plays the key role in attracting and satisfying customers for web purchase (Holloway & Sharon, 2003). Collier & Bienstock (2006) in their fundamental research work "Measuring Service Quality in E-Retailing" focused intention to construct service quality models to capture quality attributes at different stages of service of B2C EC.

Fassnacht et al. (2006)

To gain long-term success in launching B2C EC, quality is a major driving force. Comprehensive definition, assessment, and measurement of quality are the key to effective quality management. Based on extant research and findings from a qualitative study, Fassnacht *et al.* (2006) developed a broadly applicable, hierarchical quality model for electronic services and presented it in the research paper "Quality of Electronic Services Conceptualizing and Testing a Hierarchical Model".

Kim et al. (2006)

Online service quality dimensions are very important for the customers to take purchase decision. Nevertheless, the available online service quality dimensions provided by the previous works in EC service context offer a fragmented view of online service quality. Therefore, to evaluate online service quality from a consumer perspective, Kim *et al.* (2006) developed a refined model to measure service quality attributes especially designed for apparel website in the research study "Online service attributes available on apparel retail web site: an E-S-QUAL approach".

Sebastianelli et al. (2006)

Quality has long been recognized as a single most important factor to attract customers, influence purchase intention, satisfy customers, maintain future customer relationships, increase profitability, and ensure long-run survival in a rapidly changing business environment (Deming, 1986). Firms are constantly implementing service quality improvement programs in their efforts to increase profitability and attain higher levels of customer satisfaction. Quality is also important for information technology and EC. Defining service quality attributes for B2C EC is a challenging issue for both the researchers and practitioners. Sebastianelli *et al.* (2006) in the study "Perceived Quality of Internet Retailers: Does Shopping Frequency and Product Type Make a Difference?" attempted to identify general quality attributes for online retailers and incorporated some intervening variables to measure the plausible effects of these variables on service quality attributes.

The summary of the service quality dimensions derived from the above scholarly articles are presented in the following Table 3.2.

From careful observation and analysis of the explained 14 models, it is frequently found that some authors of those research models used similar scale items to form a quality dimension using different names. It is also worth noting that while some authors used a single name of a quality dimension to define several quality attributes, others used several names of quality dimensions to define that single quality dimension. It is also noted that the set of quality dimensions considered important is different in different studies, and even when the dimensions are similar, their definitions and measurements (scale items) are different.

Table 3.2. B2C EC service quality attributes investigated by various scholars

Dependent Variables	Study	Independent Variables
Quality	Bauer *et al.* (2006)	Functionality/design, enjoyment, process, reliability, and responsiveness
	Cai & Jun (2003)	Website design/content, trustworthiness, prompt/reliable service, and communication
	Fassnacht *et al.* (2006)	*Environmental quality:* Graphic quality, clarity of lay out *Delivery quality:* Attractiveness of selection, information quality, ease of use, technical quality *Outcome quality:* Reliability, functional benefit, and emotional benefit
	Kim *et al.* (2006)	Efficiency, fulfillment, system availability, privacy, responsiveness, contact, personalization, information, and graphic style
	Parasuraman *et al.* (2005)	*E-S-QUAL:* Efficiency, system availability, fulfillment, privacy *E-RecS-QUAL:* Responsiveness, compensation, contact
	Santos (2003)	*Incubative:* Ease of use, appearance, linkage, structure and layout, and content *Active:* Reliability, efficiency, support, communication, security, and incentives
	Sebastianelli *et al.* (2006)	Reliability, accessibility, ordering services, convenience, product content, assurance, and credibility
	Wolfinbarger & Gilly (2003)	Website design, fulfillment/reliability, privacy/security, and customer service
	Zhang & von Dran (2002)	Navigation, security/privacy, product and service concerns, readability/comprehension/clarity, and site technical features
Satisfaction	Collier & Bienstock (2006)	*Process quality:* Privacy, design, information accuracy, ease of use, and functionality *Outcome quality:* Timeliness, order accuracy, and order condition *Recovery quality:* Interactive fairness, procedural fairness, and outcome fairness
	Devaraj *et al.* (2002)	Usefulness, asset specifity, uncertainty, price savings, time, ease of use, and assurance
	Janda *et al.* (2002)	Performance, access, security, sensation, and information

continued on following page

Table 3.2. continued

| Intention/Intention to reuse/Intention to revisit/Intention to purchase | Loiacono *et al.* (2002) | *Usefulness:* Informational fit-to-task, tailored communications, trust, and response time
Ease of Use: Ease of understanding and intuitive operations
Entertainment: Visual appeal, innovativeness, and emotional appeal
Complimentary Relationship: Consistent image, on-line completeness, and relative advantage |
| | Yoo *et al.* (2001) | Ease of use, aesthetic design, processing speed, and security |

It is worth to note here some critical points from the above findings. These are:

1.   All the studies reviewed in Table 3.2 are conducted in USA (Yoo & Donthu, 2001; Devaraj *et al.*, 2002 ; Janda *et al.*, 2002 ; Loiacono *et al.*, 2002 ; Zhang & von Dran, 2002 ; Cai & Jun, 2003, Parasuraman *et al.*, 2005 ; Collier & Bienstock, 2006 ; Kim *et al.*, 2006 ; Sebastianelli *et al.*, 2006), or Germany (Bauer *et al.*, 2006; Fassnacht *et al.*, 2006), or UK (Santos, 2003), or USA/Canada (Wolfinbarger & Gilly, 2003). For the proper globalization of EC, quality perception of EC needs diversified attitude coming from different segmented markets which is characterized by cultural differences.

2.   If we closely look at the generic meaning of the service quality attributes organized in Table 3.2, we profoundly notice that service quality expectation and perception of consumers significantly depends on cultural differences, personal attitudes or behavioral intention, local environmental security perception (country laws and rules) which is also a function of political system, social values, organizational characteristics, economical status, frequency of purchase or purchase experience etc. These may be called as intervening variables of global quality perceptions of EC. Therefore, service quality, which is predominant factor for EC adoption and ultimately proliferation, should be analyzed with intertwined effect of cultural diversity.

3.   Globalization effect, cultural diversity, international marketing, and possible barriers for proliferation of EC are important aspects of EC service quality perceptions which are not encountered or accounted for in the existing literature of EC.

3.4. SERVICE QUALITY, CULTURAL DIVERSITY, AND EC ADOPTION AND PROLIFERATION

The rapid proliferation of information and communication technology in daily business activities is the most important long-term trend in the business world (Rust, 2001). It enables companies to open virtual channels as an alternative to traditional business channels. Operation and service of EC is now a challenging issue for market researchers. Sustainability and future expansion of these web-based retailers mostly depend on their ability to meet customers' expectations in the virtual shopping environment (Zeithaml *et al.*, 2002).The emergence of EC is significantly affecting traditional marketing patterns. Marketing experts must understand that the appearance of electronic communities is a great threat for the existing channels of business (Armstrong & Hagel, 1996). They need to understand the full range of products and services required by the electronic community. They must learn to take advantage of the technology that allows customers to move seamlessly from information gathering to completion of a transaction, interacting with the various providers of products and services as necessary (Miers, 1996). Technology acceptance model (Davis *et al.*, 1989), Delone and McLean's (1992/2003) model and the service quality models reviewed in this chapter, all show that the underpinning paradigms of EC adoption and proliferation of EC is grounded on service quality perception by consumers of EC. Service quality greatly influences customers' satisfaction and intention to shop online in the future and thus proliferation of EC. Service quality is the single most important factor for the consumers to interact with EC. Present marketing researchers agree on the point that service is gradually becoming the driving force to distinguish between the performances of two companies. In virtual marketing like EC, where direct interaction between customers and employees is absent, importance of service quality even bears more significance. Customers of traditional services usually experience service quality during transaction with the organizations. However, for online, users experience the service quality first and then decide whether to transact. A study revealed that poor service quality prevented 80 percent customers' not to go for online purchase (Dobie *et al.*, 2001). Studies have also suggested that companies who offer superior service quality can attain competitive advantage because they are able to create stronger loyalty among customers (Bell & Zemke, 1992; Zeithaml *et al.*, 1996).

Customers' perception and expectation of service quality dimensions for any field, whereas it is traditional commerce or EC, has a close relation with adoption of that system, and is significantly depend on cultural diversity of the customers (Tsikriktsis, 2002; Shareef *et al.*, 2008). Culture contains standards, ideology, values, and expectations, which develop attitudes and characteristics (Lemme, 1999). Expectation and perception are not homogeneous across customers of all countries. Over the past 40 years, several models have been developed to provide an approach for the comparative analysis of different cultures (Hofstede, 1980). Although each of the articles developed cultural models that illustrated somewhat different concepts, the core paradigms of these models provide support for their universality. Over the past three decades, validity of these findings has been confirmed in studies exploring consumer behavior, purchase intention, perception of security, and decision-making. A fundamental problem to study culture is that it is very complex and should be analyzed in comparative fashion. It is only useful in explaining differences across nations. The theories that are applied, the problems that are identified, and the solutions that are proposed are generated from a view of the world by members of the American-style society only. Most of the empirical studies of EC service quality framework have been conducted in USA or any developed countries. Although customers of EC are global, present trends of EC are focused only on the customers of developed countries. However, due to significant cultural, social, economical, and political diversity, consumers' expectation and perception of different service quality factors of EC also vary universally. Especially, we can draw a bold demarcation line between developed and developing countries. Consequently, adoption, barriers, and proliferation of EC are significantly affected by perception of service quality of EC by different segmented regions of the world market. It is also argued that the level of importance of different service quality factors might vary, even highly significantly, or non-significantly depending on cultural, social, political, and economical characteristics of those segmented regions. Therefore, adoption, cultural barriers, and proliferation of EC globally have strong connection with perception of service quality of EC.

3.5. RELATED ISSUES

The fundamental opportunity offered by B2C EC is that web retailers can communicate with the potential consumers without maintaining physical channel. In the electronic medium, consumers can buy products/services from anywhere in the world. They are not limited by any country/location. Customers' of B2C EC are global. As a result, global cultural differences develop significant disparities in behavioral intention and attitudes of consumers' of EC. A society produces some values, ideas, intentions, and speculations on human personality. These perceived psychological phenomena depend on rules, regulations, relationships, culture, tradition, etc. Depending on cultural factors, purchase behavioral can vary significantly (Engel *et al.,* 1993). Based on the literature reviews (Chase & Tansik, 1978; Kale & Sudharshan, 1987; Kogut & Singh, 1988; Li, 1994; Kettinger *et al.,* 1995; Donthu & Boonghee, 1998; Furrer *et al.,* 2000; Liu *et al.,* 2001), it is evident that those social values, which generate pre-trust disposition attitude and security concern on the customers' purchase behavior, are very important for determining service quality factors of EC and successively its adoption and proliferation. We can easily conjecture that perception of service quality which is potentially affected by cultural differences has significant relationship with adoption and proliferation of EC. Therefore, behavioral intention and culture as related issues of service quality have significant implication in the study of adoption and possible barriers of EC proliferation. The challenge of EC is to attract customers worldwide. So globalization issues and strategies should be considered in developing service quality model. In this context, exploratory studies should not be concentrated in only developed countries, it should also be extended to developing countries. Market segmentation is an important issue. It is a great challenge to develop a single model of service quality, which will serve the purpose of globalization of EC (standardize versus adaptation or customization). In this context, cultural issues have significant effects on the development of a global service quality framework.

Attitude has different aspects arising from retrospective learning, emotional views, and social values (Engel *et al.,* 1993; Shareef *et al.,* 2008). Behavioral attitude is dependent on experience, personality, and social values (Engel et al., 1993). Behavioral intention has significant implication in assessing service quality determinants. Service literatures have incorporated behavioral intention in their models for a long time to identify quality dimension (Cox & Rich, 1964; Azjen & Fishbein, 1980; Davis *et al.,* 1989; Bellizzi & Hite, 1992). Nevertheless, EC service designers have not provided enough priority to behavioral differences as an antecedent of service quality dimensions. Behavioral intentions, attitudes, and characteristics have important effects on purchase behavior. Analyzing purchase behavior of consumers is very important, because based on this retailers can develop their marketing strategy and get sustainable competitive advantage (Parasuraman *et al.,* 1985; Zeithmal, 1988; Bolton & Drew, 1991; Holbrook, 1994; Cronin *et al.,* 2000). Literature reviews on consumer behavior (Engel *et al.,* 1993) perceive purchase intention as a personal phenomenon, a situational phenomenon, a social phenomenon, and a perceived contextual phenomenon. Technology acceptance and purchase intention characteristics in the perspective of behavioral intention play significant role in the study of service quality fields of EC (van Riel *et al.,* 2001).

REFERENCES

Albrecht, K., & Bradford, L.J. (1990). The *Service Advantage: How to identify and Fulfill Customer Needs*. Richard D. Irwin, Homewood, IL.

Alpar, P. (2001). Satisfaction with a Web Site: Its Measurement, Factors, and Correlates. *Working Paper No. 99/01,* Philipps-Universität Marburg, Institut für Wirtschaftsinformatik.

Armstrong, A., & Hagel, J. (1996). The Real Value of On-line Communities. *Harvard Business Review, 74*(3), 134-141.

Azjen, I. & Fishbein, M. (1980). *Understanding Attitudes and Predicting Social Behavior.* Englewood Cliffs, NJ: Prentice- Hall Inc.

Babakus, E., & Boller, G. W. (1992). An Empirical Assessment of the SERVQUAL Scale. *Journal of Business Research, 24,* 253-268.

Balasubramanian, S., Konana, P., & Menon, N. M. (2003). Customer, Satisfaction in Virtual Environments: A Study of Online Investing. *Management Science, 7,* 871–889.

Bauer, H. H., Falk, T., & Hammerschmidt, M. (2006). eTransQual: A Transaction Process-Based Approach for Capturing Service Quality in Online Shopping. *Journal of Business Research, 59,* 866-875.

Bell, C. R., & Zemke, R. (Eds.) (1992). *Managing Knock Your Socks off Service.* Amacom, New York, NY.

Bellizzi, J. A., & Hite, R. E. (1992). Environmental Color, Consumer Feelings, and Purchase Likelihood. *Psychology & Marketing, 9,* 347-363.

Bellman, S., Lohse, G., & Eric, J. (1999). Predictors of Online Buying Behavior. *Communications of the ACM, 42*(12) 32-38.

Bolton, R. N., & Drew, J. H. (1991). A Multistage Model of Consumers' Assessments of Service Quality and Value. *Journal of Consumer Research, 17,* 375-384.

Boyer, K. K., Hallowell, R., & Roth, A. V. (2002). E-Services: Operations Strategy—A Case Study and A Method for Analyzing Operational Benefits. *Journal of Operations Management, 20*(2), 175–188.

Cai, S., & Jun, M. (2003). Internet Users' Perceptions of Online Service Quality: A Comparison of Online Buyers and Information Searches. *Managing Service Quality, 13*(6), 504-519.

Cao, M., Zhang, O., & Seydel, J. (2005). Measuring B2C eCommerce Website Quality: An Empirical Examination. *Industrial management & Data Systems, 106*(5), 645-661.

Chase, R. B., & Tansik, D. A. (1978). The Customer Contact Model for Organization Design. *Management Science, 29*(9), 673-687.

Chen, S. C., & Dhillon, G. S. (2003). Interpreting Dimensions of Consumer Trust in E-Commerce. *Information Technology and Management, 4*, 303-318.

Childers, T. L., Carr, C. L., Peck, J., & Carson, S. (2001). Hedonic and Utilitarian Motivations for Online Retail Shopping Behavior. *Journal of Retailing, 77*, 511-35.

Chiu, H. C., Hsieh, Y. C., & Kao, C. Y. (2005). Website Quality and Customer's Behavioral Intention: An Exploratory Study of the Role of Information Asymmetry. *Total Quality Management and Business Excellence, 16*(2), 185–197.

Collier, J. E., & Bienstock, C. C. (2006). Measuring Service Quality in E-Retailing. *Journal of Service Research, 8*(3), 260-275.

Cox, D. F., & Rich, S. U. (1964). Perceived Risk and Consumer Decision Making - The Case of Telephone Shopping. *Journal of Marketing Research, 1*(4), 32-39.

Cronin, J. J. Jr., & Taylor, S. A. (1992). Measuring Service Quality: A Reexamination and Extension. *Journal of Marketing, 56*(July), 55-68.

Cronin, J. J., Brady Jr. M. K., & Hult, G. T. (2000). Assessing the Effect of Quality, Value, and Customer Satisfaction on Consumer Behavioral Intentions in Service Environments. *Journal of Retailing, 76*, 193-218.

Dabholkar, P. A. (1996). Consumer Evaluations of New Technology-Based Self-Service Options: An Investigation of Alternative Models of SQ. *International Journal of Research in Marketing, 13*(1), 29-51.

Davis, F., Bagozzi, R. P., & Warshaw, P. R. (1989). User Acceptance of Computer Technology: A Comparison of Two Theoretical Models. *Management Science, 35*(8), 982-1003.

Davis, F. D., Bagozzi, R. P., & Warshaw, P. R. (1992). Extrinsic and Intrinsic Motivation to Use Computers in the Workplace. *Journal of Applied Social Psychology, 22*(14), 1111-1132.

DeLone, W. H., & McLean, E. R. (1992). Information Systems Success: The Quest for the Dependent Variable. *Information Systems Research, 3*(1), 60-95.

DeLone, W. H., & McLean, E. R. (2003). The DeLone and McLean Model of Information Systems Success: A Ten-year Update. *Journal of Management Information Systems, 19*(4), 9-30.

Deming, W. E. (1975). On Some Statistical Aids toward Economic Production. *Interfaces, 5*(4), 1-15.

Deming, W. E. (1986). *Out of the Crisis.* Cambridge. MA: MIT Center for Advanced Engineering Study.

Devaraj, S., Fan, M., & Kohli, R. (2002). Antecedents of B2C Channel Satisfaction and Preference: Validating e-Commerce Metrics. *Information Systems Research, 13*(3), 316-333.

Dobie, K., Grant, J., & Ready, K. (2001). Product Motivation and Purchasing Activity: An Exploratory Study of Consumers' Internet Purchasing Activity. *Journal of Promotion Management, 6*(1/2), 31-43.

Donthu, N., & Boonghee, Y. (1998). Cultural Influences on Service Quality Expectations. *Journal of Service Research, 1*(2), 178-186.

Edvardsson, B., Gustavsson, B. O., & Riddle, D. I. (1989). An Expanded Model of the Service Encounter with Emphasis on Cultural Context. *Research Report 89:4, CFT Services Research Centre,* University of Karlstad, Sweden.

Engel, J. F., Blackwell, R. D., & Miniard, P. W. (1993). *Consumer Behavior.* 7th edition, The Dryden Press, Harcourt Brace Jovanovich, USA.

Fassnacht, M., & Koese, I. (2006). Quality of Electronic Services: Conceptualizing and Testing a Hierarchical Model. *Journal of Service Research, 9*(1), 19-37.

Furrer, O., Liu, B. S-C., & Sudharshan, D. (2000). The Relationships between Culture and Service Quality Perceptions: Basis for Cross-Cultural Market Segmentation and Resource Allocation. *Journal of Service Research, 2*(4), 355-371.

Gartner Inc. (2001). *Report on E-Service,* www.gartner.com/symposium/canada.

Gounaris, S., & Sergios, D. (2003). Assessing Service Quality on the Web: Evidence from Business-to-Consumer Portals. *Journal of Services Marketing, 17*(5), 529-48.

Gronroos, C. (1984). A Service Quality Model and Its Marketing Implications. *European Journal of Marketing, 18*(4), 36-44.

Gronroos, C. (1990). *Service Management and Marketing: Managing the Decisive Moment in Service Competition.* Lexington, MASS: Lexington Books.

Grönroos, C., Heinonen, F, Isoniemi, K., & Lindholm, M. (2000). The Netoffer Model: A Case Example from the Virtual Market Space. *Management Decision, 38*(4), 243-52.

Gummerus, J., Liljander, V., Pura, M., & van Riel, A. (2004). Customer Loyalty to Content-Based Websites: The Case of an Online Health-Care Service. *Journal of Services Marketing, 18*(3), 175-86.

Gummesson, E. (1994). Making Relationship Marketing Operational. *International Journal of Service Industry Management, 5*(5), 5-20.

Hofstede, G. (1980). *Culture's Consequences: International Differences in Work-Related Values.* Beverly Hills, CA: Sage.

Holbrook, M. B. (1994). *The Nature of Customer Value: An Axiology of Services in the Consumption Experience.* In R. T. Rust et al. (Eds.), Service Quality: New Directions of Theory and Practice, Thousand Oaks, CA: Sage.

Holloway, B. B., & Sharon E. B. (2003). Service Failure in Online Retailing: A Recovery Opportunity. *Journal of Service Research, 6*(1), 92-105.

Janda, S., Trocchia, P. J., & Gwinner, K. P. (2002). Consumer Perceptions of Internet Retail Service Quality. *International Journal of Service Industry Management, 13*(5), 412-431.

Juran, J. M. (1962). *Quality Control Handbook.* 2nd edition, McGraw-Hill, London.

Kale, S. H., & Sudharshan, D. (1987). A Strategic Approach to International Segmentation. *International Marketing Review, 4*(4), 60-70.

Kano, N. Seraku, N., Takahashi, F., & Tsuji, S. (1984). Attractive Quality and must-be Quality, *Hinshitsu* (Quality, the *Journal of Japanese Society for Quality Control*), *14*, 39-48.

Kaynama, S. A., & Black, C. I. (2000). A Proposal to Assess the Service Quality of Online Travel Agencies: An Exploratory Study. *Journal of Professional Services Marketing, 21*(1), 63–88.

Kettinger, W. J., Lee, C. C., & Lee, S. (1995). Global Measures of Information Service Quality: A Cross-National Study. *Decision Sciences, 26*(5), 569-588.

Kim, M., & Lennon, S. J. (2004). Consumer Response to Product Unavailability in Online Shopping. Paper presented at the *International Textiles and Apparel Association Annual Meeting*, Portland.

Kim, M., Kim, J.-H., & Lennon, S. J. (2006). Online Service Attributes Available on Apparel Retail Web Site: An E-S-QUAL Approach. *Managing Service Quality, 16*(1), 51-77.

Kogut, B., & Singh, H. (1988). The Effect of National Culture on the Choice of Entry Mode. *Journal of International Business Studies, 19*(3), 411-432.

Kotler, P. (1973). Atmospherics as a Marketing Tool. *Journal of Retailing, 49*(4), 48-64.

Lee, H., Lee, Y., & Yoo, D. (2000). The Determinants of Perceived Service Quality and Its Relationship with Satisfaction. *Journal of Service Marketing, 14*(3), 217-31.

Lemme, B. H. (1999). *Development in Adulthood.* 2nd edition, Needham Heights, MA: Allyn & Bacon.

Li, J. (1994). Experience Effects and International Expansion: Strategies of Service MNCs in the Asia-Pacific Region. *Management International Review, 34*(3), 217-234.

Liljander, V., van Riel, A. C. R., & Pura, M. (2002). Customer Satisfaction with E-Services: The Case of an On-Line Recruitment Portal. In M. Bruhn & B. Stauss (Eds.), *Jahrbuch Dienstleistungsmanagement 2002–Electronic Services,* Gabler, Wiesbaden, (pp. 407-432).

Liu, C., & Arnett, K. P. (2000). Exploring the Factors Associated with Website Success in the Context of Electronic Commerce. *Information & Management, 38,* 23–33.

Liu, B. S-C., Furrer O., & Sudharshan, D. (2001). The Relationships between Culture and Behavioral Intentions toward Services. *Journal of Service Research, 4*(2), 118-129.

Loiacono, E. T., Watson, R. T., & Goodhue, D. L. (2002). WEBQUAL: A Measure of Website Quality. *In K. Evans & L. Scheer (Eds.), Marketing educators' conference: Marketing theory and applications, 13,* 432–437.

Miers, D. (1996). The Strategic Challenges of Electronic Commerce. *Electronic Commerce, Enix Consulting Limited,* (pp. 1-19).

Parasuraman, A., Zeithaml, V. A., & Berry, L. L. (1985). A Conceptual Model of Service Quality and Its Implications for Future Research. *Journal of Marketing, 49,* 41-50.

Parasuraman, A., Zeithaml, V. A., & Berry, L. L. (1988). SERVQUAL: A Multiple-Item Scale for Measuring Customer Perceptions of Service Quality. *Journal of Retailing, 64*(1), 12–40.

Parasuraman, A., & Zinkhan, G. M. (2002). Marketing to and Serving Customers through the Internet: An Overview and Research Agenda. *Journal of the Academy of Marketing Science, 30*(4), 286-295.

Parasuraman, A., Zeithaml, V. A., & Malhotra, A. (2005). E-S-QUAL A Multiple-Item Scale for Assessing Electronic Service Quality. *Journal of Service Research, 7*(3), 213-233.

Porter, M. E. (2001). Strategy and the Internet. *Harvard Business Review, 79*(3), 63-78.

Rice, M. (2002). What Makes Users Revisit a Web Site? *Marketing News, 31*(6), 12.

Rust, R. (2001). The Rise of E-Service. *Journal of Service Research, 3*(4), 283-284.

Santos, J. (2003). E-Service Quality: A Model of Virtual Service Quality Dimensions. *Management Service Quality, 13*(3), 233-46.

Schaupp, L. C., & Bélanger, F. (2005). A Conjoint Analysis of Online Consumer Satisfaction. *Journal of Electronic Commerce Research, 6*(2), 95-111.

Sebastianelli, R., Tamimi, N., & Rajan, M. (2006). Perceived Quality Of Internet Retailers: Does Shopping Frequency And Product Type Make A Difference? *EABR & ETLC*, Siena, Italy.

Shareef, M. A., Kumar U., & Kumar, V. (2008). Role of Different EC Quality Factors on E-Purchase: A Developing Country Perspective, *Journal of Electronic Commerce Research, 9*(2), 92-113.

Sirdeshmukh, D., Singh, J., & Sabol, B. (2002). Consumer Trust, Value, and Loyalty in Relational Exchanges. *Journal of Marketing, 66*(January), 15-37.

Srinivasan, S. S., Rolph, A., & Kishore, P. (2002). Customer Loyalty in E-Commerce: An Exploration of Its Antecedents and Consequences. *Journal of Retailing, 78*, 41–50.

Straub, D., & Watson, R. (2001). Research Commentary: Transformational Issues in Researching IS and Net-Enabled Organizations. *Information Systems Research, 12*(4), 337-345.

Szymanski, D. M., & Hise, R. T. (2000). E-Satisfaction: An Initial Examination. *Journal of Retailing, 76*(3), 309-322.

Taguchi, G. (1986). *Introduction to Quality Engineering*. Asian Productivity Organization, Tokyo.

Tsikriktsis, N. (2002). Does Culture Influence Web Site Quality Expectations? An Empirical Study. *Journal of Service Research, 5*(2), 101-112.

Van Riel, A. C. R., Liljander, V., & Jurriens, P. (2001). Exploring Customer Evaluations of E-service: A Portal Site. *International Journal of Service Industry Management, 12*(4), 359-77.

Wolfinbarger, M., & Gilly, M. C. (2003). eTailQ: Dimensionalizing, Measuring, and Predicting etail Quality. *Journal of Retailing, 79*(3), 183-98.

Yoo, B., & Donthu, N. (2001). Developing a Scale to Measure the Perceived Quality of an Internet Shopping Site (Sitequal). *Quarterly Journal of Electronic Commerce, 2*(1), 31-46.

Zeithaml, V. A. (1988). Consumer Perceptions of Price, Quality, and Value: A Means-End Model and Synthesis of Evidence. *Journal of Marketing, 52,* 2-22.

Zeithaml, V. A., Berry, L. L., & Parasuraman, A. (1996). The Behavioral Consequences of Service Quality. *Journal of Marketing, 60*(2), 31-46.

Zeithaml, V. A., Parasuraman, A., & Malhotra, A. (2002). Service Quality Delivery through Web Sites: A Critical Review of Extant Knowledge. *Journal of the Academy of Marketing Science, 30*(4), 362-75.

Zhang, P., & von Dran, G. (2002). User Expectations and Rankings of Quality Factors in Different Web Site Domains, *International Journal of Electronic Commerce, 6*(2), 9-33.

Chapter IV
Global Quality Management Practice for E-Commerce

ABSTRACT

Since Internet is the primary driving force of E-Commerce (EC), it has global phenomena. Consequently, Internet market is diffusing from the west to the east. Nevertheless, cultural, political, economical, technological, social, and overall attitudinal diversity create irresistible barriers for free movement of EC. In this aspect, quality standardization for EC is utmost important. Because quality experts believe that only quality improvement and standardization can provide EC acceptance by global consumers. Expansion of EC from developed countries to developing countries creates an opportunity to redefine the paradigms of quality management practice (QMP) appropriate for global diffusion of EC. This chapter illustrates some related concepts of quality, quality improvement, and different aspects of quality for EC to shed light on QMP.

4.1. INTRODUCTION

Quality management practice (QMP) is conceptualized as a set of paradigms, concepts, and interrelated practices documented by any organization to improve and standardize quality in all aspects of its process, design, production, and services to meet product and system quality and fulfill customer requirements and expectations (Bertram, 1991; Brown, 1992; Ross, 1993). To capture global market as the leader, most international E-retailers are now attempted to implement quality management principles which are completely customer focused.

QMP in traditional business sectors, either manufacturing or service systems, is investigated for decades (Parasuraman *et al.,* 2002). But QMP for EC is relatively a new topic, and after reviewing literature on the issues of quality management of EC, a limited number of scholarly studies is observed that are focused on the relevance of QMP with EC (Kumar et al., 2006). But, as we discussed in the previous chapters based on the characteristics and functions of operations, EC is inherently global. Retailers can sell and consumers can buy products through web pages from anywhere in the world. Consequently, global proliferation and global consumers' acceptance are important issues to be considered. Therefore, implementation of QMP in EC, which is an advanced step to ensure continuously global consumers preferences for quality, is a potential subject from its own merit to be discussed in this aspect .

This chapter is designed to discuss the aforementioned issues of quality management practice in EC for global proliferation and cultural adaptation with competitiveness. The chapter is divided into 5 sections with section 3 into sub-sections. The introduction section aims to provide a general background of the quality issue in EC. In the following section, we illustrate concepts of quality to provide a brief idea of the conceptual definition. In the next section, quality issues of EC are explored for QMP. In the following section, a quality management process model proposed by Kumar et al. (2006) is briefly presented to provide an illustration of QMP in EC. Finally a conclusion in this context is presented.

The proliferation of EC has magnified the importance of building a loyal customer base to an EC website (Gommans et al., 2001). Most web-based sellers rely initially on an intensive effort to create a strong global customer base. As competition for online customers grows, companies cannot simply expect that if they build websites, customers will spontaneously come (Nah et al., 2002). E-retailers are now very enthusiastic to develop quality E-services (Wang, 2003). Consumers from both developed and developing countries have diversified attitudes, cultural and social orientations, and technological beliefs. What leads to global customers' purchase decision has become a complex topic for E-retailers (Barsh et al., 2000). Previous research has explained the multidimensional and context-dependent nature of perceived value on purchase decisions (Zeithmal, 1988; Bolton et al., 1991, Shareef et al., 2008). Purchase decisions can be changed or modified with the global circumstances of the person and/or consumption situation derived from the quality attributes of vendors. Quality is the vital issue of EC. The importance of measuring and monitoring quality is now well recognized among managers (Johnson & Whang, 2002). Addressing literature on quality practice in EC (Kurtus, 2000; Chou, 2001; Yang, 2003; Field et al., 2004; Prybutok, 2005, Kumar et al., 2006), we find some interesting and challenging issues for EC globalization. These are:

1. EC is expanding very rapidly from the west to the east.
2. It is the Internet which makes the electronic market available for citizens across countries irrelevant to their geographical locations.
3. For future sustainability, E-retailers are expanding their business periphery to capture huge markets in developing countries.
4. Globalization is an inevitable reality for EC.
5. Cultural, political, technological, and economical differences among consumers across countries create potential barriers for global proliferation of EC.
6. Quality management practice(QMP) which can ensure better quality with lower price is the single most important aspect to overcome global barriers.

4.2. QUALITY AND QUALITY MANAGEMENT PRACTICE

Implementation of QMP in EC is a relatively new challenging area to researchers and management authorities. Academics and practitioners are deeply engaged in addressing and conceptualizing QMP for EC. Based on the underpinning principles of quality and quality management practice, we focus on the quality dimensions required for launching a successful global EC as the competitive edge in gaining market leadership.

Quality is defined from different perspectives. Different authors, relating to the fields of research, defined quality in different ways. Therefore, quality definition has several aspects. However, primarily quality is defined at different stages of industrial development by Deming (1975), Juran (1962), Taguchi (1986), and Crosby (1979) etc. Later on service quality is deeply analyzed and its issues are conceptualized by several researchers like, Gronroos (1984), Parasuraman et al. (1985), Cronin and Taylor (1992). The central paradigms of these conceptual definitions reflect some attributes related to:

*   Satisfy customers
*   Confirming standards
*   Provide competitive advantages in the global market
*   Lower cost
*   Effectiveness and efficiency of service
*   Cultural adaptability
*   Standardization for globalization

Shewhart (1931) defines quality, as "One of these [aspects of quality] has to do with the consideration of the quality of a thing as an objective reality independent of the existence of man The other has to do with what we think, feel, or sense as a result of the objective reality". Juran and Godfrey (1999) identified quality dimensions in two categories:

1. **Level of attributes:** Standardization of the level of product and service related attributes
2. **Absence of deficiencies:** Lowering level and decreasing number of defects to improve quality

Nielsen (1999) argues that quality is comprised of a pervasive set of attributes. On the other hand, Aladwani & Palvia (2002) consider quality to be a combination of multi-dimensional aspects related to performance. However, quality dimensions are difficult to define by any set of traits, because it is influenced by cultural, social , technological, and behavioral issues, and even time (Zhang & von Dran, 2002).

Quality can be characterized as the standardization of overall performance. Different studies assess standardization differently. Standardization which reflects the fitness for use can be analyzed shedding light on the quality concepts of information systems given by Mason and Mitroff (1973). It can be used to a web environment to empirically investigate web site quality. According to their conceptual paradigms of quality, web site quality is dependent on some specific variables. Mason and Mitroff (1973) defined an information system as consisting of "at least one PERSON of a certain PSYCHOLOGICAL TYPE who faces a PROBLEM within some ORGANIZATIONAL CONTEXT for which he needs EVIDENCE to arrive at a solution (i.e. to select some course of action) and that the evidence is made available to him through some MODE OF PRESENTATION."

Although the context in which information systems reside may have changed over time, Mason and Mitroff's characterization remains valid and can be used in web based information system's QMP. Kopcso et al. (2001) argued that Mason and Mitroff's IS characterization can be used as a basis for the development of global B2C EC service quality assessment model.

4.3. QUALITY CONCEPTS FOR EC

Studies dealing with the acceptance of technology (Meuter et al., 2001; Chen & Dhillon, 2003) reveal that customer evaluation of new technology is a distinct process. It depends on many system characteristics of EC. In the following paragraphs, some distinct quality issues relevant to EC are addressed.

4.3.1. System Quality

B2C EC system quality refers to the elements of a system that affect the end user in the way they interact and use an EC system. This is a basic dimension of EC evaluation. System quality measures the functionality of a website: usability, availability, and response time (DeLone & McLean, 2003). Smith and Merchant (2001) found that online customers are interested in getting a website which is flexible and easy to operate and interact. A user-friendly website is highly important to end-users (Robbins & Stylianou, 2003). Specifically the system quality of a website can be assessed by search facility, responsiveness, security, and ease in download.

4.3.2. Software Quality Matrix

Software quality is a field of study and practice that describes the desirable attributes of software products. From users' perspective, a software even can be treated as defected if it is not user friendly, and fails to satisfy consumers. There are several typical quality attributes related to software quality including, easy to learn and use, compatible, user-friendly, object-oriented, easy installation, error free design, fast in processing, understandable coding, easy interpretation, secured, etc. The basic objective of software quality matrices is to perform quality assessment, risk management and control, and process improvement. The matrices assist a manager in evaluating the quality of the products and services. Therefore, software quality matrix is a valuable tool which in turn contributes to QMP in B2C EC, since information and communication technology (ICT) is a fundamental attributes of system quality.

4.3.3. Total Data Quality Management

Information quality is not only dependent on system quality. It covers a vast area including software quality, data quality, and architectural design of website. For better website design in terms of aesthetic, structure, and functionality, data quality management is of utmost importance. Now managers of B2C EC realize that without data quality management, EC might not get competitive advantage in today's fierce competition. Quality is a potential and complex issue for data management. High quality EC also reflects better quality data management. To achieve a state of high data quality, total data quality management (TDQM) is now considered as an important solution. Different organizations with different objectives and working environments can develop more specific and customized programs for data quality management to suit their own needs. However, some researchers (Wolfinbarger et al., 2003; Cao et al., 2005) argue that regardless of differences in working pattern, organizations should follow certain steps in order to enable the successful implementation of TDQM:

- Basic goal, target markets, and consumer behavior should be explicitly understood.
- Required performance should be pre-fixed and evaluated regularly.
- Strategies must be explicitly objectified concerning what the organization means by quality in general.
- A set of measures for the important dimensions of data quality for the organization must be determined.

For effective and efficient data quality management, the following factors are considered to be most important (Kalakota & Whinston, 1996; Yoo & Donthu, 2001; Zhang & von Dran, 2002; Cai, & Jun, 2003; Xu & Koronios, 2004-2005): Availability, Accessibility, Appropriateness, Up-to-date, External linkage, Functionality, Credibility, Comprehensibility, Completeness, Usefulness, Organized, Consistent, Ease of manipulation, Flexibility, Accurate and free-of-error, Interpretability, Directionality, Relevancy, Security, Timeliness, Understandability, and Value-added.

4.3.4. Virtual Communal Marketing

Virtual communal marketing refers to in B2C EC as marketing in the virtual community that incorporates public involvement in the development of customer interface. A virtual community could fulfill four various kinds of needs, such as transaction, interest, fantasy, and relationship (Armstrong & Hagel, 1996; Hagel & Arthur, 1997). Virtual communal marketing enables managers to identify expectations, characteristics, and behavioral intentions of the customers, which they can utilize to develop service quality dimensions of global web based services.

4.3.5. Self-Service Technology

This technology has a significant implication in a web based system design. Self-service technology provides authorized human users to obtain or update information and perform qualified transactions from enterprise databases via communication channels, such as email, web network, and voice mail without depending upon human actions. Since dependences on human interactions are eliminated, it brings a seamless flow of information, greater efficiency, and satisfaction to users. Self-service technology is derived through management and optimization of business processes. Self-service technology helps web based system designers to assess and improve quality of website and system. This technology creates the opportunity of the electronic-vendors to identify quality of customer service and also to provide better customer service as perceived by the customers in the EC context.

4.3.6. Transactional Quality

Transactional quality is concerned with how the different phases of pre-sale to post-sale systems work together. This is crucial in B2C EC, because in absence of physical cues, customers are very much worried in these phases of total operations (Barnes & Vidgen, 2000). For example, if a customer buys a product through a company's website, then a smooth running system will correctly translate that order, payment, and delivery of the product as promised. Several researches on the context of online transaction (Hoffman et al., 1999; Jarvenpaa et al., 1999; Swaminathan et al., 1999) suggest that consumer's confidence or trust can be improved by increasing the quality of transaction. The fundamental issues for transactional quality are security issues: authentication, authorization, availability, confidentiality, data integrity, non-repudiation, and selective application services (Bhimani, 1996).

4.4. QUALITY MANAGEMENT PRACTICE

ISO 8402 defines total quality management (TQM) as a " management approach of an organization centered on quality, based on the participation of all its members and aiming at long term success through customer satisfaction and benefits to all members of the organization and to society". Kumar et al. (2006) provided a detailed conceptual model for QMP in EC named as Integrated Quality Management-EC Model. In this model, the authors have incorporated the underpinning principles of TQM in different customer interaction domains of EC to practice quality management for continuous improvement. It is grounded on the main cycle of TQM, i.e., Plan-Do-Check-Act (Shewhart, 1931; Deming, 1986; Scholtes, 1988). According to the EC quality dimension model (Kumar et al., 2006), in the major six customer-interaction domains of EC, named as Website Operation, Fulfillment /Responsiveness, Process Operation, Policy, Credibility, and Customer Service, E-retailers should implement QMP to standardize service for global consumers. Kumar et al. (2006) argue that after implementation of QMP in EC customer-interaction domains, EC is likely to experience certain benefits which can confirm competitiveness in the global market. In this regard, the authors specified some future research directions for the intended researchers in this field to focus on three different perspectives. These are:

"Management's perspective: What is the gap between management's recommended quality and quality output after integration of quality principles in EC quality dimensions?

Employee's perspective: What is the gap between specified quality and perceived quality after practicing quality in EC process?

Customer's perspective: What is the gap between perceived quality and expected quality?" (Kumar et al., 2006).

The model (Kumar et al., 2006) is presented in Figure 4.1.

4.5. CONCLUSION

In this era of globalization, E-retailers are confronting fierce competition not only from rival Electronic organizations but also from brick and mortar commerce. It is also noteworthy that B2C EC customers are generally global and they interact with websites in absence of physical customer service. Therefore, both customers and company management cannot view each other and thus fail to conceive opponent characteristics. In absence of physical cues, quality plays a significant role in EC. To achieve competitive advantages which include improving system management, differentiating service offer, improving customer service, entering new markets, availing cultural adaptability, and flourish in global market. Therefore, exploring quality issues and QMP for EC and its possible impact on customers' behavioral intention in a global context is a wide area to investigate and understand. As noted in Chapter III, service quality dimensions of B2C EC are not the same as captured in traditional service quality frameworks. As a result, though the SERVQUAL (Parasuraman et al., 1985, 1988) or Grönroos's Service Quality Model (1984) are used extensively as the primary foundations to look at service quality framework of virtual environment, identifying quality issues in different aspects of B2C EC and deriving QMP has been triggered quite extensively.

To improve quality of the EC system, E-retailers must first understand how consumers perceive and evaluate online customer service (Kumar et al., 2006). It a challenging issue to identify different segments of EC where quality improvement and thus QMP is imperative. Then TQM or any other QMP can be implemented to ensure continuous improvement of EC so that globalization of EC can maintain cultural adaptability and global standard.

Figure 4.1 Integrated quality management-EC model (source: Kumar et al. 2006)

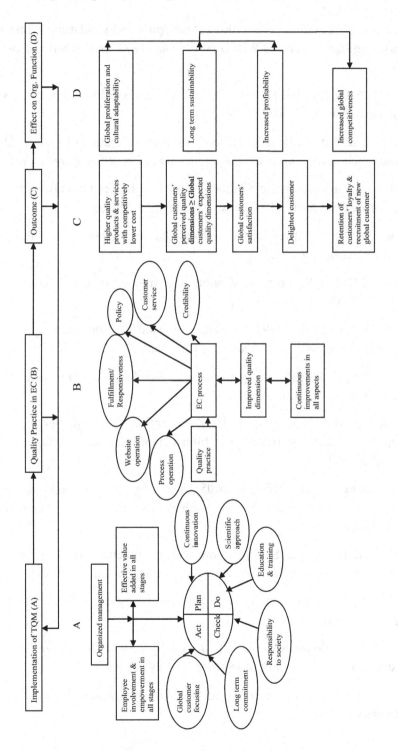

REFERENCES

Aladwani, A. M., & Palvia, P. C. (2002). Developing and Validating an Instrument for Measuring User-Perceived Web Quality. *Information and Management, 39*(6), 467-476.

Armstrong, A., & Hagel, J. (1996). The Real Value of On-line Communities. *Harvard Business Review, 74*(3), 134-141.

Barnes, S. J., & Vidgen, R. (2000). WebQual: An Exploration of Website Quality, Paper presented in the *European Conference on Information System*, Vienna.

Barsh, J., Crawford, B., Grosso, C. (2000). How E-tailing can Rise from the Ashes. *The McKinsey Quarterly.* http://www.mckinseyquarterly.com.

Bertram, D. (1991). Getting Started in Total Quality Management. *Total Quality Management, 2*(3), 279–282.

Bhimani, A. (1996). Securing the Commercial Internet, *Communications of the ACM, 39*(6), 29-35.

Bolton, R. N., & Drew, J. H. (1991). A Multistage Model of Consumers' Assessments of Service Quality and Value. *Journal of Consumer Research, 17*, 375-384.

Brown, A. (1992). Industrial Experience with Total Quality Management. *Total Quality Management, 3*(2), 147–156.

Cai, S., & Jun, M. (2003). Internet Users' Perceptions of Online Service Quality: A Comparison of Online Buyers and Information Searches. *Managing Service Quality, 13*(6), 504-519.

Cao, M., Zhang, O., & Seydel, J. (2005). Measuring B2C eCommerce Website Quality: An Empirical Examination. *Industrial Management & Data Systems, 106*(5), 645-661.

Chen, S. C., & Dhillon, G. S. (2003). Interpreting Dimensions of Consumer Trust in E-Commerce. *Information Technology and Management, 4*, 303-318.

Chou, D. C. (2001). Integrating TQM into E-Commerce. *Information Systems Management, 18*(4), 31-39.

Cronin, J. J. Jr., & Taylor, S. A. (1992), Measuring Service Quality: A Reexamination and Extension. *Journal of Marketing, 56*(July), 55-68.

Crosby, P. B. (1979). Quality is Free: *The Art of Making Quality Certain*. New York, New American Library.

DeLone, W. H., & McLean, E. R. (2003). The Delone and Mclean Model of Information Systems Success: A Ten-Year Update. *Journal of Management Information Systems, 19*(4), 9-30.

Deming, W. E. (1975). On Some Statistical Aids toward Economic Production. *Interfaces, 5*(4), 1-15.

Deming, W. E. (1986). *Out of the Crisis.* MIT Center for Advanced Engineering Study, Cambridge, MA.

Field, J. M., Heim, G. R., & Sinha, K. K. (2004). Managing Quality in the E-Service System: Development and Application of a Process Model. *Production and Operations Management, 13*(4), 291-306.

Gommans, M., Krishnan, K. S., & Scheffold, K. B. (2001). From Brand Loyalty to E-Loyalty: A Conceptual Framework. *Journal of Economics and Social Researc, 3*(1), 43-58.

Gronroos, C. (1984), A Service Quality Model and Its Marketing Implications, *European Journal of Marketing, 18*(4), 36-44.

Hagel, J. III, & Arthur G. A. (1997). Net Gain: Expanding Markets Through Virtual Communities, *Mckinsey Quarterly* (winter), (pp. 140–146).

Hoffman, D. L., Novak, T. P., & Peralta, M. A. (1999). Building Consumer Trust Online, *Communications of the ACM, 42*(4), 80-5.

Jarvenpaa, S. L., Tractinsky, N., & Saarinen, L. (1999). Consumer Trust in an Internet Store: A Cross-Cultural Validation. *Journal of Computer-Mediated Communication, 5*(2).

Johnson, M. E., & Whang, S. (2002). E-Business and Supply Chain Management: An Overview and Framework. *Production and Operations Management, 11*(4), 413–423.

Juran, J. M. (1962). *Quality Control Handbook.* 2nd edition, McGraw-Hill, London.

Juran, J. M., & Godfrey, A. B. (1999). *Juran's Quality Handbook.* 5th edition. New York: McGraw-Hill.

Kalakota, R., & Whinston, A. B. (1996). *Frontiers of Electronic Commerce.* Addison-Wesley. Reading, MA.

Kopcso, D., Pipino, L., & Rybolt, W. (2001). Factors Affecting the Assessment of Web Site Quality, Global Co-Operation in the New Millennium. *The 9th European Conference on Information Systems,* Bled, Slovenia, June 27-29.

Kumar, V., Kumar, U., & Shareef, M. A. (2006). Implementation of Quality Management Practice in EC. *Proceedings of the Administrative Sciences Association of Canada Conference*, Banff, Calgary, June, (pp. 146-163).

Kurtus, R., (2000). Using TQM and ISO 9000 in eCommerce. *Kurtus Technologies and The School for Champions,* (pp. 1-4).

Mason, R. O., & Mitroff, I. I. (1973). A Program for Research on Management Information Systems. *Management Science, 26,* 475-485.

Meuter, M. L., Bitner, M. J., Ostrom, A. L., & Brown, S. W. (2001). Choosing Among Alternative Service Delivery Modes: An Investigation of Customer Trial of Self-Service Technologies. *Journal of Marketing, 69*(2), 61-83.

Nah, F. F.-H., & Davis, S. (2002). HCI Research Issues in E-commerce. *Journal of Electronic Commerce Research, 3,* 98–113.

Nielsen, J. (1999). *User Interface Directions for the Web.* Communication of ACM, *42*(1), 65-72.

Parasuraman, A., & Zinkhan, G. M. (2002). Marketing to and Serving Customers through the Internet: An Overview and Research Agenda. *Journal of the Academy of Marketing Science, 30*(4), 286-295.

Parasuraman, A., Zeithaml, V. A., & Berry, L. L. (1985). A Conceptual Model of Service Quality and Its Implications for Future Research. *Journal of Marketing, 49,* 41-50.

Prybutok, V. R., & Ramasesh R. (2005). An Action-Research Based Instrument for Monitoring Continuous Quality Improvement. *European Journal of Operational Research, 166,* 293-309.

Robbins, S., & Stylianou, A. (2003), Global corporate web sites: an empirical investigation of content and design, *Information & Management, 40*(3), 205-12.

Ross, J. (1993). *Total Quality Management: Text, Cases and Readings,* Delray Beach, FL, St. Lucie Press.

Scholters, P. R. (1988). *The Team Handbook,* Joiner Assoc.

Shareef, M. A., Kumar, U., & Kumar, V. (2008). Role of Different Electronic-Commerce (EC) Quality Factors on Purchase Decision: A Developing Country Perspective. *Journal of Electronic Commerce Research, 9*(2), 92-113.

Shewhart, W. A. (1931). *Economic Control of Quality of Manufactured Product,* Van Nostrand Company, New York.

Smith, B. A., & Merchant, E. J. (2001). Designing an Attractive Website: Variables of Importance. *Proceedings of the 32nd Annual Conference of the Decision Sciences Institute*, San Francisco, CA.

Swaminathan, V., Lepkowska-White, E., & Rao, B. P. (1999). Browsers or Buyers in Cyberspace? An Investigation of Factors Influencing Electronic Exchange. *Journal of Computer-Mediated Communication, 5*(2).

Taguchi, G. (1986). *Introduction to Quality Engineering.* Asian Productivity Organization, Tokyo.

Wang, M. (2003). Assessment of E-Service Quality via E-Satisfaction in E-Commerce Globalization. *The Electronic Journal on Information Systems in Developing Countries, 11*(10), 1-4.

Wolfinbarger, M., & Gilly, M. C. (2003). eTailQ: Dimensionalizing, Measuring and Predicting eTail Quality. *Journal of Retailing, 79*(3), 183–198.

Xu, H., & Koronios, A. (2004-2005). Understanding Information Quality in E-Business. *Journal of Computer Information Systems*, winter, (pp. 73-82).

Yang, C. C. (2003). Improvement Actions Based On The Customers' Satisfaction Survey. *Total Quality Management & Business Excellence, 14*(8), 919-930.

Yoo, B., & Donthu, N. (2001). Developing a Scale to Measure the Perceived Quality of an Internet Shopping Site (Sitequal). *Quarterly Journal of Electronic Commerce, 2*(1), 31-46.

Zeithaml, V. A. (1988). Consumer Perceptions of Price, Quality, and Value: A Means-End Model and Synthesis of Evidence. *Journal of Marketing, 52*, 2-22.

Zhang, P., & von Dran, G. (2002). User Expectations and Rankings of Quality Factors in Different Website Domains. *International Journal of Electronic Commerce, 6*(2), 9-33.

Division III
Adoption, Proliferation, and Resistance:
Impact and Globalization

Chapter V
E–Commerce Diffusion:
Critical Factors Affecting Diffusion of E–Commerce

ABSTRACT

As we have already mentioned in the Preface of this book, mentioning EC in this chapter will signify and mean B2C EC unless it is mentioned otherwise. This chapter has primarily addressed, discussed, and conceptualized paradigms of three issues of diffusion of EC. First, we investigated the impacts of EC diffusion on overall social, political, cultural, technological, organizational, and economic relations. In this connection, we revealed seven types of prime relational changes on the effects of EC diffusion in a country context. Consequently, government-private organizations, consumers, and intermediaries (viz., the comprehensive relation of market characteristics) are reshaped. Then we traced the diffusion of EC and the role of different actors associated with this new economical and technological innovation, viz. EC, and their functional characteristics in the diffusion process. Based on the association of those stakeholders with the market economy, and the role and functions of those stakeholders in the diffusion process of EC, we conceptualized the theoretical framework for diffusion of EC. From this framework, we revealed that the government role, capability, and globalization policy; consumer preferences; private organization's capabilities; the global E-organizations mission; and the infrastructure and market mechanism factors with a set of associated variables create the ability for EC to be diffused in any country. Therefore, the diffusion of EC is not a unidimensional issue, but has multi-dimensional aspects.

5.1. INTRODUCTION

"We have a networked society and economy ... and an industrial-aged government." Stephen Goldsmith, Harvard Professor and Presidential Advisor (Turner & Desloges, 2002).

Information and communication technology (ICT) has become one of the core elements of societal, economic, cultural, organizational, and market re-formation, and E-commerce (EC) may reshape future business patterns through globalization. ICT has created many possibilities for improving managerial efficiency and the quality of service delivery to consumers (Cai and Jun, 2003; Lee and Rao, 2003). During the last decade, technology has contributed to revolutionary change in business patterns, relations, and functions (Kim *et al.,* 2006; Sebastianelli *et al.,* 2006); government structures; institutional concepts; and public administration. Technology has also radically changed the process of governance (Fountain, 2001), performance management (Brown, 1999), bureaucracy and corruption reduction (Moon and Bretschneider, 2002), and reengineering (Anderson, 1999). Various technologies have been applied to support these fundamental characteristics of EC, including electronic data interchange (EDI), interactive voice response, e-mail, voice-mail, web service delivery, virtual reality, and public key infrastructure (Moon, 2002). However, the impact of IT on the business environment in the modern market system reflects just one side of the issue. The other side is re-shaped and shaken by social and cultural thrusts. The social and cultural thrusts come from a revolutionary change in perception and speculation of business relations with consumers. Managers realize that the business system should be more dynamic, more customer focused, more open and transparent, more efficient, and more participatory. So the social aspect of forming an online business system is also vital. Therefore, we can categorize the major and fundamental aspects of EC for a government, as well as for firms who embrace online channels, by introducing EC as:

*   Clear vision, mission, and objective,
*   Structure and policy,
*   Continuous service transformation and improvement mechanism,
*   Web presence through ICT, Internet, and World Wide Web,
*   Telecommunications system,
*   Computer, and
*   Human capital.

However, these aspects are very divergent and they depend on several related factors that are based on the perspectives of a particular country. Countries are usually at different stages in building infrastructure to develop and support EC diffusion. Social, cultural, and market differences associated with the different environment and policies of governments influence and result in idiosyncratic arrangements shaping particular diffusion paths among countries and regions (McGann *et al.*, 2002). ICT, including the Internet and EC, are developed in western countries whose background, policy, and objectives are very different from those of developing countries (Kurnia, 2007). Developing countries differ significantly from developed countries in their mission, objective of developing technology, overall adaptability of government, and market economy. Developing countries also differ in their fundamental capabilities to diffuse technology in the local context. However, the success of technology acceptance and successive diffusion is heavily dependant on the adoption capability, the way it is diffused in the private and public sectors, and the way it is adopted by the adopters (Unhelkar 2003). Therefore, we suggest that the diffusion of EC has multi-dimensional aspects, and the process of diffusion is controlled by cultural diversity. In this chapter, we would like to address, reveal, and reshape those aspects of the diffusion of EC. We have divided the chapter into 6 sections. Our fundamental efforts in this chapter are designed to develop epistemological and ontological paradigms of the diffusion of EC that would contribute to form the desired framework of critical factors of EC diffusion.

The revolutionary proliferation and diffusion of ICT in the last decade, particularly the rise of the Internet and its related telecommunication and computer applications, has created unprecedented opportunities and scope for the world economy to flourish (Dedrick and Kraemer, 1998; Wong, 2002a). At the same time, it also creates the possibility of excessive disparities in terms of controlling the market economy between developed and developing countries. In terms of opportunity, the rapid proliferation of the Internet economy has leveraged the market economy of developed countries to capitalize the global market through creating a stronger and extended supply chain, integrating global customers, lowering costs, and enhancing service quality and efficiency. Developing countries are far behind in respect to creating the scope for diffusion of ICT and EC in their country. However, the history of technological evolution has shown that the leaders in an established technology have been overtaken by new, technology-intensive countries when a disruptive technological change occurs.

EC as a global phenomenon is changing social structures, cultural adaptability, market mechanisms, and economical disparity. The diffusion of information technology—such as the Internet and its business adoption, viz., EC—is considered a source of competitive advantage for national economies in the global market. EC creates enormous opportunities to expand global sales, create sales and distribution channels, target more markets without system development, reduce the cost of sales, enhance service efficiency and quality, shorten the purchasing cycle, etc. Therefore, a potential question relates to how different countries create overall opportunities to diffuse EC to embrace a future Internet economy. This situation deserves research by developed countries, because big corporations in these countries, which are now the sole owners of EC operations, are very enthusiastic to explore the huge markets of developing countries. On the other hand, it is a very important issue for developing countries who now realize the potential of the Internet economy and are taking revolutionary steps to realize the benefits of EC. Therefore, the diffusion of EC is an important research question for both developed and developing countries. The rate at which the Internet economy diffuses globally is very important to achieve the full benefits of globalization. Academicians, practitioners, and policy makers are interested in understanding the factors that drive the diffusion of EC (Kraemer, 2001; McGann *et al.,* 2002). Therefore, in this chapter, we will explore the paradigms and theoretical concepts of issues related to the global diffusion of EC.

The major thrust of this study is to explore, delineate, and conceptualize the epistemological and ontological paradigms of the diffusion of EC in developed and developing countries. In this aspect, the prime issues that we focus on and discuss here are: a) The impacts of diffusion, b) Prime stakeholders of EC diffusion, and c) Critical factors affecting the diffusion of EC from the perspective of a country. We first delineate the fundamental concept of diffusion. Then we address our research questions and conceptualize the epistemological and ontological paradigms of those research issues. Finally, we draw inferences from those conceptual findings in our conclusion and present some guidelines to advance this type of research in the future.

5.2. DIFFUSION OF E-COMMERCE

The diffusion of innovation can be defined as the "process by which an innovation is communicated through certain channels over time among the members of a social system" (Rogers, 2003). Rogers further points out (2003) that this innovation-decision process "can lead to adoption, a decision to make full use of an innovation as the best course of action available, or rejection, a decision not to adopt an innovation." Translating the principal theme of the theory of planned behavior, we find that this theory posits that most intended behaviors are subject to some uncertainty and that the success in performing a behavior depends not only on intention but also on factors that may interfere with behavior control (Netemeyer *et al.,* 1990). Therefore, diffusion of EC, (i.e., the intention to use), primary acceptance, satisfaction, and, finally, recurring use is a continuous process approach.

The adoption process is associated with a variety of factors. These include the appearance of costs and benefits over time, the role of cues to action, the problem of competing life demands, and the ways that the actual decision behavior differs from the rational ideal implicit in expectancy-value and utility theories. Therefore, adoption of a new process should be viewed as dynamic with the interactions of many determinants. According to marketing theory, in the adoption/diffusion process, sequences of events beginning with consumer awareness of a new product lead to trial usage and terminate in full and regular use of the new product. The adoption process is the "mental and behavioral sequences through which the consumer progresses and which may result in acceptance and continued use of a product or brand" (Robertson, 1974). It has four components: 1) an innovation, 2) which is communicated through certain channels, 3) over time, 4) among members of a social system (Rogers and Shoemaker, 1971).

Diffusion deals with the transfer (conversion) between an old system to a target system in an organization. A new system needs to be diffused before it can be used. Several perceived processes of diffusion can be used to implement a system. Taking the prime essence of Rogers (2003), these types include in simple terms— sudden diffusion, simultanous diffusion, and segmented diffusion—form the main speculations that are used to adopt a system. For EC, since governments or online organizations cannot impose any boundaries or rules on users of the system, this sudden diffusion is not appropriate. In the case of simultanous diffusion, the old and new systems run simultanously so all the users can get used to the new system, but can still do their work using the old system. The parallel process of traditional brick and mortar organizations and EC is a perfect example of this diffusion process. Segmented diffusion means that the adoption will happen in several stages, so after each stage, the system is a little closer to full adoption by the consumers, governments, and firms. Gallivan (1996) suggests that the appropriate diffusion process depends on these four factors:

1. Innovativeness of the individuals: Attributes of the ones that are to adopt the innovation/system
2. The type of innovation: Is it a process or product innovation?
3. Attributes of the innovation itself: Preparedness, communicability and divisibility
4. The implementation complexity: How complex is the implementation or what is its extent?

Therefore, based on the following aspects of diffusion of EC, it is imperative to reveal the impacts of diffusion on the traditional environments and market relation, the prime actors of EC diffusion, and, finally, the main issue of EC diffusion, viz., the critical factors of EC diffusion in the country context.

5.3. IMPACTS OF DIFFUSION

From the theoretical view of an industrial organization (Porter, 1985), we get the concept that the Internet as a new technology can disrupt market status quo in three ways (Evans and Wurster, 1999; Sahlman, 1999; Tiessen *et al.*, 2001). First, it dramatically changes the relative power of buyers and sellers and also the intermediaries by changing the market mechanism, lowering costs, and modifying the distribution channel. Second, the spread of information can allow competitors to offer substitute goods and services. Third, fierce competition is developing around electronic markets. So the proliferation and rapid diffusion of the Internet economy has created enormous effects on the present market structure, which reflects some drastic changes in the social, cultural, technological, behavioral, economical, and governmental policy aspects. Therefore, we can define EC diffusion in the country context as: the expansion and proliferation, i.e., the overall growth of electronic markets through market mechanism changing market structure, interaction structure, exchange structure, and payment structure based on the social, cultural, technological, and behavioral attitude of consumers and economical and governmental policy of a country. Diffusion of EC is not only the adoption or penetration rate, it is the overall growth of electronic markets. Getting insight from a study by Chwelos *et al.* (2001) on EDI diffusion, Tung and Rieck (2005) postulate that an Internet diffusion framework can be investigated from three perspectives: technological, organizational, and inter-organizational. The technological aspect deals with perceived characteristics of ICT; the organizational aspect reveals organizational characteristics of EC; and the inter-organizational perspective encompasses factors relating to the actions of other organizations and collaboration between the public and private sectors.

Different theories on this perspective provide different insights. Suppose, from the view of the neoclassical theory, technical innovation is an externally imposed independent force that has a uniform impact on all economies. As a result, the impact of ICT among countries produces common social and economic outcomes (Bell, 1973; Ohmae, 1990). Convergence theorists support this ideology and think of globalization as a universal process of homogenization in which countries converge toward a uniform and unique way of producing and organizing socioeconomic parameters with resulting common social outcomes (Bell, 1973; Ohmae, 1990, 1995). However, divergence theorists reveal that national diversity, shown in different social and economic outcomes, prevails and it prevents convergence from creating a single market where a standardized strategy can reign (Berger and Dore, 1996; Boyer, 1996; Hirst and Thompson, 1996; Wade, 1996). New growth theory encompasses a similar doctrine and reveals that, due to national characteristics, the impact of EC diffusion is not similar worldwide and it should be revealed in the country context. These national characteristics include social structure, cultural behavior, information infrastructure, government policy, technology adoption capability, financial systems, and national policies, which create different economic and legal environments and infrastructure (Boyer, 1996; Wade, 1996; Kraemer, 2001).

However, all those theories agreed on a basic point of the impacts of EC diffusion. This is: the diffusion of EC and its concurrent impact on the country environment might be similar or significantly different; however, it has social, cultural, political, organizational, economical, and technological aspects. Due to the proliferation of ICT, including the Internet and EC, the social behavior of consumers and business organizations will change. Consumers no longer have a personal interaction, go the stores physically, and use the help of customer service. The cultural habits of government, consumers, and E-organizations are also changing. Customers can buy products anytime and from anywhere in the world. Intra-organizational rearrangement is also a necessary part of this cultural change. On the other hand, governments need to enforce different rules and regulations to promote businesses as well as to control consumers' rights in terms of privacy, security, and fraud. Organizationally, E-organizations reshape, reform, and reengineer both their back and front offices. They also change supply chain management. The political effects of EC diffusion or the political impacts on EC diffusion are both very significant. In this era of globalization, though the World Trade Organization (WTO) pushes all countries to be uniform, the specific country ultimately determines its own policy. Excluding strong political commitment and government support, technology diffusion cannot be propelled in any country only from private organizations (Kraemer, 2001; McGann *et al.*, 2002; Wong, 2002a, Kraemer *et al.*, 2005). On the other hand, diffusion of the Internet economy has enormous effects on political speculation. An open information system and more participatory organizational structures basically enhance the E-government structure. Consumers' dependence on technology is also an outcome of EC diffusion. Consumers become more attached to the virtual environment where self-service is predominant. Economic change is one of the important aspects of EC diffusion (Wong, 2002b; Radaideh and Selim, 2004; Viswanathan and Pick, 2005; Jamal and Ahmed, 2007; Kurnia, 2007). The payment system for purchases and banking transactions is a vital issue. Financial rules, including the tax system, are also issues. Employment, supply chain, the distribution channel, and intermediaries are also affected by the proliferation of EC (McGann *et al.*, 2002).

The core doctrine of the socio-technical theory explains the social aspects of people and society and the technical aspects of machines and technology. This gives us insight into integrating the social, organizational, and technological aspects of the impacts of EC diffusion and adoption in the country context. This theory refers to the interrelatedness of the social and technical aspects of an organization. The discursive discourses of this theory explain the systems consist of social and organizational elements as well as technical elements, and emphasize that successful systems require the integrative interaction of 'technical,' 'organizational,' and 'social' aspects of the system (Damodaran *et al.*, 2005). The complementary theory supports the doctrine of the impacts of EC diffusion and adoption on social, cultural, technological, organizational, economical, and political aspects related to EC characteristics. Complementarity refers to the synergistic effect and integrated view of a number of variables influencing the organizational change processes. The principle of synergy states that a system can be considered comprehensively by looking at the complementary variables (Whittington and Pettigrew, 2003). In this perspective, in developing and conceptualizing the framework of EC diffusion and adoption, variables influencing this process should be considered as part of an integrated system of factors that are mutually reinforced (Massini and Pettigrew, 2003; Whittington and Pettigrew, 2003). Through shedding light on the socio-technical and complementary theories, we can encapsulate the complex interaction of market environments among various complementary variables of the role of governments, private organizations, consumers, globalization policies, and international E-organizations. Therefore, the socio-technical theory and the complementary theory adhere to all those aspects to present a comprehensive theoretical framework of diffusion speculation. Integrating and aligning the previously mentioned literature review and synthesizing different researchers' discourses and the epistemological and ontological paradigms drawn from the theoretical understanding, we observe market changes due to introduction of EC. We examine these changes from the perspectives of social, cultural, technological, organizational, economical, and political phenomena. The changes are:

1.   Seller-buyer relation,
2.   Government-consumer-seller relation,
3.   Role of government,
4.   Role of mediators,
5.   Supply-chain relation,
6.   Distribution means, and
7.   Consumers-technology relation.

However, before going further, at this stage it is vital to recognize the actors or stakeholders of EC diffusion because the previously mentioned impacts can be conceptualized on the basis of the role of different stakeholders of EC diffusion.

5.4. PRIME STAKEHOLDERS OF DIFFUSION OF E-COMMERCE ·

According to the institutional theory, institutional rules and regulations always attempt to reshape and synchronize social organizations to form isomorphism for social, organizational, and market governance (Lawrence and Suddaby, 2006). However, actors of organizational structures do not always abide by or follow these systems imposed by regulatory institutions. The institutional theory, explained by Lawrence and Suddaby (2006), primarily discusses the role of actors (individuals and organizations) in effecting, transforming, and maintaining institutions and fields, i.e., the formal structures in which organizations operate. For the operators of public administration, isomorphism is a vital aspect. Institutionalization of EC aims to develop isomorphism among E-organizations to create, maintain, and disrupt isomorphic rules. However, different actors in organizations might rule out institutional rules and, thus, isomorphism, due to non-coherence of organizational rules in favor of their group interest. Formation and implementation of EC present several fundamental attributes as the strategic option of launching. However, these strategic attributes are not always consistent with the interests of both the supply side and demand side actors of EC, since providers (i.e., private organizations) and prime users (i.e., consumers and businesses) can hold different views with regard to market relations. As a result, isomorphism of organizations cannot be implemented properly if the interests of both sides of EC and the reflection of these attributes in EC diffusion are not properly identified. Therefore, investigation of the adoption process and the role of different stakeholders is important for the proper diffusion of EC and isomorphism, especially at the aggregate level. At the aggregate level, EC includes more technological, organizational, and political sophistication as a result of both institutional isomorphism and pressures from businesses, citizens, politicians, interest groups, and other stakeholders. Therefore, the role of government is very important to manage the relation between buyers and sellers, to control and guide the market mechanism without interfering, to promote the business environment including infrastructure, and to focus on long-term commitment (Wong, 2002a; McGann *et al.*, 2002; Kraemer *et al.*, 2005).

Sometimes excessive concentration and emphasis on the technological diffusion aspects for implementation of EC distracts from the cultural and societal issues of engaging consumers in developing their ability to accept new technology, identifying real needs, and participating in decision-making regarding perceived priorities and methods of electronic transactions. A consequence, which is of concern, is that levels of understanding of user requirements are, therefore, insufficient to inform technology selection and use and the service design and delivery. While designing and selecting new technology and service for EC, private authorities and governments often create little opportunity for systematic or widespread participation of other stakeholders, particularly consumers. Consumers are the key stakeholders in systems for EC diffusion operated through ICT, yet they appear to have little input into their creation and development.

Many researchers have attempted to identify behavioral attitudes that distinguish users who accept or reject a new innovation. Alavi and Joachimsthaler (1992) suggest that the technology acceptance behaviors are grounded on cognitive style, personality, demographics, and user-situational variables. Therefore, since the ability of consumers to use and accept a new technology depends on several cultural and individual traits, it is quite relevant to address, define, and reveal the comprehensive views of consumers who are the prime users of that newly implemented technology or system. For EC to achieve its goals, there needs to be active participation of individuals and businesses as customers, interlocutors, clients and citizens (Wirtz, J. and Wong, 2001; McGann *et al.*, 2002). In this respect, the role of private organizations that are basically promoting EC and also conducting a supply chain relation with other electronic organizations is of utmost important (Gibbs *et al.*, 2003). Local private organizations can play primarily two types of roles for promoting EC: either as prime companies for EC or as intermediaries for foreign electronic organizations. The second role is especially prominent for developing countries (McGann *et al.*, 2002). Though globalization creates significant pressure on private organizations, especially local organizations, to adopt EC, it is their final choice as to whether they will embrace this ICT-based technology (Gibbs *et al.*, 2003). Financial, technological, and human resource capability are three major aspects for adoption of EC by private organizations. Several researchers reveal different factors for adopting EC by private organizations. These factors precisely articulate their organizational capability in terms of technology, finance, and human resources, and, also, in terms of a firms' mission, long-term goal, and policies (Tiessen *et al.*, 2001; Kettler and Benavides, 2002; McGann *et al.*, 2002; Gibbs *et al.*, 2003; Kraemer *et al.*, 2005; Viswanathan and Pick, 2005). However, diffusion of EC in a country context is not only formulated by local private organizations. Foreign companies and globalization policy, especially for developing countries, have potential impact on the diffusion of EC. Global production networks, internationalization policies, market stability, trade liberalization, global competition, distribution channels, and long term vision are important issues for globalization and international electronic organizations to diffuse EC from developed to developing countries. In this aspect, stakeholder and agency theories can provide deep insight.

Stakeholder theory is instrumental in offering a framework for investigating the links between conventional organizational performance and the practice of stakeholder management. The stakeholder theory (Freeman, 1984) identifies and models the groups which are stakeholders of an organization, and both describes and recommends methods by which management can recognize their participation in overall functions and provide due regard to the interests of those groups. In short, it attempts to address the real stakeholders concerning factors for the organization, what type of participation they have with that organization, and how they perform or maintain that participation. According to this theory, stakeholders are identified by their interests and all stakeholder interests are considered to be intrinsically valuable. A potential reason for incorporating the stakeholder concept in setting EC diffusion and identifying the prime users is the recognition that EC systems are extensively affected by the environment in which they operate (Chan and Pan, 2003). EC, while functioning, comes into regular contact with consumers, businesses, government agencies, employees, and special interest groups.

Agency theory is concerned with resolving the relationships of the users of a system and their purposes. Agency problems arise when the users have different interests to use that system (Eisenhardt, 1989). Several studies in political science and public administration have addressed the problems inherent in the balancing role of government to promote and also to regulate market economy. For EC, the problem is not limited only in this periphery. Here differences in agency also arise for interaction and conflicts of different stakeholders like consumers, local private organizations, and globalization policy and foreign E-corporations. Therefore, diffusion of EC through adoption of different stakeholders of EC is a complex situation. It should be resolved taking into consideration the differences in agency of the different supply side and demand side stakeholders of EC. In this aspect, we can categorize the role of the previously mentioned four actors responsible for the diffusion of EC in the country context as follows:

Supply Side:
a.   Local private organizations as the prime provider of EC or as intermediaries of foreign electronic organizations.
b.   International electronic organizations, especially based in developed countries

Demand side:
c.   Consumers and business organizations.

Intermediaries:
d.   Government role and globalization policy.

We have already addressed the plausible impacts of EC based on this paradigm: diffusion of EC impacts social, cultural, technological, economical, organizational, and political changes. We have revealed that even predominant changes are reflected in the market mechanism for both the external and internal environment. We have also identified the prime actors who influence and play in the diffusion process of EC in the country context. Now, based on the above findings and concepts, we would like to conceptualize our final and most important research question, viz., the critical factors affecting diffusion of EC.

5.5. CRITICAL FACTORS AFFECTING DIFFUSION OF E-COMMERCE

As we conceptualized in the previous section, diffusion of EC in any country depends on the associate role played by the four stakeholders. Therefore, exploring critical factors enabling diffusion of EC is finally related to defining the effective scope and performance of those four stakeholders. Models of EC diffusion driven by ICT suggest that diffusion is a function of environmental factors which are comprised of the political and social systems, and industrial policy and structure, such as technology policy and infrastructure (Dedrick and Kraemer, 1998; Tallon and Kraemer, 2000). In a developing country context, the role of government in conjunction with environmental factors and industrial policy factors are likely to have a major impact on EC, since economic capability is low (Viswanathan and Pick, 2005). Viswanathan and Pick (2005) investigated the enabling factors of EC diffusion in a comparative study of two countries, India and Mexico. They explored the related government policies, infrastructure, role of private organizations and their capability, and the scope for international organizations and global policies favoring diffusion of EC in these two countries. Finally, they compared the diffusion factors of India and Mexico based on the proposed theoretical framework of Tallon and Kraemer (2000) as the drivers of EC diffusion. According to that framework, some critical factors in EC diffusion in any country are the industrial policy of a government, environmental factors related to infrastructure and market, the growth of related industries, and the potential and nature of interaction with developed economics. Wong (2002a) explored the same issue in the context of Singapore and revealed quite similar factors required for the diffusion of EC in Singapore. McGann *et al.* (2005) examined the diffusion of EC in the U.S. and revealed the factors that enable this diffusion. They described the following 10 drivers for EC diffusion in the U.S.:

1. Demographic factors related to consumers and strength of economy,
2. Compatible market economy structure,
3. Strong technology infrastructure,
4. Uniform capability throughout the country,
5. Highest Internet user population on the world,
6. Ubiquitous availability of broadband access for both consumers and businesses,
7. Government guidance and promotion to allow EC to flourish without interference,
8. Adoption of EC by private organizations,
9. Expanding of infrastructure to strengthen and support the advent of new business initiatives, and
10. Suitable payment system for consumer purchases.

Wong (2002b) addressed ICT diffusion in Asian countries and revealed that ICT, the prime force of EC diffusion, is lower in Asian countries than in non-Asian countries. However, while detecting the enabling factors of ICT diffusion in Asian countries, he investigated only technological and infrastructure related factors. He examined Asian countries' status in respect to diffusion of various ICT goods and services relative to non-Asian countries. For the purpose of this analysis, he identified the following eight indicators of ICT diffusion:

1. Number of computers per 1,000 people;
2. Computing power in millions of instruction per second (MIPS) per 1,000;
3. Number of Internet hosts per 1,000;
4. Number of secure EC hosts per 1000;
5. Number of fixed telephone lines per 1,000;
6. Number of cellular phone subscribers per 1,000;
7. Estimated electronics goods consumption per capita; and
8. Estimated ICT expenditure per capita.

The United Nations E-government/EC readiness index is also primarily technology oriented; however, it includes a human development index. The United Nations (2003) readiness index is used to define the status *quo* of each country to provide the scope of launching E-government/EC. It includes three major components: web measure index, telecommunication index, and human capital index. So, proposing this measurement instrument, the United Nations has addressed the scope of adopting ICT and the diffusion of Internet-based public or private organizations by availability of resources, capability, and present status of a country. The web measure index is a quantitative measure applied to all 191 UN member states (this is the number of members at the time of the study; now there are 192 UN members) (UNDP, 2003). The concept used to evaluate this information revealed whether certain services were available online. The telecommunication index is a quantitative weighted measure of different electronic devices (or their usage) per 1,000 citizens such as PCs, Internet availability, televisions, telephones lines, online population, and mobile phones (UNDP, 2003). The human capital index is dependent on education measures, two thirds of which concern adult literacy and one third concerns gross enrolment ratio (UNDP, 2003).

Andersen and Bjørn-Andersen (2001) analyzed the role of the Danish government infrastructure, and global policy to demonstrate globalization, multi-national corporation (MNC) strategies, and technical innovation as incentives for industry to adopt EC and specific factors in the Danish environment that might affect the diffusion of EC. They discovered four demand drivers, each of which has some variables:

1.   Industry structure (concentration, sectoral distribution, vertical integration, size of firms, and value networks);
2.   Information infrastructure (telecommunication, wireless and Internet infrastructure, technology access and use, and technology acceptance);
3.   Financial and human resources (payment mechanisms, venture capital, population, wealth, income distribution, age, education, and IT skills); and
4.   Consumer preferences and social/cultural factors (consumption patterns, business culture, investment levels, and language).

International marketing literature examines the diffusion of EC, adaptability in country context, barriers, and driving forces of adoption (Cavusgil *et al.*, 1993; Shoham, 1999). Culture, consumer preferences, firm characteristics, and legal environments are found to be critical factors related to proper diffusion of an Internet economy, especially in developing countries. In this connection, Tiessen *et al.* (2001), revealed that environmental factors—like market structure and industry policy, firms' capabilities, and international web use, which include resources and cultural adaptation—are the diffusion and adoption criteria of EC.

Now to delineate the theoretical paradigms and accentuate the theoretical discourses of EC diffusion, we, at the beginning of this present endeavor, looked at the contingency theory. The contingency approach to management is based on the paradigm that there is no one best way to manage and that to be effective, planning, organizing, leading, and controlling must be tailored to the particular circumstances faced by an organization. The fundamental essence of contingency theory suggests that previous theories, such as Weber's bureaucracy and Taylor's scientific management, had failed because they neglected the influence on management style, management acceptance, and organizational structure by various aspects of the environment: the contingency factors. Historically and traditionally, contingency theory has sought to formulate broad generalizations about the formal structures that are typically associated with or best fit the use of different technologies. The perspective originated with the work of Woodward (1965), who argued that technologies directly determine differences in such organizational attributes as span of control, centralization of authority, and the formalization of rules and procedures. Environmental change and uncertainty, technology, different stakeholders, culture, behavioral differences, and different organizational attributes are all identified as environmental factors impacting the effectiveness of different organizational forms. Therefore, we have integrated the insights of the first issue, viz., impacts of EC diffusion; knowledge from the second issue, viz., identification of the four stakeholders and their functions associated with the diffusion of EC; literature reviews and synthesis of the developed models and critical factors for the diffusion of EC in different developed and developing countries; and information from the contingency theory. We postulate that EC diffusion is contingent on the associating role, functions of those four stakeholders, and enabling drivers of market economy and infrastructure. Our proposed theoretical framework for diffusion of EC based on these paradigms is presented in Figure 5.1.

Government role, capability, and globalization policy

Several studies conducted on diffusion criteria and driving forces in developed countries like U.S., UK, Germany, Denmark, Japan, Singapore, and in developing countries like India, Mexico, South Korea, Brazil, revealed that government policy and capability are important factors for diffusion of ICT and EC (Garcia-Murillo, 2000; Kagami and Tsuji, 2001; Tiessen *et al.*, 2001; Wong, 2002a; Jalava and Pohjola, 2002; Kiiski and Pohjola, 2002; Kettler and Benavides, 2002; McGann *et al.*, 2002; Kraemer *et al.*, 2005 ; Viswanathan and Pick, 2005). In this context, we add the globalization policy imposed by WTO, different regional or economical treaties with some countries, and the globalization policy of a country as determinants of diffusion of EC in that country context. In our proposed framework we define government role for EC diffusion by consumer policy, financial policy, market policy, and promotional policy. Consumer policy refers to different rules and regulation imposed by a government to guide electronic business for the sake of protecting consumer rights and business legal environment. In EC, since the transaction is virtual and consumers can purchase any product or service from anywhere in the world, customers always feel insecure, a lack of privacy, uncertainty, and a lack of trust. Several researchers observed that lack of trust, privacy, and security are three major factors that affect consumer interest in online transaction (Ranganathan and

Figure 5.1. E-commerce diffusion framework

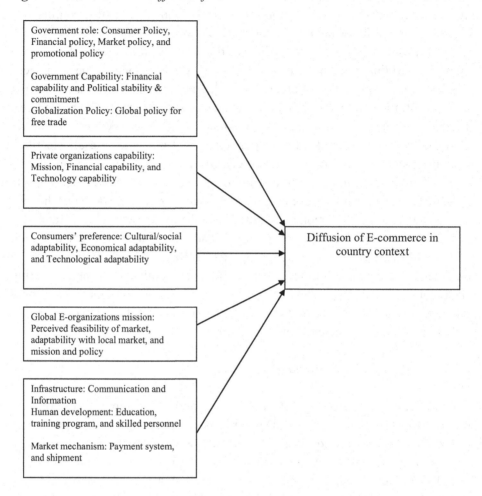

Ganapathy, 2002; Zhang and von Dran, 2002; Balasubramanian *et al.,* 2003; Soat, 2003; Brown and Muchira, 2004; Al-adawi *et al.,* 2005; Parent *et al.,* 2005). Though online companies use several policies to impart confidence among consumers regarding security, privacy, and developing trust, still the role of government in this connection is very important (McGann *et al.,* 2002; Warkentin *et al.,* 2002; Parent *et al.,* 2005). If we explore the national innovative capacity theory (Furman *et al.,* 2002) which focuses on the ability of a country to produce and commercialize a flow of innovative technology over the long term, we find logical underpinnings to integrate government capability with the process of adopting new innovation like EC. National innovative capacity depends on the strength of a country's common innovation infrastructure, the environment of innovation in a country's industrial clusters, and the strength of linkages between these two (Nelson, 1993; Furman *et al.*, 2002). Therefore, based on this theory, we can argue that, government intention to develop appriopriate infrastructure and implement strategic supporting market policy can create friendly environment for the proliferation of EC in the country context.

Strict government rules and regulations can build trust among consumers in online transactions and also bind electronic organizations to protect consumers' rights and develop trust. Therefore, this is a vital issue for EC diffusion. Financial policy refers to government regulations regarding financial rules for EC transactions both for foreign and local companies. The most important part in this field is the government tax and duty policy for online transactions. Allowing a rebate for tax and several sales duties in online transaction or financial incentives can expedite proliferation of EC and acceptance among consumers (McGann *et al.*, 2002). Due to differences in tax systems among different countries, the diffusion of EC is restricted severely (Wong, 2002a; McGann *et al.*, 2002). The market policy of government refers to creating facilities for markets operated by the Internet. Government is primarily authorized and responsible for this function. Including an Internet act, company registration, government business policy for Internet economy, the overall formalization of an Internet economy is a vital issue for systematic diffusion of EC in a country. Promotional policy is one of the potential and favoring factors for diffusion of EC (Wong, 2002a; Kettler and Benavides, 2002; McGann *et al.*, 2002). Traditional business operations have a long history. But EC has experienced business operation for only a few years. So this new business needs some efforts to promote and to expedite usage and guidance from the government side to be nurtured properly (Andersen and Bjørn-Andersen, 2001; McGann *et al.*, 2002; Viswanathan, and Pick, 2005). The U.S. has experienced an enormous diffusion of EC due to the excellent promotion of this business by the federal government (McGann *et al.*, 2002). With proper guidance and offers of financial incentives, governments can leverage proliferation of EC globally.

Government financial and political capabilities are two major pillars for systematic diffusion of EC (Andersen and Bjørn-Andersen, 2001). Countries where EC is extensively diffused have strong and stable financial and political capability (Andersen and Bjørn-Andersen, 2001; McGann *et al.*, 2002). Initially, a huge investment is required to develop the online environment. Several scholarly articles (Madu, 1989; Bhatnagar, 2002; Heeks, 2002; Dada, 2006) identified that information technology is still not suitable as a means of communication in developing countries. They also observed that it was a pragmatic mistake to implement the models of ICT in developing countries by copying directly from developed countries. The technology absorption capacity of developing countries, from both the government and citizen perspective, is quite different from that in developed countries. The prime reason for this observed difference between developed and developing countries is due to financial capability. Political stability is also an important difference between developed and developing countries. Generally, developed countries have a very stable political and government scene. Creating online facilities and aiding and promoting virtual business are long-term missions that need goals and strategies that cannot be attained without political and governmental stability (Dada, 2006). A sustainable policy for commerce is required to ensure foreign investment. So, it is also an important aspect for diffusion of EC in the long run.

The globalization policy and the compatibility of a national trade policy with the globalization policy introduced by WTO are important for diffusion of any business globally. This is especially true for EC, since it is inherently global (Kettler and Benavides, 2002; Yip, 2003). If the trade policy of any country follows economic protection, it is really difficult for international online organizations to extend their business operation to that country; additionally, consumers of that country cannot participate in external EC operation. As a result, this creates a major barrier for global EC diffusion (McGann *et al.,* 2002; Yip, 2003).

Private organizations' capability

Initiatives by local private organizations are primary ways to boost the Internet economy (Andersen and Bjørn-Andersen, 2001; Tiessen *et al.,* 2001; Wong, 2002a; McGann *et al.,* 2002; Viswanathan and Pick, 2005). Basically, in a market economy and in the era of globalization, private organizations are the primary initiators of EC adoption, proliferation, and diffusion among consumers. However, adoption criteria offered by different researchers for private organizations note that a firms' mission and objective as well as financial and technological capabilities are the main parameters (Kettler and Benavides, 2002; Gibbs *et al.,* 2003; Kraemer *et al.,* 2005; Viswanathan and Pick, 2005 ; Kurnia, 2007). The mission of a firm, whether it is ready and aimed to implement EC, is the primary determinant of EC adoption by firms. Their financial capability—including size, structure, business pattern, and resources to launch EC as the primary entity or as the intermediary—are also a vital to adoption (Bonaccorsi, 1992; Calof, 1994). Technological capability includes skilled and experienced manpower, availability of technology, competence in use of modern ICT, software, compatibility of company and long term objective with the use of ICT determine acceptance, use, and adoption of EC by private entities (Kettler and Benavides, 2002). Therefore, diffusion of EC is primarily dependent on private organizations' capability to adopt and use ICT and, thus, EC.

Consumers' preference

Ultimately, for business-to-consumer EC, consumers are the final users of EC products and services. If, for any cultural/social, economical, and technological reasons, consumers of any country are not ready to adopt ICT and thus EC, diffusion of EC is not at all possible (Internet Week, 2000; Kurnia, 2007; Jamal and Ahmed, 2007). Even the existence of versatile facilities favorable for EC growth cannot ensure proliferation unless consumers are ready to accept it. Due to cultural/social diversity, consumers of some countries lack an interest in conducting business in the virtual environment. As previously mentioned, lack of trust, privacy, security, and uncertainty might also deter them from adopting EC (Ranganathan and Ganapathy, 2002; Zhang and von Dran, 2002; Balasubramanian *et al.,* 2003). Economically, the majority of consumers in developing countries are not capable of transacting in EC due primarily to the unavailability of credit cards (Viswanathan and Pick, 2005). They also do not have an Internet connection, personal computers, and telecommunications. Without ensuring the development of those economic capabilities, the diffusion of EC, especially in developing countries, is hardly possible or feasible. The technological capability of consumers is another important aspect (Heeks, 2002). If consumers are not capable of handling ICT, the diffusion of EC will be stagnant, will be limited to certain groups, and will create a digital divide. Consumers' education, computer literacy, Internet experience, and availability are vital factors of EC diffusion countrywide (McGann *et al.,* 2002; Viswanathan and Pick, 2005).

Global E-organizations' mission

For extensive diffusion of EC in any country, the entrance of international E-organizations in that country is imperative. This is especially true for developing countries, because these countries are not well equipped to launch versatile EC organizations. If international E-organizations start operating their business functions globally, viz., if consumers of any country can purchase products/services from those well-established international E-organizations that have enormous distribution channels, then EC diffusion will be enhanced in any country context. However, a global E-organization's mission to extend their business periphery to any country includes the feasibility of markets in that country, which is comprised of market demand, and the strength, growth, stability, and supply chain entities of that country. If the market is large enough, has a strong demand, is growing fast, is very stable, and also has a sufficient supply chain, foreign E-organizations will definitely be attracted to intervene in that market. Adaptability with local markets in terms of the tax system; currency exchange; banking system; and the language, cultural, and social aspects are also prime issues for diffusion of EC (McGann *et al.,* 2002; Travica, 2002; Kurnia & Johnston, 2003).

Infrastructure, human development, and market mechanism

Infrastructure, human development, and market mechanism are three general issues for diffusion of EC in any countries (Andersen and Bjørn-Andersen, 2001; McGann *et al.,* 2002; Kraemer *et al.,* 2005; Viswanathan and Pick, 2005). Infrastructure is a major issue for ICT and EC diffusion. Since EC is very technology oriented, proper development of communication and information infrastructure can develop the scope to flourish, accept, use, and adopt EC, and, thus, diffusion is possible. Communication infrastructure includes computers, Internet connection with reasonable cost and speed, and telecommunications. Human development is also an important aspect of EC diffusion (Madu, 1989; Bhatnagar, 2002; Heeks, 2002; Dada, 2006). An ICT-intense business operation needs skilled personnel. Awareness of EC, an extensive computer/Internet and training education program, and developing skilled personnel are the core driving forces of EC diffusion (Wong, 2002a; McGann *et al.,* 2002). A UNDP survey (2003) of 191 countries revealed that developing countries lag far behind in terms of those mandatory facilities for diffusion of EC and, thus, determined that those countries are not ready to adopt ICT and EC.

The market mechanism refers to offering the scope to electronic organizations and also a financial instrument and shipment method for online transactions. This is a great issue observed by many researchers that, due to the unavailability of credit cards in most of the developing countries, consumers in those countries cannot enter into the global EC business arena (Radaideh and Selim, 2004). For primarily international EC, shipment of products and return are vital business functions. Without creating systematic and stable payment and shipment methods, EC transactions cannot be optimized globally, and, thus, extensive operation of EC will fail.

5.6. CONCLUSION AND FUTURE RESEARCH DIRECTION

This chapter has primarily addressed, discussed, and conceptualized paradigms of three issues of diffusion of EC. First, we investigated the impacts of EC diffusion on overall social, political, cultural, technological, organizational, and economical relations. In this connection, we revealed seven types of prime relational changes on the effects of EC diffusion in a country context. From a theoretical background and the functional characteristics of EC diffusion, we postulate that diffusion of EC might significantly affect social, cultural, organizational, technological, economical, and political behavior. Consequently, government-private organizations, consumers, and intermediaries (viz., the comprehensive relation of market characteristics) are reshaped.

Then we traced the diffusion of EC and the role of different actors associated with this new economical and technological innovation, viz. EC, and their functional characteristics in the diffusion process. The government role and globalization policy, local private organizations, consumers, and international online organizations play controlling roles in the diffusion of EC in the country context. Based on the association of those stakeholders with the market economy, and the role and functions of those stakeholders in the diffusion process of EC, we conceptualized the theoretical framework for diffusion of EC. From this framework, we revealed that the government role, capability, and globalization policy; consumer preferences; private organization's capabilities; the global E-organizations mission; and the infrastructure and market mechanism factors with a set of associated variables create the ability for EC to be diffused in any country. Therefore, the diffusion of EC is not a unidimensional issue, but has multi-dimensional aspects. When all the associated stakeholders of market mechanism, demand side, supply side, and intermediary function favor adoption of EC, then only systematic diffusion of EC is possible and also feasible in a country context. This view is supported by the different socio-technical theories and evidences from different countries. EC diffusion is a complex phenomenon, and it is strongly related to country phenomena. All the five prime categories of factors with a set of variables in the proposed theoretical framework of EC diffusion are dependent on any country's specific social, cultural, economical, technological, organizational, and political characteristics. Therefore, from these findings, policy makers, practitioners, and academicians get insights into EC diffusion. These are:

1. EC diffusion possibility and pattern is country dependent. We cannot copy or transfer a successful diffusion model from developed countries to developing countries, since social, cultural, economical, technological, organizational, and political characteristics of developed and developing countries differ significantly.
2. EC diffusion is a multidimensional and complex issue. It should be resolved considering the favoring roles of all the stakeholders associated with the market economy in any country.
3. Private organizations that are launching EC play a pivotal role in the diffusion process; however, the capability of government and consumers is very important in promoting, guiding, and embracing that effort.
4. The compatibility of the globalization policy introduced by the WTO with country-specific trade policy has leverage in formalizing EC diffusion.

5.   Long-term vision, mission, objectives, and strategic planning of any govern-
      ment are of utmost important for diffusion of EC, which are evidenced from
      experiences in several developed and developing countries.

The proposed framework to explore diffusion factors of EC is a relative theoretical framework. The identified factors, role of different stakeholders, and associated
set of variables do not bear any particular standard. For example, infrastructure,
availability of Internet, government policy, capability, etc. do not provide any numeri-
cal standard based on which we can evaluate the scope for diffusion of EC in any
country. Therefore, several benchmarking empirical studies are essential in some
developed countries where EC has been successfully diffused. Then, in the light
of this theoretical framework, exploring the factors with their associated variables
and comparing with the benchmarking information of developed countries, we can
address, identify, and reveal conditions, the scope, opportunities, and barriers for
diffusion of EC in any country.

REFERENCES

Al-adawi, Z., Yousafzai, S., & Pallister, J. (2005). Conceptual Model of Citizen
Adoption of E-Government. *The Second International Conference on Innovations
in Information Technology (IIT'05)*.

Alavi, M., & Joachimsthaler, E. A. (1992). Revisiting DSS Implementation Research: A Meta-Analysis of the Literature and Suggestions for Researchers. *MIS
Quarterly, 16*(1), 95-116.

Anderson, K. (1999). Reengineering Public Sector Organizations Using Information Technology. In R. Heeks (Ed.), *Reinventing Government in the Information
Age* (pp. 312-30). New York, Routledge.

Andersen, K. V., & Bjørn-Andersen, N. (2001). *Globalization and E-Commerce:
Growth and Impacts in Denmark*. Center for Research on IT and Organizations
University of California, Irvine.

Balasubramanian, S., Konana, P., & Menon, N. M. (2003). Customer, Satisfaction
in Virtual Environments: A Study of Online Investing. *Management Science,
7*(July), 871–889.

Bell, D. (1973). *The Coming of Post-Industrial Society*. New York: Basic Books.

Berger, S., & Dore, R. (Ed.). (1996). *National Diversity and Global Capitalism*.
Ithaca, NY: Cornell University Press.

Bhatnagar, S. (2002). E-government: Lessons from Implementation in Developing Countries. *Regional Development Dialogue*, *24*, UNCRD, (Autumn Issue, 2002), 1-9.

Bonaccorsi, A. (1992). On the Relationship between Firm Size and Export Intensity. *Journal of International Business Studies*, *23*, 605-635.

Boyer, R. (1996). The Convergence Hypothesis Revisited: Globalization But Still the Century of Nations?. In S. Berger and R. Dore (Ed.), *National Diversity and Global Capitalism* (pp. 29–59). Ithaca, NY: Cornell University Press.

Brown, D. (1999). Information Systems for Improved Performance Management: Development Approaches in U.S. Public Agencies. In R. Heeks (Ed.), *Reinventing Government in the Information Age* (pp. 113-34). New York, Routledge.

Brown, M., & Muchira, R. (2004). Investigating the Relationship between Internet Privacy Concerns and Online Purchase Behavior. *Journal of Electronic Commerce Research*, *5*(1), 62-70.

Cai, S., & Jun, M. (2003). Internet Users' Perceptions of Online Service Quality: A Comparison of Online Buyers and Information Searches. *Managing Service Quality*, *13*(6), 504-519.

Calof, J. L. (1994). The Relationship between Firm Size and Export behavior Revisited. *Journal of International Business Studies*, *25*, 367-387.

Cavusgil, S. T., Zou, S., & Naidu, G. M. (1993). Product and Promotion Adaptation in Export Ventures: An Empirical Investigation. *Journal of International Business Studies*, *24*(4), 479-506.

Chan, C. M. L., & Pan, S. L. (2003). Managing Stakeholder Relationships in an E-Government Project. *9th Americas Conference on Information Systems*, (pp. 783-791).

Chwelos, P., Benbasat, I., & Dexter, A. S. (2001). Research Report: Empirical Test of an EDI Adoption Model. *Information Systems Research, 12*(3), 304–321.

Dada, D. (2006). *The Failure of E-government in Developing Countries.* http://www. lse.ac.uk/collections/informationSystems/iSChannel/Dada_2006b.pdf. [Accessed: 2006].

Damodaran, L., Nicholls, J., & Henney, A. (2005). The Contribution of Sociotechnical Systems Thinking to the Effective Adoption of e-Government and the Enhancement of Democracy. *The Electronic Journal of e-Government*, *3*(1), 1-12.

Dedrick, J., & Kraemer, K. L. (1998). *Asia's Computer Challenge: Threat of Opportunity for the United States and the World.* Oxford University Press, New York.

Eisenhardt, M. K. (1989). Agency Theory: An Assessment and Review. *Academy of Management Review, 14*(1), 57).

Evans, P., & Wurster, T. S. (1999). Getting Real about Virtual Commerce. *Harvard Business Review, 77*(6), 85-94.

Fountain, J. (2001). *Building the Virtual State: Information Technology and Institutional Change.* Washington, DC, Brookings Institution Press.

Gallivan, M. J. (1996). Strategies for Implementing New Software Processes: An Evaluation of a Contingency Framework. *SIGCPR/SIGMIS '96*, Denver Colorado.

Garcia-Murillo, M. (2000). Information Technology in Latin America. *AMCIS Proceedings, Association for Information Systems*, Atlanta, GA, (pp. 1883–1886).

Gibbs, J., Kraemer, K. L., & Dedrick, J. (2003). Environment and Policy Factors Shaping E-Commerce Diffusion: A Cross-Country Comparison. *The Information Society, 19*(1), 5-18.

Heeks, R. (2002). Information Systems and Developing Countries: Failure, Success, and Local Improvisations. *The Information Society, 18*, 101–112.

Hirst, P., & Thompson, G. (1996). *Globalization In Question: The International Economy And The Possibilities Of Governance.* Cambridge: Polity Press.

Internet Week. (2000). Consumer Behavior Varies Widely By Country, Study Says. *Internet Week*, December 12.

Jamal, A. S., & Ahmed, A. F. (2007). Socio-cultural Factors Influencing Consumer Adoption of Online Transactions. *8th World Congress on the Management of eBusiness* (WCMeB 2007).

Jalava, J., & Pohjola, M. (2002). Economic Growth in the New Economy: Evidence from Advanced Economies. *Information Economics and Policy, 14*(2), 189–210.

Kagami, M., & Tsuji, M. (Eds.). (2001). *The 'IT' Revolution and Developing Countries: Late-Comer Advantage.* Institute of Developing Economies, Japan External Trade Organization, Tokyo.

Kiiski, S., & Pohjola, M. (2002). Cross-country Diffusion of the Internet. *Information Economics and Policy, 14*(2), 297–310.

Kettler, H. F., & Benavides, E. (2002). E-Business Globalization. *Analyzing Foreign Countries for E-Commerce Opportunities*. www.hipermarketing.com/nuevo%204/columnas/efrain/ebus. pdf.

Kim, M., Kim, Jung-Hwan, & Lennon, S. J. (2006). Online Service Attributes Available on Apparel Retail Web Site: An E-S-QUAL Approach, *Managing Service Quality, 16*(1), 51-77.

Kraemer, K. L. (2001). *Globalization of E-Commerce*. Center for Research on IT and Organizations, University of California, Irvine. E-Business Center Director's Forum, Chicago.

Kraemer, K. L., Gibbs, J., & Dedrick, J. (2005). Impacts of Globalization on E-Commerce Use and Firm Performance: A Cross-Country Investigation. *The Information Society, 21*, 323-340.

Kurnia, S. (2007). *E-Commerce Adoption in Developing Countries: an Indonesian Study*. http://www.dis.unimelb.edu.au/staff/sherahk/Papers/SISC_developing%20countries_Final.doc. [Last Accessed December, 2007].

Kurnia, S., & Johnston, R. B. (2003). Adoption of Efficient Consumer Response: Key Issues and Challenges in Australia. *Supply Chain Management: An International Journal, 8*(2), 251-262.

Lawrence, T. B. & Suddaby, R. (2006). Institutions and Institutional Work. In S. R. Clegg, C. Hardy, T. B. Lawrence, & W. R. Nord (Eds.), *Handbook of Organization Studies* (pp. 215-254). 2nd Edition: London: Sage.

Lee, J. K., & Rao, H. R. (2003). A Study of Customer's Trusting Beliefs in Government-To-Customer Online Services. *9th Americas Conference on Information Systems*, (pp. 821-826).

Madu, C. N. (1989). Transferring Technology to Developing Countries – Critical Factors for Success. *Long Range Planning, 22*(4), 115-124.

Massini, S., & Pettigrew, A. M. (2003). Complementarities in Organizational Innovation and Performance: Empirical Evidence from the INNFORM Survey. In A. M Pettigrew, R. Whittington, L. Melin, C. Sanchez-Runde, F. Van den Bosch, W. Ruigrock, & T. Numagami (Ed.), *Innovative Forms of Organizing: International Perspectives*. SAGE Publications.

McGann, S., King, J., & Lyytinen, K. (2002). Globalization of E-Commerce: Growth and Impacts in the United States of America. Sprouts: *Working Papers on Information Environments, Systems and Organizations, 2*(2) (Spring), 59-86.

Moon, M. J. (2002). The Evolution of E-Government among Municipalities: Rhetoric or Reality?. *Public Administration Review, 62*(4), 424–433.

Moon, M. J., & Bretschneider, S. (2002). Does Perception of Red Tape Constrain IT Innovativeness in Organizations: Unexpected Results from Simultaneous Equation Model and Implications. *Journal of Public Administration Research and Theory, 12*(2), 273–91.

Netemeyer, R., Johnston, M., & Burton, S. (1990). Analysis of Role Conflict and Role Ambiguity in a Structural Equations Framework. *Journal of Applied Psychology, 75*, 400-410.

Furman, J. L., Porter, M. E., & Stern, S. (2002). The Determinants of National Innovative Capacity. *Research Policy, 31*, 899-933.

Nelson, R. R. (Ed.) (1993). *National Innovation System: A Comparative Analysis.* Oxford University Press.

Ohmae, K. (1990). *The Borderless World: Power and Strategy in the Interlinked Economy.* New York: Harper Perennial.

Ohmae, K. (1995). *The End of the Nation State.* New York: Free Press.

Parent, M., Vandebeek, C. A., & Gemino, A. C. (2005). Building Citizen Trust through E-Government. *Government Information Quarterly, 22*, 720–736.

Porter, M. E. (1985). *Competitive Strategy: Techniques for Analyzing Industries and Competitors.* New York, NY: Free Press

Radaideh, M. A., & Selim, H. M. (2004). E-Commerce: Adoption, Acceptance, and Prototyping in Abu Dhabi. *The 5th Annual U.A.E. University Research Conference.*

Ranganathan, C., & Ganapathy, S. (2002). Key Dimensions of Business to Consumer Web Sites. *Information and Management, 39*, 457-465.

Robertson, T. S. (1974). A Critical Examination of Adoption Process Models of Consumer Behavior. In J. N. Sheth (Ed.), *Models of Buyer Behavior.* New York: Harper & Row.

Rogers, E. M., & Shoemaker, F. F. (1971). *Communication of Innovations: A Cross-Cultural Approach* (2nd edition). New York: Free Press.

Rogers, E. M. (2003). *Diffusion of Innovations* (5th Edition). New York, NY: Free Press. ISBN 0-7432-2209-1.

Sahlman, W. A. (1999). The New Economy is Stronger than You Think. *Harvard Business Review, 77,* 99-106.

Sebastianelli, R., Tamimi, N., & Rajan, M. (2006). Perceived Quality of Internet Retailers: Does Shopping Frequency and Product Type Make a Difference? *EABR & ETLC,* Siena, Italy.

Shoham, A. (1999). Bounded Rationality, Planning, Standardization of International Strategy, and Export Performance: A Structural Model Examination. *Journal of International Marketing, 7*(2), 24-50.

Soat, J. (2003). Privacy, Security, Identity Still Matter. *InformationWeek, 936,* 75.

Tallon, P.P. & Kraemer, K.L. (2000). Information Technology and Economic Development: Ireland's coming of Age with Lessons for Developing Countries. *Journal of Global Information Technology Management, 3*(2), 4–23.

Tiessen, J. H., Wright, R. W., & Turner, I. (2001). A Model of E-commerce Use by Internationalizing SMEs. *Journal of International Management, 7,* 211-233.

Travica, B. (2002). Diffusion of Electronic Commerce in Developing Countries: The Case of Costa Rica. *Journal of Global Information Technology Management, 5*(1), 4–24.

Tung, L. L., & Rieck, O. (2005). Adoption of Electronic Government Services Among Business Organizations in Singapore, *Journal of Strategic Information Systems, 14,* 417–440.

Turner, M., & Desloges, C. (2002). *Strategies and Framework for Government On-Line: A Canadian Experience.* World Bank E-Government Learning Workshop, Washington D.C., June 18.

UNDP (United Nations Department of Economic and Social Affairs Report). (2003). *World Public Sector Report 2003: E-Government at the Crossroads.* NewYork: United Nations Publication.

Unhelkar, B. (2003). Understanding the Impact of Cultural Issues in Global e-Business Alliances. *4ᵗʰ International We-B Conference,* 24-25 Nov, Perth, Western Australia.

Viswanathan, N. K., & Pick, J. B. (2005). Comparison of E-commerce in India and Mexico: An Example of Technology Diffusion in Developing Nations. *International Journal on Technology Management, 31*(1/2).

Wade, R. (1996). Globalization and its Limits: Reports of The Death of the National Economy are Greatly Exaggerated. In S. Berger & R. Dore (Ed.), *National Diversity and Global Capitalism* (pp. 60–88), Ithaca, NY: Cornell University Press.

Warkentin, M., Gefen, D., Pavlou, P., & Rose, G. *(2002). Encouraging Citizen Adoption of e-Government by Building Trust.* Electronic Markets, *12*(3), 157-162.

Whittington R., & Pettigrew A. M. (2003). Complementarities Thinking. In A.M. Pettigrew, R. Whittington, L. Melin, C. Sanchez-Runde, F. van den Bosch, W. Ruigrok & T. Numagami (Eds.), *Innovative Forms of Organizing: International Perspectives* (pp. 125-132), London: Sage.

Wirtz, J., & Wong, P. K. (2001). An Empirical Study on Internet-Based Business-To-Business E-Commerce in Singapore. *Singapore Management Review, 23*(1), 87-112.

Wong, P. K. (2002a). Globalization of American, European and Japanese Production Networks and the Growth of Singapore's Electronics Industry. *International Journal of Technology Management, 24(7/8), 843-869.*

Wong, P-K. (2002b).ICT Production and Diffusion in Asia Digital Dividends or Digital Divide?. *Information Economics and Policy, 14*(2002) 167–187.

Woodward, J. (1965). *Industrial Organization: Theory and Practice.* London: Oxford University Press.

Yip, G. S. (2003). *Total Global Strategy II.* Prentice Hall, Upper Saddle River, New Jersey.

Zhang, P., & von Dran, G. (2002). User Expectations and Rankings of Quality Factors in Different Web Site Domains. *International Journal of Electronic Commerce, 6*(2), 9-33.

Chapter VI
Diffusion of E–Commerce in Developed and Developing Countries:
Comparative Studies

ABSTRACT

Based on the theoretical framework revealed in Chapter V, this chapter is intended to investigate the country-specific roles of governments, private organizations, and consumers and the status of infrastructure development and the market mechanism of some developed and developing countries in terms of EC diffusion. In this connection, EC diffusion status and role of different stakeholders are analyzed for developed countries: USA and Denmark, developing countries with stronghold in ICT: Mexico and India, and developing countries: Bangladesh and Ghana.

6.1. CASE STUDIES

Drawing inference from the proposed E-commerce (EC) diffusion framework in Chapter V, in this chapter we aim to investigate, identify, and illustrate the overall condition of some developed and developing countries in terms of EC diffusion. In Chapter V, we noted that EC diffusion depends on the critical roles of the stakeholders of EC. We also developed a framework of diffusion comprising some critical factors, namely *Government role, capability, and globalization policy; Private organizations' capability; Consumers' preferences; Global E-organizations' mission; Infrastructure, human development, and the market mechanism.* Now in this chapter, we will view some cases of EC diffusion in the light of that framework. As cases, we will analyze the business-to-consumer (B2C) EC diffusion status of several developed and developing countries, grounded on the theoretical framework of diffusion proposed in Chapter V. Then we will contrast those factors for different countries, which we will analyze in the case studies section, in respect to the diffusion in the respected countries. We will divide this chapter into 2 sections with the second section in subsections.

National environment and country demographics that represent government policy, consumer preferences, social and cultural values, and overall country status in terms of technology infrastructure and economical strength are key features for globalization of the Internet-based economy (Gibbs, Kraemer, and Dedrick, 2003). Different countries have significantly different positions in respect to their capability of adopting and also diffusing B2C EC in their domestic environment. In this section, we aim to investigate country-specific roles of governments, private organizations, and consumers and the status of infrastructure development and the market mechanism. Shedding light on those factors in any specific country and the globalization policy, we then contrast international E-retailers mission for that country. Finally, we will evaluate EC diffusion status in that country based on the observed roles of the stakeholders of EC.

Developed countries are in a good position to develop their capability in relation to diffusion of EC. North American, Western European, and some Asian countries show strength in this respect. However, some developing countries also exhibit bright promise concerning diffusion factors for an ICT-based Internet economy. These countries include India, Brazil, China, Mexico, South Africa, Singapore, Taiwan, and Hong Kong. Nevertheless, most of the developing countries are really at a premature stage in light of the roles of different stakeholders of EC diffusion identified in Chapter V. So, we will investigate several countries, selecting from the previously mentioned three groups, viz., developed countries, developing countries with a stronghold in the ICT sector and high prospects for diffusion of EC, and less developed countries. We will investigate the status of six countries in the light of the diffusion framework. The countries that we plan to focus on—based on social, cultural, political, technological, and economical variability—are:

1.   Developed countries: USA and Denmark,
2.   Developing countries with stronghold in ICT: Mexico and India, and
3.   Developing countries: Bangladesh and Ghana.

6.1.1. Developed Countries

Robust market economy, financial capacity, advancement in modern ICT, extensive proliferation of and penetration by the Internet, strong social and governmental guidance, active role of big corporations, and tremendous purchasing power of consumers place the developed countries in a high position in relation to embracing and diffusing EC. In this context, in the next subsections, we will look at the anatomy of some developed countries shedding light on the theoretical framework developed for diffusion of EC in Chapter V. However, before going into a case-by-case study of different countries, we should look at the globalization policy administered by the United Nations to briefly demonstrate its support in the proliferation of B2C EC. This globalization policy, particularly enhanced and guided by the World Trade Organization (WTO), is apparently common for all member countries.

6.1.1.1. Globalization Policy

The Working Group on Internet Governance (WGIG) infrastructure paper noted that, "Internet governance was inextricably linked to the larger issue of globalization …" (United Nations, 2005). Since, the Internet economy is gradually expanding from the west to the east; we expect a revolutionary change in the Internet economy. One of the questions raised in the WGIG background report is: "whether the rules and practices developed to govern trade in physical goods and services can and should be applied to EC?" (United Nations, 2005). The Internet and globalization both facilitate global open competition (MacLean, 2004). This phenomenon does not easily lend itself to regulation as such but certainly requires constant review and upgrading of international policy frameworks. The successful completion of the Uruguay Round Agreement in 1993 and the establishment of the WTO in 1995 were expected to have crucial implications for globalization of trade across countries. The new areas of trade negotiations with concomitant changes in legal and administrative structures include rule making and rule breaking under the WTO, which ensure and promote proliferation of the Internet economy globally.

Globalization and the impact of rapid advances in technologies present new opportunities and new challenges to all countries, regions, societies, and citizens. Public interest in globalization has focused on the multilateral system. Enhanced openness, free movement, mobility, political and trade liberalism, and transparency are central to the task of demonstrating the benefits that flow from open markets. Public understanding of the linkages and complementarities between trade liberalization and the range of issues arising in other policy areas are deepening through the strengthened Internet economy (Rao, 2001). The rules-based multilateral trading system supported by WTO provides the best framework for global growth and prosperity. In November 2001, the WTO Ministerial Conference at Doha agreed: "to continue the Work Program on EC. The work to date demonstrates that EC creates new challenges and opportunities for trade for members at all stages of development, and we recognize the importance of creating and maintaining an environment which is favorable to the future development of EC....... We declare that members will maintain their current practice of not imposing customs duties on electronic transmissions" (WTO, 2001). WTO agreed that the term EC meant the production, distribution, marketing, sale, or delivery of goods and services by electronic means. Member countries of WTO have discussed the issues of globalization of the Internet economy in the General Council, the Council for Trade in Services, the Council for Trade in Goods, the Council for TRIPS, the Committee on Trade and Development, and the work of other inter-governmental organizations.

WTO, International Monetary Fund (IMF), World Bank, International Labor Organizations (ILO), and the United Nations Conference on Trade and Development (UNCTAD) are all working to liberalize trade across countries by proposing or advising a consistent tariff and tax system, zero or minimum subsidies, and open competition through open trade. The Doha Development Agenda required that all countries prepare for negotiations on agreements of consistent market economic policy with open competitive trade. After Doha, the WTO and all associated organizations of the United Nations are working in favor of globalization of the Internet economy. However, there are several complications in defining goods and services for the Internet economy, which is governed electronically. "The rules governing trade in goods fall under the General Agreement of Tariffs and Trade (GATT) while the rules governing trade in services fall under the General Agreement on Trade in Services (GATS). The fact that neither "goods" nor "services" are defined in the GATT and GATS respectively seriously complicates the already complicated matter of the electronically delivered product. WTO recognizes that it is products previously traded only as physical goods but are now also tradable as digital information that present the challenges" (United Nations, 2005).

WTO rules now treat goods and services differently. Conventionally, GATT reflects its principle in proposing reduction of tariffs applied to all members. On the other hand, member countries are very reluctant to comply with that principle, and are more enthusiastic to progressively liberalize custom duties, particularly that imposed on services.

Fundamentally, WTO always advocates for waiving or at least reduction of border taxes on products shipped across countries electronically; however, it must be noted that import duties and border taxes are important sources of revenue for most developing countries. Currently, most goods ordered using online channels are delivered by traditional means and are, therefore, accessible for inspection and charging as appropriate. "However, a rapidly increasing volume and variety of soft goods—music, movies, books, architectural and engineering drawings, etc.—are being shipped electronically and delivered over the Internet" (United Nations, 2005). The physical equivalents of some of these products can be apparently assumed as goods, and therefore, tariff can be imposed on these intangible products ignoring its contents.

Most of the delivery systems of B2C EC still rely on traditional shipment methods, viz. physical delivery. But, the problem is electronic delivery of software, movies, songs, etc. In 1995, the WTO committee on customs valuation adopted a 1984 Tokyo Round Committee decision which allows members to levy taxes either on the value of the "carrier media"—i.e., tape, and CDs—or on the combined value of the carrier media and its contents—i.e., software, songs, and movies. (WIPO, 2005). So there is a consensus on electronic ordering and physical delivery. However, electronic delivery is still a potential issue of conflict among member countries. Labeling the term "intangible" goods is considered as a prospective solution (Cadbury Committee, 1992).

Another conflicting issue, especially raised by developing countries, is the existence of intellectual property in both goods and services. Consequently, the application of Trade-Related Aspects of Intellectual Property Rights (TRIPS) rules may defy any general solution to EC disciplines in trade.

While continuing to work on this issue, the member countries of WTO remain aware of work being done elsewhere. To develop Internet taxation proposals, several reports are being developed by Organization for Economic Cooperation and Development (OECD), the European Union (EU), and the U.S. UNCTAD (2000) has prepared a report on "Tariffs, Taxes and Electronic Commerce: Revenue Implications for Developing Countries". There is also an OECD report (1998) on "Electronic Commerce Taxation Framework Conditions." These reports explored and analyzed rigorously issues concerning across border taxation, tariffs, and import duty policies, and they proposed some harmony and consistency in global EC. However, it is still an issue of severe challenge raised from several developing countries, including China, India, and Brazil.

In the light of the global EC system, security, privacy, and Internet fraud, countries across the world have still not reached a consensus to develop uniform rules and regulations to protect consumers' rights, which is essential for the global proliferation of B2C EC. The international community must create truly global agreements regarding cyber-crime that will specifically target identity theft. In addition, the international community should create an international body to enforce laws on cyber identity theft and to work through the kinks of international cooperation (Davis, 2003). Arguably, the WTO has not really tackled Internet and convergence regulatory issues.

The Internet is an "electronic medium that disregards geographical boundaries and throws the law into disarray by creating entirely new phenomenon that need to become the subject of clear legal rules but that cannot be governed, satisfactorily, by any current territorially-based sovereign" (Jackson, 1989). Therefore, for the Internet economy, we earnestly need a global solution. WTO rules, at present, are working in this connection, and are considered controversially by some, important protection against any aggressive operations led by multinational corporations.

The previously mentioned discussion of globalization policy, administered by different international organizations for the sake of guiding and supporting the global diffusion of EC, reflects clear evidence that, though the globalization policy is working in favor of EC diffusion, its present situation is complicated and under construction. However, this globalization policy, particularly governed by WTO, is apparently common for diffusion of EC in all the countries discussed below.

6.1.1.2. Denmark

Government role and capability

The Danish government has been very enthusiastic in the rapid adoption, imple-mentation, and exploitation of EC in all sectors of the economy. Consequently, the government has a long-term mission and set of objectives to develop a compatible environment, business-centric policy, and technology infrastructure, and to guide private sectors and educate customers in the Internet economy by establishing a proper education system. The government's prime policy is to explore IT in both public and private sectors and to educate citizens in IT beginning in primary and secondary schools. The Danish government also worked to develop a partnership between the public and private sectors to meet the challenge of organizing and financing ICT-based projects. Another central policy issue is to develop the capac-ity to offer competitive outline provisions for enterprises in the network society (Ministry of Information Technology and Research, 1999). The government has strong guidance and initiatives to promote a countrywide Internet economy.

Denmark is a leading developed country. The annual output of the Danish economy amounts to US$ 256.3 billion, a GDP per capita of US$ 57,035, and the productivity of the Danish workforce is one of the highest among the developed countries (IMF Report, 2007). According to the per capita income and financial capability of Denmark government, this country is placed at the very top level in world economic activities. Denmark has a strong and well-established political and democratic movement. The country's political and economical policy is very stable with long-term goals.

Private organizations' capability

The Danish economy is dominated by more small enterprises than large corporations. Sixty percent of the private sector labor force works in companies with less than 100 employees (Andersen and Bjørn-Andersen, 2001). According to a cross-country study made by (Kraemer, Gibbs, and Dedrick, 2002), small business firms are more likely interested in business-to-business (B2B) EC than business-to-consumer (B2C) EC. This finding is also obvious in Denmark's overall market structure. Most of the private organizations in Denmark are engaged in extensive B2B EC operations, whereas their average engagements in B2C EC operations are lower than the Scandinavian average (Andersen and Bjørn-Andersen, 2001). However, if we look at the information infrastructure in the private sector, we see more than 90 percent of all Danish enterprises have access to the Internet, and more than 80 percent of companies with more than 10 employees have their own homepage (Andersen and Bjørn-Andersen, 2001).

Consumers' preference

A United Nations report (UNPAN, 2005) indicates that Denmark has a high literacy rate (around 100 percent) and they are skilled in Internet and computer operations. The population is financially solvent and educated, beginning in elementary school, about computers and the Internet. It is worth emphasizing that Denmark also has well-organized vocational training for general citizens, and public and private employees. Culturally and socially, Danish consumers have a positive attitude towards ICT uses.

Global E-organizations' mission

The European e-action plan has three fundamental initiatives to promote the Internet economy across Europe. These include: 1) cheaper, faster, and more secure networks for the Internet; 2) investment programs in people and skills; and 3) e-acceleration programs and transportation media to stimulate use of the Internet (European Commission, 2001). Adoption of EU legislation on copyrights, e-marketing, e-money, and jurisdiction is a key priority for the commission. There is a strong emphasis on protecting consumer privacy and security. The European Data Protection Act, which mandates that companies use a specific standard for collecting and using private data, ensures consumer privacy; however, it significantly inhibits the mobility of EC. The extensive Internet regulation in Europe is in contrast to the market-driven approach in the U.S., and has been criticized as slowing EC diffusion (Lewell, 1999). In addition, the Danish job market is highly unionized (more than 85 percent), which is a unique feature of the industrial relations in the Scandinavian countries. The consequence, however, might be reduced structural flexibility and an inability to attract global E-retailers. So, the presence of international B2C E-retailers is not very common in Denmark. Government policy and the tax system in Denmark are also in favor of B2B EC and not very focused on B2C EC.

Infrastructure, human development, and market mechanism

Based on the web measure index (0.9731), human capital index (0.9800), and infrastructure index (0.7642) prepared by the United Nations (UNPAN, 2005), which are the measures for the Internet economy and also E-government (EG), Denmark is at the very top level (0.9058 out of 1, which placed them at the second rank after the U.S.) among other developed countries. These parameters indicate that Denmark has extensive infrastructure to implement an ICT-based economy. Denmark's telecommunication infrastructure and Internet penetration rate (68.8 percent) (Internet World Stats, 2007) are very high compared to other European countries. For availability of the Internet with better speed at lower cost, government cyber cafés, call center, computers, telecommunications, Denmark is extremely competent in comparison to other developed countries.

In terms of credit cards, payment for EC, return of goods, Denmark is in a very convenient position. More than 30 percent of the total population have debit and credit cards. Electronic banking, payment, transactions, and money exchange to the U.S. dollar are all well-established in Denmark.

Diffusion of EC

It is apparent that government policy, capability, stability, infrastructure, and market mechanisms are strong drivers for the diffusion of EC in Denmark. Consumer preferences, private organizational initiatives, and global E-retailers motives toward Denmark are moderate drivers. Global policy is a strong catalyst for the diffusion of EC globally, in general. However, so many conflicting issues regarding this have yet to be resolved for actual free and open trade operations of B2C EC globally and to offer sustainable benefits of globalization to all consumers of all countries. Consequently, B2C EC, in general, is still not a significant contributor to the world economy and has not diffused as extensively as was anticipated. However, in comparison to the world average, diffusion of B2C EC is very significant and has a stronghold in Denmark. It is just not as extensive as it could be in a developed country.

In 2000, approximately one out of ten companies in Denmark performed sales transactions through the Internet, which comprises DKK 12 billion (US$ 1.5 billion). However, it is mostly from local markets (81 percent). Thirteen percent of the sales were B2C EC. If we compare the B2B and B2C turnover with the overall figures in Scandinavia, Europe, the United States, and the OECD, the Danish economy is at an average EU level in terms of B2C trade and at a higher than average level in B2B trade. However, the B2C turnover in Denmark, compared to the U.S., is smaller. A survey by Taylor Nelson Sofres (Sofres, 2000) showed that only 16 percent of Internet users purchased online in the past month, whereas the corresponding figure in the U.S. was about 27 percent. Measured in percentage of GDP, the Danish B2C trade was only 0.1 percent; in the U.S. it was 0.4 percent (Forrester Research, 2000). A small population (5.4 million) is a big problem for the proliferation of B2C EC.

6.1.1.3. USA

Government role and capability

From the beginning of 1990, the Department of Commerce emphasized that the U.S. government saw the importance of EC and IT to U.S. society and businesses. The government characterized the online dynamic that is occurring as "a transformation of America's economy and society." The U.S. government helps the Internet economy to boost productivity and global competitiveness. According to the government's EC website (www.ecommerce.gov), the five primary guiding principles held by the U.S. government with regards to this area are as follows:

- The private sector should lead.
- Governments should avoid undue restrictions on EC.
- Where governmental involvement is needed, its aim should be to support and enforce a predictable, minimalist, consistent, and simple legal environment.
- Governments should recognize the unique qualities of the Internet.
- EC over the Internet should be facilitated on a global basis.

The U.S. government also put forth the following initiatives to facilitate the growth of the EC:

- Tripled investment in community technology centers from $10 million in FY99 to $32.5 million in FY00.
- Supported innovative applications of information technology to link job seekers and workers with employers to fill jobs and upgrade skills through a suite of online services called America's Career Kit.
- Supported the private sector to develop new business strategies for low-cost computers and Internet access to make universal access at home affordable for all Americans.

- Increased the number of classrooms connected to the Internet from 3 percent in 1994 to 51 percent in 1998 through the implementation of the "E-Rate Program," which leverages a universal service fund to provide significant capital for disadvantaged schools to narrow the digital divide. The funds are allocated to give these schools telecommunications services, internal connections, and infrastructure as well as Internet access.

The U.S. government also subsidizes several infrastructure and market-related resource factors to increase EC proliferation. Also, at the present, B2C EC transaction has been enabled by the taxation policy. Currently, there is no tax on state-to-state transactions; a situation which adds tremendous appeal to the option of online shopping (McGann, King, and Lyytinen, 2002).

Security, fraud, and privacy are important reasons for consumers not to accept B2C EC. In this context, the U.S. is a leading country in setting many rules and regulations to protect consumers rights and interests. The U.S. has passed legislation for digital signatures, privacy, consumer protection, copyright, content regulation, and taxation (Gibbs et al., 2003). Also, market and telecommunication liberalization seem to be significant enablers because they drive down costs of access and use, and increase resource availability.

The U.S. has had the highest market economy and yearly turnover in the world for decades. The perspectives of stability and financial capability of the U.S. government to set structures for the Internet economy is well known. The U.S. is the largest economy in the world. Its GDP is $13,220 billion U.S., which is the largest and far ahead of the second largest economy represented by Japan as $4,911 billion U.S. Per capita income is also at the top level, $45,594 U.S. dollar. At different times, the U.S. government has allocated billions of dollars to develop, support, and guide the Internet economy. The U.S. is one of the pioneer countries of democracy and has a long history of stable government and long-term, object-oriented planning. All these criteria work in favor of extensive diffusion of EC countrywide and, also, globally.

Private organizations' capability

Globally, the U.S. is the first country to promote and adopt EC. This feature reflects the overall capability of private organizations to manage venture capital, invest, and properly enhance and intervene in the market economy as well as societal tendencies towards collaboration. Private organizations of the U.S. have immense credibility to engage the consumers in liberal credit card spending, though there exists fear of the risks inherent in EC, and to establish a role for the U.S. as a leader in the IT industry. U.S. private organizations are well established, well funded, and well organized to manage new online business, which are originally derived from the U.S.

Most of the leading organizations of the Internet economy—such as eBay and Amazon.com; search engines like Yahoo and Google; Internet browsers like Internet explorer and Netscape Navigator—are U.S. based. Therefore, in promoting EC, U.S. private organizations lead the world.

Consumers' preference

From the cultural, financial, social, and technical perspectives, U.S. consumers have a high attitudinal coherence with the Internet economy. U.S. consumers have a high propensity to engage in liberal spending, especially with the use of credit cards. The U.S. has top ranking worldwide in credit card utilization. This is highly significant when considering the fact that nearly all online consumers require a valid credit card. According to Forrester Research, the average American who utilizes the Internet for EC spends about $250 a month online. Cahners In-Stat report, issued in March of 2000, reveals that U.S. consumers are less sensitive to online security risks in shopping than are citizens of many countries (McGann *et al.,* 2002). Hofstede's (1991) findings of cultural attributes also support this statement. Literacy rate, skill in computer and Internet usage, social values to online purchase, behavioral attitude of consumers are all factors that support consumers' preference to EC.

Global E-organizations' mission

Basically, the global E-organizations' mission for diffusion of EC in the U.S. is not an important aspect. The reason is that the U.S. is the leader in the Internet economy. Most of the leading businesses who are operating B2C EC, are situated in the U.S. However, in the light of collaboration, globalization, and foreign investment, the U.S. always is a lucrative market. Although the higher wage rate inhibits investment, a stable market and free trade opportunities, along with a strong legal framework, are convenient factors. The strong purchasing power of consumers, highest number of transactions, and the largest market economy are great drivers for seeking opportunity from the U.S. market. Therefore, foreign E-retailers can always find a reason to invest in and collaborate with U.S.-led private organizations to capitalize on the U.S. Internet market.

Infrastructure, human development, and market mechanism

From the perspective of infrastructure, the availability of resources with competitive prices and features, and market mechanism, the U.S. has a leading position in the world market. A key factor in the ability of the U.S. to lead the proliferation of EC is its position in the global IT arena. The average investment and infrastructure development of the U.S. is comparable with the average of OECD countries in some areas, but leads in most of the parameters. The U.S. has less of its GDP represented by telecommunications investment than the OECD average, but more of its GDP in IT generally. This country is the central market of software manufacturing. All of the giant manufacturers of software are located in the U.S., and the U.S. is also the main consumers and users of that software. The U.S. represents nearly 40 percent of the OECD total in IT hardware production. This country has a highly developed wire line telephone infrastructure (approximately 1/3 more lines per 1,000 people), and about the same proportion of its lines are digital. Table 6.1 shows the comparative features of the U.S. with respect to other OECD countries.

According to a United Nations report (UNPAN, 2005) on EG readiness index, we find that the web measure index, infrastructure index, and human capital index are 1.0000, 0.7486, and 0.9700, respectively. This reflects the extremely high position of the U.S. in preparation to embrace and develop the capacity to engage in the world Internet economy. In the U.S., the number of PCs available per 100 citizens is 66. The Internet penetration rate is 71.4 percent (Internet World Stats, 2007). All these figures indicate an extremely competitive position for the U.S. to launch EC.

In light of the market mechanism, the U.S. always has the upper position in the world due to several reasons. In terms of availability and usage of credit card, the U.S. has the highest position. According to the U.S. Bureau of Labor Statistics (2004), the percentage of individuals who have a general-purpose credit card in the U.S. is 71.5. Payment, shipment, return, and money exchange are not an issue for the consumers in the U.S. to interact in B2C web pages. The U.S. Dollar hege-

Table 6.1. OECD and U.S.: Telecommunications indicators (Source: McGann et al., 2002)

	Telecom investment as % of GDP	IT as % of GDP	IT hardware production, USD billion	IT hardware exports USD billion (1998)	Main phone lines/1K population	Cell phone subscribers/1K population	Digital as % of all phone lines	CATV subscribers/1K population	PCC/1K population	Internet users per 1K population	Internet hosts/1K population
US	0.3%	4.1%	$85.10	$38.00	673	315	91.6%	251.34	517.07	271.74	195
OECD	0.5%	3.1%	$221.20	$170.00	508	325	93.8%	140.02	285.55	180.05	62.63

mony always provides an upper hand for U.S. consumers. Most of the international E-retailers are located in the U.S. Therefore, in terms of payment, shipment, and return, the U.S. is the most convenient location for E-retailers.

Diffusion of EC

The prime factors that enhance B2C EC in the U.S. are the consumer culture, attitude, and preferences for convenience and lifestyle-enhancing products and services, and the business desire to reach new markets or protect existing markets. In addition, other favoring factors and strong enablers are Internet diffusion; a high IT literacy and a strong IT infrastructure; a strong market mechanism; and government promotion, guidance, and vigorous assistance. Online shopping at night presents a more convenient option in countries where citizens are truly busy, such as the U.S. For the U.S., local E-retailers are strong, well-funded, and capable of boosting the national Internet-based economy and able to expand globally. The large economy and lucrative purchasing power of U.S. consumers always attract foreign E-retailers to enter the U.S. market. Finally, the U.S. government plays a role through initiatives aimed at building consumer acceptance of Internet and promoting IT literacy. The large U.S. market is also a driver for Internet economy to flourish. The total population of the U.S. is almost 301 million, the third largest in the world. The purchasing power of the consumers is the highest in the world.

Total EC sales in the U.S. for 2007 were estimated at $136.4 billion, an increase of 19.0 percent from the same figure of 2006. EC sales in 2007 accounted for 3.4 percent of the total sales (U.S. Census Bureau, 2007). Basically, B2C EC sales in the U.S. have increased by almost 20 percent in every year since 1999. The total retail sales in 2007 increased 4.0 percent from 2006. So, E-retail sales have increased almost five times more than the total retail sales. Although, E-retail sales still represent a small percentage of total retail sales, its growth rate is extraordinary. Due to the presence of all enablers for the diffusion of EC, it is expected that in the U.S., B2C EC will diffuse extensively in the coming future.

6.1.2. Developing Countries with Stronghold in ICT

In this section, we will address and explore the condition of two developing countries from two distant continents where ICT has a stronghold. We will examine them from the perspective of diffusion parameters as described in our proposed EC diffusion framework in Chapter V.

6.1.2.1. India

Government role and capability

The Indian government has, until recently, been an obstacle, especially in terms of its policies in providing telecommunications infrastructure and its lack of strong support for the hardware industry. However, the rapid proliferation of its market economy and the fall of the Soviet Union have made the Indian government realize the need for change and it has taken some steps towards supporting the growth of the telecommunications sector. Some important government policies that have guided, explored, and benefited the Internet economy include allowing private Internet service providers (ISP), enabling Internet access through cable, taking steps to set up a National High Speed Telecom Backbone (NHSTB), and early implementation of cyber laws. India has also encouraged foreign business firms to invest in local markets and create joint ventures, incorporated computer education in the school syllabus, provided extensive training and awareness programs countrywide, and taken initiatives to convert the existing Public Call Offices (PCOs) to intelligent info-kiosks. These changes could result in the spread of Internet access to rural areas as well as increasing the adoption rate. The central government has also prompted the creation of an autonomous society called Software Technology Parks of India (STPI) that primarily assists to the needs of the software industry. STPI provides enormous ICT-based facilities to the software industries, including high-speed data connectivity at internationally competitive rates and speed. All basic and value-added services have been opened up to the private sector with the total foreign investment limit raised to 74 percent of the capital. To ensure overall balanced development of ICT in all the regions and reduce the digital divide, the universal service obligation fund has been created to support the funding of expansion of services in rural and remote areas (UNESCAP, 2006).

India has a long history of political stability as one of the most advanced democratic countries. But in terms of economic and market protection policy, investors are still not very comfortable due to India's history, especially during the era of the Soviet Union. Financially, India is not a rich country to support countrywide technology infrastructure. It needs collaboration from the private sector in this context. Its GDP is 796 billion and per capita income is around $965 U.S.

In conclusion, we note that at the present the Indian government has taken extensive policies to reform their market to promote an ICT-based economy, guide private organizations, and protect consumers' rights. As a developing country, India has overcome many obstacles to reach this connection; however, it has yet to pass many hurdles to be competitive in the world.

Private organizations' capability

Seybold (1998) suggested simple tests to determine whether an entity has engaged in EC. These activities include the use of e-mail; using the web to get technical support for a product, to solve a customer problem, or to purchase goods and services; and a signature on a handheld computer to obtain delivery of a package. Based on these parameters, most major business enterprises, many medium enterprises, and some small enterprises in India are engaged in EC functions either as suppliers, buyers, or entities in search of information. A 1999 survey of EC in India carried out by the Indian Market Research Bureau (IMRB) composed of medium to large size organizations indicated that the primary use of the internet has been for the purpose of e-mail, file transfer protocol (FTP), and website monitoring (IMRB, 1999). Among those with a website of their own, 84 percent use it primarily for advertising, while 38 percent say they are selling products and services through the website (IMRB, 1999). Overall, 20 percent of the organizations surveyed indicated that they use EC at least to some extent.

India's private business enterprises are very enthusiastic at this moment to capitalize on the world market by investing and attracting foreign collaboration in the domestic Internet economy. So local E-retailers are launching B2C EC and encouraging buyers to interact on their websites. However, foreign collaboration in the software industry, though enormous, is not significant in B2C EC.

Consumers' preference

Culturally, Indians are not used to electronic purchase. In consideration of consumers' rights, government policy, cyber crime, security, and privacy, Indian consumers are still not very realistic about and trustful of web purchasing. Although, this phenomenon is changing gradually, if we consider countrywide sentiment in this respect, the change is still insignificant.

The main strength from the consumer side in the proliferation of the Internet economy is the size of the Indian market. The Indian population is almost 1,130 million (Internet World Stats, 2007). The Internet penetration rate in India is very low, around 5.3 percent, but the growth rate is almost 1,100 percent from 2000 to 2007. According to a United Nations report (UNPAN, 2005) on the EG readiness index, we find that the web measure index, infrastructure index, and human capital index are 0.5827, 0.0277, and 0.5900, respectively. This reflects India's average position in the preparation to embrace and develop the capacity to engage in the world Internet economy. A study conducted by IMRB on consumer use of the Internet indicates that among households, more than 90 percent viewed it primarily as a source of information, communication, learning, and entertainment (IMRB 1999). Only 60 percent of the households with PCs and 47 percent of the households without PCs viewed the Internet as a source for the purchase of products and services. Preliminary survey data from International Data Corporation indicated that one third of survey respondents from India had made online purchases (Internet Week, 2000).

Global E-organizations' mission

India has a long history of protecting its market from penetration by international corporations. However, recently, due to the imminent thrust of globalization, market liberalization has been strongly encouraged by the Indian government. Since India has a huge market, international corporations are always eager to intervene in the Indian market and are very interested in developing collaboration with some world-class Indian business giants. However, due to strong protection by Indian government in several areas, the presence of international E-retailers in the Indian market is still not profound.

Infrastructure, human development, and market mechanism

According to the connectivity and technology infrastructure score for selected Asian and Pacific countries and areas, India's score is 1.40, while the score for Hong Kong and China in the same parameter is 8.10 out of 10 (UNESCAP, 2006). ICT expenditure as a percentage of GDP in India is 3.8, whereas the global average is 6.4 (Viswanathan and Pick, 2005). However, the Indian IT sector has been growing very fast over the last decade with a compounded annual growth rate of over 20 percent in the last ten years. About 30 percent of the world's software engineers come from India, and India has over 20 percent of the global cross-country customized software development market (Viswanathan and Pick, 2005). The growth of the IT industry in India has a potential impact on the growth of EC in India by increasing awareness of it, by providing a source of skilled manpower, and by enhancing the penetration of associated hardware in the business and customer segments. Before 1999, only a public organization named Videsh Sanchar Nigam Limited (VSNL) provided telecommunication services to India. This has definitely hindered progress in developing technology infrastructure countrywide. However, in 1999, private ISP was allowed to enter the market and recently have gained permission to set up international gateways. Their entry has reduced the cost of Internet access to the customer by almost 50 percent. Now, in terms of developing infrastructure for an ICT-based economy and providing resources to consumers to participate in B2C EC, India is moving fast and has already developed competence, at least in metropolitan areas.

However, the payment system, availability of credit cards, shipment methods, and return policy are still the major barriers for proliferation of the Internet economy.

To participate in global B2C EC, Indian consumers need a strong money exchange policy, international payment methods, an explicit taxation system, and shipment and return mechanisms.

Diffusion of EC

As a developing country, EC in India is a relatively recent phenomenon that is beginning to expand its reach from metropolitan areas to the countryside in select regions of the country. A number of drivers—including government's role and policies, especially the recent trade liberalization—have expedited the promotion of private organizations. In particular, this has been true in the computer and telecommunications industries where consumers have been gradually involved in the Internet economy and the foreign E-retailers continuing interest in the Indian market have reflected the importance of EC for the economic development of the country. India's global strength in the areas of ICT-based technology and skilled personnel, as well as the success of many Indian entrepreneurs in Silicon Valley and their interaction with the Indian government and local Indian industry have provided enormous encouragement in the growth and proliferation of EC. Government stability and guidance, the role of private organizations, and consumer preference are moderate drivers for the proliferation of B2C EC in India. The huge population and, consequently, the interest of international E-retailers to capture the Indian market are strong parameters for diffusion of EC. However, the government market protection policy and financial incapability, overall market mechanism, and technology infrastructure are still barriers for the proliferation of B2C EC in the whole country.

Although the growth of EC in the business and consumer sectors has created substantial interest and excitement, at least for the upper middle class and educated youth segments of the population in the metropolitan areas, in the country as a whole it is still not very significant. India has the potential to remove key barriers—such as a lack of consumer culture of electronic payments, the absence of international payment system, countrywide telecommunications infrastructure, and protection of consumer rights. However, the country has yet to achieve global readiness to extensively participate in international B2C EC.

6.1.2.2. Mexico

Government role and capability

Financially, Mexico is in a better position than most of the developing countries. Its GDP is $741 billion U.S. Due to the proximity of the U.S. market and the free trade agreement (the North American Free Trade Agreement—NAFTA), the Mexican government has adopted strong initiatives to develop and guide the market for the Internet economy. The ICT-based public administration reformation strategy in Mexico started after the year 2000. However, Mexico has made significant gains in delivering more services online over the last few years. Since the beginning of the use of ICT, it had been assigned the mission of "leading Mexico towards the information and knowledge society, integrating the efforts of all the social parties to be incorporated to this process, with technologies at the service of society" (ICA Report, 2006). Public-private collaboration initiatives target provision of access to ICT, specialized contents, and basic skills to the people for the use of ICT. It has four main pillars: E-health, E-learning, E-economy, and E-government (EG). The easing of federal regulation has led to an environment of EC that is largely unfettered by the government, but it is restricted by business and cultural constraints (Travica, 2002). Government regulatory framework for EC is now favorable for diffusion (Garcia-Murillo, 2000; Palacios, 2003). For instance, the telecommunications sector was privatized and partially de-regulated in the 1990s (Garcia-Murillo and Pick, 2003). Legislative reforms in 1999 allowed legal recognition of most electronic documents and signatures (Dedrick, Kraemer, and Palacios, 2001).

Private organizations' capability

The support for EC in Mexico has come more from the private sector than government (Palacios, 2003). Private sector industry associations such as AMECE and AMITI, consulting companies such as Select-IDC, portals, standards organizations, and major vendor firms such as Microsoft have worked together as active promoters of EC (Palacios, 2003). Due to its location, Mexican private organizations have the automatic privilege of launching joint ventures with U.S.-based E-retailers to capitalize on domestic and international markets. Low labor wages are also a strong incentive for U.S. E-retailers to penetrate the Mexican market.

Consumers' preference

Mexican culture has a positive impact on the proliferation of B2C EC. Though Mexico is a developing country, the impact of neighboring countries like the U.S. and Canada makes the consumers of Mexico more prone to American culture. The Mexican diaspora also has a strong impact on consumer culture. During the 1980s and 1990s, there was a large immigration of Mexicans to the U.S. Mexicans and Mexican Americans send an estimated $5 billion annually from the U.S. to Mexico. Many Mexican Internet companies hope to capitalize on this market by helping Mexican Americans purchase goods and services for their families in

Mexico through the Internet. The Hispanic population in the U.S., most of them of Mexican descent, makes them the largest minority group (U.S. Census, 2001). The per capita income in Mexico is also high enough, as a developing country (U.S. $8,426), to give its citizens a high purchasing power. However, the population of Mexico is very low, 108 million. So the market in Mexico is not very big. Mexico's major potential lies in the prevalence of the Internet, the business use of EC, close proximity to the United States, and the huge Mexican-American EC market that could be potentially leveraged into the Mexican domestic market.

Global E-organizations' mission

Global E-organizations, more specifically U.S.-based E-retailers, play a comprehensive supporting role in the enhanced diffusion of EC in Mexico in terms of providing much needed venture capital as well as an incentive to middle class Mexicans to become entrepreneurs. Due to NAFTA, trade movement between the U.S. and Mexico is open and frequent. The Mexican market is very lucrative for U.S.-based E-retailers for several reasons; these include distance, a known culture, ease of money exchange, ease of shipment and return, influence on the political system, a uniform taxation policy, lower wage, and free trade. Since the U.S. is the primary and major source of international E-retailers, Mexico receives the full benefits of collaboration with global E-organizations to diffuse EC countrywide. NAFTA is expected to influence the use of EC in sectors such as banking, insurance, automotive, electronics, and the chemical industry.

Infrastructure, human development, and market mechanism

The hardware industry in Mexico is fairly advanced with over two-thirds of IBM's laptops, for example, being produced in Mexico. The total Mexican information technology market had revenues of US $6.5 billion in 2003, and grew during the period 1998–2003 at 8.9 percent per year (INEGI, 2003). The Internet penetration rate is moderate for a developing country— 21.3 percent. The high cost of local telephone charges and the relatively low level of computer penetration, at 83 per 1,000 persons (UNPAN, 2005), is a constraint in the growth of the Internet economy. In 2001, there were 13.6 million fixed telephones and 21.5 million mobile phones in Mexico, while Internet users stood at seven million people (World Bank, 2003). In 2002, 3.7 million Mexican households, or 15 percent, had a computer, of which 1.98 million (53 percent) were connected to the Internet (INEGI, 2003). Although the figure continues to increase rapidly, the low number of Internet-connected households puts a constraint on the B2C EC market. Mexico's web measure index, infrastructure index, and human capital index are, respectively, 0.8192, 0.1491, and 0.8500, which indicate its potential promise in the future proliferation of the ICT-based economy.

Since Mexico is very close to the U.S. and Canada, this country has an advantage in the shipment and return of goods and services. Money exchange has been a drawback because Mexico is a developing country; however, the free trade zone has been a great help in resolving that problem. However, as a developing country, Mexico has a weak credit card and payment system for interaction with U.S.-based E-retailer web pages.

Diffusion of EC

Mexico is not a leading technological country. As a developing country, government guidance is still not very transparent in accomplishing effective collaboration between the public and private sectors. The Internet penetration rate, availability of resources, and development of skilled personnel are going forward, however, but still not at a high rate. Mexican cultural adherence to EC is a major plus for the diffusion of EC. INEGI (2003) estimates that 1 percent of the Mexican population uses EC. In light of the government policy and capability, infrastructure, market mechanism, and the role of private organizations, Mexico has fairly a moderate position for developing EC further. Consumer preference, cultural adaptability, and the interest of foreign organizations in penetrating the Mexican market are strong parameters. However, the small market, low Internet penetration rate, underdeveloped market economy, and the unstable government policy and mission are potential barriers for the diffusion of B2C EC in Mexico.

6.1.3. Developing Countries

In this section we focus on developing countries that are less developed in the areas of government policy and capability, technology adoption and usage, infrastructure, resource availability, private entrepreneurs, market mechanism, and consumer adherence and adaptability for online transaction. In this context, we will discuss two countries: Bangladesh and Ghana, which are also from two less-developed continents—Asia and Africa, respectively.

6.1.3.1. Bangladesh

Government role and capability

Bangladesh got its independence from Pakistan in 1971, and the country is still struggling to establish a stable political and democratic environment. The government mission and long-term policy towards the market economy and adoption of technology is not clear. Due to frequent local military activities and foreign political invasions, the democratic environment does not yet have an institutional base. As a result, long-term planning for policies towards implementing an ICT infrastructure is not well developed because the government has not had sufficient control of the market. As a result, from the financial and legal perspectives, consumers' rights and security are not well protected by government and law enforcement authorities. However, the government now has a five-year plan to develop a technology infrastructure; it is devoted to establishing certain features, including:

- Connecting a submarine cable link throughout the country,
- Developing technology infrastructure and making resources available publicly,
- Adopting the Internet in public offices,
- Implementing EG and offering government services through the Internet
- Providing tax holidays (sometimes zero tax) for businesses related to computers, computer accessories, and Internet operations, and
- Promoting ICT-based education beginning in the elementary school.

Economically, Bangladesh is a poor country. It has little financial capability to boost national economy by developing a proper Internet-based market economy solely from the government side. This country is still dependent on foreign investment and support. Government guidance in developing an ICT-based market economy is also not sufficient.

Private organizations' capability

Just one decade ago, it could be safely said that private enterprises in Bangladesh are more or less not interested and engaged in an Internet-based economy. However, the scenario is now changing very rapidly. Although it can still not connect a significant percentage of the population of Bangladesh to the Internet economy, the progress in this sector has created some future prospects. Now there are many cyber cafés where citizens can interact with and explore the Internet. Several private organizations are hosting a few websites and operating business through the Internet. Just within the last few years, this has increased quite dramatically. According to the Bangladesh Bureau of Statistics (2007), more than 100 private organizations are now operating online businesses countrywide.

Consumers' preference

Culturally, socially, technologically, and financially, the consumers of Bangladesh do not have a strong commitment to engage in an Internet-based economy. The Internet penetration rate is very low. The availability of computers and other resources that assist consumers in developing an interest in adopting certain behaviors is even lower. The financial capability of consumers is also insignificant. Per capita income is only $444 U.S. and the country GDP is $69 billion U.S. Therefore, excluding a very insignificant percentage of the population, most Bangladeshi citizens are not habituated to online purchasing. However, this scenario is gradually changing. The increasing availability and usage of mobile phones in Bangladesh, and thus the availability of the Internet, has drastically changed the attitude of Bangladeshi consumers; in the near future this might push them to turn to online purchasing.

Global E-organizations' mission

Population density in Bangladesh is very high. The total population is almost 150 millions (Internet World Stats, 2007). In addition, the wage rate is very low. These are the strengths of domestic market economy for foreign companies to invest in Bangladeshi market. So international E-retailers might be interested in intervening in the Bangladeshi market. However, due to political instability, an underdeveloped market economy, a lack of infrastructure, and few initiatives from local private enterprises, foreign organizations do not put a top priority in launching EC operations that collaborate with local private organizations.

Infrastructure, human development, and market mechanism

Despite existing microwave links and optical fiber routes, as of 2003, Bangladesh still has a very low telephone density (0.51 percent) and a very small percentage (0.3 percent) of the population has access to the Internet (Pipattanasomporn, 2007). Several problems have been detected: 1) the readily available IT infrastructures are located primarily in major cities and towns; 2) resource availability in rural areas is insignificant; however, the rural population comprises the majority of citizens, 3) the financial capability of consumers in Bangladesh to interact in modern ICT is very limited, 4) literacy, education, and skill in technology oriented activities are very poor, and 5) the telecom backbone of the country, which consists of microwave radio, only has an available bandwidth of 34-155 Mbps. This will not be enough to support broad-based IT services throughout the country.

Bangladesh has only been connected by a submarine cable link since 2006. In 1991-92, this country first rejected being connected with this superhighway due to a lack of government policy. The optical fiber line connects the capital city to a south coast submarine cable landing station, which takes the nation to the information superhighway. It serves as the backbone of international communication, while satellite services with limited bandwidth act as a backup. Presently, the Bangladesh Telephone and Telegraph Board (BTTB), the government-owned public organization, is using 2799 Mbps voice and 1244 Mbps data bandwidth through the optical fiber and submarine cable lines. The availability of PCs per 100 citizens is only 0.80. According to a UN survey report (UNPAN, 2005), the web measure index, infrastructure index, and human capital index for Bangladesh are, respectively, 0.0731, 0.0055, and 0.4500. This is even far below regional average.

In Bangladesh, the market economy is not yet fully mature and the Internet economy is in the infancy stage. The payment system, money exchange rate, availability of international credit cards, shipment and return methods, market security, consumers' rights and protection—all are backdated and present barriers for EC diffusion in Bangladesh.

Diffusion of EC

Bangladesh is still not at a stage to embrace and diffuse B2C EC in domestic market. This is shown in the governmental role, policy, and capability; private organization initiatives; and the role of foreign E-retailers to intervene in the Bangladeshi market. Other possible barriers for Bangladeshi consumers to interact in EC technology are the lack of infrastructure and a market mechanism; consumer cultural, social, financial, and technological affairs; and security and breach of contract. A survey conducted by Shareef *et al.* (2008) observed that a low percentage of people in Bangladesh have experience in Internet purchasing, and they are mostly afraid of the security of their payment. Nevertheless, some driving forces are working in Bangladesh that indicate future prospects in this arena. These are:

1. Extensive diffusion of mobile phones in Bangladesh in both urban and rural areas. At present five private mobile phone companies are working in Bangladesh. These companies' total subscribers, quite surprisingly, increased from thousands in the last decade to millions (around 15 million) in 2008.
2. The new generation, especially high and high-middle class consumers are very interested in web purchasing.
3. The electronic banking sector, which comprises several foreign and local banks, is emerging quite strongly in Bangladesh. These banks now provide several options for credit card and international payment systems.
4. Although it was very late, now the government realizes the potential of the Internet and is interesting in developing a countrywide ICT-based technology.

5.   As a developing country, the education standard is competent enough to develop personnel skilled in technology.

So, based on the findings of the parameters of Bangladesh, it is still in an infancy stage in the adoption and diffusion of B2C EC. However, the foreseeable future might tell a different story if the country can develop certain standards in the areas pointed out here.

6.1.3.2. Ghana

Government role and capability

In recognition of the potential of science and technology in socio-economic development, the government of Ghana established the Council for Scientific and Industrial Research (CSIR). With the proper guidance and assistance of the United Nations, the government of Ghana continues to promote technology infrastructure countrywide by recognizing the role of science and technology in development and by enacting science and technology legislation to guide a national market economy (Siamwiza, 2002). Ghana, looking to tap into the potential of ICT generally and the Internet economy specifically, is very eager to enact legislation to enable and encourage the adoption of EC. However, although initially the efforts were tremendous, ultimately these projects could not attain the desired results. Several causes lie behind this failure; they include:

•   Lack of long-term political commitment,
•   Lack of political stability,
•   Strategic mistake in implementation methods,
•   Lack of financial ability,
•   Shortage of human capital resources,
•   Lack of collaboration with private entities, and
•   Corruption in the public sector.

Ghana's GDP is 10.18 billion and per capita income is $682 U.S. Financially, Ghana is a poor country. Its financial capability to develop countrywide technology infrastructure is limited. Politically Ghana is not stable. Its democracy is still not mature, and the country is still suffering from its lack of momentum to attain its long-term goal.

Private organizations' capability

Private organizations in Ghana are not well engaged in the Internet economy. The population of Ghana is 23 million, so the country does not have a big market. The cultural habits of Ghanaian consumers are oriented towards offline business. As a consequence, private enterprises in Ghana are not focused on B2C EC. This scenario is changing at a slow pace. Some information and technology-based private organizations have started working in this arena and are hosting several domestic web pages. These private organizations are the primary source of the domestic Internet economy. However, local organizations have not collaborated with international E-retailers to bring consumers in Ghana into the global economic environment.

Consumers' preference

Consumers in Ghana are gradually starting to interact with foreign E-retailers' web pages. However, they have a more serious attitude toward use of the Internet, rather than personal entertainment or purchase. Internet is expensive. Consequently, it may impart a perception that Internet is for serious work, not suitable for general interaction. A recent survey by NCS found that 38.4 percent of Internet subscribers cited communication as the main reason for using the Internet. The survey also cited the ability to access databases (32.9 percent) and research (16.6 percent) are the two rest major reasons to use the Internet. So more than 85 percent of users mentioned these three functions as key reasons for subscribing to the Internet (Quaynor *et al.*, 2008).

Cultural habits, language, social values, technological unfamiliarity, and security concerns are potential barriers for diffusion of EC in Ghana. Consumers in Ghana still perceive the Internet as the medium of getting required global information, not for simple purchases. Local private organizations are also not capable of providing online commercial/shopping impressions to consumers. The presence of domestic B2C EC is very limited and mostly organized among the consumers of the capital city.

Global E-organizations' mission

Since Ghana's market is small, the purchasing power is low, the market economy is underdeveloped, and the technology infrastructure is weak, foreign E-organizations are not focused towards investing in Ghana's Internet economy or to creating joint ventures with local private organizations. Lack of political commitment is also a problem that foreign investors perceive in Ghana. So the initiative and role of international E-retailers to boost Ghana's Internet economy are weak. However, due to extensive opportunity in African countries, recently international organizations have looked to this region to explore the resources hidden in the under side of the market economy.

Infrastructure, human development, and market mechanism

According to the report of Quaynor *et al.* (2008), in 1995, Network Computer Systems (NCS), an information technology company, was the first organization to achieve full Internet connectivity in West Africa. NCS is currently working on a satellite gateway. They are working with the Ministry of Transport and Communication of Ghana and Ghana Telecom to set up the first alternate international gateway in Ghana. This Gateway is operating with an INTELSAT approved 3.8m F1 station having a capacity of 2 Mb data transfer. In this context, NCS has primarily developed an alternate VSAT connection to the Internet backbone (Quaynor *et al.*, 2008). It is worthwhile to note that Ghana has installed kiosks that are wireless payphones in order to help people in rural areas have access to phones (Evans and Yen, 2006).

Nevertheless, infrastructure development is not extended countrywide in Ghana, and it is still underdeveloped. According to a UN survey report (UNPAN, 2005), the web measure index, infrastructure index, and human capital index for Ghana are, respectively, 0.1885, 0.0214, and 0.6500. The infrastructure index is especially very low. The Internet access rate is 2.7 percent. The number of computers available is 0.40 for 100 of the population. However, Ghana is achieving slow but steady progress in allocating resources to develop a technology orientation.

In the area of human development, Ghana lags far the African average (Evans and Yen, 2006). The education standard, literacy rate, and adoption of technology education in elementary school are not well managed. Many skilled professionals go abroad for higher education and then do not return. Brain drain is an acute problem for African countries in developing sustainable technology infrastructure. A lack of regular electronic banking system, money exchange, online payment system, internationally accepted credit cards, and shipment and return methods from western countries are the possible barriers for global diffusion of EC in Ghana, and for the consumers of Ghana to be connected globally to interact with international E-retailers.

Diffusion of EC

Diffusion of EC in Ghana has not yet achieved any significant progress. It is still at the infant stage. Government role, policy, guidance, and capability; consumers preferences; private organizational initiatives; the foreign E-retailers role; infrastructure; and the market mechanism all create barriers and make diffusion of B2C

EC in Ghana difficult. However, Ghana's strong economic growth over the past ten years and constant growth rate of over 5 percent a year suggest that Ghana has the potential to develop technology infrastructure to capitalize on the full benefits of modern ICT-based economy in the foreseeable future. The growth of ICT-based infrastructure with the strong demand for Internet services from companies and individuals in Ghana develops a strong base for future prospects of the Internet economy.

6.2. COMPARATIVE STATEMENT

We have analyzed six countries in the light of the parameters of diffusion framework of EC. Based on the readiness of different parameters of diffusion of EC, we have explored and anticipated the possible diffusion of EC in any specific country. Now we would like to develop a precise comparative statement, in tabular format, that is grounded on the observations and fact-finding, as shown in Table 6.2.

From the above table—which shows comparative statements of diffusion of B2C EC in some countries with different cultural, social, financial, behavioral, political, and technological aspects—we can draw some conclusions.

1. We have analyzed the countries based on the diffusion framework of EC as presented in Chapter V.
2. Focusing on the parameters of a diffusion framework of EC, we have addressed and explored the status of six countries and then conjectured the probable diffusion of EC in those countries.
3. We have also attempted to visualize the actual diffusion of B2C EC in those countries. Contrasting both figures, viz., what degree of diffusion we can anticipate based on the analysis of the parameters of diffusion of EC as proposed in Chapter V and what diffusion we actually observe, we get very compatible results.
4. The proposed theoretical framework of diffusion of EC can be practically used to analyze the position and probable future trend of diffusion of B2C EC in any country.
5. Based on all the parameters, the U.S. is the leading country for the diffusion of EC. Denmark as a developed country is overall doing well and has a significant diffusion of EC. India and Mexico are developing countries; however, for some convenient parameters and active roles of different stakeholders of EC, these countries are promising for diffusion of EC. However, as developing countries with a poor infrastructure and lack of modern ICT absorption capacity, Bangladesh and Ghana are still not active participants in the Inter-

Table 6.2. Comparative statement of EC diffusion countrywide

Parameters	Denmark	U.S.	India	Mexico	Bangladesh	Ghana
Government role and capability	Policy, role, capability, and stability are very strong.	Policy, role, capability, and stability are very strong and extremely supportive.	Long term policy, role, capability, and stability are moderate, however, market economy, to some extent, is still protected.	Policy, role, capability, and stability are moderate and not very dynamic.	Policy, role, capability, and stability are a very weak connection for diffusion of Internet economy.	Policy, role, capability, and stability are weak, however, slow but steady progress is observable.
Private organizations' capability	Private organizations are acting and promoting Internet economy but it is still not very significant for B2C EC.	Strong and dynamic contribution of private E-retailers is visible both in domestic and global Internet market.	Indian private organizations are hosting several Internet-based business operations domestically. However, as a global phenomenon, it is still not very strong.	In terms of location, Mexico has some advantages and private organizations utilize those advantages to get moderate benefits.	This sector is still under construction. However, it is expanding.	This sector is still under construction and does not yet reflect a strong promise.
Consumers' preference	Consumers are culturally and socially habituated in Internet economy, however, global exposure is moderate.	Consumers are highly habituated in Internet economy and have the highest potential in E-purchase.	Culturally, socially, technologically, and financially consumers are still not very active in web purchasing. But the tradition is changing very rapidly.	Culturally, socially, technologically, and financially consumers are still not very active in web purchase. But tradition is changing very rapidly.	Culturally, socially, technologically, and financially overall consumers are not familiar with web purchase.	Culturally, socially, technologically, and financially consumers are overall not familiar with web purchase.

continued on following page

Table 6.2. continued

Parameters	Denmark	U.S.	India	Mexico	Bangladesh	Ghana
Global E-organizations' mission	Market is not very big and business functions are mostly limited among European countries. So, global E-retailers have a moderate interest in collaborating with domestic private organizations to capture Danish market.	USA is the largest economy and has well-established market mechanism. So, global E-organizations are extremely interested in U.S. on-line market.	Strong market economy and huge population are the drivers. At the same time overall country development for ICT-based economy is not superb. So, this parameter is moderate for India.	For cultural and social affiliation of Mexico with U.S., and also as a neighboring country of U.S. with lower wage, Mexico is a choice for global E-retailers. However, constraints arising from other sources make Mexico a moderate choice.	Large population and lower wage are strong issues for global E-organizations to look at Bangladeshi market. However, this market is still under construction	Technologically, Ghana is advancing in respect to several African countries. So, international E-organizations are now evaluating Ghana to promote their business functions in Ghana. However, it is still at an immature stage.
Globalization policy	Global policy and role of different international organizations who are acting for promoting globalization are very strong. However, overall institutional, organizational, financial, and legislative policies are actually under experiment for Internet economy.					
Infrastructure, human development, and market mechanism	This is a strong parameter for driving EC in Denmark.	U.S. is the leader in this sector. For market mechanism, dollar hegemony is always a plus point for U.S.	Infrastructure development is moderate, especially in major cities. However, market mechanism in favor of diffusion of B2C EC is not well established.	Infrastructure development is moderate. However, market mechanism in favor of diffusion of B2C EC is not well established.	Diffusion of modern ICT and resources availability are very poor. Market mechanism is a weak connection for diffusion.	Diffusion of modern ICT and resource availability are very poor. Market mechanism is a weak connection for diffusion.
Diffusion of EC	Overall diffusion of B2C EC and participation in global Internet economy is moderate.	Highest diffusion of B2C EC is observed. It is expanding much faster than traditional retail sales.	Diffusion of B2C EC is not very significant yet. However, it can be anticipated from the recent trend that diffusion will quickly increase in the foreseeable future.	With the help of the U.S. and NAFTA, the future of the Internet economy in Mexico might be significant. However, at present, it is diffusing as a moderate symptom.	Diffusion of B2C EC is really insignificant.	Diffusion of B2C EC is really insignificant.

net-based economy. Some developing countries who are highly equipped in modern ICT-based market mechanism—such as India, Mexico, Brazil, South Africa, South Korea, Malaysia, Thailand—have high prospects for diffusion of EC in the global market. However, the majority of developing countries, like Bangladesh and Ghana, have the identical circumstantial evidence in the parameters of diffusion framework of EC. Therefore, diffusion of B2C EC as a global phenomenon still has a long way to go.

REFERENCES

Andersen, K. V., & Bjørn-Andersen, N. (2001). *Globalization and E-Commerce: Growth and Impacts in Denmark.* Center for Research on IT and Organizations, University of California, Irvine.

Bangladesh Bureau of Statistics. (2007). *Industrial Production Statistics* (IPS), http://www.bbs.gov.bd/

Cadbury Committee. (1992). *The Cadbury Committee Report on Financial Aspects of Corporate Governance.*

Davis, E. S. (2003). A World Wide Problem on the World Wide Web: International Responses to Transnational Identity Theft via the Internet. *Journal of Law & Policy, 12*(2003), 201-227.

Dedrick, J., Kraemer, K. L., & Palacios, J. J. (2001). Impacts of Liberalization and Economic Integration on Mexico's Computer Sector. *The Informat6ion Society, 17*, 119–132.

Evans, D., & Yen, D. C. (2006). E-Government: Evolving Relationship of Citizens and Government, Domestic, and International Development. *Government Information Quarterly, 23*, 207–235.

European Commission. (2001). *eEurope 2002 - Accelerating E-commerce. Brussels: European Commission.* http://europa.eu.int/information_society/eeurope/action_plan/ecommerce/indexen. htm.

Forrester Research, Inc. (2000). *Global E-Commerce Model.*

Garcia-Murillo, M. (2000). Information Technology in Latin America. *AMCIS Proceedings* (pp. 1883–1886), Association for Information Systems, Atlanta, GA.

Gibbs, J., Kraemer, K. L., & Dedrick, J. (2003). Environment and Policy Factors Shaping E-Commerce Diffusion: A Cross-Country Comparison. *The Information Society, 19*(1), 5-18.

Hofstede, G. (1991). *Cultures and Organizations: Software of the Mind*, London: McGraw-Hill.

ICA REPORT. (2006). *MEXICO.* http://www.ica-it.org/conf40/docs/Conf40country_reportMexico.pdf.

IMF Report. (2007). *Global Financial Stability Report.* Market Developments and Issues.

IMRB. (1999). *Survey of E-Commerce in India.* Indian Market Research Bureau, New Dehli, India.

INEGI. (2003). *Indicadores Sobre Tecnologia de la Información.* Instituto Nacional de Estadisticas, Geografía, e Informática, available at http://www.inegi.gob.mx, Aguasca-lientes: Aguascalientes, Mexico.

Internet Week. (2000). Consumer Behavior Varies Widely by Country, Study Says. *Internet Week*, December 12.

Internet World Stats. (2007). http://www.allaboutmarketresearch.com/internet.htm.

Jackson, J. H. (1989). *The World Trading System: Law and Policy of International Economic Relations,* (p. 34). Cambridge: MIT Press.

Kraemer, K. L., Gibbs, J., & Dedrick, J. (2002). Impacts of Globalization on E-Commerce Adoption and Firm Performance: A Cross-Country Investigation. *Center for Research on IT and Organizations.* University of California, Irvine. E-Business Center Director's Forum, Chicago.

Lewell, J. (1999). Forrester Slams Internet Regulations in Europe. *Internet News.* 19 February. http://www.internetnews.com/intl-news/article/0,6_70291,00.html.

MacLean, D. (2004). *Internet Governance: A Grand Collaboration* (p. 345). New York, UNICT Task Force.

McGann, S., King, J., & Lyytinen, K. (2002). Globalization of E-Commerce: Growth and Impacts in the United States of America. *Sprouts: Working Papers on Information Environments, Systems and Organizations, 2*(2) (Spring), 59-86.

Ministry of Information Technology and Research. (1999*). Digital Denmark - Conversion to the Network Society.* Copenhagen: Danish Ministry of Information Technology and Research.

OECD report. (1998). Electronic Commerce Taxation Framework Conditions, *A Report by the Committee on Fiscal Affairs, as presented to Ministers at the OECD*

Ministerial Conference, A Borderless World: Realizing the Potential of Electronic Commerce on 8 October 1998.

Palacios, J. J. (2003). The Development of E-Commerce in Mexico: A Business-Led Passing Boom or a Step toward the Emergence of a Digital Economy? *The Information Society, 19*, 69–79.

Pipattanasomporn, M. (2007). *Existing Telecommunications Infrastructure and Applicable Technologies for Bangladesh*, http://www.ari.vt.edu/internet/Impression/ Manisa-notes.pdf. [Retrieved December, 2007]

Quaynor, N., Tevie, W., & Bulley, A. (2008). *Expansion of the Internet Backbone in Ghana*, http://www.isoc.org/INET97/proceedings/E5/E5_2.HTM. [Retrieved on February, 2008].

Rao, T. P. R. (2001). E-Commerce and Digital Divide: Impact on Consumers. *Presented in the Regional Meeting for the Asia-Pacific: New Dimensions of Consumer Protection in the Era of Globalization*. Goa, India, 10-11 September 2001.

Seybold, P. B. (1998). *Customers.com*. (p. 360). New York, NY: Random House

Shareef, M. A., Kumar, U., & Kumar, V. (2008). Role of Different Electronic-Commerce (EC) Quality Factors on Purchase Decision: A Developing Country Perspective. *Journal of Electronic Commerce Research*, 9(2), 92-113.

Siamwiza, M. N. (2002). The Impact of Globalization on Science and Technology in Sub-Saharan African countries. *African Technology Policy Studies Network (ATPS)*, Special Series No. 3.

Sofres, T. N. (2000). *Global eCommerce Report*, http://www.tnsofres.com.

Travica, B. (2002). Diffusion of Electronic Commerce in Developing Countries: The Case of Costa Rica. *Journal of Global Information Technology Management, 5*(1), 4–24.

UNCTAD. (2000). *Tariffs, Taxes and Electronic Commerce: Revenue Implications for Developing Countries*. Working Paper Series, 2000.

UNESCAP. (2006). *Enhancing Regional Cooperation in Infrastructure Development Including that Related to Disaster Management.* Poverty and Development Division (PDD).

United Nations. (2005). *The Working Group on Internet Governance (WGIG) infrastructure report on Intellectual Property, e-Commerce, Competition Policy, and Internet Governance*, www.wgig.org.

UNPAN. (2005). *From E-government to E-inclusion*. UN Global E-government Readiness Report, 2005.

U.S. Bureau of Labor Statistics. (2004). Division of Labor Force Statistics.

U.S. Census Bureau Report. (2007). USA. http://www.census.gov.

Viswanathan, N. K., & Pick, J. B. (2005). Comparison of E-commerce in India and Mexico: An Example of Technology Diffusion in Developing Nations. *International Journal on Technology Management, 31*(1/2), 2-19.

WIPO. (2005). *Development Agenda*. World Intellectual Property Organization. WO/GA/31/15, at http://www.wipo.org.

WTO. (2001). *World Trade Organization, Doha Declaration*, November 2001, Paragraph 34, http://www.wto.org.

World Bank. (2003). *World Development Indicators*, World Bank, Washington, D.C. Intellectual Property, e-Commerce, Competition Policy, and ...

Chapter VII
E–Commerce Adoption in Developing Countries

ABSTRACT

This chapter is aimed to provide a fundamental conceptual framework for adoption of EC by the consumers of developing countries. Through extensive review of literature and different related theories, we suggest that Awareness, Availability of infrastructure, Relative advantage, Compatibility, Website quality, Information quality, Multi-lingual option, and Trust have positive and Complexity has negative relations with adoption of EC by consumers of developing countries. These constructs can also measure the status of developing countries whether B2C EC could pursue consumers to use their systems.

7.1. INTRODUCTION

The notion of explicit and long term objective, globalization, appropriate selection of technology, cultural and social paradigms of developing countries, fundamental capabilities of EC to extend their service, customers to adopt that service, and quality of E-service has been increasingly identified and accepted by both researchers and practitioners, as being the significant determinants in successful E-commerce

(EC) implementation (Gefen *et al.,* 2003; Ribbink *et al.,* 2004). In order to develop customer focused EC services, which provide participants with accessible relevant information and quality services that are more expedient than traditional 'brick and mortar' transactions, E-retailers must first understand the factors that influence citizen's adoption of this innovation. Until now, the need for increased efficiency in private sector and the potential in information technology seem to have been the primary drivers of EC. However, little information is presented in literature on identifying distinct characteristics of consumers from developing countries, addressing their involvement pattern, evaluating fundamental capabilities of these consumers, and realizing and developing the framework of adopting EG systems by these consumers. This may be justified at an early stage of implementing new services. However, as users mature, it is argued that their input is increasingly valuable in terms of improving the services, suggesting new opportunities, and developing successful system. We have aimed to provide a fundamental conceptual framework for adoption of EC by the consumers of developing countries in this chapter. We have divided this chapter into 5 sections. After the introduction section, we will address and discuss existing literature to get deep insight of adoption criteria of EC. Then we will explain adoption process and develop our theoretical framework for factors enabling adoption of EC among consumers of developing countries. Then we will draw the conclusion.

Citizens' behavior in terms of adopting a new technology driven system is a very complex and robust subject (Bélanger *et al.,* 2002). Therefore, a growing body of research is now focusing on citizens' adoption criterion for successful implementation of EC. According to agency and contingency theories, citizens' adopting criteria and intentions are greatly affected and diversified by their attitudes, behavioral intent, local environmental security perception, service quality, and criteria of involvement of different stakeholders in the system. Therefore, understanding and estimating citizens' adopting criteria, which lead to successful implementation of EC, would have important managerial implications for globalizations.

EC is an innovative way to present a business with the extensive use of ICT. It is the use of information technology to enable and improve the efficiency with which business organizations' services are provided to customers and other businesses. Over the past few years, an increasing amount of scholarly attention has been focused on EC. It is basically the provision of information and services by business organization 24 hours per day, seven days per week (Norris *et al.,* 2001). EC is, in simple concept, the presence of business organizations in online to display, interact and transact with different stakeholders including other business organizations like supply chain and customers. The first stakeholder in the above definition of EC, viz., other business organizations and supply chain represent business-to-business (B2B) EC. The latter stakeholder, viz., customer interaction with E-retailers represents business-to-customer (B2C) EC. This chapter is primarily designed to conceptualize the diffusion and adoption of EC by customers of developing countries. As Internet is the main vehicle of EC operation, so viewing, interacting, and transacting in web pages of any E-retailers can be conducted from anywhere in the world. This specific characteristic of EC defines it as inherently global. From the perspective of mission, objective, and operation, EC is global. However, from real market perspective, B2C EC operation is quite limited to developed countries including North America and Europe with little exception (Balasubramanian *et al.*, 2003; Vehovar, 2003). The convergence of computer and ICT in developed countries has revolutionized and reshaped how we view, store, retrieve, interact, and share information. Consumers of developed countries are now quite familiar with EC function and operations. Governments of those countries are also very supportive, and binding rules and regulations are prompted to encourage diffusion of EC (Davis, 2003). These countries have extensive knowledge supported services, maintain a considerable ICT and government infrastructure to offer these, and are well funded. Consumers of developed countries now routinely use computer and Internet to receive information, identify sellers, evaluate products and services, compare prices, and exert market leverage. They are very much accustomed with functional characteristics of B2C EC. Though the money value of EC transactions is still small relative to the size of the world economy, it continues to show strong growth despite a recent economic downturn (US census Bureau, 2007). Consequently, many new Internet-based companies and traditional producers of goods and services are working to transform their business processes into EC processes in an effort to lower costs, improve customer service, and increase productivity with competitive advantage. However, due to technological pitfalls, socio-cultural barriers, and economical inability, huge potential consumers of developing countries are outside of this new technology based economic market. Several scholars since last one decade have attempted to discover and conceptualize the characteristics of consumers and their adoption criteria. However, although these studies revealed customers characteristics and adoption behavior, in general, their overall engagement was concentrated to conceptualize consumers of developed countries only (Kurnia, 2007). Very few researchers have attempted to address and identify the adoption framework for EC for the consumers of developing countries, which might be the primary source of success for globalization of EC. Moreover there are significant differences between consumers of developed and developing countries in terms of cultural, social, political, technological, and economical aspects of adoption and diffusion criteria of e-commerce (Heeks, 2003; Basu, 2004; Ndou, 2004; Krishna *et al.*, 2005; Dada, 2006). Without very advanced technical, financial, political, social, and individual ability, it is really difficult to progress and achieve fundamental mission of EC implementation, viz., diffusion in developing countries. Numerous studies on ICT adoption (Basu, 2004; Ndou, 2004; Dada, 2006) have shown that ICT in general abruptly fails in developing countries. Success stories can be cited in literature, but failures are more frequent (Krishna *et al.,* 2005). Why did this happen or is still happening? Several scholarly articles (Madu, 1989; Bhatnagar, 2002; Heeks, 2002; Dada, 2006) identified that information technology is still not suitable in developing countries as a means of communication, and they also observed that it was a pragmatic mistake to implement the models of ICT in developing countries directly by copying them from developed countries. The technology absorption capacity of consumers of developing countries is quite different from that of developed countries. Before funding and implementing ICT and extending business periphery from developed to developing countries, it is a challenging issue to identify the generic and distinctive characteristics of consumers of developing countries in terms adoption of EC and overall technology absorption capabilities. In this era of globalization, the answer to these issues, and thus the development of a framework regarding the plausible adoption criteria of EC for consumers of developing countries is of utmost important. Therefore, we attempt, as the first objective of this chapter, to track and comprehend the perspectives and paradigms of EC diffusion and adoption, especially in developing countries. Then, to accomplish the second objective of this chapter, we address, identify and conceptualize the critical factors that enable stakeholders to adopt EC system.

The next section deals with literature review on EC adoption, diffusion, and possible barriers in developing countries. The following section describes concepts of adoption and its perspectives and paradigms. Then a conceptual framework is presented to conceptualize adoption of EC by consumers, especially of developing countries. We then present a conclusion and offer future research direction.

7.2. LITERATURE REVIEW ON EC ADOPTION

A number of scholarly studies have been conducted on EC and technology adoption. However, most of these studies have been conducted in developed countries. Developing countries show inert reflection in fitting into the global digital market (Chowdhury 2003; Kurnia, 2007). As a result, the effects of EC on globalization of economic activities have created opportunity as well as threat of digital divide with a bold division between developed and developing countries. Developing countries substantially fail to adopt Internet based economy. The problems are located by numerous studies (UNCTAD, 2003; Radaideh & Selim, 2004). Studies show that both governments and consumers are not ready to embrace a technology based economy. Several reasons lie behind this failure of diffusing ICT in developing countries including political speculation, development of technological and social capability, cultural unfamiliarity, and economical condition. Nevertheless, more and more governments as well as consumers in the developing countries are beginning to eliminate obstacles to the adoption of ICT and grasp the potential of Internet economy (UNCTAD, 2003). While the immediate effects and present status are not seemingly dramatic, future trend in improvements in adaptability of virtual environment reflects some drastic revolution in case of some developing countries like India, Brazil, China, Singapore, Taiwan, Honk Kong, South Korea, Malaysia etc. However, many other developing countries still face difficulties in identifying, accepting, and implementing the potential benefits of ICT and thus adopting B2C EC for domestic economic development (UNCTAD, 2003).

Several researchers have addressed the issue of EC adoption criteria in developed countries; however, a few scholars have investigated the issue from developing country perspective (Radaideh & Selim, 2004). Additionally, those who encapsulate this issue, reveal fragmented reasons for the adoption of EC through incorporating constructs from different segmented views of literature like information technology, technology adoption model, diffusion of innovation theory, service quality models, and behavioral study. However, comprehensive view is explicitly absent. Since extension and proliferation of EC from developed to developing countries is a recent phenomenon in Internet economy, so the reason is quite understandable. But EC adoption reflects government system, political view, technology usage, economic reformation, social aspect, and cultural impacts. Therefore, inclusion and exclusion of different major aspects and related constructs definitely require logical and sequential literature review from different fields, detailed explanation of used paradigms, and screening through established theoretical framework. To explore the relevance and epistemological and ontological perspective of issue of EC adoption and the opportunity of its growth in developing countries, it is imperative to understand national, cultural, technological, behavioral, political, and financial factors that affect EC adoption.

Kurnia (2007) conducted a case study in Indonesia and investigated EC adoption criteria in the basis of Indonesian Internet market. He identified that EC adoption criteria in developing countries is contingent on different social, cultural, political, government initiatives, and technological factors. Some other scholarly studies conducted in developing countries address the issue of consumers' adoption of B2C EC and explore this from fragmented perspective (Radaideh & Selim, 2004; Viswanathan & Pick, 2005; Jamal & Ahmed, 2007). They hardly comprehend social, technological, cultural, behavioral, political, and other aspects of adoption criteria. Synthesizing their findings, the following prime sources of critical factors of B2C EC are identified: Government Initiatives, Public Awareness, External Influence,

Socio-cultural Condition, Geographical Condition, Technology Infrastructure, Political Condition, and Economic Condition. Wong (2002) studied ICT adoption criteria in Asian countries and observed that social, cultural, and political factors are predominant for EC adoption in Asian developing countries. Viswanathan and Pick (2005) addressed the barriers of EC adoption in India and Mexico and revealed that poor information infrastructure, lack of consumer credit, low penetration of computers, relatively low usage of credit cards, lack of incentives for consumers to purchase products or services over the Internet, and cultural habit are the significant barriers for EC adoption and proliferation in these two major developing countries. Radaideh and Selim (2004) capture the critical factors that affect the adoption of EC in the United Arab Emirates, particularly in the emirate of Abu-Dhabi.

Some researchers have conceptualized adoption factors of B2C EC by consumers from theoretical perspectives. Grounded on different theories related to information systems, these adoption criteria include organizational, technological, government oriented, behavioral, and economical issues (Radaideh & Selim, 2004). Technology related aspects which are quite similar to technology adoption model (Davis, 1989) are very popular for EC adoption factors by consumers addressed by different scholars (Karakaya, & Charlton, 2001; Sohail & Shanmugham, 2003). Some authors prioritized behavioral characteristics for adoption of EC (Bhattacherjee, 2001; Eastin, 2002). Organizational, governmental, and economical factors are also identified and conceptualized in EC adoption models (Koyuncu & Lien, 2003; Sohail & Shanmugham, 2003). However, the major weaknesses of these models are:

1. Theoretical backgrounds of these models are either absent or very poor and scattered.
2. These adoption studies copied the theme of adoption from developed countries, thus fail to conceptualize the specific and distinct characteristics of cultural, governmental, and social aspects of developing countries.
3. Often these studies are concentrated in technological and economical aspects. However, comprehensive view of different adoption studies suggests integration of technological, socio-cultural, governmental, and economical aspects.
4. Most of the empirical studies for adoption criteria are conducted in developed countries, and from analogical study, the adoption factors are justified for developing countries.
5. Most of the studies are conceptual. The studies which have empirical support also often used secondary data.
6. Primary data are collected mostly from the students who might not be a fully representative sample of actual customers of EC.

7.3. PERSPECTIVES AND PROCESS OF ADOPTION

This section is organized to identify and figure out perspectives and process of design of the adoption framework for explanatory variables. We, at this stage, attempt to investigate the prime aspects of B2C EC adoption by consumers. Then after analyzing those prime aspects of EC adoption, successively we set our efforts to recognize and postulate the plausible explanatory variables for adoption of EC.

7.3.1. Perspective of Adoption Factors

While investigating and revealing the prime perspectives of explanatory variables of EC adoption, this book chapter explores two major fields as theoretical background. The first attempt is engaged in reviewing literature addressing B2C EC adoption, implementation, and related issues. The second field is extensive cultivation of theories related to technology adoption, public administration and organization, psychology, sociology, political science, culture, and marketing.

From the literature review, the comprehensive view of critical factors for adoption of B2C EC by consumers of developing countries is already encapsulated. Precisely these include technological, social, behavioral, governmental, cultural, and economical perspectives.

Now to delineate the theoretical paradigms and accentuate at theoretical discourses, this research, at the outset of this present endeavor, looks at the contingency theory. The contingency approach to management is based on the paradigm that there is no one best way to manage, and that to be effective, planning, organizing, leading, and controlling must be tailored to the particular circumstances faced by an organization. Environmental change and uncertainty, technology, different social and governmental aspects, culture, behavioral differences, and different economical attributes are all identified as environmental factors impacting the effectiveness of adoption.

EC's acceptance, intention, usage, satisfaction, and recurring adoption attributes also have some prime perspectives, like   driven from behavioral or attitudinal intention, social epistemological and ontological paradigms, cultural phenomena, political aspects, economical behavior, and governmental issues. EC offers enormous benefits to its end users which include economical incentives, speed, time and alternative of choices, round the clock availability, and improvement of service. Therefore comparative economical and social behavior reflects consumers' preferences to adopt EC. Transactional cost analysis (TCA) and capability theory also shed light on these perspectives of EC adoption criteria.

From the core principle of TCA, motivation for behavioral intention to interact with different organizational structure is significantly influenced by economical parameters. (Shelanski *et al.,* 1995). With the rapid growth of the ICT and the advent of EC, government organizations play an important role in economic activities, and individuals participate in various types of interactions. Therefore, while measuring adoption criteria of EC, economical benefits, attitudinal benefits, and governmental interaction are important aspects to be encountered. In the electronic medium, competitors can emerge from anywhere in the world with significant differences in attitude, especially in adopting new information and communication technology, which is the main vehicle of EC. As a result, national and also global cultural attributes develop significant disparities in behavioral intention and attitudes of users of EC. A society prescribes some values, ideas, intentions, and speculations on human personality. These perceived psychological phenomena depend on rules, regulations, relationships, culture, tradition, etc. Depending on cultural factors, behavioral intention to adopt EC operated through ICT can be affected vividly (Engel *et al.,* 1993). Beliefs and attitudes about a system direct human beings toward an intention. If we translate the core doctrine of Socio-technical theory, which explains the social aspects of people and society and technical aspects of machines and technology, we get deep insight of integrating social, organizational, and technological aspects of EC adoption framework. Therefore, based on these theoretical discourses and literature review, it is explicit that consumers' adoption of B2C EC must be explored, addressed, and conceptualized from the core perspectives of behavioral, technological, social, cultural, governmental, and economical perspectives.

However, these perspectives, where we have to put our enthusiasm to investigate, identify, and reveal critical factors of adoption framework of EC, are not mutually exclusive phenomena. These are interrelated speculations. According to actor network theory, different influential functions are acting around a system acted by both human and non-human entities which are connected by networks. The integrated functions and all related factors produce the stabilized system. Several researchers (Grönlund, 2003/2005; Green & Pearson, 2005) have shed light on this theory to conceive the network functions of different constituents, i.e., stakeholders, and non-human beings, i.e., societal factors, cultural factors, and most importantly embracing of technological factors. Similarly adoption perspectives are intertwined with different explanatory variables. Therefore, our investigation for identifying critical factors of EC will not track those perspectives of EC adoption factors separately; rather we will look for interdependent and comprehensive effects.

7.3.2. Adoption Process

We encompass adoption of EC as a continuous process starting from beliefs of benefits, attitude toward using it, intention to use, actual use, satisfaction, and recurring use. This speculation is also supported by Watson *et al.* (2000). According to

Watson *et al.* (2000), EC adoption process based on performance can be classified into five stages as follows: awareness, popularity, contact, conversion, and retention. The first indicator is consumers' awareness of the system. The second indicator is website popularity. The third indicator is contact efficiency refers to site content and convenience. After visitors register, they should be able to e-mail a request for information, file a claim, buy an item or make a transaction. The fourth indicator is conversion refers to transactions and customer satisfaction. The fifth indicator is retention or customer loyalty. A successful site must be able to move a one-time visitor to a return customer. The implementation of an IT system goes through six stages: initiation, adoption, adaptation, acceptance, use, and incorporation (Kown & Zmud, 1987). The adoption process as suggested by Spence (1994) goes through five sequential steps.

Depending on the aforementioned paradigms of EC adoption process, we find logical underpinnings on the premise that the adoption process of EC is the frequent and recurring use of online services by consumers for obtaining information, interaction and/or transaction with E-retailers. Therefore, for an elementary precondition of EC, that is to act customer oriented is to have knowledge about customer needs and to have market sensing capability (Day, 1994).

7.4. THEORETICAL FRAMEWORK FOR EC ADOPTION

Classic diffusion theory (Rogers, 1995) postulates that for systematic diffusion of progress, public awareness (Knowledge of the existence of the innovation) is one of the primary steps. According to information management principles, creating awareness among the customers, i.e., the end users about implementation of innovation, concerning factors and issues, basic paradigms of the new system, comprehensive view of advantages and disadvantages, and overall security of the system is a prime factor for adoption (Internet Week,2000; Viswanathan & Pick, 2005). Awareness is defined by Okot-Uma & Caffrey (2000) as "Providing information about the political process, about services and about choices available, the time horizons for the decision-making process and about the exponents of the decision-making process". Long history of offline service shows that customers are traditionally habituated to use brick and mortar business organizations for information collection, interaction, and all types of transaction. The evolution history of EC is very new and mostly adapted by several developed countries not more than 10-15 years ago. Most of EC customers are coming from developed countries (Koenig & Wigand, 2004). Even majority of population of developing countries are not at all aware of EC—its functional characteristics and benefits (Viswanathan & Pick, 2005). Consumers of developing countries mostly do not know the operation of EC, virtual environment, and E-retailers (Kurnia, 2007). As a result, they have little information about reputation and reliability of those E-vendors. Therefore, due to unfamiliarity with E-retailers, EC operation, and ultimately E-purchase, consumers are not ready to adopt EC. For adoption of EC, consumers need to be aware of EC characteristics. Awareness of EC has governmental aspect, behavioral aspect, and social aspect. Government guidance, publication, and supervision have significant implications for consumers' awareness about operations, security, and functional advantages of EC (Karakaya & Charlton, 2001; Kim & Lee, 2002). Due to backward social system and relations, consumers of developing countries are not socially habituated to adopt ICT and rely on any virtual system. If the consumers perceive social values related to strategic implementation of EC, service quality and competitive advantages of EC, and attitudinal or behavioral motivation of EC system, then they might have intention to adopt EC system. Several researchers asserted awareness as the significant independent variable to create attitude to use EC system (Watson *et al.,* 2000; Jamal & Ahmed, 2007). Absorptive capacity theory ((Cohen and Levinthal, 1990; Liu and Whiter, 1997) also supports the argument that prior knowledge of existing technology, which reflects the awareness of new technology, positively affect individuals' ability to adopt new technology system. The concepts of adoption capabilities are extensively explored by the absorptive capacity theory. The theory emphasizes the prior knowledge as the foundation base for adopting new knowledge and concepts. This theory has received attention by several studies in innovation adoption. The theory was first introduced by Cohen and Levinthal (1990). It is applicable in multilevel of organizational structure including individual level, group level, and firm level. Based on this theory, absorption capability of individuals for any information technology intense system depends rigorously on prior knowledge (knowledge stocks and knowledge flows) as well as communication. Prior knowledge supports and accelerates the ability of individuals to acquire new information. Because, through a cognitive process, individuals can assimilate existing knowledge with new knowledge and decide whether to adopt it or not. This prior knowledge about the similar technology can create awareness of the new technology. So, we categorize the construct awareness as the explanatory variable for adoption of EC and defined it as: having sufficient knowledge and experience about functional characteristics of EC. Depending on the above arguments, we propose:

Proposition-1: Awareness has a positive relation with adoption of EC

Several researchers asserted that adoption of new technology is closely related to availability of resources, viz., overall infrastructure (Radaideh & Selim, 2004; Viswanathan & Pick, 2005). This is especially a practical aspect for developing countries. Several studies and United Nations report affirms that infrastructure related to implementation of ICT in public and private sectors in developing countries are mostly inadequate and availability of computers, Internet, telecommunications system to majority of consumers is insignificant (United Nations, 2003; Viswanathan & Pick, 2005). While consumers can secure and achieve traditional business service without modern ICT and infrastructures including computers, Internet connection, and telecommunications, adoption of EC implies acceptance, use, and adoption of Internet, virtual environment, software, and computer. Several researchers point out that due to scarcity in computers, Internet with competent features like access, speed and cost, and government supports like call-center, resource-center, cyber-café, EC implementation in several countries especially in developing countries could not attain desired success (Madu, 1989; Bhatnagar, 2002; Heeks, 2002; Dada, 2006). Following Nussbaum & Sen (1993), the capability approach is defined as the ability to adopt some systems with freedom of choice. If we look at Capability theory, it highlights that consumers cannot achieve capability of using a system unless they have freedom of utility of using that system (Nussbaum & Sen, 1993). Therefore, if we cannot reduce digital divide, promote equality in resources of using EC, make available of all components of EC system and knowledge, adoption of EC will not be successful. Infrastructure required for use of EC has behavioral, economical, cultural, social, and technological aspects. Generally, where computers, Internet, and modern information and communication technology are not available, they are economically poor, less educated, and unaware of modern technology, socially and culturally are not familiar, and technologically are not skill. Therefore, there is an obvious relation between availability of infrastructure and adoption of EC. We define Availability of overall infrastructure (AOI) for implementation of ICT and operation of EC as the development of overall facilities for successful implementation of ICT and availability of using Computers, Internet, Information and communication technology (ICT) with competitive features like access, speed, and cost across the country among overall consumers. We argue that Availability of overall infrastructure (AOI) creates beliefs of using EC system operated through ICT which in turn creates attitude to use EC. This is also asserted by several scholars addressed the adoption issue of EC (Kraemer & Dedrick, 2000; Bhatnagar, 2002; Heeks, 2002; Dada, 2006). Drawing conclusion from the above arguments, we propose here:

Proposition-2: Availability of infrastructure (AOI) has a positive relation with adoption of EC.

According to Diffusion of Innovation Theory (DOI), the rate of diffusion is affected by an innovation's relative advantage, complexity, compatibility, trialability, and observability. Rogers (1995) addresses relative advantage as "the degree to which an innovation is seen as being superior to its predecessor". For EC, it is the relative advantage (as perceived by the consumers) of viewing, interacting, and transacting through online instead of using traditional offline channel for conducting the same functions. It is quite similar to the construct perceived usefulness (PU) of technology adoption model (TAM) by Davis (1989). Several researchers revealed that perceiving relative advantage and usefulness of EC enhances consumers' intention to use EC system (Yoo *et al.* 2001; Wolfinbarger *et al.,* 2003). Complexity, comparable to TAM's perceived ease of use (PEOU) construct, is "the degree to which an innovation is seen by the potential adopter as being relatively difficult to use and understand" (Rogers, 1995). Complexity captures the essence of difficulties in viewing, interacting, and transacting in ICT, computer and EC due to system function of EC and personal inability. Due to several drawbacks of consumers of developing countries including less education, unfamiliarity with ICT, lack of experience and skill in using ICT, majority of population are unable to use ICT and interact with EC. Therefore, complexity in using ICT and EC is a major cause for consumers of developing countries not to adopt EC (Alpar, 2001; Devaraj *et al.*, 2002; Collier *et al.* 2006; Jamal & Ahmed, 2007). Consumers will not accept a system if they do not perceive it useful and easy to use (Davis, 1989). The constructs Relative advantage and Complexity have technological and social perspectives. Due to revolutionary re-engineering of traditional business system, perception of online organizational structure which is apparently new has an important social aspect to perceive relative advantage and usefulness of using the system. Technology is very much predictable aspect to get insight of Relative advantage and Complexity (Fichman and Kemerer, 1997).

Compatibility refers to "the degree to which an innovation is seen to be compatible with existing values, beliefs, experiences and needs of adopters" (Rogers, 1995). This construct has cultural, behavioral, and social aspects. It is dependent both on individual characteristics like avoiding personal interaction and social influence. Several researchers indicated that specific characteristic of EC that allows consumers to avoid personal interaction might create perception of compatibility among consumers to adopt EC system (Gilbert *et al.,* 2004). Shedding light on the theory of planned behavior, theory of reasoned action, and capability theory, compatibility of EC system with adopters' beliefs, values, and attitudes reflect behavioral aspect. From socio-technical and complementary theory, beliefs and attitudes of adopters of a new technology system also has social and cultural aspects. Several researchers use this construct as the significant predictor of EC adoption of virtual transaction (Devaraj *et al.* 2002; Carter & Bélanger, 2005; Shareef *et al.,* 2007). For EC systems, we conjecture Compatibility as the degree of preference of consumers of viewing, interacting, and transacting in EC websites that match with behavioral and cultural values, social needs, and overall attitudes. Based on theoretical discourses and previous literature on online behavior, we argue that Compatibility (C) creates among consumers'- attitudes to use EC system.

Trialability is the "degree to which an idea can be experimented with on a limited basis" (Rogers, 1995). And observability is the "degree to which the results of an innovation are visible" (Rogers, 1995). Several literature reviews suggest that relative advantage, compatibility, and complexity are the most relevant constructs to determine the adoption characteristics of online systems (Rogers, 1995; Gilbert *et al.* 2004; Carter & Bélanger, 2005; Gil-García, & Pardo, 2005). These authors, especially Tornatzky & Klein (1982), in their meta analysis of research on the adoption of innovations, argue that Trialability and observability are not related constructs for online adoption. Hence, we are interested in relative advantage, complexity, and compatibility in our study. Therefore, the three dimensions relative advantage, complexity, and compatibility are investigated here and assumed that these might affect EC adoption. Therefore, we propose

Proposition-3: Relative advantage has a positive relation with adoption of EC

Proposition-4: Complexity has a negative relation with adoption of EC

Proposition-5: Compatibility has a positive relation with adoption of EC

B2C EC website quality refers to the elements of a system that affect the end user in the way they interact and use an EC system. This is a basic dimension of EC evaluation. Website quality measures the functionality of a website: usability, availability, and response time (DeLone & McLean, 2003). Smith and Merchant (2001) found that online customers are interested in getting a website which is easy to read, as well as easy to navigate. A responsive website is highly important to end-users (Robbins & Stylianou, 2003). Specifically quality of a website can be assessed by search facility, responsiveness, and multi-media capability. Website quality has technological aspect. Several researchers have show that if a website is user friendly and can provide some basic quality, like easy navigation, organized content, easy access, links, availability, and quick download, then customers have better attitude toward adopting the system (OECD, 2000; Bosworth & Triplett, 2001; Jalava & Pohjola, 2002; Liljander *et al.,* 2002). The attitude, in turn, leads to intention to use ICT and the eventual acceptance of the information technology (Davis *et al.,* 1989; Bhattacherjee, 2001, Moon, 2002). Several scholarly articles (Yoo & Donthu, 2001; Collier & Bienstock, 2006) dealing with acceptance of web based transactions by customers reveal that for online interaction facilitation factors such as: communication quality, technical quality, loading quality, organization of the web etc., are important for B2C EC adoption. Thus, web site quality is a basic dimension of EC quality evaluation. Website quality encapsulates "the degree to which the design of the website and software, i.e., overall technology of the website functions and facilitates customers during website interaction". Depending on the above aspects of website quality, it is argued that this quality construct is related to the appearance of the user interface, thus this study proposes:

Proposition-6: Website quality has a positive relation with adoption of EC

Content and structure of information, i.e., Information quality including accuracy, up to date, relevancy, completeness, integration, organization, and timelines plays a significant role to accept virtual interaction offered in EC (Rainer & Watson, 1995; Ehikioya, 1999). This imparts assurance and confidence to stakeholders to use EC. In order to assure the success of an information system, Delone and McLean (2003) proposed the Information System Success Model (IS Model). The model asserted that information quality is the determinant of system use and user satisfaction that affects individual and organization impact (Wangpipatwong *et al.,* 2005). Information quality asserts service requirements of consumers and economical benefits of viewing and collecting information from website in lieu of verbal interaction from traditional government offices. Therefore, it has an economical aspect. Behaviorally, if consumers find information in websites is not accurate, up-to-data, and necessary, they might loose their intention to use EC. Mason and Mitroff's characterization can be used to an online environment to empirically investigate information quality. Mason and Mitroff (1973) defined an information system as consisting of "at least one PERSON of a certain PSYCHOLOGICAL TYPE who faces a PROBLEM within some ORGANIZATIONAL CONTEXT for which he needs EVIDENCE to arrive at a solution (i.e. to select some course of action) and that the evidence is made available to him through some MODE OF PRESENTATION." Therefore, information quality has behavioral aspect. Technological aspect of information quality is obvious, since display, organization, links, customization, up-to-date-----all are related to technology.

Information quality has been considered as a relevant topic in web-based service and critical in determining information system success (DeLone & McLean, 2003). Wang and Strong (1996) categorize 20 sub-dimensions of data quality into four major groups as information quality. These are, accessibility quality: examines access and security of data; contextual quality: considers the timeliness, amount, completeness, and relevancy of data; representational quality: examines the understandability, interpretability, and consistency of data; and intrinsic quality: looks at the accuracy, objectivity, and believability of data. Information Quality is considered to be one of the most important elements of EC service dimensions (Turban & Gehrke, 2000). This construct captures and describes the status of information collection, gathering, arrangement, and comparison. DeLone and McLean's conceptual model (2003) captures the essence of information quality as a driver of individual's impact on adoption of information system. Information quality is dependent on users' perception of quality and objective of use. Information quality also captures the website content issues (Cao *et al.*, 2005). Information is a basic tool of a website by reading which customers advance further. Deciding what content to place, how to place it, how to arrange, organize, and update on a website are extremely important. Lin and Lu (2000) reveal that customers' acceptance is positively affected by the features and accurate information in the website. Presentation of information about products, services, people, events, or ideas affect customers' decision whether they further interact or not with the website. It is, thus, imperative for online service providers to extend attentions to the possible factors to enhance the information quality (Lin & Lu, 2000). The information on the website should be accurate, informative, and updated. Information relevance, i.e., the extent to which the information on the website is related to the information needs by the stakeholders is also an important aspect for them to interact and thus to move further with recurring use. Therefore, information quality construct includes content, accuracy, up-to-date, and systematic arrangement of information of the website provided for users. This research defines Information Quality (IQ) as: "Information quality covers the extent to which complete, accurate, organized, understandable, up to date, users' agency based, and timely information is provided in the website for the customers to get information about any of their intended objective." Grounded on aforementioned arguments, we propose

Proposition-7: Information quality has a positive relation with adoption of EC

Practitioners and academics are showing growing interest in the service sector's operations and in service quality in particular. It is the difference between customer expectations of service and perceived service. If expectations are greater than performances, then perceived quality is less than satisfactory, and hence customer dissatisfaction occurs (Parasuraman *et al.*, 1985). Service quality is higher perception of consumers about the performance of the online retailer. As communication and information technology push markets, people and products ever closer, it is the single most effective and sustainable means of differentiation between competing organizations.

Demand of service quality basically includes many perceived components required by consumers. In online transaction, since different physical cues are absent, virtual transaction desires some extra facilities to perform transaction with different ethnic background. Generally English is the predominant language for Internet interaction. There are also some other languages like Chinese, Spanish, French etc. used in Internet, however, generally majority of consumers of developing countries do not have fluency and skill in those languages (Kettler & Benavides, 2002; Viswanathan & Pick, 2005; Internet World Stats, 2007,). This criterion is especially very important for a country where literacy and education rate are very low. Since EC has global aspect, multi-lingual option is considered a very significant aspect for global adoption of EC. Service quality research of EC also augmented this phenomenon as a desired criterion for consumers (Stefani & Xenos, 2003). Nantel *et al.* (2005) conducted an empirical study about customers' adoption of online purchase. Their research shows that the perceived usability increases when the website is originally conceived in the native language of the user. Therefore, marketing literature is now very enthusiastic to verify multilingual option in marketing thrust (Hartzer, 2006). Processing and understanding of information is closely linked with language and cognitive schemas (D'Andrade, 1992), which help us to store information in specific categories. These schemas result from adaptation to a certain environment and are shared by all members of a specific culture (D'Andrade, 1987). Hence, the cognitive effort required to comprehend a system decreases when a website is congruent with the user's culture (Luna *et al.*, 2002). Therefore, a culturally adapted website with native language results in greater ease of navigation and a more positive attitude towards the site. Singh *et al.* (2005) investigated this concept by analyzing 93 websites for the cultural content from local companies in China, India, Japan and the USA. Their findings provided evidences in support of the cultural dimensions established by Hofstede (1980, 1991). They, therefore suggest international E-retailers for localizing their websites. For less educated consumers, single language option for viewing, collecting, interacting, and transacting with EC websites might create a significant barrier. This is an important cultural aspect (Scollon & Wong, 2001; Michon & Chebat 2004). It can be argued that digital divide is also a collective aspect for language barrier. If we borrow speculation of Technology acceptance model and Diffusion of innovation theory, usefulness of EC will trigger inclusion of multilingual option in EC web pages. From technological perspective, this might be proved important. Though, EC research did not put enough consideration in this aspect, however, beliefs in competence with EC interaction which further promotes attitude towards adoption of EC according to theory of planned behavior can be exaggerated if known language option prevails in EC websites. Therefore, multilingual option has behavioral aspect. If we look at capability theory, multilingual option in EC might create equal and competitive capability which ultimately enhances economical power of consumers of developing countries. Therefore, from economical perspective, multi-lingual option in EC can create level playing field for major users groups with multilingual background.

From marketing, technological, behavioral, and cultural perspectives, we argue that multi-lingual option in EC might enhance processing and understanding capability of EC. We define Multilingual Option (MLO) as "Customers ability to view, interact, and transact in EC through local dominating language in absence of human interaction." Therefore, since this criterion promotes ability to use EC, we thus propose

Proposition-8: Multi-lingual option has a positive relation with adoption of EC

Reviewing Gefen's framework (Gefen, 2002), it is found that trust is related to familiarity and disposition to trust which affect adoption behavior. Lee *et al.* (2001) view comprehensive information, shared value, and communication as antecedents of trust which affect customers' revisit to a website. Belanger *et al.* (2002) found that pleasure, privacy, security, and web features are related matters to perceived trustworthiness to website. Trust has root in technological, governmental, social, behavioral, cultural, and economical perspectives. Governmental supervision, rules and regulations are very important aspects to build trust for adoption of EC (Mc-Gann *et al.,* 2002). Virtual environment has a great influence on trust perception in ICT. From social perspective, social and market rules and regulations impart some perception about social system which is a predictor of perceived trustworthiness. People's individual beliefs about a system also form trust about a system. Trusting behavior is an important aspect for final trust disposition attitude (Balasubramanian *et al.,* 2003; Shareef *et al.,* forth coming). Different culture has different trusting attitude and privacy concept (Tsikriktsis, 2002). For developed and developing countries, privacy concept sometimes reflects different traits (Vehovar, 2003).

Trust disposition attitude is dependent on personal experience, prior knowledge, behavioral attitude, and social values (Engel *et al.,* 1993). Actually trust disposition attitude plays a significant role toward perceived trustworthiness (Balasubramanian *et al.,* 2003). The research conducted by Shareef *et al.* (forth coming) in developing country found that trust disposition attitude has a significant effect on online purchase intention. Prior research in EC and EG also found uncertainty, security, privacy, and risk are all antecedents of perceived trust (Yoo *et al.,* 2001; Devaraj *et al.,* 2002; Balasubramanian *et al.,* 2003; Shareef *et al,* 2008). From the light of above discussion, we define trust as "The degree to which users of EC have attitudinal confidence on overall EC performance". Thus, we propose

Proposition-9: Trust has a positive relation with adoption of EC

Therefore, we suggest that Awareness, Availability of infrastructure, Relative advantage, Compatibility, Website quality, Information quality, Multi-lingual option, and Trust have positive effect on adoption of EC in developing countries. On the other hand, Complexity has negative relations with adoption of EC by consumers of developing countries. Our objective of finding these 9 explanatory variables are to suggest international E-retailers to investigate those variables in any developing countries to conceptualize the adoption status and also to provide those facilities for capturing global Internet economy.

7.5. CONCLUSION AND FUTURE RESEARCH DIRECTION

Though many companies are still just beginning to grasp the potential uses and impacts of B2C EC, advances in technologies and their applications continue. Observing the proliferation of B2C EC, companies are increasingly turning to the Internet to market products and services to gain competitive advantage. However, the effectiveness and efficiency of such online commerce systems largely depend on the degree of comfort that customers feel with the technology-based interactions. Because of the expansion and increasing reliance on corporate websites, research-ers and practitioners are equally concerned with the issues of understanding and managing B2C EC. In addition, diffusion, proliferation, and globalization of EC from developed to developing countries is finally grounded on the adoption of EC by the consumers of huge population of developing countries. If for any reason, revealed in this study, consumers of developing countries are not ready to adopt B2C EC from behavioral, technological, social, cultural, governmental, and eco-nomical aspects, endeavors aiming to diffuse and globalize will not be successful. Therefore, investigating, identifying, revealing, and conceptualizing the theoreti-cal perspective of EC adoption, especially for consumers of developing countries have significant implication for EC policy makers, practitioners, and academicians (Uzoka *et al.*, 2007).

This study has developed a theoretical framework exploring behavioral, tech-nological, social, governmental, cultural, and economical perspectives for adoption of B2C EC by consumers, especially of developing countries. The fundamental paradigms of this framework are grounded on extensive review of literature and theories and concepts related to information system, psychology, marketing, eco-nomics, sociology, and organizational behavior. The study identified 9 predictor variables for adoption of B2C EC. It is plausible that all these variables have inte-grated effect on adoption process. Since, study regarding the adoption of B2C EC for the consumers of developing countries is at an early stage, this study attempts to identify explanatory variables in a comprehensive manner which in turn affect adoption intention. As a result this study reviews literature and theories very rig-orously and incorporates several factors depending on special characteristics of consumers of developing countries which might influence their adoption process. Basically majority of population of most of the developing countries (some exceptions of developing countries might include Singapore, Taiwan, Hong Kong, India, South Korea, Malaysia, Thailand etc. which have advanced experience in diffusion of ICT across countries) are unaware of Internet economy, its functional characteristics and competitive benefits. They are also unfamiliar with how to interact with EC. Therefore, awareness might be a strong predictor for adoption of EC in developing countries. For developing countries, digital divide is very profound and majority of population are deprived of using computers and getting access to Internet economy. Overall infrastructure in developing countries is not suitable for diffusion, proliferation, globalization, and adoption of B2C EC. Availability of infrastructure including computers, Internet, and telecommunication systems might be a potential factor for adoption of EC. Compatibility, complexity, and relative advantage, which are incorporated in adoption framework from diffusion of innovation theory and have theoretical references from perceived ease of use and perceived usefulness of technology adoption model, are three important predictors of adoption of ICT and thus EC. Consumers of developing countries have specific social, cultural, behavioral attitudes, and their capability to use ICT is also discrete. Majority of population of most of the developing countries are not accustomed with values, beliefs, and characteristics of modern technology intense economy, have less skill and experience to interact in websites, and cannot understand functional advantages of adopting EC. Therefore, these three factors might have significant relation with adoption of EC. Since literacy and education rate in developing countries are very less, language is identified by several researchers as a serious barrier for consumers of less advanced population to interact in Internet where language is predominantly English. So, provision of local language, viz., multi-lingual option might be a plausible adoption criterion for consumers of developing countries. If the website is not well organized, not always available, difficult and slow to download, browsing is not easy, contents are not easily manageable, information are not accurate, up-to-date, and well linked, generally from technological, behavioral, and economical perspectives, consumers might be deterred to accept EC. Therefore, website quality and information quality are two important predictors for adoption and are thus incorporated in the adoption framework. For online transactions, factors such as security, uncertainty, risk, privacy are often cited by literature as important causes for consumers to interact in EC. Positive perception of all those phenomena develops trust among consumers about an E-retailer. If consumers cannot trust an E-retailer, most probably they will not interact with that E-retailer. Consumers of developing countries, due to unfamiliarity and less experience with interaction in Internet and due to social and cultural perception of risk and security, are more risk averse. So, trust on EC might be a significant factor for adoption of EC and thus this construct has been incorporated.

For developing countries, this theoretical framework for identifying EC adoption has important implication. The reasons include:

1. This framework has rigorously reviewed literature on information system, EC service quality, purchase intention, and adoption factors. All the explanatory variables have some literature background.
2. All the explanatory variables are significantly rooted in strong theoretical perspectives of information system, psychology, economics, sociology, and organizational behavior.
3. Different technological, behavioral, governmental, social, cultural, and economical perspectives of adoption for consumers of developing countries are cultivated. So, the framework is very comprehensive.
4. Very few studies have been conducted addressing adoption criteria for consumers of developing countries. However, for diffusion, proliferation, and globalization of EC, understanding unknown adoption criteria for consumers of developing countries is single most important issue for both practitioners and academicians.

This is a conceptual framework. Integration of several explanatory variables in the adoption framework is predictive, and yet not validated. Even, empirical study in a single developing country is not enough to validate the framework. In future, rigorous empirical studies should be conducted in different developing countries located in different regions to generalize the understanding of EC adoption criteria for consumers of developing countries. Because, this is a very important aspect for successful globalization of EC and integrating consumers of both developed and developing countries under the unique umbrella of Internet economy.

REFERENCES

Alpar, P. (2001). *Satisfaction with a Website: Its Measurement, Factors, and Correlates.* Working Paper No. 99/01, Philipps-Universität Marburg, Institut für Wirtschaftsinformatik.

Balasubramanian, S., Konana, P., & Menon, N. M. (2003). Customer, Satisfaction in Virtual Environments: A Study of Online Investing. *Management Science*, *7*(July), 871–889.

Basu, S. (2004). E-government and Developing Countries: An Overview. *International Review of Law Computers & Technology*, *18*(1), 109–132.

Bélanger, F., Hiller, J., & Smith, W. (2002). Trustworthiness in Electronic Commerce: the Role of Privacy, Security, and Site Attributes. *Journal of Strategic Information Systems, 11*(2002), 245-270.

Bhatnagar, S. (2002). E-government: Lessons from Implementation in Developing Countries. *Regional Development Dialogue, 24*(Autumn Issue), 1-9.

Bhattacherjee, A. (2001). An Empirical Analysis of The Antecedents of Electronic Commerce Service Continuance. *Decision Support Systems, 32*, 201 –214.

Bosworth, B. P., & Triplett, J. E. (2001). *What's New about the New Economy?* IT Economic Growth and Productivity. Tokyo Club Papers 14.

Cao, M., Zhang, O., & Seydel, J. (2005). Measuring B2C eCommerce Website Quality: An Empirical Examination. *Industrial management & Data Systems, 106*(5), 645-661.

Carter, L., & Bélanger, F. (2005). The Utilization of E-government Services: Citizen Trust, Innovation and Acceptance Factors. *Information Systems Journal, 15*, 5-25.

Chowdhury, A. (2003). Information Technology and Productivity Payoff in the Banking Industry: Evidence from the Emerging Markets. *Journal of International Development, 15*(6), 693-708.

Cohen, W., & Levinthal, D. (1990). Absorptive Capacity: A New Perspective on Learning and Innovation. *Administrative Science Quarterly, 35*, 128-152.

Collier, J. E., & Bienstock, C. C. (2006). Measuring Service Quality in E-Retailing. *Journal of Service Research, 8*(3), 260-275.

Dada, D. (2006). The Failure of E-government in Developing Countries. http://www.lse.ac.uk/collections/informationSystems/iSChannel/Dada_2006b.pdf. [Accessed: 2006].

D'Andrade, R. G. (1987). A Folk Model of the Mind. In D. Holland & N. Quinn (Eds.), *Cultural Models in Language and Thought*. London: Cambridge University Press.

D'Andrade, R. G. (1992). Schemas and Motivation. In R. D'Andrade and C. Strauss (Eds.), *Human Motives and Cultural Models*. London: Cambridge University Press.

Davis, F. (1989). Perceived Usefulness, Perceived Ease of Use and User Acceptance of Information Technology, *MIS Quarterly, 13*(3), 319-340.

Davis, F, Bagozzi, R. P., & Warshaw, P. R., (1989). User Acceptance of Computer Technology: A Comparison of Two Theoretical Models. *Management Sd., 35*(8), 982-1003.

Davis, E. S. (2003). A World Wide Problem on the World Wide Web: International Responses to Transnational Identity Theft via the Internet. *Journal of Law & Policy, 12,* 201-227.

Day, G. S. (1994). The Capabilities of Market-Driven Organizations. *Journal of Marketing, 58* (October, 37-52.

DeLone, W. H., & McLean, E. R. (1992). Information Systems Success: The Quest for the Dependent Variable. *Information Systems Research, 3*(1), 60-95.

DeLone, W. H., & McLean, E. R. (2003). The Delone and Mclean Model of Information Systems Success: A Ten-Year Update. *Journal of Management Information Systems, 19*(4), 9-30.

Devaraj, S., Fan, M., & Kohli, R. (2002), Antecedents of B2C Channel Satisfaction and Preference: Validating e-Commerce Metrics. *Information Systems Research, 13*(3), 316-333.

Eastin, M. S. (2002). Diffusion of e-Commerce: An Analysis of the Adoption of Four E-Commerce Activities. *Telematics and Informatics, 19,* 251–267.

Ehikioya, S. A. (1999). A Characterization of Information Quality Using Fuzzy Logic. *Proceeding of International Conference on Fuzzy Information Processing Society,* (pp. 635-639).

Engel, J. F., Blackwell R. D., & Miniard, P. W. (1993). *Consumer Behavior.* 7th edition, The Dryden Press, Harcourt Brace Jovanovich, USA.

Fichman, R. G., & Kemerer, C. F. (1997). The Assimilation of Software Process Innovations: An Organizational Learning Perspective. *Management Science, 43*(10), 1345–1363.

Gefen, D. (2002). Customer Loyalty in E-Commerce. *Journal of the Association for Information Systems, 3,* 27-51.

Gefen, D., Karahanna, E., & Straub, D. W. (2003). Trust and TAM in Online Shopping: An Integrated Model. *MIS Quarterly, 27,* 51-90.

Gilbert, D., Balestrini, P., & Littleboy, D. (2004). Barriers And Benefits In The Adoption Of E-Government. *The International Journal of Public Sector Management, 14*(4), 286-301.

Gil-García, J. R., & Pardo, T. A. (2005). E-Government Success Factors: Mapping Practical Tools to Theoretical Foundations. *Government Information Quarterly*, *22*(2), 187–216.

Green, D. T. & Pearson, J. M. (2005). Social Software and Cyber Networks: Ties That Bind or Weak Associations within the Political Organizations? *Proceedings of the 38th Hawaii International Conference on System Sciences.*

Grönlund, A. (2003). Emerging Electronic Infrastructures. *Social Science Computer Review, 21*(1), 55-72.

Grönlund, A. (2005). What's in a Field – Exploring the eGovernment Domain. *Proceedings of the 38th Hawaii International Conference on System Sciences.*

Hartzer, B. (2006). Translating Web Sites Considerations for Multilingual Online Businesses, *Internet Serach Engine Database*, http://www.isedb.com/db/articles/ 1385/1/Translating-Web-Sites--Considerations-for-Multilingual-Online-Businesses/ Page1.html.

Heeks, R. (2002). Information Systems and Developing Countries: Failure, Success, and Local Improvisations. *The Information Society, 18*, 101–112.

Heeks, R. (2003). *Most eGovernment-for-Development Projects Fail: How Can Risks be Reduced?* iGovernment Working Paper Series, Paper no. 14.

Hofstede, G. (1980). *Culture's Consequences: International Differences in Work-Related Values.* Beverly Hills, CA: Sage.

Hofstede, G. (1991). *Cultures and Organizations: Software of the Mind.* London: McGraw-Hill.

Internet Week. (2000). Consumer Behavior Varies Widely by Country, Study Says. *Internet Week*, December 12.

Internet World Stats. (2007). http://www.allaboutmarketresearch.com/internet. htm.

Jalava, J., &Pohjola, M., (2002). Economic Growth in the New Economy: Evidence from Advanced Economies. *Information Economics and Policy, 14*(2), 189–210.

Jamal, A. S., & Ahmed, A. F. (2007). Socio-Cultural Factors Influencing Consumer Adoption of Online Transactions. *8th World Congress on the Management of eBusiness* (WCMeB 2007).

Karakaya, F., & Charlton, E. T. (2001). Electronic Commerce: Current and Future Practices. *Managerial Finance, 27*(7), 42-53(12).

Kettler, H. F., & Benavides, E. (2002). *E-Business Globalization. Analyzing Foreign Countries for E-Commerce Opportunities.* www.hipermarketing.com/nuevo%204/columnas/efrain/ebus. pdf.

Kim, J., & Lee, J. (2002). Critical Design Factors for Successful e-Commerce Systems. *Behavior & Information Technology, 21*(3), 185-199.

Koenig, W., & Wigand, R. T. (2004). Globalization and E-Commerce: Diffusion and Impacts of the Internet and E-Commerce in Germany. *Center for Research on Information Technology and Organizations.* University of California, Irvine.

Kwon, T. H., & Zmud, R. W. (1987). *Unifying the Fragmented Models of Information Systems Implementation, Critical Issues in Information Systems Research,* John Wiley & Sons, Inc., New York, NY.

Koyuncu, C., & Lien, D. (2003). E-Commerce and Consumer's Purchasing Behavior. *Applied Economics, 35,* 721– 726.

Kraemer, K. L., & Dedrick, J. (2000). Information Technology in Southeast Asia: Engine of Growth or Digital Divide. *Paper presented at the ASEAN Roundtable 2000, New Development Paradigms in Southeast Asia: The Challenge of Information Technology,* 12–13 October. Institute of Southeast Asian Studies, Singapore.

Krishna, S., & Walsham, G. (2005). Implementing Public Information Systems in Developing Countries: Learning From a Success Story. *Information Technology for Development, 11*(2), 123-140.

Kurnia, S. (2007). E-Commerce Adoption in Developing Countries: an Indonesian Study.http://www.dis.unimelb.edu.au/staff/sherahk/Papers/SISC_developing%20countrisFinal.doc. [Last Accessed December, 2007].

Lee, D., Park, J., & Ahn, J. (2001). On The Explanation of Factors Affecting E-Commerce Adoption. *Proceedings of the 22nd International Conference in Information Systems,* New Orleans, USA, 109-120.

Liljander, V., van Riel, A. C. R., & Pura, M. (2002). Customer Satisfaction with E-Services: The Case of an On-Line Recruitment Portal. In M. Bruhn & B. Stauss (Eds.), *Jahrbuch Dienstleistungsmanagement 2002 – Electronic Services* (pp.407-32), Gabler, Wiesbaden.

Lin, C. J., & Lu, H. (2000). Towards an Understanding of the Behavioral Intention to Use a Web Site. *International Journal of Information Management, 20*(3), 197-08.

Liu, X., & Whiter, R. S. (1997). The Relative Contributions of Foreign Technology and Domestic Inputs to Innovation in Chinese Manufacturing Industries. *Technovation, 17*, 119-125.

Luna, D., Peracchio, L. A., & de Juan, M. D. (2002). Cross-Cultural and Cognitive Aspects of Web Site Navigation. *Journal of the Academy of Marketing Science, 30*(4), 397-410.

Madu, C. N. (1989). Transferring Technology to Developing Countries – Critical Factors for Success. *Long Range Planning, 22*(4), 115-124.

Mason, R. O., & Mitroff, I. I. (1973). A Program for Research on Management Information Systems. *Management Science, 26*, 475-485.

McGann, S., King, J., & Lyytinen, K. (2002). *Globalization of E-Commerce: Growth and Impacts in the United States of America.* Sprouts: Working Papers on Information Environments, Systems and Organizations, *2*(2), 59-86.

Michon, R., & Chebat, J.-C. (2004). Cross-Cultural Mall Shopping Values and Habitats: a Comparison Between English- and French-Speaking Canadians. *Journal of Business Research, 57*(8), 883-892.

Moon, M. J. (2002). The Evolution of E-government among Municipalities: Rhetoric or Reality. *Public Administration Review, 62*(4), 424-33.

Nantel, J., Sénécal, S., & Mekki-Berrada, A. (2005). The Influence of "Dead-ends" on Perceived Website Usability. *Journal of E-Business, 5* (1), 1-12.

Ndou, V.D. (2004). E-government for Developing Countries: Opportunities and Challenges. *Electronic Journal of Information Systems in Developing Countries, 18*(1), 1-24.

Nussbaum, M. & Sen, A. (Ed.) (1993). *The Quality of Life.* Oxford: Clarendon Press.

OECD. (2000). *A New Economy?: The Changing Role of Innovation and Information Technology in Growth.* OECD, Paris.

Okot-Uma, R. W-O., & Caffrey, L. (Ed.) (2000). *Trusted Services and Public Key Infrastructure. Commonwealth Secretariat,* London.

Parasuraman, A., Zeithaml, V. A., & Berry, L. L. (1985). A Conceptual Model of Service Quality and Its Implications for Future Research. *Journal of Marketing, 49*, 41-50.

Radaideh, M. A., & Selim, H. M. (2004). E-Commerce: Adoption, Acceptance, and Prototyping in Abu Dhabi. *The 5th Annual U.A.E. University Research Conference.*

Rainer, R. K. Jr., & Watson, H. J. (1995). The Keys to Executive Information System Success, *Journal of Management Information System, 12*(2), 83-93.

Ribbink D., Riel, A. C. R. V., Liljander, V., & Streukens, S. (2004). Comfort Your Online Customer: Quality, Trust and Loyalty on the Internet. *Managing Service Quality, 14*(6), 446-456.

Robbins, S., & Stylianou, A. (2003). Global Corporate Web Sites: An Empirical Investigation of Content and Design. *Information & Management, 40*(3), 205-12.

Rogers, E. (1995). *Diffusion of Innovations.* The Free Press, New York, USA.

Scollon, R., & Wong, S. (2001). *Intercultural Communication.* 2nd edition. Blackwell Publishing, Oxford.

Shareef, M. A., Kumar, U., & Kumar, V. (2007). Developing Fundamental Capabilities for Successful E-Government Implementation. *Proceedings of ASAC Conference*, Ottawa, (pp. 159-177).

Shareef, M. A., Kumar U., & Kumar, V. (2008). Role of Different EC Quality Factors on E-Purchase: A Developing Country Perspective, Journal of Electronic Commerce Research, *9*(2), 92-113.

Shelanski, H. A., & Klein, P. G. (1995). Empirical Research in Transaction Cost Economics—A Review and Assessment. *Law Economics Organization, 11*(2), 335-361.

Singh, N., Zhao, H., & Hu, X., (2005). Analyzing the Cultural Content of Web Sites. A Cross-Cultural Comparison of China, India, Japan, and US. *International Marketing Review, 22*(2), 129-146.

Smith, B. A., & Merchant, E. J. (2001). Designing an Attractive Web Site: Variables of Importance. *Proceedings of the 32nd Annual Conference of the Decision Sciences Institute*, San Francisco, CA.

Sohail, M. S., & Shanmugham, B. (2002). E-Banking and Customer Preferences in Malaysia: An Empirical Investigation. *Information Sciences, 150,* 207 –217.

Spence W. (1994) Innovation: *The Communication of Change in Ideas, Practices and Products.* London, UK: Champn and Hall

Stefani, A., & Xenos, M. (2003). Greek vs. International E-commerce Systems: An Evaluation Based on User-centered Characteristics. *Proceedings the 9ᵗʰ Panhellenic Conference in Informatics,* PCI2003, Thessaloniki, (pp. 70-79).

Tornatzky, L. G., & Klein, K. J. (1982). Innovation Characteristics and Innovation Adoption-Implementation: A Meta-Analysis of Findings. *IEEE Transactions on Engineering Management EM-29*(1).

Tsikriktsis, N. (2002). Does Culture Influence Web Site Quality Expectations? An Empirical Study. *Journal of Service Research, 5*(2), 101-112.

Turban, E., & Gehrke, D. (2000). Determinants of E-commerce Website, *Human Systems Management, 19,* 111-120.

UNCTAD Report. (2003). *E-Commerce in Developed Countries Continues On Strong Growth Path.*

United Nations. (2003). *World Public Sector Report: E-Government at the Crossroads.* Department of Economic and Social Affairs, New York, United Nations Publication.

U.S. Census Bureau Report. (2007). U.S.

Uzoka, F-M. E., Seleka, G. G., & Khengere, J. (2007). E-Commerce Adoption in Developing Countries: A Case Analysis of Environmental and Organizational Inhibitors, *International Journal of Information Systems and Change Management (IJISCM), 2*(3), 232 - 260.

Vehovar, V. (2003). Security Concern, and Online Shopping. http://www.consumerweb watch.org/pdfs/Slovenia.pdf. (Accessed 8-9 June 2003).

Viswanathan, N. K., & Pick, J. B. (2005). Comparison of E-commerce in India and Mexico: An Example of Technology Diffusion in Developing Nations. *International Journal on Technology Management, 31*(1/2).

Wang, R. Y., & Strong, D. M. (1996). Beyond Accuracy, What Data Quantity Means to Data Consumers. *Journal of Management Information Systems, 1294,* 5-34.

Wangpipatwong, S., Chutimaskul, W., & Papasratorn, B. (2005). Factors Influencing the Adoption of Thai eGovernment Websites: Information Quality and System Quality Approach. *Proceedings of the 4ᵗʰ International Conference on eBusiness,* November 19-20, 2005, Bangkok, Thailand

Watson, R., Berthon, P., Pitt, L., & Zinkhan, G. (2000). *Electronic Commerce—The Strategic Perspective.* Harcourt College Publishers, 2000.

Wolfinbarger, M., & Gilly, M. C. (2003). eTailQ: Dimensionalizing, Measuring, and Predicting etail Quality. *Journal of Retailing, 79*(3), 183-98.

Wong, P-K. (2002).ICT Production and Diffusion in Asia Digital Dividends or Digital Divide? *Information Economics and Policy, 14*(2002) 167–187.

Yoo, B., & Donthu, N. (2001). Developing a Scale to Measure the Perceived Quality of an Internet Shopping Site (Sitequal). *Quarterly Journal of Electronic Commerce, 2*(1), 31-46.

Zhan C., & Dubinsky, A. J. (2003). A Conceptual Model of Perceived Customer Value in E-Commerce: A Preliminary Investigation. *Psychology and Marketing, 20*(4), 323– 347.

Zhang, P., & von Dran, G. (2002), User expectations and rankings of quality factors in different Web site domains. *International Journal of Electronic Commerce, 6*(2), 9-33.

Chapter VIII
Influencing Factors and the Acceptance of Internet and E-Business Technologies in Maritime Canada's SMEs:
An Analysis

Princely Ifinedo
Cape Breton University, Canada

ABSTRACT

This chapter examines the influence of some relevant factors on the acceptance of internet and E-Business technologies in Maritime Canada's SMEs (small- and medium-sized enterprises). To examine the influence of the factors, a research framework was developed and nine hypotheses formulated to test the various relationships. A survey was conducted and a total of 162 valid responses were obtained from mainly business owners and managers. The data supported five out of the nine hypotheses formulated. The key findings are as follows: The sampled SME's organizational readiness is positively related to their intent to use Internet/business technologies (dependant variable); the two constructs of the technology acceptance model (TAM) were found to be important mediators in the relationship between the management support construct and the dependant variable. Further, no evidence was found to suggest that management support positively influences the intent to use Internet/ business technologies among Maritime Canada's SMEs. The implications of the study's findings for policy making and research were discussed.

8.1. INTRODUCTION

More and more businesses around the world are realizing the critical importance of using information and communication technologies (ICT) in their operations (Net Impact Study Canada, 2002; 2004; Sadowski *et al.,* 2002). Such technologies are being used to reduce operational costs, improve management capabilities, access the global market, among others (Sadowski *et al.,* 2002; Mehrtens *et al.,* 2001; Martin and Milway, 2007). Accordingly, management in both large and small enterprises have realized the beneficial impacts of adopting, accepting, and investing in ICT applications including internet and e-business technologies (Wade *et al.,* 2004; Davis and Vladica, 2006; Martin and Milway, 2007). Further, data and reports continue to highlight the importance of such technologies in global e-commerce and e-business engagements, and for national economic developments (Net Impact Study Canada, 2002; 2004; Davis and Vladica, 2006; Martin and Milway, 2007). Specifically, business organizations in Canada (a developed country) are beginning to reap the benefits of employing such technologies in their commercial activities (Net Impact Study Canada 2004; Noce and Peters, 2006; The Daily, 2006). For example, Noce and Peters (2006) note that the value of e-commerce engagements alone in Canada for the year 2004 was $28 billion, an amount which Statistics Canada (2006) expects to grow in the next decade.

Despite the positive trend being reported for Canada, it has to be mentioned that it has not been clear sailing for the country's businesses – large and small – to adopt and use ICT products, including internet and e-business technologies. In fact, the widely publicized Net Impact Study Canada (2002; 2004) reports showed that small and medium enterprises (SME) lag behind larger businesses on the adoption of internet business solutions (IBS), a term that we accept as being a connotation of internet and e-business technologies. The phrase "internet and e-business technologies" was borrowed from a study conducted by Davis and Vladica (2006) in the same region as this study's, wherein such technologies as email, the Internet, and Website were given as examples. These are related, useful technologies for e-commerce and e-business engagements, and in fact Sadowski *et al.* (2002, p.76) note that "in establishing a new connection to the Internet [business environment], new users are required to adopt a series of related new technologies."

The focus of this chapter will be on the acceptance of such technologies in Canadian SMEs. It is appropriate to pay attention to SMEs, given the universal knowledge of the relevance of such businesses. In a nutshell, SMEs serve as engines for employment generation and national economic growth. According to the Net Impact Study Canada (2002, p.2), "Canadian SMEs deliver 60% of Canada's economic output, generate 80% of national employment and 85% of new jobs." Suffice it to say that a broader understanding of the adoption of internet and e-business technologies in Canadian SMEs will benefit both policy makers and researchers. Importantly, the Net Impact Study reports sought to alert Canadian policy makers to two debilitating issues: a) the reluctance of some SMEs in the country to adopt IBS, b) SMEs lag behind larger businesses on the adoption of internet business solutions. It comes as no surprise, therefore, when the Net Impact Study Canada (2004, p.1.) sounded a note of caution to policy makers and industry leaders in the country by stating that:

"A lukewarm SME response to IBS adoption may weaken any national strategy to bolster Canada's international competitiveness. The challenge for industry leaders and policy makers is to bring lagging SMEs online and deepen the capabilities of those already online. The cost of inaction is to have this vital sector of the economy stall at current levels of engagement while other nations catch up or increase their lead."

This call is pertinent to and, to some extent, has motivated this study. It is worth noting that this study is not designed to provide all the answers as to why some Canadian SMEs appear reluctant to adopt internet and e-business technologies. An attempt to address those concerns would be beyond of the scope of this paper. On the other hand, this research aims at shedding light on the nature of relevant factors affecting the acceptance of internet and e-business technologies among SMEs in a particular geographical region of Canada. Larger firms are excluded from this exploratory study because the literature suggests that SMEs differ from larger enterprises on how resource, i.e., financial and knowledge considerations impact ICT adoption and success issues (Thong *et al.,* 1996; Daniel and Grimshaw, 2002; Ifinedo, 2006). This research will draw on a theoretical framework in the information system (IS) literature as well as other relevant insights.

8.2. BACKGROUND INFORMATION

Reports in Canada indicate that the country's international competitiveness may be negatively impacted if efforts are not directed towards addressing the reticence of some SMEs to adopt relevant internet commerce technologies (Net Impact Study Canada, 2002; 2004). It was also shown that half the number of SMEs in the country has adopted such technologies. How are SMEs defined in Canada, and why are they important for the country? Statistics Canada (2006), generally defines SMEs as firms with fewer than 500 employees. Canadian SMEs provide more jobs to the population than do larger firms, and they contribute significantly to national economic growth (Net Impact Study Canada, 2004). Without a doubt, one of the major concerns for Canadian's policy makers would be to gain some understanding of the nature of relevant factors that might impact the acceptance of internet and e-business technologies among the country's SMEs.

This study was designed to provide insights in this regard. Due to the limited resource available for this study, it would be impossible to sample views on the research's theme across the country. Rather, a region of the country, i.e., the Maritime or Atlantic region, which apparently lags behind the rest of the country on variety of issues including the use of the Internet for business and commerce (Industry Canada, 2001), is chosen for illustrative purposes. This study will include views of SMEs in the Maritime region with provinces including Nova Scotia, Newfoundland and Labrador, Prince Edward Island, and New Brunswick. Indeed, larger and more economically endowed regions such as Alberta and British Columbia are among the leaders regarding the use of Internet for business and commerce (The Daily, 2006; Statistics Canada, 2006). Such regions are excluded in this preliminary study for obvious reasons.

Other researchers in Canada have discussed themes similar to this one. For example, Noce and Peters (2006) examined the barriers to e-commerce adoption in Canadian small-sized business organizations. Davis and Vladica (2006) reported findings on the distribution and use of internet technologies and e-business solutions in one of the provinces in Maritime Canada. Using Canadian businesses, Wade et al. (2004) studied the net impact of e-commerce on firms' performances. Others have investigated the business value of ICT products in SMEs (e.g., Davis and Vladica, 2006; Martin and Milway, 2007). None has studied the nature of some relevant factors impacting the adoption internet and e-business technologies among Canadian SMEs as this research intends to do. This work will draw on the technology acceptance model (TAM) as well as the suggestion that other factors including management support and organizational readiness of the adopting organization are relevant in the discourse. Next, well briefly discuss the TAM and the other factors.

8.2.1. The Theoretical Framework: The Technology Acceptance Model (TAM) and the Other Influences

Various researchers have used different theoretical frameworks in discussing technology acceptance and adoption (Igbaria *et al.,* 1997). Without a doubt, the technology acceptance model (TAM) is regarded as the most widely used theoretical framework for assessing the acceptance of technologies in the literature (see e.g. Legris *et al.,* 2003). The TAM was developed by Davis (1989). Additionally, the TAM has been shown to be relevant for small organizations in particular (Igbaria *et al.,* 1997). The TAM is illustrated in Figure 8.1 below. It proposes that users' acceptance of a new IS can be predicted by the users' perceptions. These perceptions include the ease of use and usefulness of Information technology (IT) (Davis, 1989). The three core constructs in TAM include the following: perceived ease of use, perceived usefulness, and usage. The conception of the TAM shows that perceived usefulness mediates the effect of perceived ease of use on the intention to use, and at the same time directly influences the construct of intention to use (Davis, 1989). The perceived ease of use describes "The degree to which a person believes that using a particular system would be free of effort" (Davis, 1989, p. 320). Perceived usefulness describes the user's perceptions of the expected benefits derived from using a particular IS system (Davis, 1989). Intention to use is the dependent variable in TAM.

There are limitations in the TAM. In critically reviewing the literature on the use of the TAM in explaining why people accept IS. Researchers, including Igbaria *et al.* (1997) and Legris *et al.* (2003), argue that the TAM may be too simplistic in predicting intention to use of computer technologies. Accordingly, Igbaria *et al.* (1997) and others modeled factors as "Management support" as an external influence on the TAM. Indeed, the literature has suggested that top management support, commitment, and knowledge of technological innovations are crucially important for the success of IT adoption in small-sized businesses in general (Thong *et al.,* 1996; Igbaria *et al.,* 1997), and for the successful acceptance of e-commerce and internet technologies adoption by SMEs in particular (e.g. Mirchandani and Motwani, 2001; Yu, 2006; Al-Qirim, 2007). Likewise, the acceptance of e-commerce and related IT innovations has been known to be strongly influenced by the organization's ability to understand and assimilate the importance of such applications in their operations (Boynton *et al.,* 1994). In particular, Boynton *et al.* (1994) asserts that the organizational environment in which a business operates is linked to its ability to absorb and use IT-related technologies. In other words, the firm's culture, values, etc. would impact its ability to use new innovations (Grandon and Pearson, 2004). Mirchandani and Motwani (2001), Mehrtens *et al.* (2001), and Grandon and Pearson (2004), discussing the adoption of internet and e-commerce, referred to this competence as organizational readiness, and they noted strongly the influence of the adoption of e-commerce solutions by SMEs. In brief, organization readiness refers to the knowledge of IT and Internet among organizational members. The research framework with the hypotheses is illustrated in Figure 8.1. The discussion of the formulation of the hypotheses follows in the next section.

8.2.2. The Research Hypotheses

It has been accepted that perceived usefulness mediates the effect of perceived ease of use on intention to use (Davis, 1989). And, the constructs of perceived usefulness and perceived ease of use have been reported to positively impact intention to use of IT (Davis, 1989). Evidence of this is readily available in the relevant literature (Igbaria *et al.* 1997). With respect to e-business and internet technologies, research (Mirchandani and Motwani, 2001; Daniel and Grimshaw, 2002; Grandon and Pearson, 2004) have indicated that when both perceived ease of use and perceived usefulness of internet-enabled applications are high, this usually leads to such technologies being accepted by organizational members. In light of the foregoing discussion, we predict that the acceptance of internet and e-business technologies among SMEs in the Maritime region of Canada will be positively influenced by perceived ease of use and usefulness of such technologies. We therefore hypothesize that:

H1: Perceived ease of use will have a positive effect on perceived usefulness of internet/e-business technologies

H2: Perceived usefulness of internet/e-business technologies is positively related to the intent to use such technologies

H3: Perceived ease of use of internet/e-business technologies is positively related to the intent to use of such technologies

Regarding the two non-traditional TAM constructs, past research suggests that support from top managers and the readiness of the firm to absorb new ideas tend to augur well for the acceptance of technological innovations (e.g., Iocovou *et al.,* 1995; Igbaria *et al.,* 1997; Grandon and Pearson, 2004; Yu, 2006; Al-Qirim, 2007). This is because top managers act as change agents in the adoption process of technological innovations (Thong *et al.,* 1996; Igbaria *et al.,* 1997). When top managers in SMEs understand the importance of a computer technology, they tend to play a crucial role in influencing other organizational members as well as committing resources to the adoption of such technologies (Thong *et al.,* 1996; Yu, 2006). Conversely, where management support is low or unavailable, technology acceptance and adoption tend to be placed on the back-burners of organizational issues (e.g. Igbaria *et al.,* 1997; Yu, 2006). Likewise, the acceptance of IT-related technologies tend to be more favorable in organizations where the right type of culture and values exist, and where there is a good understanding of the relevance and benefits of the technology in question (Boynton *et al.,* 1994; Grandon and Pearson, 2004; Mirchandani and Motwani, 2001; Al-Qirim, 2007). The foregoing discussion permits us to formulate the set of hypotheses below:

Figure 8.1. The research framework

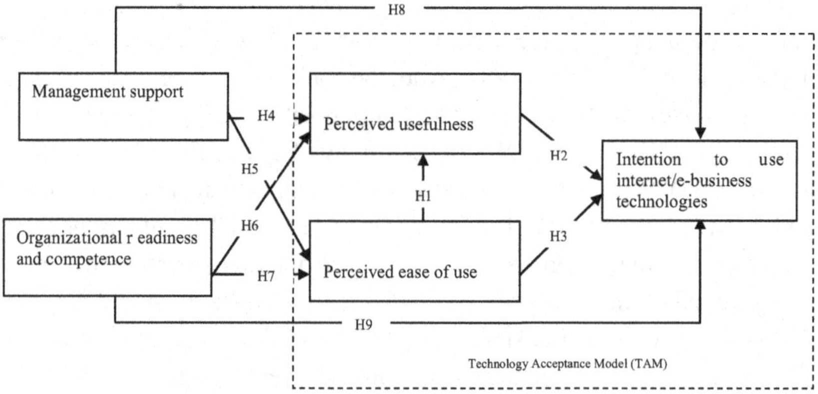

H4: Management support will positively influence the perceived usefulness of internet/e-business technologies

H5: Management support will positively influence the perceived ease of use of internet/e-business technologies

H6: Organizational readiness and competence will positively influence the perceived usefulness of internet/e-business technologies

H7: Organizational readiness and competence will positively influence the perceived ease of use of internet/ e-business technologies

H8: Organizational readiness and competence will positively influence the intention to use internet/e-business technologies

H9: Management support will positively influence the intention to use internet/e-business technologies

8.3. RESEARCH METHODOLOGY

The researcher sampled SMEs generated from telephones directories in the four provinces in Maritime Canada. Two research assistants used a variation of the stratified sampling method -- i.e., every odd number firm was included, and larger firms omitted if it falls on such -- was used to select participating SMEs from across such industries as auto dealership, insurance, manufacturing, retail, and so forth. Organizational informants including owners and presidents were contacted. Each received a packet consisting of a cover letter, a questionnaire, and a self-addressed, stamped envelope. In all, one thousand and seven hundred (1700) questionnaires were mailed in November, 2007 and responses were collected until February, 2008.

8.3.1. Data Collection

Of note, participation in the study was voluntary. Respondents were assured that their individual responses would be treated as confidential. A part of the question- naire is provided (See Appendix). To ensure data validity and reliability, sixteen (16) knowledgeable individuals (i.e., 4 faculty, 2 SMEs top managers, and 10 col- lege students) completed the initial draft of the questionnaire. Comments received improved the quality of the questionnaire mailed to participants. The majority of the measures used were taken from previously validated sources (e.g. Davis, 1989; Thong *et al.*, 1996; Yu, 2006) and were anchored on a 6-point Likert scale, ranging from Strongly disagree (1) to Strongly agree (6), on which participants were asked to indicate an appropriate choice. An extra column was also provided, which was labeled "Not Applicable" (NA). The measures in the TAM constructs came from Davis (1989) and Igbaria *et al.* (1997).

The measures used to operationalize organizational readiness and competence were modified from Mirchandani and Motwani (2001) and Grandon and Pearson (2004). The Appendix shows the measures in the questionnaire, and their reliabili- ties scores. Clearly, the Cronbach alpha for each dimension is above the 0.70 limit recommended by Nunnally (1978), indicating reasonably high reliability of the research measures and constructs. A total of 170 responses were received, of which, 162 were considered valid. The excluded eight (8) responses were either not filled out properly or had a high number of missing entries. From the number sent out, 121 questionnaires were returned as undeliverable due to changed or incomplete addresses. Thus, the effective response rate for the survey is 10.3%., which is good for a study of this nature. Table 8.1 shows the participants' demographics and the characteristics of the responding firms. The participants' average work experience was 13.4 years. The workforce ranged from 1 to 500 employees, with a median of 5 employees.

8.4. DATA ANALYSIS AND RESULTS

The PLS (Partial Least Squares) approach of the structural equation modeling (SEM) technique was used to examine the relationships among the factors or constructs. There are two main approaches: PLS (Partial Least Squares) and covariance-based SEM. The PLS approach was chosen for its capability in accommodating small-sized samples (Chin, 1998). Furthermore, PLS recognizes two components of a causal model: the measurement model and the structural model. The measurement model consisted of relationships among the factors of interest (the observed variables) and the measures underlying each construct. PLS demonstrates the construct validity of the research instrument (i.e. how well the instrument measures what it purports to measure). The two main dimensions are the convergent validity and the discriminant validity. The convergent validity (also known as the composite reliability) assesses the extent to which items on a scale are theoretically related. On the other hand, the structural model provides information on how well the hypothesized relationships predict the theoretical model. The R2 indicates the percentage of a construct's variance in the model, while the path coefficients (β) indicate the strengths of relationships among constructs (Chin, 1998).

Table 8.1. Demographic information of the sample (n = 162)

	Freq.	(%)		Freq.	(%)
Gender			Education		
Male	94	58	Primary school	6	3.7
Female	66	40.7	High school	36	22.2
Missing	2	1.2	College/university	79	48.8
			Post-graduate	31	19.1
			Others	10	6.2
Age			Annual sales revenues ($)		
Less 20 year	1	1.2	Less $500, 000	75	46.3
21 - 30	23	14.2	$500,000 - $ 1 million	32	19.8
31 - 40	27	16.7	$ 1.1 - $5 million	35	21.6
41 - 50	55	34	$ 5.1 - $ 10 million	7	4.3
51- 60	47	29	$ 10.1 - $ 20 million	9	5.6
Above 60 year	8	4.9	$ 20.1 - $50 million	4	2.5
			"$" = Canadian dollar		
Job Titles			Workforce		
Manager, Accountant	43	26.6	Less 50 employees	146	90.1
Owner, Proprietor	64	39.5	51 – 99 employees	10	6.2
Vice President, Director	29	17.9	100 – 500 employees	5	3.1
Others	26	16	Missing	1	0.6
Type of business					
Adverting,, Marketing	12	7.4			
Auto Dealership,	12	7.4			
Repairs	6	3.7			
Construction	8	4.9			
Design outfits, Decora-	4	2.5			
tor	6	3.7			
Education, Driving	17	10.5			
School	17	10.5			
Hotel, Hospitality	33	20.4			
Insurance, Accounting	9	5.6			
firms	38	23.4			
Manufacturing					
Retailer, Wholesaler					
Real estate, Legal firms					
Others					

8.4.1. Assessing the Structural Model

The squared R (R2) and the paths' coefficients (β) were generated by PLS Graph 3.0 and are shown in Figure 8.2. The R2 is 0.36 which suggests that the contingency factors explained 36 of the variance in the intent to use internet/e-business technologies construct. Indeed, the R2 of 0.36 is adequate for the study, indicating that the results in general are supportive of the research model. Chin (1998) notes that both the β and the R2 are sufficient for analysis, and β values between 0.20 and 0.30 are adequate for meaningful interpretations.

8.4.2. Assessing the Measurement Model

PLS Graph 3.0 – the PLS software developed by Prof Chin – was used to compute the composite reliability (convergent validity) of each construct; the item loadings were also provided (see the Appendix). Chin (1998) notes that item loadings and composite reliabilities greater than 0.7 are considered adequate. In assessing the discriminant validity, the square root of the average variance extracted (AVE) for each construct, which provides a measure of the variance shared between a construct and its indicators, is checked. Chin (1998) recommend AVE values of at least 0.50 and that the square root of AVE should be larger than off-diagonal elements. Table 8.2 presents the inter-correlations among the constructs, AVE and the square root of AVE. The research's measures indicate that the constructs are distinct and unidimensional.

Figure 8.2. The PLS graph 3.0 results for the research framework

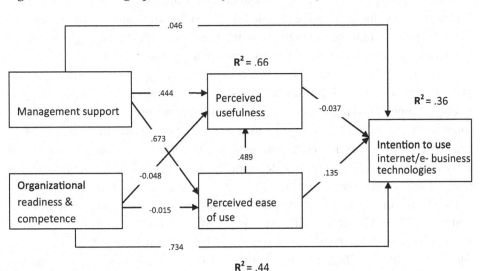

Table 8.2. The correlations among the constructs and the AVE

	AVE	1	2	3	4	5
1: Management support	0.511	0.715				
2: Organizational readiness and competence	0.531	0.636	0.729			
3: Perceived usefulness	0.685	0.727	0.591	0.828		
4: Perceived ease of use	0.559	0.660	0.548	0.756	0.748	
5: Intent to use internet/e-business technologies	0.765	0.722	0.824	0.533	0.540	0.877

8.5. FINDINGS AND DISCUSSIONS

Table 8.3 provides a summary of the results. The data strongly supports four of the nine (9) hypotheses (i.e., H1, H4, H5, and H9) and moderately supports one: H3. The results, however, do not support the other four hypotheses (H2, H6, H7, and H8). Next, we discuss the set of supported hypotheses, which is then followed by discussions of the unsupported ones.

In accordance with hypothesis H1, perceived ease of use will have a positive effect on perceived usefulness of internet/e-business technologies. This prediction suggests that a higher level of the usefulness of internet/e-business technologies would be brought about when SMEs perceived such technologies were not difficult to use. This seems to be the viewpoint of the sampled SMEs in this study. Hypothesis H2 stated that perceived ease of use of internet/e-business technologies is positively related to the intent to use of such technologies. This hypothesis is moderately supported by the data. As Legris *et al.* (2003) noted in their study, it is not uncommon for studies using the TAM to produce results that are not totally clear or inconsistent. Suffice it to say that among the sampled SMEs in the Maritime region of Canada, the data suggests that the intent to use of internet/e-business technologies is higher when firms perceive such applications as not being difficult to use.

In Hypothesis H2, it was stated that management support will positively influence the perceived usefulness of internet/e-business technologies. The data analysis strongly supports this prediction. The result could be interpreted as meaning that the intention to use internet technologies in an SME is higher when the management of such an enterprise has an understanding of the benefits and impacts of such technologies, and then are able to provide the necessary support for the entrenchment of such applications in its organization. Other studies investigating the diffusion of ICT among SMEs in Canada have presented a finding similar to this study's (e.g., Noce and Peters, 2006; Martin and Milway, 2007). Similarly, studies from other regions of the world have offered results consistent with the foregoing (e.g., Mirchandani and Motwani, 2001; Yu, 2006; Al-Qirim, 2007). The data analysis strongly supported

Table 8.3. Summary of the results

Hypothesis	Path coefficient (β)	t-Value for the path	Result
Perceived ease of use → Perceived usefulness (H1)	0.489	1.8643*	Supported
Perceived usefulness → Intention to use internet/ e-business technologies (H2)	-0.037	0.1423	Not Supported
Perceived ease of use → Intention to use of internet/e-business technologies (H3)	0.135	1.0179	Moderately Supported
Management support → Perceived usefulness of internet/e-business technologies (H4)	0.444	1.8951*	Supported
Management support → Perceived ease of use of internet/e-business technologies (H5)	0.673	5.0135**	Supported
Organizational readiness → Perceived usefulness of internet/e-business technologies (H6)	-0.048	0.2415	Not Supported
Organizational readiness → Perceived ease of use of internet/e-business technologies (H7)	-0.015	0.0791	Not Supported
Management support → Intention to use internet/e-business technologies (H8)	0.046	0.2642	Not Supported
Organizational readiness → Intention to use internet/e-business technologies (H9)	0.734	4.9620**	Supported

* significant at p< 0.01,   ** significant at p< 0.001 (two-tailed)

hypothesis H9. The result shows that a positive relationship organizational readiness and the intent to use internet and e-business technologies exist. That is, the acceptance of ICT tends to be more favorable in SMEs with a good understanding of the relevance and benefits of the technology being considered (Boynton *et al.,* 1994; Grandon and Pearson, 2004). To some extent, the result here corroborates the findings on the adoption of ICT products in Canada that researchers in the country, including Martin and Milway (2007), have made public. They noted that one of the biggest problems facing the growth of ICT use among SMEs is a lack of organizational readiness, as well as poor levels of information awareness of the benefits and impacts of relevant technologies among owners and employees of such businesses. A plausible explanation for the lack of support for the remaining hypotheses might be related to the study's design, the diversity in the industry sampled firms, among others. With regard to hypothesis H2, which is related to the TAM core, studies have shown that it may not be out of place to have dissenting results (Legris *et al.,* 2003). The direct link between management support and the dependent construct is unsupported, perhaps as result of the foregoing insights.

8.6. CONCLUSION

This chapter aims at providing empirical information on the nature of some relevant factors affecting the intent to use internet/e-business technologies by SMEs based in Maritime Canada. The research study has both practical and academic implications. In the context of the research setting in particular and for the country in general, the results may suggest that SMEs would be inclined to adopt internet/e-business technologies and related ICT solutions if they perceived such applications to be easy to use. The implication of this is that external agents, including suppliers and vendors of such e-business technologies, have to emphasize the ease of use of such technologies rather than merely underscore their usefulness. This viewpoint is consistent with that espoused by local researchers (Martin and Milway, 2007) suggesting that the supply side (vendors of such application) could do more for the growth of internet/e-business solution among SMEs in the country if these providers paid more attention to the wares that they offer SMEs in the country. It could be argued that less complex products and appropriate education would go a long way here. Interestingly, the relationship between the management support construct and the intention to use internet/e-business technologies for sampled SMEs is not supported.

However, the data analysis indicated that when management provide necessary support, interest, and have a clear vision as to use of such applications, the perceived usefulness and ease of use of such technologies tend to be high. (The two core constructs of the TAM act as mediators in the relationships between the management support variable and the dependant construct). This would suggest that for the use of internet business solutions to grow in the Maritime region and perhaps in other regions of the country, the management of small businesses would have to acquire attitudes supportive of emerging ICT innovations. In the same vein, SME's management could benefit from education designed to accentuate the impacts of such technological innovations in their operations. Needless to say, the apparent reluctance in adopting IBS reported in the Net Impact Study Canada (2004) might have stemmed from a lack of proper education as well as negative attitudes among decision makers in SMEs regarding the impact of internet technologies on their businesses. Feedback from one owner of an SME reads, "My business is very small and I keep quite busy with word of mouth and the yellow pages." This might be indicative that the right kind of information may not be available to small businesses owners. In order for small businesses in the Maritime region (and for Canada as a whole) to change the unimpressive statistics noted in the opening section of this paper, owners need to be made aware of the benefits of using e-business solutions. Organizational readiness and competence with respect to knowledge about ICT benefits lead invariably to higher levels of need to use internet/e-business technologies. Other local authors (Martin and Milway, 2007) seem to echo this sentiment.

Similarly, the academic community benefits from this discourse as well. A study of this nature expands the discussion on factors affecting the use of internet/e-business technologies in a relatively poor part of a developed country, Canada. Results from this study may be pertinent to theory development in global IT management as it relates to the adoption of internet business solutions. In general, the study's results lend support to some prior studies in the literature. For example, the importance of management support and organizational readiness were found to be vitally important in the adoption of internet and e-business technologies by other researchers (Mirchandani and Motwani, 2001; Mehrtens *et al.,* 2003; Yu, 2006; Al-Qirim, 2007). Evidence from this work affirms this viewpoint. Most importantly, this work showed that the amount of variation explained by the TAM model can be improved upon significantly by the inclusion of relevant factors. Igbaria *et al.* (1997) and others have made assertion in this regard. There are inherent limitations in this study. It is exploratory and the sample selected may not have been random. Personal bias may have been an issue, as only the views of a single respondent were used per firm. The measures for some of the constructs could be improved. This study presents the viewpoints of SMEs in Maritime Canada; it is difficult to say whether the findings can be replicated in other regions of the country. The research did not control for the types of internet/e-business technologies in use by the SMEs. The study lumped together the various internet/e-business technologies such as email, website ownership, internet, and so forth. It is possible that by not distinguishing between technologies in the study, the findings might have been amplified or downplayed.

It has to be noted that future studies examining a similar theme could incorporate the impact of relevant inter- and intra-organizational factors such as market pressures and government support. Also, this present study could be replicated in other Canadian regions. When results from such endeavors begin to emerge, will we be able understand why Canadian businesses, especially smaller ones, appear to lag behind in accepting e-business. Additionally, studies are needed to affirm or reject the findings in this study. E-business technologies' acceptance in both large and SMEs could be compared. Lastly, better insights and easily verifiable results could emerge if a single internet/e-business technology were used for a given study. This would ensure that confounding effects emanating from the use of diversified technologies would be controlled. Future research should take note of this detail.

ACKNOWLEDGMENT

Funding for this research was provided by RP grant (#8241) of Cape Breton University (CBU), Canada. Of note, a version of this article was presented at AMCIS 2008, Toronto, Canada.

REFERENCES

Al-Qirim, N. (2007). An Empirical Investigation of a Usage Model of E-Commerce Technologies in Small Businesses in New Zealand: Theory Extension and Implications. *IJEB, 5*(1), 42-64.

Boynton, A., Zmud, R., & Jacobs, G. (1994). The Influence of IT in Large Organizations. *MIS Quarterly, 18*(3), 299-320.

Chin, W. (1998). Issues and Opinion on Structural Equation Modeling. *MIS Quarterly, 22*(1), vii-xvi.

Daniel, E. M., & Grimshaw, D. J. (2002). An Exploratory Comparisons of E-Commerce Adoption in Large and Small Enterprise. *JIT, 17*(3), 33-147.

Davis, F. D. (1989). Perceived Usefulness, Perceived Ease of Use, and User Acceptance of Information Technology. *MIS Quarterly, 13*(3), 319-339.

Davis, C. H., & Vladica, F. (2006). Use of Internet Technologies and E-Business Solutions: A Structural Model of Sources of Business Value among Canadian Micro-Enterprises. *Proceedings of the 39th Annual HICSS Conference,* Hawaii.

Grandon, E. E., & Pearson, J. (2004). Electronic Commerce Adoption: An Empirical Study of Small and Medium U.S. Businesses. *Information and Management, 42*(1), 197-216.

Igbaria, M., Zinatelli, N., Cragg, P., & Cavaye, A. L. M. (1997). Personal Computing Acceptance Factors in Small Firms: A Structural Equation Model. *MIS Quarterly, 21*(3), 279-305.

Ifinedo, P, (2006). Key Information Systems Management Issues in Estonia for the 2000s and a Comparative Analysis. *JGITM, 9*(2), 22- 44.

Industry Canada (2001). Micro-Enterprises Survey 2000: A Progress Report Small Business Policy http://www.ic.gc.ca/epic/site/sbrp-rppe.nsf/en/rd01992e.html.

Legris, P. Ingham, J. & Collerette, P. (2003). Why Do People Use Information Technology? A Critical Review of the Technology Acceptance Model. *Information and Management, 40*(3), 191-204.

Martin, R. L., & Milway, J. B. (2007). Enhancing the Productivity of Small and Medium Enterprises through the Greater Adoption of Information and Communication Technology. *Information and Communication Technology Council Report*, http://www.ictc-ctic.ca/en/.

Mehrtens, J., Cragg, P. B., & Mills, A. M. (2001). A Model of Internet Adoption By SMEs. *Information and Management, 39*(3), 165-176.

Mirchandani, A. A., & Motwani, J. (2001). Understanding Small Business Electronic Adoption: An Empirical Analysis. *JCIS, 41*(3), 70-73.

Net Impact Study Canada (2002). *The SME Experience - A Preliminary Report - November 2002 - Canadian e-Business Initiative.* http://www.cebi.ca/epic/site/ecic-ceac.nsf/vwapj/NISME-e.pdf/$file/NI SME-e.pdf.

Net Impact Canada IV (2004). *Strategies for Increasing SME Engagement in the e-Economy.* (Net Impact IV). http://www.cebi.ca/epic/site/ecic-ceac.nsf/vwapj/NI4-e.pdf/$file/NI4-e.pdf.

Noce, A., & Peters, C. (2006). Barriers to Electronic Commerce in Canada: A Size of Firm and Industry Analysis (III-C). *Industry Canada Electronic Commerce Branch*, Ottawa, Canada.

Nunnaly, J. C. (1978). *Psychometric Theory.* New York, NY: McGraw-Hill

Thong, J. Y. L., Yap, C. S., & Raman, K. S. (1996). Top Management Support, External Expertise and Information Systems Implementation in Small Business. *ISR, 7*(2), 248-267.

The Daily (2006). *E-commerce: Shopping on the Internet.* http://www.statcan.ca/Daily/English/061101/d061101a.htm.

Sadowski, B. M., Maitland, C., & van Dongen, J. (2002). Strategic Use of the Internet by Small- Ad Medium-Sized Companies: An Exploratory Study. *Information and Economic Policy, 14*(1), 75-93.

Statistics Canada (2006). Survey of Electronic Commerce and Technology. http://e-com.ic.gc.ca/epic/ site/ecic-ceac.nsf/en/gv00152e.html.

Wade, M., Johnston, D., & McClean, R. (2004). Exploring the Net Impact of Internet Business Solution Adoption on SME Performance. *IJEB, 2*(4), 336-350.

Yu, C-S. (2006). Influences on Taiwanese SME E-Marketplace Adoption Decisions. *JGITM, 9*(2), 5-21.

APPENDIX

Table A1. The questionnaire measures and the reliability scores

	Item loading	Cronbach alpha	Composite reliability
Ease of Use			
Eou1: The use of internet/e-business technologies would be clear and understandable for us	0.7590		
Eou2: Learning to use internet/e-business technologies would be easy for our employees	0.8874	0.940	0.832
Eou3: Overall, internet/e-business technologies would be easy to use in our organization	0.7503		
Eou4: It would be easy to become skilful at using internet/ e-business technologies in our firm.	0.7543		
Perceived Usefulness			
PUS1: Using internet/e-business technologies would make work easier for our employees/managers.	0.8558		
PUS2: Using internet/e-business technologies would increase employees' & managers' productivity.	0.7050	0.937	0.913
PUS3: Using internet/e-business technologies would increase the performance of our employees.	0.8893		
PUS4: Our employees and managers would find internet/ e-business technologies useful in their jobs.	0.9020		
PUS5: Using internet/e-business technologies would provide information for strategic decisions.	0.9127		
Management Support			
MS1: Management is interested in the use of internet/e-business technologies in our operations.	0.6667		
MS2: Management is supportive of the use of internet/ e-business technologies in our operations.	0.7343	0.943	0.794
MS3: Our business has a clear vision regarding the use of internet/e-business technologies.	0.6772		
MS4: Management communicates the need for internet/ e-business technologies usage in the firm.	0.8150		
Organizational Readiness and Competence			

continued on following page

Table A1. continued

OCR1: Our firm knows how information technology (IT) can be used to support our operations.	0.6489		
OCR2: Our firm has a good understanding of how internet/ e-business technologies can be used in our business.	0.8625	0.911	0.814
OCR3: We have the necessary technical, managerial and other skills to implement internet/e-business technologies.	0.7148		
OCR4: Our business values and norms would not prevent us from adopting internet/e-business technologies in our operations.	0.7658		
Intention to Adopt Internet/e-business Technologies			
IntAD1: I am certain my firm/organization will adopt Internet/e-business technologies someday.	0.8954	0.943	0.907
IntAD2: My firm is committed to adopting Internet/e-business technologies in the future.	0.8481		
IntAD3: There is likelihood that my firm will adopt Internet/ e-business technologies in the future.	0.8793		

To what extent do you agree or disagree with the following statements. (Not Applicable (N/A) = 0, 1 = Strongly disagree, 2 = Disagree, 3 = Somewhat disagree, 4 = somewhat agree, 5 = Agree, 6 = Strongly agree)

Chapter IX
Effect of Proliferation and Resistance of Internet Economy:
Understanding Impact of Information and Communication Technology in Developing Countries

ABSTRACT

Information and communication technology (ICT) is the prime driving force of Internet economy. Therefore, before implementing E-Commerce (EC) and E-Government (EG) projects, it is a vital issue to investigate the capability of developing countries to adopt ICT and reveal the impact of adopting ICT among society. However, it is observed that in developing countries, rural and urban population have significant digital divide. We argue that the purposes of implementing Internet-based projects, particularly EG, can only be accomplished and full benefits can be realized if rural population of developing countries has that ability to adopt ICT, the main driver of EG, and if ICT has positive impact on rural population in technological, economical, and social perspectives. Therefore, it is the prime motive of policy makers of developing countries to study the impact of ICT in capability development among citizens prior to launching EG. To study the impact of ICT on both rural and urban population separately through a vertical survey, this research proposes separate ad-hoc and post-hoc frameworks.

9.1. INTRODUCTION

Virtual communal marketing in Internet economy refers to managing, organizing, and marketing in the virtual community that incorporates public involvement in the development of Internet economy in stakeholders interface. A virtual community could fulfill various kinds of needs, such as transaction, interest, fantasy, and relationship (Armstrong and Hagel, 1996; Hagel and Arthur, 1997). Virtual communal marketing enables public administrators to identify the expectations, characteristics, and behavioral intentions of different stakeholders, which they can utilize to develop the service quality dimensions of global web-based services. The Internet potentially offers individuals, institutions, small and large businesses, all communities, and all levels of governments with new opportunities for learning, interacting, transacting business, and developing their social and economic potential. Information and communication technology (ICT) and the advent and proliferation of the Internet has changed the structure and performance of the global market and consumers' perceptions and purchasing behavior.

Internet-based economy has created enormous opportunities not only for business corporations which is generally termed as Electronic-business or customer oriented Electronic-commerce but also for governments in wider space particularly known as Electronic-government (EG). An EG or EC transaction is any transaction completed over a computer-mediated network that involves the transfer of ownership or rights to use goods or services. Transactions occur within selected transaction processes, and are completed when agreement is reached between buyers and sellers to transfer the ownership or rights to use the goods or services. However, the sphere of the scope of EG is much wider than EC. Alternatively, EC is only a fragmented part of EG. EG is about complete relationships with civic institutions and the foundation of our next-generation states and communities. Understanding what citizens and businesses want and how government, the private sector, and other institutions will be integrated is the vital function of EG. Benchmarking the online revolution in public and private sectors requires new discourses about policy issues, political realities and their impact on the satisfaction of different stakeholders (Sakowicz, 2007). The EG model should also comprehend the evolution of ICT, the reformation of public administration, and the integration of stakeholders. In this chapter of the book, we will explore and illustrate the overall impact of the Internet economy among developing countries. The chapter does not focus much on the developed countries, because the positive effect of ICT on developed countries is quite obvious. Moreover, developed countries already have utilized and also are capitalizing full features of ICT in the Internet economy by launching EG in public sector and also guiding EC in private sector. However, developing countries are at the preliminary stage in this context. And in terms of capability to capitalize and use ICT in government and private sectors, the status of developing countries is not explicit. There is a controversy whether ICT intense projects either in public level or in private level would spur digital divide and would it ultimately fail to get the desired result in developing countries. So, we feel it is a challenging issue to address and evaluate the impact of proliferation of the Internet economy on the developing countries for the sake of globalization.

Internet economy is the latest business model both for corporations and governments. International or domestic business organizations, especially of developed countries--- all are very much enthusiastic to explore Internet based business operations for supply chain management known as E-business and customer-based transactions known as E-commerce. At the same time different governments, especially of developed countries are also very aggressive in implementing Internet-based government service which also includes business operations, known as E-government (EG). Throughout the world, governments are realizing the potential of placing traditional government services online. This shift is considered to be a major transformation, not only an introduction of new technology. Varying degrees of complexity and success are reported from different parts of the world. State-of-the-art examples include Canada, Singapore, and the USA. Depending on the interaction between government and the prospective users, EG has been classified with different names by researchers. European Union (2002) classified EG into two major groups depending on the services offered by EG. These are: G2C: Government to Citizens and G2B: Government to Business. The most popular form of EG is G2C, i.e., government to citizen. By G2C EG governments provide services to citizens and access to government information through government web pages. On the other hand, citizens can receive effective and efficient services from these government communications. It formulates the traditional model of EG, and is the most widespread use.

The G2B category focuses on the interaction between government and businesses on the ability to reduce cost and gather better information. This allows the government to perform different commercial activities related to business organizations, like purchase items, pay invoices, and conduct business in a more cost-effective method. This also helps the government in obtaining data to assist in decision making. Now, it is the responsibility of governments to post information for business organizations in their websites (US Department of Justice, 2002). Private organizations collect information and interact with these websites according to their needs.

Proliferation of Internet-based economy operated through EG and EC especially in developed countries is noteworthy. Business organizations are always striving to succeed in their Internet-based business model and are very much enthusiastic to extend their business periphery from local to international markets. Challenges and competitive advantages of launching Electronic-based business operations for private organizations are addressed, discussed, and revealed in chapters five and six of this book. However, from country and customer perspectives, while developed countries are very keen and devoted to expand Internet-based economy both in public and private services, developing countries and also their citizens are sometimes reluctant to explore and adopt Internet-based economy. Therefore, it is a challenging issue to conceptualize the purposes of proliferation of Internet-based economy and possible resistance from country and customer perspectives. Consequently, the very important intertwined topic which might reflect the ontological and epistemological paradigm of reluctant behavior of consumers and governments of developing countries is a potential issue to be discussed here. This is: understanding the effect of information and communication technology (ICT) in developing countries. Since ICT is the main driving force for both EG and EC, its adoption and impact on developing countries is a significant and relevant issue to be discussed to conceptualize such issues as i) purposes of proliferation of Internet-based economy, ii) resistance or barriers against this proliferation, and iii) impacts of dual forces on globalization. Therefore, this chapter is designed to identify and conceptualize the following specific objectives:

1. To evaluate the prime purposes of proliferation of Internet based economy, especially EG and EC,
2. To explore the possible barriers against and impacts of this proliferation especially among citizens of developing countries, and,
3. To develop theoretical frameworks to identify the adoption capability and the impacts of ICT adoption on the society in developing countries.

We have divided the chapter into six sections to conceptualize the purpose of proliferation of the Internet economy, possible barriers, different outcomes of the effect of this proliferation and barriers, and theoretical paradigms of impact of the Internet economy. Then we would provide the conclusive remarks of our analysis.

9.2. PURPOSES OF PROMOTING INTERNET ECONOMY

International corporations of developed countries launch their business operations through electronic media to get competitive advantage of present market economy.

There are many business organizations that currently operate EC in North America and Europe. Although, any customer can interact and buy products and services theoretically from those E-retailers 24 hours a day and 7 days a week from any where in the world, however, practically due to several constraints including payment method, credit card acceptability, shipment, return, cultural inadaptability etc., global aspect of those E-commerce is very limited. For business-to-business transactions, like supply chain management, so many B2B companies explore and extend their market throughout the world. However, for B2C EC, it is mostly operated regionally which includes North America and Europe. In some developing countries where infrastructure is strong enough to launch and operate B2C EC, and where overall technology availability, adoption, and adaptability is extensive, several business organizations take the scope to float local EC among domestic consumers. We can cite examples from China, India, Brazil, Taiwan, Hong Kong, South Korea, Malaysia, Thailand, South Africa, etc. Several authors, who have worked on proliferation of B2C EC, have shown several factors behind launching E-retailing locally, regionally, and internationally (Szymanski *et al.,* 2000; Srinivasan *et al.,* 2002; Zhang and von Dran, 2002). However, globally many countries like USA, Canada, and West Europe are very much responsible to encourage and guide their B2C EC to extend globally. World Trade Organization (WTO) takes many initiatives to open the global market for free trade and to take consistent trade policy for all the countries of United Nations. This organization from Uruguay Round Table deals with the rules of trade among nations at a global level. WTO addresses custom, tax, and subsidy policies of different countries and attempts to develop harmonic rules for globalization under the Doha Development Agenda (DDA). However, several countries, based on several paradigms like subsidy policy, market regulation, tax and duty policy, digital divide, incapability to adhere with globalization in terms of cultural differences, technology non-readiness, disparity in competition etc., are reluctant to encourage, accept, and boost up proliferation of B2C EC. Therefore, it is a potential research question to address the purposes of proliferation and barriers against this proliferation of B2C EC from country and customer perspectives.

Technologically advanced countries like USA, Japan, UK, Germany, France, Italy, Canada, Singapore, South Korea, and Taiwan are potentially playing the leading role in information and communication based market. These countries including so many developing countries are struggling to achieve advantages and sustain in fierce competitive market through grasping potentials of Internet economy. Therefore, these countries, especially USA, as a leader of Internet economy, encourage, develop, and guide to flourish their B2C EC. A potential benefit of Internet economy is globalization. Fundamentally, through operation of EC, any country can promote domestic E-retailers to launch their business operations globally and capture international market. USA is actively a leader in capitalizing benefits of globalization. Although private organizations have separate entity and in market economy, governments have no authority to intervene in market, however, protecting consumers and ensuring better service for consumers are also pivotal managerial issues for any good government. By promoting ICT-based economy, governments of different countries ensure and expedite quality and cost effective service for citizens. Digital divide is another popular concept which is targeted by different governments to reduce among citizens by promoting countrywide electronic economy. The term digital divide refers to differentiate people to get rights and freedom to learn, avail, and use resources of ICT. Since customer policies are well written and displayed in B2C EC, so transparency is a common aspect of Internet economy. Additionally, customers can enjoy interaction with B2C EC from anywhere in the world which increases scope for participation. Therefore, reviewing several researchers' findings of purposes of promoting B2C EC from country and consumers perspectives, precisely the following causes can be summarized:

1. To gain country competitiveness and market advantage by boosting national economy
2. To adhere with potentials of globalization
3. To promote ICT
4. To ensure better quality and cost effective service for consumers/citizens
5. To reduce digital divide and expedite capability
6. To promote transparency and increase participation

Now, at this stage, we would like to accentuate readers on another aspect of Internet economy, viz. E-government (EG). Although, prospective and function of EG is fundamentally oriented towards domestic periphery, its globalization aspect to focus country image outside, attract foreign investments and resources including immigrants cannot be overlooked. EG refers to government's use of information technology to exchange information and services with citizens, businesses, and other arms of government. It is a tool to transform and rationalize public sector work through the use of ICT, which may include wide area networks, the Internet, mobile computing, and mobile telephony (Schware and Deane, 2003). It enables government to provide citizens with easier and electronic access to information and modernized services through personal computers, kiosks, telephones, and other resources (Banerjee and Chau, 2004). This suggests that citizens no longer need to claim services over the counter. EG involves using ICT to deliver public services through digital channels. So, EG promotes efficient, cost effective, and better quality services, and increased participation and democratization. Throughout the world, governments are realizing the potential of placing traditional government services online. Moreover, since its main mission is citizen driven, its implementation, development, and performance should be such that it should and must meet the criteria and facilitating factors that enable citizens to adopt this modern technology driven government system—EG. EG should also win citizens approval after initial resistance. Therefore, for the comprehensive performance of EG and successful proliferation, the acceptance of EG system of a country by different national and international stakeholders is of utmost important.

The strategy and objectives of EG development have technological, social, economical, organizational, marketing, and political aspects. From the technological point of view, different countries strategically implement EG to institutionalize modern ICT in government, make citizens familiar with ICT, and capitalize on the benefits of this technology. From the social point of view, the implementation strategy of EG focuses on changing the social relation between government and citizens, creating more opportunity for citizens to participate in government decision making, and developing living standard. The economical aspect of developing EG relies on boosting national development, keeping a leading position in the global economy, integrating the domestic market, and promoting international investment. All of these will improve economical capability at the micro level. From the organizational perspective, the objective of EG is to reform and reengineer public administration, which is very bureaucratic, corrupt, and stagnant. Improving the quality of service, which ensures its competence with the private sector, drives the marketing aspect of EG. This agenda includes efficient, cost effective, dynamic, extensive, easy, and higher quality government services to citizens and businesses. The objectives of the political aspect of EG are to enhance public participation and access in government information and decision making, promote a cohesive government to all stakeholders of the government, improve government transparency and accountability, and, thus, establish good governance. After the advent of the Internet, information technology and electronic communication played a very important role in fulfilling the vision of reforming government in an entirely different way. Innovations in ICT have dramatically transformed organization-customer, government-citizen, and inter-state communications. The Internet gradually has matured into a universally accepted and user-friendly platform for government organizations to communicate directly with citizens and deliver information without any time interruption. Therefore, ICT is believed to be conducive to the movement of government reinvention. It has transformed the way government operates. EG is the pragmatic use of ICT to improve the way that government performs its business. It is a commitment by government decision-makers to strengthen the partnership between citizens and public sectors through using EG for enhanced, cost-effective, and efficient delivery of services, information, and knowledge. Since government departments have a monopoly in their functions, their services and procedures are commonly held to be inefficient. They traditionally have little motivation to meet citizen expectations, and citizens do not have an alternative provider for government services. The revolutionary development and increased usage of technology and communication in government organizations has changed some of these attitudes. A more enlightened view has emerged from different governments and their successive organizations to treat citizens like business consumers where transaction satisfaction is important. This change in attitude is actually more efficient for governments, as well as for citizens, as it allows governments to process information and to provide service more efficiently and effectively (Evans and Yen, 2006).

The automating of government functions helps to increase customer service levels and decrease costs. The development of an EG system helps to disseminate information and further the attitude that citizens are customers and that their satisfaction is important, not irrelevant. Further, it aids in the collection of information that helps decision makers serve citizens more effectively. EG allows government agencies to centralize decision making and purchasing to reduce costs. The centralization of certain activities eliminates inefficient and costly redundancies. Furthermore, the presence of EG structures may cause the government to operate in a more transparent and accountable manner (Evans and Yen, 2006). Therefore, EG can be seen as a modern government organizational structure operated through ICT to transform and rationalize public sector work to provide citizens easier and electronic access to information and modernized services through personal computers, kiosks, telephones, and other resources (Schware and Deane, 2003; Banerjee and Chau, 2004).

According to the European Union (European Union Report, 2002), EG is a tool not a goal in itself. It should help to deliver better government service. In other words, EG, perceived by the European Union, should help democracy to function better through the realization of an open government and should aim to deliver public services in such a way that they are accessible and relevant for each individual citizens and company. EG should also increase productivity through higher efficiency and better quality services. The purposes of EG set by European Union (European Union Report, 2002) are as follows:

1. EG should make it possible for citizens to follow and participate in their government's functions – central, regional, and local, participate in decision making from the early phases onwards, and verify that public money is being spent well. EG is a means to realize open government.
2. EG should help to provide citizens with personalized and customized public services that meet their specific needs.
3. EG should help public administrations to deliver more value for taxpayer money by increasing efficiency and upgrading productivity.

There is an explicit inter-connection between the expressed mission of the modernization and democratization agenda through the application of ICT and that of the EG agenda. For instance, within a proposed national strategy for EG in England, the term EG has been conceptualized as "exploiting the power of information and communications technology to help transform the accessibility, quality and cost-effectiveness of public services, and to help revitalize the relationship between customers and citizens and public bodies who work on their behalf" (Local Government Association, 2002). The UK Government's statement on electronic government establishes four guiding principles:

1. Building services around citizens' choices.
2. Making government and its services more accessible.
3. Social inclusion.
4. Using information better.

On 24 June 2000, the US government unveiled a series of new initiatives to give the American people – what President Clinton in his first-ever Saturday web cast address to the Nation claimed to be – "the 'Information Age' government they deserve." Clinton stated that the new initiatives will "cut red tape, make government more responsive to the needs of citizens, and expand opportunities for participation in our democracy." (Clinton, 2000). By the end of 2000, citizens must be able to search all online resources offered by the federal government from a single web site called "firstgov.gov." The citizen-centered EG strategy set by the US government (GAO, 2002) plans to improve the quality of the services to the citizens and businesses. The primary goals for the US President's "Expanding E-Government" initiative are to:

1. Make it easy for citizens to obtain services and interact with the federal government,
2. Improve government efficiency and effectiveness, and
3. Improve government's responsiveness to citizens.

After reviewing different articles addressing missions, objectives, and purposes of EG implemented in different countries at different stages, the following generalized targets can be summarized at the outset of implementation (Okot-Uma and Caffrey, 2000; Jaeger and Thompson, 2003; Parent, *et al.,* 2005; Evans and Yen, 2006; Gil-Garcia and Martinez-Moyano, 2007; Heeks and Bailur, 2007):

1. To use ICT in public organizations and capitalize on the benefits of this technology,

2.   To diffuse ICT among citizens from government level,
3.   To reform and reconstruct public administration,
4.   To promote domestic economy,
5.   To improve competitiveness of the country globally,
6.   To provide cost effective and dynamic services of government to citizens and businesses,
7.   To provide efficient and better quality service,
8.   To enhance public participation and access in government information and decision making, improve transparency and accountability, and, thus, establish good governance.

9.3. BARRIERS AGAINST PROLIFERATION OF INTERNET ECONOMY

Although most of the countries in the world are now members of WTO, and thus they are forced to be rational to adhere with free trade policies established by WTO, so many countries are not actively interested in embracing the proliferation of Internet economy. Especially developing countries are accused of creating barriers for globalization of International E-retailers and reluctant in promoting EG countrywide. There is a Russian proverb, 'When one person becomes rich, at least ten people become poor'. This is a reality and paradigm of world economy in both micro level and macro level. It is an axiom for both intra-country and inter-country economy.

It is already mentioned that one of the fundamental purposes of promoting EC or EG by especially developed countries is to achieve the potentials of Internet economy. Globalization of Internet economy is an umbrella term that refers to a complex of economic, trade, social, technological, cultural, and political interrelationships, convergence, and integration. This process has fierce implications on the environment, on culture, on political systems, on economic development and prosperity, and on living standards in societies around the world. However, globalization – its policy, trend, and implications are deeply controversial. Scholars who advocate for globalization argue that it allows poor countries and their citizens to develop economically, raise their standards of living, unveil greater opportunity globally, create competitiveness, greater quality, and improved product and service at lower price, establish homogeneous market, and consider world as a global village. On the other hand, opponents of globalization claim that the creation of a so-called free international market has benefited multinational corporations in the industrialized world at the expense of local enterprises, local cultures, and poor people.

Positive side of globalization and its inevitable proliferation has been announced and advocated by WTO. Some compelling and interesting paradigms based on universal business ethics, norms and values, humanity, equal rights, humankind, and equal universal community are generally highlighted when advertising in favor of globalization. While agreeing on many of the doctrines of the globalization, several scholars reject certain paradigms, which they think, are based on fallacy. The primary contexts are:

1. Level playing field and equalization
2. Cultural integration
3. Equal employment opportunity for deserved personnel
4. WTO operates globalization theme impartially
5. Regional organizations, like NAFTA, EU, and ASEAN etc. are pursuing globalization
6. Uniform business globalization, no political power
7. Open competition, not monopoly etc.

9.3.1. Level Playing Field and Equalization

Several scholars dealing with globalization advocate that globalization creates the level playing field for all the nations to play globally. Giddens (1990) recognized globalization as a process of interdependence in which states are increasingly interconnected and social relations are stretched across national boundaries, and he viewed this as an equalizing process. It is true to some extent. However, are all the countries from north to south playing in the same level? The obvious answer is negative. International financial and trade organizations, like International Monetary Fund (IMF), World Bank, WTO regulate tariff systems for developing countries and suggest them (or order?) to open their market for all for the sake of globalization, however, politically powerful countries, like USA, China, Japan, UK, France, Germany subsidize local vulnerable industries (for example, sugar industry in USA, semiconductor industry in China, some fruits in Japan). By using political power, capital, information technology, and influence in WTO, industrialized countries are inherently positioning them in the upper field before the actual international race starts. Let us consider the role of information technology. Since predominant language used on the web is US English and search engines, news media, and advertisements in the Internet are mostly controlled by the organizations of USA, it is obvious that they are getting some extra advantage for globalization through the Internet. The debate is not that whether the Internet language will be English or French, or Chinese. Since the Internet and international media are mostly operated, funded, and owned by the USA, there should be universal consensus that it will be controlled by their language. However, when we are concerned about globalization and when we are talking about equalization, we should also argue that north and south are not playing in the same level.

9.3.2. Cultural Integration

A widely published paradigm of globalization is cultural integration. By globalization itself, barriers between countries, societies, and cultures are broken and a homogeneous and integrated culture, living standards, values, norms, attitudes are creating among the whole world. However, this paradigm has also some flaws. It is plausibly true that cultural integration is a practical phenomenon of globalization. However, is it multidirectional? For most of the cases, this is not the true picture. Actually cultural standards mostly dominated by the westerns are infiltrating in the third world by globalization. It is a controversy that the American view of globalization is that people all over the world will be habituated with American consumer market. And this ideology is getting well support from prominent world media's. Americans are proud of Asians wearing blue jeans; however, they are quite suspicious of Americans wearing Asian costumes. Therefore, we can comment that cultural integration through globalization, to some extent, has unidirectional flow.

9.3.3. Equal Employment Opportunity for Deserved Personnel

Developed countries generally are not very much eager to evaluate skilled personnel, who are coming from developing countries, in the same weighing machine in terms of their education and experience. So, for globalization, sometimes skilled personnel of developing countries who are searching for jobs, especially in managerial level, cannot avail equal opportunity.

9.3.4. WTO Operates Globalization Theme Impartially

WTO, IMF, and World Bank, are widely believed to bear the interest of powerful countries and are acting for the good of large transnational (or multinational) corporations. In practice, most of the WTO's vulnerable decisions are made in informal meetings, often called "Green Room" meetings, to which most members are not invited. Several WTO treaties have been accused of a partial and unfair bias toward multinational corporations and wealthy nations. Critics believe that small countries have little impact on WTO, and though one of the official aims of WTO is to help the developing countries, the influential nations in the WTO focus on their own commercial interests. We can cite some examples of these disparities which should have been addressed impartially by the WTO for globalization; however, real pictures were different.

1.   Rich countries are able to impose higher import duties and quotas in certain products, blocking imports from developing countries (e.g. clothing).
2.   Anti-dumping measures are widely considered as a strong tool against developing countries.
3.   Developed countries are protecting their agriculture while developing countries are pressed to open their markets.
4.   The TRIPs (Trade-Related Intellectual Property Rights) agreement which limits developing countries from utilizing some technology that originates from abroad in their local systems (including medicines and agricultural products).

9.3.5. Regional Organizations, like NAFTA, EU, and ASEAN etc. are Pursuing Globalization

These organizations are frequently creating barriers for other countries in terms of globalization and also raising disputes among the participating countries which are also against globalization. In this aspect, we can review NAFTA. Canada and USA have long disputes for several industries in term of tariffs, subsidy etc. Suppose USA imposed countervailing duty tariff on Canadian softwood lumber on the point that Canada is subsiding this industry, while Canada denied it (Ultimately a tentative solution is reached recently). Canada has a complaint that USA is subsiding agricultural products, while USA is complaining the same for Canadian wheat products. For several products by subsiding, EU is protecting their markets from USA, Canada, China, and Japan. For example, EU has banned import fur from Canada, genetically modified organisms (GOM) from USA. USA banned Canadian beef on the ground of mad cow. In this connection, it is very interesting to see that powerful countries can create some issues to ban import of some products from some specific countries, especially when the defendant country is a developing country.

9.3.6. Uniform Business Globalization, No Political Power

It is witnessed that business globalization is seriously dominated by political power. The countries that have political power can create pressure on weak countries to open market for their large corporations. At the same time powerful countries open their market for developing countries only for those products they need for their market stability. From the study of WTO dispute settlement case, thousands of examples can be cited which reflect subtle influence of political power in decision making.

9.3.7. Open Competition, not Monopoly

Though it is a popular saying that globalization, under the banner of free trade, is pursuing open competition, however, reality is not always like that. Powerful countries are always creating some extra spaces for their own international industries. When developing countries protect small farmers by reducing tariff– a key source of income for developing countries, WTO criticizes it, while rich countries are still paying their farmers massive subsidies. Developing countries cannot afford this subsidy. For example, in many occasions, as one of the most powerful countries in the world, China is subsiding many sectors, like agricultural products, semiconductor. When the conflict starts between USA, China, France, Japan, UK, Germany etc., we might get some global solutions. However, if the complaining party is a developing country with less power, solution for the sake of globalization is beyond reality.

We conclude this ongoing debate with the famous saying of Abraham Lincoln, "You can fool some of the people all of the time, and all of the people some of the time, but you can not fool all of the people all of the time".

Therefore, as a consequence, so many developing countries are basically reluctant or creating barriers in proliferation of B2C EC to save their countries from imperialist Internet-based economy. Additionally, cultural difference is also an important aspect for some countries to resist extension of B2C EC. Lack of skilled people, technology infrastructure, and financial ability to achieve global competitiveness are also potential causes for so many countries not to embrace unstoppable wave of globalization of Internet economy (UNCTAD, 2000). The technology absorption capacity of developing countries and its impact on them is quite different than in developed countries.

Now, if we look at paradigms of EG, we precisely observe that EG provides participants accessible and relevant information and high quality services that are faster than traditional "brick and mortar" transactions. Until now, the need for increased efficiency in the public sector and the potential in information technology seem to have been the primary drivers of EG. However, little information is presented in the literature on identifying the different stakeholders of EG; addressing their involvement pattern; evaluating the fundamental capabilities of a government, especially of a developing country; and realizing and developing the framework of adopting EG systems by the prime users, viz. the citizens. This may be justified at an early stage of implementing these new services. However, as users mature, it is argued that their input is increasingly valuable in terms of improving the services, suggesting new opportunities, and developing a successful system. Developing countries are especially vulnerable in the adoption of EG, since its primary driving force is

ICT. Due to significant digital divide in developing countries, between urban and rural populations, accomplishing the primary objectives of EG depends on the adoption capability of ICT among the less advanced population. If it is learned that the impacts of implementing ICT at the national level reflects discrimination and a digital divide with respect to the social, technological, and financial aspects, it is rarely possible to achieve the objectives of implementing EG.

Therefore, if we conclude all of those factors which prompt several countries as well as millions of citizens to be reluctant, or are actively creating barriers against the proliferation of Internet economy including both EC and EG, we can precisely reach one single aspect of the negative side of Internet economy. This is the digital divide. It can arise internationally and it can also strike equal rights and freedom of citizens domestically. We would like to define digital divide for Internet economy as "Creating discrimination among countries internationally and among citizens internally (inside a country) which is against the level playing field for all nations to get access in the Internet economy and use the same ICT-based resources. It imparts privilege for privileged countries globally and for privileged people locally through operation and function of Internet economy". The possible digital divide due to proliferation of Internet economy can arise from two sources, i) internationally: In this case some privileged countries, especially economically and politically powerful countries utilize their positions to gain extraordinary advantages over less powerful developing countries through launching ICT based Internet economy, and ii) nationally: In this case privileged groups of citizens, especially urban citizens gain and utilize their positions to achieve extraordinary benefits over less powerful rural people. Although, one of the basic arguments and premises of launching Internet-based economy like EC and especially EG was to reduce digital divide between privileged and non-privileged countries internationally and between urban and rural citizens internally. However, it is a deep rooted controversy whether proliferation of Internet economy reduces this ill-fashioned characteristic of world politics, viz., digital divide, or it basically promotes and accelerates long-time prevailed digital divide internationally and nationally. Proponents of globalization and proliferation of Internet economy deny this doctrine. On the other hand, it is also a popular speculation that digital divide is deeply rooted in the proliferation of Internet economy including EC and EG. Therefore, it is a challenging issue for WTO, United Nations, and policy makers of developing countries to address, identify, and conceptualize the impact of ICT, the main driving force of Internet economy, among less privileged citizens of less privileged countries.

9.4. READINESS, DIGITAL DIVIDE, AND CAPABILITY

EG would not be successful nationally, and developing countries would not support proliferation of B2C EC if the majority of population of developing countries who live in rural areas do not have the ability to use technology and useful information and services. This would lead to a low user base, as the system would not be equally accessible by all citizens. Linked to this is the lack of skills and training required to effectively use an ICT-based system that are available to urban consumers. This problem has been mentioned by numerous academics (Heeks, 1999; Moon, 2002; Ho, 2002, Ebrahim and Irani, 2005). Disparity in access to Internet economy operated through ICT and discrimination in facilitating the same scope of opportunity are potential managerial issues (Bertot, 2003). Gaps in access to and use of Internet economy can be related to a number of characteristics, including location, gender, race, color, political involvement, income level, education level, language, and disability. Rural communities have the same right as citizens to get government services through EG that are available to urban communities. However, in real sense, already there exists disparity in getting and using ICT resources between urban and rural population, and EG is promoting further digital divide. Typically, it is a very common phenomenon that rural communities have restraints in getting all types of communications than that of urban population (Parker, 2000). Due to low population density in rural areas, investment to construct information technology infrastructures is not economically feasible (Hollifield and Donnermeyer, 2003). However, as a government structure, EG should create the same level of playing field for both urban and rural populations, otherwise the proliferation of EG in the modern world cannot be capitalized. At the same time, globalization basically prompted through Internet economy like EC. EC should create the same level of playing field for both powerful developed countries and developing countries; otherwise the proliferation of EC in the modern world cannot be capitalized and urge for emancipation of developing countries cannot be ruled out only by imposing different regulations from WTO. Developing skill in having and using technology, appears to be a key element of successful ICT-based market economy.

In this context, if we shed light on the capability theory, we can observe that without equal capability defined by awareness and availability of resources and skill, the scope of the same opportunity cannot be either created or justified. Following Nussbaum and Sen (1993), the capability approach is defined here as a normative development objective of United Nations and individual governments that seeks to enhance its stakeholders' ability. It does this by expanding and procuring modern ICT and providing good governance with the earnest cooperation of United Nations and individual governments in the actual freedoms and capabilities of individuals and groups to voluntarily engage in sustainable state development. It is a philosophical, political, and organizational approach to human development, which transcends traditional macroeconomic growth indicators as benchmarks for development. The capability approach as a development paradigm of government departs from traditional development economics in a significant way, because it does not equate human freedom and development to national economic growth. Depending on this phenomenal concept of welfare economics, we can develop our paradigms, because without creating the same capability for both developed and developing countries internationally and for both urban and rural population nationally to access and use ICT, the adoption and purpose of implementing Internet economy cannot be accomplished or justified (Gigler, 2004; Harris, 2005). Rather, proliferation of Internet economy and globalization internationally, especially in developing countries, might be accused of importing inequality, digital divide, and discrimination. Therefore, it is the single most important issue for the policy makers of International bodies and developing countries to study the impact of ICT, especially in the rural population in developing countries, before supporting the proliferation of Internet-based economy promoting EC globally and EG nationally where ICT is the main driver (Bhatnagar, 2000; Madon, 2000; Krishna and Madon, 2004).

The United Nations has attempted to find out the digital divide among world countries. Through an extensive survey among the 191 member countries (this is the number of members at the time of the study; now there are 192 UN members), they addressed the issue by developing an EG readiness factor. This parameter is used to define the progress of each country to provide the scope of adopting online system and launching EG. It includes three major components: web measure index, telecommunication index, and human capital index. So, proposing this measurement instrument, the United Nations has addressed the scope of adopting ICT and launching EG by availability of resources, capability, and present status of a country. The web measure index is a quantitative measure applied to all 191 UN member states. The concept used to evaluate this information revealed whether certain services are available online. The telecommunication index is a quantitative weighted measure of electronic devices (or their usage) per 1,000 citizens such as PCs, Internet users, televisions, telephones lines, online population, and mobile phones. The human capital index is dependent on education measures, two thirds of which relate to adult literacy (United Nations, 2003). However, while attempting to identify the digital divide among different countries, this survey missed one potential aspect of readiness of adopting ICT and, thus, Internet economy. This is the extreme digital divide and unequal availability and distribution of resources between the rural and urban populations in developing countries. In developing countries, the majority of the populations live in rural areas, and they lag far behind the urban population in terms of availability, awareness, and capability of using ICT. For that reason, the average result of any empirical study of readiness conducted in urban areas or even in both rural and urban areas cannot produce an accurate indication of the actual readiness of the major population of that country. The rural population, which comprises the major percentage of the population, might be individually far behind the average of the country (Adam and Wood, 1999). As a result, the statistical average might be meaningless for developing countries. Basically, it is a strong argument that this type of Readiness Index measure initiated by United Nations is conducted to misguide developing countries internationally and rural populations nationally in getting actual idea of the capability of adopting ICT-based economy. United Nations do this type of survey to promote globalization and Internet economy to support the positions of developed and powerful countries internationally. AT the same time, urban populations of developing countries also, like developed countries, are the privileged and powerful groups of a nations over rural populations. Consequently this type of survey measurement index is also conducted to support the positions of urban populations. The strong paradigm behind this argument is that the readiness index measured through empirical study in developing countries gives a significant intentional flaw of statistical analysis. In most of the developing countries, a majority of the population lives in rural areas. Additionally, disparity in income, resource availability and uses, scope and opportunities for employment, especially in relation to modern ICT-based market economy between rural and urban are extremely and alarmingly high. Therefore, a statistical report which is comprised of national average conducted by United Nations to show readiness of developing countries to promote Internet economy like EC internationally and EG nationally, is extremely biased and provides misleading information about the actual readiness to develop the capability to adopt ICT-based market economy. Therefore, this type of readiness index measure conducted by the United Nations cannot justify removing the barriers against the proliferation of Internet-based economy and reflecting the actual picture of digital divide due to proliferation of Internet economy. To justify that proliferation of Internet-based economy is not enhancing digital divide, like EC internationally between developed and developing countries and EG nationally between urban and rural population, we should first address and reveal the impact of ICT in rural population of developing countries who comprises the majority of the population of the world.

9.5. IMPACT OF ICT AND CONCEPTUAL FRAMEWORK

As Information System (IS) researchers, policy makers, and United Nations organizations have been addressing the challenge of the digital divide and technology failure in developing countries, the ICT impact research concerning development interventions in developing countries has become a prominent issue (Madon, 1991;

Adam and Wood, 1999). While researchers and the United Nations report on the strategy of implementation of ICT, the ICT impact research towards overall capability of both rural and urban populations of developing countries is very limited (Meso and Mbarika, 2006). In recent years, the United Nations, non-government organizations (NGO), and some researchers (Madon, 1997; Sein and Ahmad, 2001; Sahay and Avgerou, 2002; Heeks, 2002; Walsham and Sahay, 2006) have been addressing the issue in scattered ways. However, most of these studies have some significant weaknesses. These can be listed as:

1.   These studies are conducted to capture the average impact of the overall population in a developing country. However, it is revealed in several studies and also in the light of capability theory (Nussbaum and Sen, 1993) that technology adoption capability and performance of technology in rural and urban population is remarkably different (Harris, *et al.,* 2003; Harris, 2005; United Nations, 2005). Additionally, a majority of the population in developing countries live in the rural area, and their average employment opportunity, cultural characteristics, education, awareness, and technology adaptability and overall rural infrastructural development are far behind from not only urban average but also remarkably lower than national average on the same parameters. Therefore, an average impact study cannot reveal the actual status of rural areas in developing countries in respect to technology adoption capability and technology performance. Average impact of ICT on rural population of developing countries should be addressed and revealed separately to evaluate, estimate, and anticipate impact of Internet economy on developing countries in relative to developed countries internationally. Since, rural population in developing countries represents the majority. And also average impact of ICT on rural population of developing countries could be compared with the same of urban populations domestically.

2.   Most of those reports and studies have paradigms focused on a techno-centric approach to evaluate ICT development. Other dimensions – like social parameters, economical aspect, and cultural change – have hardly been addressed. However, it is argued that social, economic, and cultural aspects are very important to examine in an impact analysis of ICT (Engel, *et al.,* 1993, Titah and Barki, 2005). It has been suggested that measuring ICT development in developing countries should take into account two factors: the number of electronically connected individuals (Macome, 2002) and social progress conducive to universal access to basic welfare systems and the "knowledge society" (Mansell and Wehn, 1998; Mansell, 2002; Dixit, 2006).

3.   All of these studies have been conducted within a short timeframe. However, to capture the impact of ICT in rural populations in developing countries,

these studies should be conducted over a long period of time. As we need to know the impact of ICT, we require prior knowledge of implementing ICT in public projects in rural areas and also we need knowledge sometime after ICT has been implemented in those projects. Therefore, to learn the actual picture of the impact of ICT on rural areas in developing countries, we argue that the study should be conducted in two phases: the pre-implementation and post-implementation phases.

Madon (2003) developed an exploratory framework for assessing the impact of ICT-based projects through an empirical study in a developing country. The author adopted a social constructivist perspective for this study, however, it did not account for the pre-implementation perspective and the post-implementation perspective separately. Impact assessment requires a vertical study to inspect the possible outcomes or changes in society due to ICT adoption. Moreover, many aspects of the initial situation prior to ICT implementation must be known so that the impact of ICT among populations can be compared with the condition of the pre-implementation phase (Menou and Potvin, 2007). Therefore, impact assessment is a long-term continuous process that is contingent upon a variety of factors, and requires a rigorous monitoring at the field level for a reasonable length of time.

Based on literature reviews and the discourses drawn from the above discussion, we suggest that the impact of ICT in developing countries should be conducted separately in rural and urban areas and it should be carried out in two phases. Before using ICT extensively in different economic, social, cultural, political, and organizational projects, an ad-hoc study is essential to investigate and realize whether rural people are ready and capable of adopting ICT. Getting insight from the capability theory, we define capability of adoption as: *the ability of populations of a country to become familiar with modern technology, get access to the resources required for use, achieve the skill to use, and perceive functional benefits of ICT.*

9.5.1. Ad-Hoc Phase

Rural people in developing countries are mostly less educated and unfamiliar with modern technology. As a result, they also do not have the belief to acquire benefits by using an ICT system (Mansell and When, 1998; Mansell, 2002; Dixit, 2006). At the beginning, to create beliefs and intention to use ICT, rural people must be aware of the characteristics of ICT and its functional benefits. Perception of functional benefits is a construct of technology acceptance model ((Davis, *et al.* 1989; Davis, 1989). From the implied essence of the theories of planned behavior, diffusion of innovation, and transaction cost analysis (TCA), a user will not achieve that belief towards intention to use ICT system to get competitive advantage unless he/she perceives functional benefits of using that system. It is essential that the user has competence to use it and perceives the functional benefits of modern ICT. This is especially true for the rural population of developing countries who are less educated, not at all skilled, and have no idea about the characteristics and functional benefits of ICT. If the rural populations do not get sufficient skill and knowledge to use it without complexity and perceive absolute and relative functional benefits, they will not invest time and money in such a mysterious activities (Mansell and When, 1998; Mansell, 2002; Dixit, 2006).

Additionally, rural people have different employment scopes and opportunities which mostly are not compatible to technology-based economy. Consequently, rural populations of developing countries have different types of cultural and behavioral characteristics which mostly do not show resemble to technology adoption belief. This concept can be explained by compatibility construct from the diffusion of innovation theory (Rogres, 1995). Compatibility refers to "the degree to which an innovation is seen to be compatible with existing values, beliefs, experiences and needs of adopters". For ICT systems, we assume compatibility as the preference of rural population of using ICT-based projects that match with the cultural, behavioral, and economical demand of the population. Infrastructures of rural areas in developing countries are extremely underdeveloped, even so many areas, in an average, are not equipped with modern electricity. Due to significant differences in employment types, skill in technology operation is very limited in terms of human resources in rural areas in developing countries. These characteristics of rural areas, such as technological infrastructure and human resources can be measured through telecommunication index and human capital index of readiness index addressed by United Nations (2003). All these aspects which can be used to measure overall readiness and adoption capability of citizens, here we termed as "Social belief". As a result, social belief of rural population of developing countries might potentially differ from developed countries as well as urban population of the same country. Therefore, Social belief, defined here as: *developing beliefs to use, awareness to use, perception of benefits to use, capability to use, and compatibility to use in terms of employment pattern and characteristics and cultural and behavioral characteristics*, is very important. An overall readiness by awareness, ability, intention, and preparation is a contributing factor for the capabilities to absorb ICT. The attitude, in turn, leads to an intention to use ICT and the eventual acceptance of the information technology (Davis, *et al.,* 1989; Lucas and Spitler, 1999; Venkatesh, 2000; Bhattacherjee, 2001; Moon, 2002). Unavailability of resources – including computers, Internet connection, electricity, and telecommunications – is one of the main barriers for rural population of developing countries to adopt and use ICT (Dada, 2006). Several researchers asserted that adoption of new technology is closely related to knowledge and experience of that system as well as availability of resources (Parent, *et al.,* 2005; Titah and Barki, 2005; Kumar, *et al.,* 2007). From the technological, behavioral, economical, and organizational perspectives, it is anticipated that failing to get enough resources to use ICT will not create a behavioral attitude to adopt the system. Several researchers pointed out that ICT implementation in public projects in several countries, especially developing countries, could not attain desired success or would fail because of a number of factors (Madu, 1989; Bhatnagar, 2002; Heeks, 2002; Dada, 2006). These factors include a scarcity of computers; Internet with competent features such as access, speed, and cost; and government supports like call-center, resource-center, and cyber-café. The Capability theory suggests that citizens can not achieve capability of using a system unless they have the freedom of utility of using that system. Generally, where computers, Internet, and modern ICT are not available, the residents are economically poor, less educated, unaware, socially and culturally are not familiar with modern technology, and lack technological skills. We encompass readiness and adoption of ICT as: *a continuous process starting from an awareness of benefits, attitude toward using it, skill in using it, and availability of resources to use and adopt ICT-based market economy.* Based on the above arguments, we now propose the following framework of Social belief to evaluate the overall readiness and adoption capability of rural population of developing countries. The model is termed here as the Ad-Hoc framework to evaluate the readiness of citizens of adoption capability of ICT. The term adoption capability is already defined in the end of the previous section. We use the term Ad-Hoc to capture the concept that the framework would be used to evaluate the overall readiness of citizens of a country to adopt ICT-based system at the pre-implementation phase of massive ICT intense projects, like EG. Compatible to United Nations readiness index (2003), this ad-hoc framework can be used to measure the constructs of social beliefs to reflect the overall readiness of citizens' adoption capability of ICT. The four constructs of social beliefs which have derived from literature review and theoretical perspectives in this section are briefly listed in the following paragraphs. The Adoption Capability Readiness Index is a composite index of Social beliefs comprising:

1. Consciousness Index
2. Interest Index
3. Human Index
4. Technology Index

Awareness and beliefs to ICT (**Consciousness Index**): This index can be measured through scale items related to i) Awareness to technology, ii) Beliefs to technology, and iii) Overall knowledge to technology.

Perceived functional benefits and compatibility in relation to cultural, behavioral, and economical characteristics of rural population (**Interest Index**): This index can be measured through scale items related to i) Behavioral interest in using technology, ii) Perception of functional benefits of using technology, iii) Cultural adaptability to technology, and iv) Employment pattern of rural areas and compatibility with Internet economy.

Human Capital Index: This index can be taken from the United Nations readiness study (2003). This is dependent on education measures concerning adult literacy. Human Capital Index relies on the UNDP "education index", which is a composite of the adult literacy rate and the combined primary, secondary and tertiary gross enrolment ratio with two thirds of the weight given to adult literacy and one third to gross enrolment ratio. "Adult literacy is the percentage of people aged 15 years and above who can, with understanding, both read and write a short simple statement on their everyday life. Combined primary, secondary and tertiary gross enrolment ratio is the total number of students enrolled at the primary, secondary and tertiary level, regardless of age, as a percentage of the population of school age for that level" (United Nations, 2003).

Technology Index: This construct is quite similar to Telecommunication Index as defined by United Nations Readiness Study (2003). Telecommunication Index defined by United Nations is a composite, weighted average index of six primary indices based on basic ICT-related infrastructure indicators. These are: PCs/1,000 persons; Internet users/1,000 persons; Telephone lines/1,000 persons; Online population/1,000 persons; Mobile phones/1,000 persons; and TVs/1,000 persons. However, some measurement items should be added to capture comprehensive view of rural areas of developing countries to adjust with actual condition of rural areas. These additional items over existing items of Telecommunication Index are: i) Speed and Cost of Internet in rural areas, ii) Infrastructure of electricity, iii) Availability of electricity in terms of time, and iv) Cost of electricity.

Our intention is to measure adoption capability of rural population of developing countries by measuring the social beliefs of rural population. Therefore, the framework of "Readiness of Adoption Capability" is as follows (Figure 9.1).

This Ad-Hoc model is a theoretical framework to study the adoption capability of ICT of rural and urban population of developing countries in the pre-implementation phase of massive ICT-based projects, and it can also be used in developed countries. From the operationalization of the four independent constructs and one dependent construct, we can measure the ICT adoption capability of population of developing countries, especially of the rural population. We argue that those four Index – Consciousness, Interest, Technology, and Human Capital – can comprehensively measure the ICT adoption capability of rural and urban populations of

Figure 9.1. Ad-hoc framework: Readiness of adoption capability of ICT

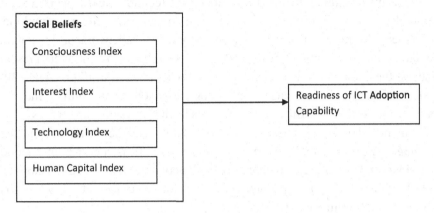

developing countries separately and also populations of developed countries at the ad-hoc phase.

9.5.2. Post-Hoc Phase

According to our paradigms, the study of the impact of ICT in developing countries should be carried out in two different segmented areas separately. To capture the development of two significantly distinguishable areas, it should be carried out in both the urban and rural populations. The study should also be conducted in two phases: the ad-hoc phase and the post-hoc phase. In the post-hoc phase, the study should capture not only the technological aspect but also the economic and social aspects. Economic development through ICT could be gained primarily through the following sectors: economic opportunity, production growth, and infrastructure building (Madon, 2000). In developing countries, ICT enables people and enterprises to capture economic opportunities by connecting businesses globally, improving market access, and creating opportunities for employment (Bhatnagar, 2000; Jerinabi and Arthi, 2005; Anwer, 2006). From the core principle of TCA, the motivation for behavioral intention to interact with different organizational structures is significantly influenced by economic parameters. The fundamental doctrine of TCA is that while measuring the economic performance, the institutional structure is a dominant factor, and different institutional structures have different influences on economic performance (Shelanski, *et al.,* 1995). With the rapid growth of ICT and the advent of EG, government organizations play an important role in economic activities, and individuals participate in various types of interactions. Therefore, while measuring the impact of ICT, economic benefits and attitudinal benefits are important aspects to be examined.

We have already explained socio-technical and complementary theories in chapter seven to get deep insight into integrating social and technological aspects of the ICT adoption framework. The socio-technical and complementary theories combine all those aspects to present a comprehensive theoretical framework of development speculation due to the impact of ICT. Several researchers who conducted research to address the impact of ICT on developing countries (Avgerou, 1998; Gigler, 2004; Heeks, 2005) argue that a focus on technological factors or non-human indicators (similar to the economic indicators), should not be the only solution towards ICT-led development in developing countries. These technological factors include the rate of technology adoption, establishment of technological infrastructure, Internet hosting, and volume of computer ownership. Both economic and social developments should be integrated in this framework of development (RIRDC, 1997; Mansell and Wehn, 1998; Johnston, 2003).

Therefore, depending on the above arguments and theoretical references, we propose that in the post-hoc phase, the overall development of rural and urban population should be studied. Factors that should receive attention in any empirical study of these segmented populations are the adoption, implementation, and usage of ICT in different domestic Internet-based projects, like domestic EC and EG. This could be accounted for by researching the following aspects:

1. **Economical parameters:** Economical development and changes of both rural and urban population separately including income, job opportunity, purchasing power, etc.
2. **Social parameters:** Social development and changes of both rural and urban population separately including cultural development, social relation, social consciousness, standard of living, welfare, etc. It could be similar to the Human development Index of the United Nations.
3. **Technological parameters:** Educational and Skill development and changes of both rural and urban population separately, including literacy rate, technology familiarity, technology skill, education, rate of technology usage, etc.

Most of the countries, to some extent, have Internet-based economic operations. Depending on the variables, as mentioned in those three perspectives, the overall development impact of the rural and urban population can be measured as the result of ICT adoption, implementation, and usage in private and public Internet-based projects like EC and EG. Studies regarding the impact of ICT in rural and urban populations due to the implementation of ICT in different private and public projects can be explored using insight from this theoretical framework. Measuring the impact of ICT, especially on rural areas in developing countries, through the above mentioned three parameters, we can get detailed knowledge of whether the rural population is capable to achieve benefits of using modern ICT. This post-hoc framework can also contribute to a study of the changes in the overall economic, social, and technological aspects of the rural and urban population.

Therefore, the relation among the three objectives of this chapter is obvious. In the first and second objectives, we described the purposes of promoting Internet economy like EC and EG and possible barriers against proliferation of B2C EC and globalization. Different countries, especially developed countries, set so many citizen-centric purposes for promoting Internet economy globally. At the same time, different countries, especially developing countries, sometimes resist globalization and Internet economy. The primary reason of resisting Internet economy and thus globalization is digital divide. Strong paradigm lies behind this argument that Internet economy is basically nursing and enhancing digital divide between west and east internationally and between rich and poor citizens nationally. Therefore, it is a prime issue to investigate whether citizens of developing countries, especially rural populations, have that capability to adopt Internet economy. However, since ICT is the main driver of Internet economy, competence in ICT is a vital issue for adopting EC and EG. We argue that the rural population of developing countries might not be capable of adopting ICT. Also the impact of ICT implementation on different public projects in rural areas of developing countries is not explored comprehensively. Studies like overall country readiness in adopting ICT do not provide meaningful insight, because it is quite obvious that there is a significant digital divide between rural and urban populations in developing countries. Therefore, to accomplish the third objective, we propose two theoretical frameworks: an ad-hoc phase framework to identify separately the adoption capability of rural and urban population and a post-hoc phase to identify the impact of implementing ICT on different private and public projects among the rural and urban populations separately.

9.6. CONCLUSION AND FUTURE RESEARCH DIRECTION

The purpose of this chapter, as mentioned earlier, is threefold. In the first section, we have attempted to conceptualize the purposes for proliferation of Internet economy like EG and EC and possible barriers against globalization of Internet economy. Then we argued that those purposes of Internet economy can only be accomplished if the rural population of developing countries has the ability to adopt ICT, which is the main driver of Internet economy. And, if ICT would have a positive impact among rural populations under technological, economical, and social perspectives, then the arguments of the proponents of globalization can be justified that Internet economy is not a cause for increasing global digital divide. The Ad-hoc framework to evaluate readiness of adoption capability of ICT should be used instead of only Techno-centric 'Readiness Index" proposed by United Nations. By using our proposed framework, which specifies condition of rural population of developing countries, overall readiness of adoption capability can be addressed, revealed, and summarized for rural and urban populations of developed and developing countries separately. From the Post-hoc framework, overall impact of Internet economy can be evaluated on rural and urban populations of developed and developing countries separately. Empirical studies among rural and urban populations based on the two proposed frameworks can give comprehensive comparative pictures of readiness for adoption capability of and impact of Internet economy on rural and urban popula- tions of developing countries in contrast to developed countries. If the empirical evidences observed through these two Ad-hoc and Post-hoc frameworks show that in inter-country comparison, readiness for adoption capability and impact of ICT on developed countries are far above than that of urban and rural populations (especially of rural population) of developing countries, we assume that anti-glo- balization movement especially against Internet economy like B2C EC might get potential strength standing on the argument that Internet economy is a vital cause to increase digital divide between West and East. In that case, invariably proliferar- tion and globalization of Internet economy by mainly developed countries would be resisted by so many developing countries. By developing only rules and regulations, WTO cannot help removing those barriers.

Another aspect can be revealed from empirical studies using these two frame- works. This issue is related to launching EG nationally. It is the prime motive of policy makers of developing countries to study the impact of ICT on capability development among citizens prior to launching an EG project. Otherwise, there is a great possibility that EG projects could not accomplish the purpose of implementa- tion and could abruptly fail to reduce the digital divide, establish equal rights for all citizens, and promote good governance. Both the proposed ad-hoc and post- hoc frameworks for studying the impact of ICT in the development of developing countries are based on an explicit paradigm. Based on this paradigm, the studies should be conducted separately in urban and rural population to capture the impact on development of capability separately, not the average of the country. This study argued from literature reviews and the theoretical perspective that the impact of ICT on the capability development of rural and urban populations in developing countries could be significantly different. However, if the impact of ICT on capa- bility development of the rural population, captured from the two-phase studies proposed in this research, does not signal important positive prosperity for the majority of the people, it can be argued that that country is not ready to implement EG. Therefore, to capitalize on the full benefits of EG and fulfill the purposes of EG as revealed in this research, developing countries should conduct empirical studies in both ad-hoc and post-hoc phases of ICT implementation among both rural and urban populations separately. This will allow them to understand the capability of adoption of the rural population in ad-hoc phase and the impact of development in post-hoc phase. If, from studies, it is revealed that, especially, the rural population of developing countries is still not capable of adopting ICT; those countries might not be at the stage of implementing EG. Otherwise, the purpose of EG implementation might be jeopardized.

The proposed concepts and models address the theoretical understanding of development from both the economic and social perspectives. It provides a mechanism to identify the readiness of implementing EG by investigating the capability of adoption and performance of development of ICT for all countries, especially separately in rural and urban populations of developing countries. We expect that these theoretical frameworks might provide a deep insight into the study of digital divide, a prime issue related to Internet economy. We hope that those two frameworks can contribute to existing knowledge of evaluating the impacts of ICT on the rural and urban populations separately. It is an important aspect for both policy makers and the United Nations who are engaged in exploring the scope of implementing globalization of Internet economy in developing countries to provide better service, establish good governance, and reduce the digital divide. However, if we fail to evaluate the adoption capability of ICT of rural population of developing countries and the impact of ICT implementation, the issue of digital divide would not be resolved. This information is essential because ICT is the driving force of Internet economy. Without achieving the capability of adopting ICT countrywide in developing countries, globalization of EC internationally and diffusion of EG nationally will further increase the digital divide. Moreover, if digital divide increases due to proliferation of EC internationally and implementation of EG nationally, increased discrimination, digital divide, and suppression will always create issues for majority of the populations of the world to resist Internet economy globally and nationally for their urgent emancipation. And this is a challenging issue for world civilization.

REFERENCES

Abanumy, A., Mayhew, P., & Al-Badi, A. (2003). An Exploratory Study of E-Government in two GCC Countries. *Proceedings of the International Business Information Management Conference*, December 16-18th Cairo, Egypt.

Accenture Report. (2003). E-Government Leadership – Realizing the Vision. *The Government Executive Series*.

Adam, L., & Wood, F. (1999). An Investigation of the Impact of Information and Communication Technologies in Sub-Saharan Africa. *Journal of Information Science, 25*(4), 307-318.

Ajzen, I. (1991). The Theory of Planned Behavior. *Organizational Behavior and Human Decision Processes, 50*(2), 179-221.

Anwer, M. (2006). ICT for Better Society. *9ᵗʰ International Conference on Computer and Information Technology*, Dhaka, Bangladesh.

Avgerou, C. (1998). How can IT Enable Economic Growth in Developing Countries?. *Information Technology for Development, 8*(1), 15.

Banerjee, P., & Chau, P. (2004). An Evaluation Framework for Analyzing E-government Convergence Capability in Developing Countries. *Electronic Government, 1*(1), 29-48.

Basu, S. (2004). E-government and Developing Countries: An Overview. *International Review of Law Computers & Technology, 18*(1), 109–132.

Bhatnagar, S. (2002). E-government: Lessons from Implementation in Developing Countries. *Regional Development Dialogue, 24*, UNCRD, (Autumn Issue), 1-9.

Bhatnagar, S. C. (2000). Social Implications of Information and Communication Technology in Developing Countries: Lessons from Asian Success Stories. *Electronic Journal of Information Systems for Developing countries, 1*(4), 1-9.

Bhattacherjee, A. (2001). Understanding Information Systems Continuance: An Expectation-Confirmation Model. *MIS Quarterly, 25*(3), 351-370.

Bertot, J. C., McClure, C. R., & Owens, K. A. (1999). Universal Service in a Global Networked Environment: Selected Issues and Possible Approaches. *Government Information Quarterly, 16*(4), 309-327.

Bertot, J. C. (2003). The Multiple Dimensions of the Digital Divide: More than the Technology "haves" and "have nots. *Government Information Quarterly, 20*(2), 185-191.

Carter, L., & Bélanger, F. (2005). The Utilization of E-government Services: Citizen Trust, Innovation and Acceptance Factors. *Information Systems Journal, 15*, 5-25.

Clinton, B. (2000). http://www.whitehouse.gov/WH/New/html/e-government.html.

Cresswell, A. M., & Pardo, T. A. (2001). Implications of Legal and Organizational Issues for Urban Digital Government Development. *Government Information Quarterly, 18*, 269–278.

Dada, D. (2006). *The failure of E-government in Developing Countries.* http://www.lse.ac.uk/collections/informationSystems/iSChannel/Dada_2006b.pdf. [Accessed: 2006].

Damodaran, L., Nicholls, J., & Henney, A. (2005). The Contribution of Sociotechnical Systems Thinking to the Effective Adoption of e-Government and the Enhancement of Democracy. *The Electronic Journal of e-Government, 3*(1), 1-12.

Davis, F. (1989). Perceived Usefulness, Perceived Ease of Use and User Acceptance of Information Technology, *MIS Quarterly, 13*(3), 319-340.

Davis, F, Bagozzi, R. P., & Warshaw, P. R., (1989). User Acceptance of Computer Technology: A Comparison of Two Theoretical Models. *Management Sd., 35*(8), 982-1003.

Dawes, S. S., Pardo, T. A., & Cresswell, A. M. (2004). Designing Electronic Government Information Access Programs: A Holistic Approach. *Government Information Quarterly, 21*(1), 3–23.

Dixit, K. (2006). *Does Information Technology Really Promote Knowledge?* [cited 2006 10 July]; Available from: http://sade.sdnp.undp.org/rc/forums/mgr/sdnpmgrs/msg 01283.html.

Engel, J. F., Blackwell R. D., & Miniard, P. W. (1993). *Consumer Behavior.* 7th edition, The Dryden Press, Harcourt Brace Jovanovich, USA.

Ebrahim, Z., & Irani, Z. (2005). E-government Adoption: Architecture and Barriers. *Business Process Management Journal, 11*(5), 589-611.

Evans, D., & Yen, D. C. (2006). E-Government: Evolving Relationship of Citizens and Government, Domestic, and International Development. *Government Information Quarterly, 23*, 207–235.

European Union. (2002). Evolution of E-government in the European Union. *Report Commissioned by the Spanish Presidency of the Council of the European Union,* Available at http://www.map.es/csi/pdf/eGovEngl_definitivo.pdf.

Fountain, J. (2001). *Building the Virtual State: Information Technology and Institutional Change.* Washington, DC, Brookings Institution Press.

Gigler, B.-S. (2004). Including the Excluded - Can ICTs Empower Poor Communities? *4th International Conference on the Capability Approach,* Italy.

GAO. (2002). *Implementing the President's Management Agenda for E-Government*. Available at http://www.whitehouse.gov/omb/inforeg/egovstrategy.pdf.

Gil-García, J. R., & Pardo, T. A. (2005). E-Government Success Factors: Mapping Practical Tools to Theoretical Foundations. *Government Information Quarterly*, *22*(2), 187–216.

Gil-Garcia, J. R., & Martinez-Moyano, I. J. (2007). Understanding the Evolution of E-government: The Influence of Systems of Rules on Public Sector Dynamics. *Government Information Quarterly*, *24*, 266–290.

Gupta, M. P., & Jana, D. (2003). E-government Evaluation: A Framework and Case Study. *Government Information Quarterly*, *20*(4), 365–387.

Harris, R. W., Kuman, A., & Balaji, V. (2003),. Sustainable Telecentres? Two Cases from India. In S. Krishna & S. Madon, (Ed.), *Digital Challenge: Information Technology in the Development Context*, ASHGATE: Aldershot, (pp. 124-155).

Harris, R. W. (2005). Explaining the Success of Rural Asian Telecentres. In R. M. Davison, R. W. Harris, S. Qureshi, D. R. Vogel, & G-Jd. Vreede. (Eds.), *Information Systems in Developing Countries: Theory and Practice* (pp. 83-100), Hong Kong: City University of Hong Kong Press.

Heeks, R. (2002). Information Systems and Developing Countries: Failure, Success, and Local Improvisations. *The Information Society*, *18*, 101–112.

Heeks, R. (2003). *Most eGovernment-for-Development Projects Fail: How Can Risks be Reduced?* iGovernment Working Paper Series, Paper no. 14.

Heeks, R., & Bailur, S. (2007). Analyzing E-government Research: Perspectives, Philosophies, Theories, Methods, and Practice. *Government Information Quarterly*, *24*, 243–265

Ho, A.T-K. (2002). Reinventing Local Governments and the E-government Initiative. *Public Administration Review, 62*(4), 434-444.

Hollifield, C. A., & Donnermeyer, J. F. (2003). Creating Demand: Influencing Information Technology Diffusion in Rural Communities. *Government Information Quarterly, 20*, 135–150.

Irkhin, IU. V. (2007). Electronic Government and Society: World Realities and Russia (A Comparative Analysis). *Sociological Research, 46*(2), (March–April), 77–92.

Jaeger, P. T., & Thompson, K. M. (2003). E-government around the World: Lessons, Challenges, and Future Directions. *Government Information Quarterly, 20*, 389–394.

Jerinabi, U., & Arthi, J. (2005). Impact of Information Technology and Globalization on Women's Career. *International Conference on Information and Communication Technology of Management,* Melaka, Malaysia.

Johnston, J. (2003). The Millennium Development Goals and Information and Communications Technology. *United Nations Information and Communication Technologies Task Force,* Berlin.

Krishna, S., & Madon, S. (2004). *The Digital Challenge: Information Technology in the Development Context (Voices in Development Management).* Ashgate Publishing Company, Brookfield, VT.

Krishna, S., & Walsham, G. (2005). Implementing Public Information Systems in Developing Countries: Learning From a Success Story. *Information Technology for Development, 11*(2), 123-140.

Kumar, V., Mukerji, B., Butt, I., & Persaud, A. (2007). Factors for Successful e-Government Adoption: A Conceptual Framework. *The Electronic Journal of e-Government, 5*(1), 63-76.

Local Government Association. (2002). *egov@local: Towards a National Strategy for Local E-government.* Local Government Association, London.

Lucas, H. C., & Spitler, V. K. (1999). Technology Use and Performance: A Field Study of Broker Workstations. *Decision Science, 30*(2), 291-311.

Macome, E. (2002). *The Dynamics of the Adoption and Use of ICT-Based Initiatives for Development: Results of a Field Study in Mozambique.* In Faculty of Engineering, Built Environment and Information Technology, University of Pretoria: Pretoria, (p. 279).

Madon, S. (1991). *The Impact of Computer-Based Information Systems on Rural Development: A Case Study in India.* Imperial College of Science, Technology & Medicine: London.

Madon, S. (1997). Information-Based Global Economy and Socioeconomic Development: The Case of Bangalore. *Information Society, 13*(3), 227-244.

Madon, S. (2000). The Internet and Socio-Economic Development: Exploring the Interaction. *Information Technology & People, 13*(2), 85-101.

Madon, S. (2003*). Studying the Developmental Impact of E-governance Initiatives in Internationals Federation of Information Processing, IFIP.* Working Group 8.2 and 9.4, Athens,Greece.

Madon, S., (2004). Evaluating the Developmental Impact of E-Governance Initiatives: An Exploratory Framework. *Electronic Journal of Information Systems in Developing Countries, 20*(5), 1-13.

Madu, C. N. (1989). Transferring Technology to Developing Countries – Critical Factors for Success. *Long Range Planning, 22*(4), 115-124.

Mansell, R., & Wehn, U. (1998). *Knowledge Societies: Information Technology for Sustainable Development.* Oxford, New York: Published for and on behalf of the United Nations by Oxford University Press.

Mansell, R. (2002). From Digital Divides to Digital Entitlements in Knowledge Societies. *Current Sociology, 50*(3), 407-426.

Massini, S., & Pettigrew, A. M. (2003). Complementarities in Organizational Innovation and Performance: Empirical Evidence from the INNFORM Survey. In A. M. Pettigrew, R. Whittington, L. Melin, C. Sanchez-Runde, F. Van den Bosch, W. Ruigrock, & T. Numagami (Ed.), *Innovative Forms of Organizing: International Perspectives.* SAGE Publications.

Mbarika, V. W. A., Okoli, C., Byrd, T. A., & Datta, P. (2005). The Neglected Continent of IS Research: A Research Agenda for Sub-Saharan Africa. *Journal of the Association for Information Systems, 6*(5), 130-170.

Meso, P., Datta, P., & Mbarika, V. (2006). Moderating Information and Communication Technologies' Influences on Socioeconomic Development with Good Governance: A Study of the Developing Countries. *Journal of the American Society for Information Science & Technology, 57*(2), 186-197.

Moon, M. J. (2002). The Evolution of E-government among Municipalities: Rhetoric or Reality. *Public Administration Review, 62*(4), 424-33.

Ndou, V. D. (2004). E-government for Developing Countries: Opportunities and Challenges. *Electronic Journal of Information Systems in Developing Countries, 18*(1), 1-24.

Nedovic¢-Budic¢, Z., & Godschalk, D. (1996). Human Factors in Adoption of Geographic Information Systems. *Public Administration Review, 56,* 554–567.

Nussbaum, M., & Sen, A. (Ed.) (1993). *The Quality of Life.* Oxford: Clarendon Press.

Okot-Uma, R. W-O., & Caffrey, L. (Ed.) (2000). *Trusted Services and Public Key Infrastructure. Commonwealth Secretariat,* London.

Parker, E. B. (2000). Closing the Digital Divide in Rural America. *Telecommunications Policy, 24,* 281–290.

Parent, M., Vandebeek, C. A., & Gemino, A. C. (2005). Building Citizen Trust through E-Government. *Government Information Quarterly, 22,* 720–736.

Prattipati, S. (2003). Adoption of E-Governance: Differences between Countries in the Use of Online Government Services. *Journal of American Academy of Business, 3*(1), 386-391.

Reddick, C. G. (2006). Information Resource Managers and E-government Effectiveness: A Survey of Texas State Agencies. *Government Information Quarterly, 23,* 249–266.

Rogers, E. (1995). *Diffusion of Innovations.* New York, USA: The Free Press.

RIRDC, A. (1997). *Framework for Developing Regional Communications Initiatives,* (Ed.) Centre for International Research on Communication and Information Technologies (South Melbourne Vic.), Melbourne.

Sahay, S., &. Avgerou, C. (2002). Introducing the Special Issue on Information and Communication Technologies in Developing Countries. *Information Society, 18*(2), 73-76.

Schware, R., & Deane, A. (2003). Deploying E-government Program the Strategic Importance of 'I' Before 'E'. *Info, 5*(4), 10-19.

Sein, M., & Ahmad, I. (2001).A Framework to Study the Impact of Information and Communication Technologies on Developing Countries: The Case of Cellular Phones in Bangladesh. In *BITWORLD 2001,* Cairo, Egypt.

Spence, W. (1994). *Innovation: The Communication of Change in Ideas, Practices and Products.* London, UK: Champn and Hall

Srinivasan, S. S., Rolph, A., & Kishore, P. (2002). Customer Loyalty in E-commerce: An Exploration of Its Antecedents and Consequences. *Journal of Retailing, 78,* 41–50.

Szymanski, D. M., & Hise, R. T. (2000). E-satisfaction: An Initial Examination. *Journal of Retailing, 76*(3), 309-322.

Titah, R., & Barki, H. (2005). E-government Adoption and Acceptance: A Literature Review. *HEC Montréal.*

Taylor Nelson Sofres. (2002). *Annual Global Report on Government Online an International Perspective.* http://unpan1.un.org/intradoc/groups/public/documents/APCITY/UNPAN007044. pdf.

UNCTAD. (2000). Barriers of Internet Economy: E-commerce and LDCs. *Round Table Katmandu – Nepal – 30-31 MAY*, Electronic Commerce Section, SITE / UNCTAD.

United Nations. (2003). *Department of Economic and Social Affairs Report World Public Sector 2003: E-Government at the Crossroads*. New York, United Nations Publication.

United Nations, (2005). The Digital Divide: ICT Development Indices. *United Nations Conference on Trade and Development*, New York and Geneva: UN.

Venkatesh, V. (2000). Determinants of Perceived Ease of Use: Integrating Control, Intrinsic Motivation, and Emotion into the Technology Acceptance Model. *Information Systems Research*, *11*(4), 342-365.

Walsham, G., & Sahay, S. (2006). Research on Information Systems in Developing Countries: Current Landscape and Future Prospects. *Information Technology for Development*, *12*(1), 7-24.

Warkentin, M., Gefen, D., Pavlou, P., & Rose, G. (2002). Encouraging Citizen Adoption of E-Government by Building Trust. *Electronic Markets*, *12*(3), 157-162.

Watson, R., Berthon, P., Pitt, L., & Zinkhan, G. (2000). *Electronic Commerce—The Strategic Perspective*. Harcourt College Publishers.

Whittington, R., & Pettigrew, A. M. (2003). Complementarities Thinking. In A.M. Pettigrew, R. Whittington, L. Melin, C. Sanchez-Runde, F. van den Bosch, W. Ruigrok & T. Numagami (Eds.), *Innovative Forms of Organizing: International Perspectives* (pp. 125-132), London: Sage.

West, D.M. (2004). E-Government and the Transformation of Service Delivery and Citizen Attitudes. *Public Administration Review*, *64*(1), 15–27.

Wilhelm, A. G. (2004). *Digital Nation: Towards an Inclusive Information Society*, MIT Press.

Zhang, P., & von Dran, G. (2002). User Expectations and Rankings of Quality Factors in Different Web Site Domains. *International Journal of Electronic Commerce*, *6*(2), 9-33.

Division IV
Globalization of E-Commerce:
Cultural Adaptation

Chapter X
Globalization and Relevant Strategy for E-Commerce

ABSTRACT

This current conceptual study reviews the literature of globalization and EC, and reveals three independent variables that help to determine, initially, whether a regionalization or globalization approach is most compliant with B2C EC. These variables are customer adoption of B2C EC across countries, the external environment, and customer perception of EC quality. If globalization is currently complying with the EC operation, then this study suggests a sequential adoption of a globalization strategy. It should begin with customization for segmented markets, then modify the marketing mix for integrated segmented markets, and end with a standardized globalization approach for a homogenous market.

10.1. INTRODUCTION

The Internet potentially offers individuals, institutions, businesses, communities, and all levels of governments with new global opportunities for learning, educating, interacting, transacting business, and developing their social and economic potential (Adam & Wood, 1999). Especially, developed countries with extensive telecommunication, skilled personnel, computers, Internet, and technology infrastructure, like USA, Canada, Western Europe, Japan, Singapore, Hong Kong can get the privilege of globalization through the Internet. It plays a significant role in the present information and knowledge based market by planning, generating, managing, and transmitting information in the most effective way to provide easy access and availability across the countries. Therefore, as the most topical issue, proliferation of EC and globalization captures the attention of the practitioners, academicians, policy makers, and readers substantially which leads to development of new theoretical framework to encompass globalization strategies of EC. In this chapter, we hope to provide a theoretical framework for the globalization strategy of EC. We have divided this chapter into 6 sections to explain the related concepts of EC globalization, issues of globalization, existing literature of globalization of Internet economy, and globalization framework with conclusion. If readers follow this chapter sequentially, they will get a clear picture of the issues and paradigms of globalization of EC.

Globalization – the growing integration of trades, societies, culture, and human beings around the world – has been one of the most controversial topics in international economics over the past few years. Rapid growth of economies, extensive adoption and implementation of information and communication technology (ICT), openings of market bearing enormous opportunities, dramatic shift in political flexibility, and poverty reduction are some aspects of globalization. In countries like China, Brazil, India, South Korea, Malaysia, Thailand, Taiwan, Singapore, Hong Kong and others, that were poor decades ago, globalization has led to seamless transformation of economic activities. Globalization has generated significant international interaction across countries over the years and even skeptical analysts are foregoing to anticipate its barrier breaking movements (Andersen, & Bjørn-Andersen, 2001; Kraemer, 2001, Wong, 2002; Kettler, & Benavides, 2002; Kraemer *et al.,* 2002; Koenig & Wigand, 2004). Globalization is an umbrella term that refers to a complex of economic, trade, social, technological, cultural, and political interrelationships, convergence, and integration. This process has fierce implications on the environment, on culture, on political systems, on economic development and prosperity, and on living standards in societies around the world. EC is one of the drivers of globalization and has helped to capitalize the competitive advantages from market economy worldwide. Therefore, exploring globalization strategies, possible barriers and its possible impact on E-commerce' functional characteristics is a broad area to investigate and understand. Some scholarly researchers have explored, identified, and evaluated strategies of globalization and its adherence and adaptability with business operations (Levitt, 1983; Kustin, 1994; Kraemer *et al.,* 2002; Tsikriktsis, 2002; Balasubramanian *et al.,* 2003; Yip, 2003; Koenig & Wigand, 2004).

Globalization of traditional brick and mortar business organizations has been studied extensively for more than 20 years. The study of globalization came to prominence after Levitt (1983) announced his well established doctrine about the uniform approach of globalization in his seminal study. According to the synopsis of this discursive discourse, business organizations can simply adopt and launch a uniform and standardized product/service specification with similar marketing procedure across the countries. Global customers are not divided according to culture and social values (Levitt, 1983). Rather the global customers show similar adaptability with quality and price. However, this authoritarian marketing strategies targeted to capture global market with lower cost does not go unchallenged. Several marketing theorists (Porter, 1986; Kustin, 1994; Alden *et al.,* 2006) argue that ignoring cultural and social diversity in marketing strategy of globalization can be dangerous. In response to the controversial and one-dimensional paradigm of Levitt, these scholars including others have suggested different compromising globalization approaches which balance and ensure trade off between diversity in global market and uniformity in marketing strategy. These include customization, modified marketing mix, and regionalization. These strategies encompass very close meaning and in broader sense, these paradigms of globalization suggest differentiation in marketing strategy for segmented market as an approach of globalization considering overall diversity among those segmented markets. These diversities among segmented and sometimes regional markets can be treated as possible barriers for uniformity in marketing strategy. However, all those aforementioned controversies are mostly grounded on paradigms of traditional business methods, which is suitable for offline business. Few scholarly articles have addressed a globalization approach that is relevant to business-to-consumer (B2C) EC. Therefore, considering the gaps in this field and absolute importance of the issue, we would like to review the literature of globalization, functional characteristics of EC, and attempts to identify the perspectives of globalization strategy for B2C EC in this chapter.

Two contemporary and sometimes controversial social, cultural, and economic trends are globalization and the widespread proliferation of Internet economy. Many scholars, engaged in research on globalization trends, suggest that these two trends are so closely associated that they might be considered as mutually inclusive (Andersen, & Bjørn-Andersen, 2001; Kraemer, 2001, Wong, 2002; Kettler, & Benavides, 2002; Kraemer *et al.,* 2002; Koenig & Wigand, 2004). They even play as the driving catalysts for each other, while both are being driven or obstructed by other common forces, such as trade liberalization and government policy, regionalization and business treaty, deregulation, migration, and the expansion of the market economy

(Held *et al.,* 1999). Globalization and EC revolution are restlessly enthusiastic to create a functioning single universal market (Pohjola, 2002). To some extent, both have supplementary initiations. The seamless movement of globalization creates new challenges and opportunities for competitive online firms. The opportunities include access and intervene in new markets that were previously closed due to cost, distance, unfamiliarity, and regulation as well as cultural, political, and business barriers. Free market doctrine initiated by World Trade Organization (WTO) also enhances the ability of countries to tap resources such as labor, capital, and knowledge on a worldwide basis and the opportunity to participate in global production and distribution networks. On the other hand, Internet economy has generated seamless movement for business organizations across countries and developed close relationships between customers and business organizations which ensure and possibly create the playing field for globalization.

EC customers are inherently global; in fact, this is one of the major aspects of EC. Since, customers can interact with EC without crossing borders, online presence of any EC apparently is open worldwide. However, we should be focused on the term used in the previous sentence, "EC apparently is open for worldwide". However, there are many barriers to the way of accomplishing assumed globalization advantages. Enormous barriers can suspend the enormous opportunities postulated in the literature of the proponents of globalization and functioning of EC and also deroute the possible strategies of globalization. These barriers and perspectives of globalization may arise from political differentiation among countries, differences in trade policies, significant disparities in technology diffusion, pragmatic views of different societies, and cultural diversity. Also depending on diversity in cultural and social aspects, customers from different countries vary widely in response to some quality factors of EC; their differences depend on their perception of social values, trust disposition attitude, security and privacy concerns, and overall adoption of virtual interaction. Empirical evidence shows that cultural differences limit the ability of service providers to expand their operations globally (Li, 1994). Basically the aforementioned strategic controversies (like standardized versus marketing mix or customization or regionalization) have the primary roots grounded on these inevitable barriers of globalization. Therefore, successful globalization of EC demands a continuing understanding of changing global aspects, customer characteristics, and the fundamental paradigms that contribute to understand the strategic suitability of globalization for seamless movement of EC. In this perspective, it is imperative that E-retailers who aim to capture global market should identify the critical issues of globalization that are most concerned with their business pattern, and develop suitable and appropriate strategies to sustain, expand, and get a competitive advantage while adopting the opportunities of globalization. This current issue is, therefore, very important and has significant implications for both researchers and practitioners.

In this chapter, we attempt to investigate these issues and hence would like to address, investigate, and manifest the following twofold objectives:

1.   To address, identify, and conceptualize the issues, functional characteristics, and barriers of B2C EC related to globalization.
2.   To analyze contemporary globalization strategies and recognize the synchronization of functional characteristics of EC with globalization strategies for possible adoption and proliferation

Consumers now have divergent attitudes, versatile bargaining power, extensive varieties of available choices, and lower switching costs. However, at the same time, web operations are very vulnerable to security threat, identity theft, privacy, and trust. As a result, customers are very critical and sensitive in conducting online purchase. Nevertheless, customers of developed countries are gradually becoming aggressive in EC purchase. EC has gained dramatic importance in world retail markets. Though, EC encompasses a very little percentage of world total retail sales still now, EC retail sale is increasing every year more than 20% in USA, whereas total retail sale increases by around 4-5% (U.S. Census Bureau Report, 2007). Actually, among the developed countries, this trend of tremendous growth rate of EC is observed. EC is gradually becoming a significant part of commercial transactions. Nevertheless, EC operation and customer interaction among developing countries is still very low or sometimes insignificant. Inactive participation of developing countries which comprise a major percentage of world consumers seems to be one of the major barriers of B2C EC globalization (Wong, 2002; Kettler, & Benavides, 2002; Kraemer *et al.,* 2002; Koenig & Wigand, 2004). EC has already captured and extended throughout retail markets of developed countries. Now, it is the potential challenges of EC to extend their business periphery among developing countries for globalization and to gain competitiveness through global operation. Therefore, it is imperative that identifying and encapsulating globalization strategy of EC basically focused on revealing strategy for extending EC operation throughout the developing countries has potential merit.

The following section provides the definitions of the strategic words used in this book chapter. Then functional characteristics of B2C EC are comprehend and explained to conceptualize and relate the underlying paradigms of EC with globalization. The next section describes the literature underlying the globalization strategies so far have been discussed by the scholars in the literature. The section that follows contains the detail description of different perspectives related to barriers of globalization and theoretical concepts of conjoined relation of these barriers with prospective adoption and possibility of globalization for EC. Then the study addresses aspects of EC for globalization strategy. The final section discusses conclusion, study limitations and guidelines for future research.

10.2. DEFINITION OF RELATED CONCEPTS

This study contains four core terms: EC, B2C EC, Globalization, and Regionalization. Before going further, it is important to explain the different views held by researchers and institutions about these terms and define the specific meanings of these terms used throughout the paper. However, since we have already discussed and defined the first two terms in chapter two, we do not like to repeat here. So, we will illustrate the other two concepts.

10.2.1. Globalization

Globalization, which has arisen basically in the last two decades, is an important issue both for politicians, United Nations, and international business organizations. According to the International Monetary Fund (IMF), "globalization is the growing economic interdependence of countries worldwide through increasing volume and variety of cross-border transactions in goods and services, free international capital flows, and more rapid and widespread diffusion of technology." Held *et al.,* (1999) also illustrated globalization from this trading paradigm and defined it as the growing interconnectedness of the world through cross-border flows of information, capital, and people. Giddens (1991) defined the concept of globalization as "the intensification of world-wide social relations that links distant localities in such a way that local developments become a function of events occurring many miles away and vice versa." Castells (1996) described the trend of globalization as an increasing interconnection of economic activities and social relations. We view globalization for EC as *the economic, social, and cultural interconnectedness and interdependencies among the countries of the world. It is carried out in such a way that a uniform business approach throughout the world, interconnecting different nations as a single market or clustered markets as a segment, can prevail, sustain, and flourish.* In this chapter, we are mostly focused on economic globalization, which can be measured in different ways. Globalization espouses the following main economic, social, and political flows that characterize the pragmatic views of globalization:

Economical movement for globalization:

- Trading of goods and services, e.g. exports and imports globally across countries with global positioning view.
- Marketing and advertisement including pricing and quality of products and services among countries in the world with consistent and uniform approach that views global customers as a single entry point.
- Capital Investment globally to conduct global business considering unique approach.
- Uniformity and consistency in domestic subsidies, tariff, and customs duty globally.
- Open market sustainable with competition, no protectionism.

Social movement for globalization

- Labor/people migration inward or outward across countries
- Technology transfer, branding, diffusion, and. international research & development flow across countries considering open boundaries
- Cultural adaptation and mobility throughout the world

10.2.2. Regionalization

Regionalization is another strategy, sometimes opposing to globalization. Before taking global approach, some regional countries, due to similarities in economic and market pattern, rules and regulations, and customers' characteristics, and due to cost effectiveness and close distance, initiate a common free zone market for mutual trading benefits. This is called regionalization. European Union (EU), North American Free Trade Agreement (NAFTA), Association of Southeast Asian Nations (ASEAN) are prominent examples of regionalization. There are some valid reasons for clustering some areas, zones, or countries that exhibit similar economical, cultural, social, political, and marketing trends as a single market for a specific industry or a group of industries. This clustering can be based on many similarities, such as demographic characteristics, purchasing behaviors, cultural convergences, trade policies and agreements, history, forms of government, and development perspectives (Yip, 2003). Other important similarities are geographic proximity, economic performances, and financial indicators such as GDP, per capita income, infrastructure, and cross investment. Depending on these commonalities, uniform, discrete, and standardized drivers and strategies can be applied on a regional basis (Yip, 2003). A standardized business policy, which is developed and used for a specific region only, is defined in the study as regionalization. Among the trade alliances in a region, an integrated strategy can be adopted opposed to the fundamentals of globalization. Papadopoulos (1992) extended the regionalization and trade block concepts by contrasting globalization versus regionalization and suggesting that regionalization is a distinct entity for which neither global nor national strategies may be appropriate.

10.3. FUNCTIONAL CHARACTERISTICS AND ISSUES OF EC FOR GLOBALIZATION

It is worthwhile to mention here that the formation, operation, functionality, and customer interaction of EC are quite different from that of traditional businesses. In EC, the interaction between a customer and a business takes place with the Internet as the interface. As a result, customers from anywhere in the world can interact in this interface. So, global phenomenon is a visible aspect of EC. EC provides virtual environment. Virtual communal marketing enables managers to identify expectations, characteristics, and behavioral intentions of the customers, which they can utilize to develop service quality dimensions of global web based services (Armstrong & Hagel, 1996; Hagel & Arthur, 1997). Traditionally, in EC there is no human interaction or it has no substantial implication. Self service is one of the major aspects of EC operation. Customers buy, interact, and transact in EC website through self service. This technology has a significant implication in a web based system design. Self-service technology provides authorized human users to obtain or update information and perform qualified transactions from enterprise databases via communication channels, such as email, web network, and voice mail without depending upon human actions. Since dependencies on human interactions are eliminated, it brings a seamless flow of information, greater efficiency, and satisfaction to users. Self-service technology is derived through management and optimization of business processes. Self-service technology helps web based system designers to assess and improve quality of website and system. This technology creates the opportunity of the Electronic-vendors to identify quality of customer service and also to provide better customer service as perceived by the customers in the EC context. Another important difference between offline service environment and online interface is that companies in traditional business are able to customize their service to individuals, particularly when they interact directly with the customer. For EC, the opportunity to customize is not automatic because the website must first receive and processes customer information before it can provide customization. In EC, while interacting with the website of the retailer physically, customers do not buy goods or services in the traditional sense. They apparently purchase a website offer for a product (Gummesson, 1994). EC is significantly dominated by modern ICT. Skill, affluence, familiarity, awareness, availability of resources, viz., overall capability on using technology is a major aspect that EC requires. Customers' cultural and social values, attitudes, and beliefs are important issues for EC operation. Acceptance and usage of technologies across customers depend on their technology beliefs, and similar differences might exist in the evaluative process (Cowels & Crosby, 1990). Since EC operation is virtual without human physical presence and Internet, a sensible component for identity theft is the major media of EC, service quality factors, especially trust, security, and privacy play a very distinctive role in internet-based purchase for true globalization (Tsikriktsis, 2002; Kettler, & Benavides, 2002; Kraemer *et al.*, 2002; Balasubramanian *et al.*, 2003; Gefen *et al.*, 2003). Therefore, studying globalization of EC provides different insights which are not very similar for globalization of brick mortar business organization (Bauer *et al.*, 2006; Collier & Bienstock, 2006; Kumar *et al.*, 2006). In turn, to promote globalization and capitalize full competitive benefits of EC, policymakers are likely to face the increasingly complex issues of possible barriers and different perspectives of globalization of EC.

10.4. LITERATURE REVIEW: GLOBALIZATION STRATEGY

Globalization is the phenomenal subject for this era. All the big companies are now considering pushing their markets throughout the world. However, with regard to cost of product and service, business operation, marketing, and other related issues, country based market policy has been proved inefficient (Levitt, 1983; Kustin, 1994). As a result, international corporations are now very eager to adopt a consistent and uniform business policy which can sustain and prevail with competitive advantage throughout the world, viz., globalization .There are several business strategies which different organizations follow for globalization of services and products. One approach to globalization gives priority to a standardized marketing strategy to global homogenous market, while the other focuses on a modified marketing mix strategy to global diverse markets (Levitt, 1983; Kustin, 1994, Yip, 2003). It is still debatable whether a standard marketing strategy considering the whole world as a homogenous market or a mix marketing strategy considering different segments of the world heterogeneous is appropriate. There are several driving forces, like organization, market, and industry related factors should be considered before choosing any specific strategy of globalization (Yip, 2003). The literature focused on strategies of globalization often refers to regionalization as another concept of internationalization which somewhat opposes absolute meaning of globalization (Papadopoulos & Denis 1988, Papadopoulos, 1992). However, researchers conceptualizing different globalization strategies are keen to observe the presence or absence of commonalities across countries rather than in whether these countries are formally networked as a regional trade group (Papadopoulos, 1992). Regionalization as an opposing theory and practice argues that instead of targeting the global market, it is opportunistic to select a regional market with interconnectedness among countries in that selected area and form a business treaty to mutually operate that regional market. This middle approach to international market selection is region-based (Papadopoulos & Denis 1988, Papadopoulos, 1992). The world from the couple of decades started globalizing, and due to invention of Internet and fall of communism, continues to globalize in an inevitable, irresistible movement (Levitt, 1983; Holt *et al.,* 2004). Different potential aspects have substantially contributed to globalization. These factors include stable market, political synchronization (emancipation of east Europe from controlled market), rapid proliferation of market economy, worldwide investment, economic advances in several developing countries, a supply chain of production and marketing, advances in telecommunication technologies and the Internet, increases in world travel, and the growth of global media (Steenkamp *et al.,* 2002; Ozsomer *et al.,* 2004; Stremersch *et al.,* 2004; Van Everdingen *et al.,* 2005). Scholars, who are proponents of a standardized globalization approach (Hannerz, 1990; Levitt, 1983), have predicted that globalization leads to the creation of a "global consumer culture" (Alden *et al.,* 1999, Crane, 2002). These scholars believe world can be treated, without much risk, as a single point of marketing. Cultural, social, political, and economical barriers will be traded off with lower price and better quality which can be ensured by capitalizing huge global market. According to this discourse of globalization, if a company offers better quality and reliability with a lower price, customers from different cultures and behaviors will be united in a single global standard. In other words, customers will not influence the corporations' global strategy; rather corporations will format and reshape the consumers' behavior and culture. Convergence theorists support this ideology to create a harmony among different segmented markets (Bell, 1973; Ohmae, 1990, 1995). On the other hand, other scholars, who view the globalization trend as a marketing mix of adaptation, have argued that local culture, social, political, and economical status provide a very powerful influence to differentiate the global market (Kotler, 1973; Porter, 1986; Sheth, 1986; Wind *et al.,* 1986; Kustin, 1994; Hermans *et al.,* 1998; Alden *et al.,* 2006). These researchers predict that due to significant variations between countries, especially developed and developing countries, a homogenous and standardized business strategy cannot function properly. These profound variations include factors like political differences, market rules and protectionism, distribution of tariffs and subsidies, social values and perception, consumer needs and tastes, quality standards, economic development and purchasing power, commercial infrastructure and capability, traditions, and technological development. Presence of substantial differences on these aspects among global countries, in particular, between developed and developing countries potentially prove the unacceptability of standardized or homogenous globalization approach. Although these scholars support globalization, instead of a standardized strategy throughout the whole world, these researchers propose somewhat modified marketing mixes. This globalization theory considers globalization with a local strategy. They suggest global organizations can modify and adjust products, service, quality, advertisement strategies, processes, packaging, price, and customer policies including payment, return, and service etc following the traits of those countries. Divergence theorists affirm that national diversity. Their logic lies on the paradigms that profound differences among different countries in social, political, cultural, and economic patterns prevail and these restrict convergence by creating a single market where a standardized strategy can reign (Berger *et al.,* 1996; Boyer, 1996; Hirst *et al.,* 1996; Wade, 1996).

10.5. THEORETICAL FRAMEWORK FOR STRATEGY

Global concept is an inherent aspect for the functional characteristics of B2C EC. However, practically, contemporary B2C EC is operating locally or regionally between North America and Europe. But, traditional business organizations, especially large corporations are very much enthusiastic and keen to develop global approach as their marketing strategy. Since EC, in terms of functional characteristics are more prone and supportive to globalization, and also developing countries comprising a major percentage of potential consumers who are gradually adopting the Internet, globalization for EC will soon become a pivotal question for the policy makers, practitioners, and academicians.

To set the business strategies of globalization, Electronic-retailers should first conceptualize several factors of global market. Yip (2003), a leading author of global strategy, mentioned that globalization strategy is multidimensional. Developing strategy for a global business requires choices along a number of strategic dimensions. These dimensions basically determine whether the business strategy should focus regional or global. Further, if an E-retailer takes a global approach; it is a meritorious question to identify which strategy of globalization namely standardized or marketing mix is suitable. The following paragraphs of this section will be engaged to identify a theoretical framework to determine whether globalization or regionalization approach is suitable for globalization of EC. Then if it observed that EC can take, at present, globalization approach, the second question arises to resolve and determine the strategy of globalization. The basis of this theoretical framework is grounded on two potentially segmented markets, namely developed and developing countries. based on recommendations from different literature reviews and reports conducted on developing countries, this research argues that technological, political, social, and financial parameters are the major differences between developed and developing countries for extending EC operation from developed to developing countries, and thus are the potential barriers for EC globalization (Madon, 1997; Sein & Ahmad, 2001; Sahay & Avgerou, 2002; Heeks, 2002; Walsham & Sahay, 2006). Since globalization has multi-dimensional aspects, Swiss think tank KOF (2007) has proposed a composite index to measure globalization. The index measures the three main perspectives of globalization: economic, social, and political aspects. However, from the light of capability theory (Nussbaum & Sen, 1993), due to unavailability of technological infrastructure in developing countries, technology aspect also plays a significant role in globalization of EC. Therefore, the argument of this study lies on the ground that if developing countries are at a position to adopt EC technologically, socially, politically, and financially, then EC, mostly prevailed and dominated in developed countries, can be targeted to capture huge consumers of developing countries by extending into developing countries through a suitable globalization approach. So, the first question which will be addressed here is that whether globalization approach or regionalization approach is appropriate for EC companies. This concern will be resolved by shedding light on the above mentioned aspects of developing countries.

10.5.1. Technological and Social Aspect

The compelling characteristics and pragmatic scope of globalization, unlike traditional internalization or even multinational views, are often facilitated by information and communication technology and the Internet, the main drivers of EC. Majority consumers of developing countries (exceptions may apply in some developing countries which have got profound advancement in diffusion of ICT like China, South Korea, Hong Kong, Taiwan, Malaysia, Singapore, South Africa, Brazil, India etc.) are generally

1. Socially not familiar and aware of ICT, computer, and the Internet. As a result they are not conscious about EC interaction and purchase. Without adoption of ICT by consumers, EC can not be sustained and accentuated in a market.
2. Less educated and language is a potential barrier.
3. Consumers are mostly incapable of operating and conducting EC transaction due to lower skill in web browse.
4. Availability of infrastructure like the Internet, computers, and telecommunication is very limited among consumers.

In this context, if we shed light on capability theory, we can observe that without equal capability defined by awareness and availability of resources and skill, scope of same opportunity cannot either be created or justified. Depending on this phenomenal concept of welfare economics, it can be argued that without having competitive capability for consumers of developing countries socially and technologically to avail and use ICT, adoption of EC and purpose of globalization cannot be accomplished or justified (Gigler, 2004; Harris, 2005). Rather globalization of EC in developing countries might be accused of propelling inequality, digital divide, and discrimination. Technology adoption model (Davis *et al.* 1989; Davis 1989) and Diffusion of innovation theory (Rogers, 1995) also support the arguments. Since technology is the driving force of EC interaction, identifying technology adoption capability of consumers of developing countries is a single most important issue for EC practitioners to launch globalize operation (Madon, 2000; Bhatnagar, 2002; Krishna & Madon, 2004). Several scholarly researchers have confirmed that the digital divide based on technological and social aspects between developed and developing countries is a potential barrier for globalization of EC (Balasubramanian *et al.,* 2003; Vehovar, 2003). Since most of the developing countries are generally economically less advanced, socially less educated, and technologically less habituated in using modern ICT, technological and social aspects are two pre-dominated factors for developing adoption capability of EC. Technological barriers include less skill in using ICT, Internet, and computers (Heeks, 2002/2003). Social barrier for developing countries include unfamiliarity with and unavailability of resources related to EC operation and website language (Kettler, & Benavides, 2002). Since B2C EC has already expanded among the developed countries (UNCTAD, 2004), the following arguments are targeted toward factors relating to the adoption of B2C EC by customers in developing countries. We define technological capability as "the ability of consumers of developing countries achieving skill to use and interact in EC". We view social capability as "the ability of consumers of developing countries becoming aware and familiar with modern technology, having resources required to access in ICT and interact in EC, and understanding language used in EC". Technological capability aspect can be measured through some constructs getting insight directly from technology adoption model (Perceived Ease of use, Perceived usefulness) and diffusion of innovation theory (Compatibility). Social capability can be operationalized through some constructs in the light of capability theory, theory of planned behavior, like awareness of the consumers of developing countries and availability of resources socially to get access and interact in EC. Therefore, we propose the following paradigm:

P₁: If the consumers of developing countries do not have the technological capability, globalization approach for EC operation extending from developed to developing countries cannot, at present, be feasible; rather present regionalization approach is still justified.

P₂: If the consumers of developing countries do not have the social capability, globalization approach for EC operation extending from developed to developing countries cannot, at present, be feasible; rather present regionalization approach is still justified.

10.5.2. Political Aspect

Although WTO is engaged and very much enthusiastic to liberalize the world market and create harmony among developed and developing countries, in terms of rules and regulations prevailing to control the market, subsidies, duty, and tariffs, still different countries are protecting their markets and local entrepreneurs by applying controlling rules, subsidies, and tariffs. Also due to political instability and presence of different doctrines including other potential factors, many developing countries are often against proliferation of market economy and globalization.

The political aspect needed to facilitate globalization of B2C EC is also extremely important. It includes country-specific rules and regulations, policies, market parameters, and political legislation. Several researchers noted that country-specific government policy, duty and tariff systems, and subsidies in domestic market are the potential barriers of globalization of B2C EC (Tiessen *et al.,* 2001; Gibbs *et al.,* 2003). Even, sometimes different rules and regulations of some countries like North Korea, Burma, Cuba protect consumers from purchasing through EC completely. As a result, potentially EC cannot be extended to these markets and sustained through adopting globalizing strategy. Therefore, political adoption of developing countries which is defined here as "the political system synchronized with the policy of WTO, viz., open market policy, to allow foreign companies to interact in local market without government intervention" is one of the foundations for successful launching and extension of EC in developing countries. This political adoption of developing countries can be measured through some variables like government support and policy consistent with non-protectionism, government-political stability, open market, systematic subsidy and tariff system. Proliferation of EC to developing countries depends on market rules, regulations, tax systems, subsidies, and commercial barriers which are implemented through political speculation. Though the WTO is eager to open the world market by reducing obstructive rules and regulations, introducing flat duty/tariff system, and removing hidden subsidy systems, countries across the world are still not operated under a harmonized system. Without the cooperation of different governments, WTO cannot create the ideal structure for the globalization of B2C EC. Uniformity of government systems is associated with democratization, political openness, transparent vision, higher level commitment, huge resource allocation, a radical change of government service systems, and smooth financial strategies that conform to a universal system. Depending on the above arguments, we hereby propose,

P_3: *If the developing countries do not politically adopt B2C EC and allow them to be operated enjoying free market as regulated by WTO, consumers of developing countries ultimately cannot avail the full benefits of EC and thus will not adopt EC. As a result, globalization approach for EC operation extending from developed to developing countries cannot, at present, be feasible; rather present regionalization approach is still justified.*

10.5.3. Financial Tool Aspect

Since EC operation is virtual and one of the major functional characteristics of EC is that it can be conducted from anywhere in the world, EC transaction needs some specific financial arrangements. These include payment system and shipment system. Most of the EC payment is conducted by some credit cards. But, most of the developing countries do not have credit card system which is internationally accepted. Also money exchange and money transfer are also vital problems for developing countries. Exchanging from US dollar to local currency is not a problem, however, opposite exchange is always a problematic issue in developing countries. Also, most of the developing countries put some barriers to exchanging local currency into US dollar to maintain US dollar reserve which is very important for developing countries to pay international debts. Therefore, without authenticated and internationally acceptable credit card system and easy money exchange system without intervention, consumers of developing countries cannot participate in global operation of EC. Financial transaction tools are also potential factors that could hinder the global transaction of EC. As a result, globalization approach of EC cannot be justified without arranging especial financial tools to settle the problems. Another real concern arises when there is a question for shipment and especially for return of items. E-retailers have some arrangements with shipping companies. Among these shipping companies, some are not operated in some developing countries, or even if operated, for a long travel and less frequency of order volume, they charge excessively. Consequently, total payment goes far above than expectation, and consumers of developing countries loose interest in interacting in EC. Same type of problem, but sometimes detrimental than the previous one, is return of items. If customers are not satisfied with their purchase, it is really difficult for consumers of developing countries to return their purchased items. We here address the financial tool aspect as "the availability of payment and exchange system and shipment and return policy and modes". Therefore, without solving these problems, adoption of EC in terms of financial aspect cannot be possible in developing countries and thus globalization of EC in developing countries is not feasible (Tiessen *et al.,* 2001; Gibbs *et al.,* 2003). It is possible, however, for global E-retailers to adopt alternative payment methods in developing countries by, for example, setting up a transaction mechanism with the local banks. Based on the above findings, we propose:

P$_4$: If the developing countries do not have adoption capability in terms of financial tool aspect, consumers of developing countries ultimately cannot avail the full benefits of EC and thus will not adopt EC, and as a result, globalization approach for EC operation extending from developed to developing countries cannot, at present, be feasible; rather present regionalization approach is still justified.

So, this study offers a theoretical framework of technological, social, political, and financial adoption capability of developing countries to identify whether EC operated in developed countries can decide to extend their market periphery to developing countries by adopting globalization approach or they will continue to operate as it is now through regionalization. Now the second question arises from the solution of the first problems. If the developing countries have that technological, social, political, and financial capability in relation to EC operation, E-retailers can expand their operation from developed to developing countries taking a suitable globalization strategy. But what will be that globalization strategy? The answer will be resolved through looking into cultural aspect and service quality perception of consumers of developing countries.

10.5.4. Cultural Aspect and Service Quality Perception

Studies dealing with interactions in virtual environment (Meuter *et al.,* 2001; Chen & Dhillon, 2003) reveal that customer evaluation of online interaction is a distinct process. It depends on many behavioral characteristics like personality, belief, attitude, experience, education, and different external environmental stimulus, which comprehensively represent culture of a nation. It plays a distinctive role in quality perception (Cowles 1989; Cowles & Crosby 1990; Dabholkar 1996; Eastlick 1996; Tsikriktsis, 2002). Culture and its effect on globalization is a vast area and needs more attention from both the researchers and practitioners. Hofstede (1994) defined culture as the "collective programming of the mind which distinguishes the members of one group or category of people from those of another." A society produces some values, ideas, intentions, characteristics, attitudes, and speculations on human personality. This is a perceived psychological phenomenon that depends on both internal and external stimulus which comprise culture of a nation. Depending on cultural factors, globalization can be affected vividly. Therefore studying globalization always demand close observation of cultural attributes, cultural interaction, cultural negotiation, and its global impact. It is argued that culture influences business negotiation, conflict resolution, mergers & acquisition, organization policy. On the other hand, culture affects purchase decision, product choice, and customers' evaluation of complex services. To set the business strategies of globalization, E-retailers attempt to conceptualize several factors of the global market. Yip (2003) mentioned that the globalization strategy is multidimensional. Developing a strategy for a global business requires choices along a number of strategic dimensions. Among these dimensions, service quality is the single most important factor for conceptualizing online behavior (Parasuraman *et al.*, 2005; Bauer *et al.*, 2006; Fassnacht *et al,* 2006; Kim *et al.*, 2006; Sebastianelli *et al.*, 2006; Shareef *et al*, 2008).

Levitt (1983) and other proponents of homogeneous globalization approach throughout the world anticipated that better quality and lower price push customers throughout the world to adopt a product or service in a singular manner. However, different authors addressing quality of EC revealed that perception of quality of EC play the most significant role in online purchase which is significantly differ-ent from offline purchase (Devaraj *et al.,* 2002; Janda *et al.,* 2002; Loiacono *et al.,* 2002; Zhang & van Dran, 2002; Cai & Jun, 2003; Santos, 2003; Wolfinbarger & Gilly, 2003; Parasuraman *et al.*, 2005; Bauer *et al.*, 2006; Kumar *et al.*, 2006; Se-bastianelli *et al.*, 2006, Shareef *et al.,* 2008). Some scholars also revealed that price is not a very important aspect in online environment as it is in offline environment (Rust, 2001; Parasuraman *et al.*, 2005). Scholars who are conducting research in modeling service quality, postulate that cultural differences in developed and de-veloping countries play a significant role in quality perception of EC (Tsikriktsis, 2002; Collier & Bienstock, 2006 Balasubramanian *et al.,* 2003; Zhan *et al.,* 2003; Ribbink *et al.,* 2004; Chiu *et al.,* 2005; Schaupp *et al.,* 2005; Shareef *et al.,* 2008). It is explicitly observed that on the perspective of technological, social, financial, political, cultural issues, consumers of developed and developing countries show remarkable differences in relation to online behavior (Bhatnagar, 2000; Heeks, 2003; Vehovar, 2003; Dada, 2006; Shareef *et al.,* 2008). However, these findings related to differences in quality perception of EC between developed and developing countries are very much fragmented and cannot provide a generalize view. Therefore, from the above findings, these following synopses can be organized:

1.   Price is not as important in online purchase as in offline purchase. Therefore, one of the most potential arguments for standardized globalization approach is not assured in online behavior.

2. Quality perception is a potential factor for interacting in EC.
3. Culture has enormous effect on perception of quality.
4. Developed and developing countries might show differences in quality perception of EC.

Therefore based on the arguments of globalization strategists (Levitt, 1983; Hannerz, 1990; Kotler, 1973; Porter, 1986; Sheth, 1986; Wind *et al.,* 1986; Kustin, 1994; Holt *et al.,* 2004) of both standardized and customization, perception of service quality of B2C EC can be introduced in theoretical framework of globalization to investigate whether developed and developing countries show harmony and parity in perception of service quality. If it is revealed that the service quality framework of B2C EC is homogenous throughout the world according to the perception of the customers, then B2C Electronic-retailers might consider standard marketing strategy for global market; otherwise, they will launch marketing mix (customization) strategy as the globalization approach for developed and developing countries. Several scholars have investigated and formulated quality models of EC as described in chapter three (Devaraj *et al.,* 2002; Janda *et al.,* 2002; Loiacono *et al.,* 2002; Zhang & van Dran, 2002; Cai & Jun, 2003; Santos, 2003; Wolfinbarger & Gilly, 2003; Parasuraman *et al.,* 2005; Bauer *et al.,* 2006; Fassnacht *et al,* 2006; Kim *et al.,* 2006; Sebastianelli *et al.,* 2006). However, these models are validated only based on the perception of consumers of developed countries. Therefore, we are familiar with the quality perception of developed countries. Now, it is imperative that these models can be tested in some different developing countries. If the empirical studies find quite similarities in quality perception between developed and developing countries, Levit's (1983) seminal globalization approach, viz., standardize marketing strategy can be considered to be suitable for online interaction. Dissimilarities in quality perception between developed and developing countries will lead to provoke the alternative strategy of globalization which several authors advocated for (Porter, 1986; Douglas *et al.,* 1989; Kustin, 1994; Alden *et al.,* 2006), viz., marketing mix strategy. Therefore, we propose:

P₅: If the consumers of developed and developing countries show similarities in perception of service quality, a standardize globalization approach can be adopted by B2C EC, otherwise customization (marketing mix) is the alternative globalization approach for developed and developing countries.

However, disparity in quality perception between developed and developing countries observed at present, might not predict future trend. As several scholars revealed, difference in culture in relation to quality perception gradually synchronizes among the segmented markets and might ultimately ensure unique purchasing culture based on single market (Bell, 1973; Ohmae, 1990, 1995; Holton, 2000).

10.6. CONCLUSION

The global adoption of websites makes it cheaper and easier for firms to satisfy their customers, manage their operations, and coordinate value chains across borders (Globerman *et al.*, 2001; Cavusgil, 2002). EC enhances globalization by reducing transaction and coordination costs, creating new and expanded markets with economies of scale, and providing better quality service (Steinfield *et al.*, 1999; Mann *et al.*, 2000). Globalization can provide EC the full benefits as expected from its implementation as perceived by functional characteristics. Firm globalization is heralded as a key driver in expanding the use of EC (Steinfield *et al.*, 1999). Due to the worldwide proliferation of the Internet, the main vehicle of B2C EC, EC has a great opportunity to spread throughout the world among the consumers of both developed and developing countries. Therefore, adoption of B2C EC by customers among developing countries can be considered as a crucial factor for proper globalization. However, due to several barriers and constraints, EC functionally focuses primarily on local or regional markets as termed in this study as regionalization. At the present, most of the E-retailers operate within North America and Europe. Developing countries are not integrated within the operation arena of B2C EC. However, globalization is an important aspect for EC, since large consumer populations from developing countries might be ready to interact with EC. But on the other hand, if developing countries are not ready to adopt EC, globalization approach for EC must be considered as abandoned and wasteful. Therefore, identification of the strategy of globalization, or regionalization for EC proliferation is the burning question for operation of B2C EC. We have identified the plausible perspectives of barriers for globalization of EC and extension from developed to developing countries. If developing countries have technological, social, political, and financial (tool) capabilities simultaneously to adopt EC, then E-retailers can extend their business periphery from developed countries to developing countries and adopt globalization strategy. Otherwise present status of regionalization is the appropriate solution for EC operation. Therefore, we postulate that EC operation strategy, globalization or regionalization, is contingent on technological, social, political, and financial (tool) aspect of developing countries.

Now, from empirical studies among different developing countries, should we observe that developing countries are more or less equipped and ready technologically, socially, politically, and financially to adopt EC. This study suggests implementing globalization approach in EC operation by extending present EC operation to developing countries from regionalization which is limited in developed countries. Now the second concern is which strategy of globalization is more suitable for present EC operation. Proponents of standardized globalization approach, though, advised that culture is not a potential factor to differentiate market, rather better quality and lower price ensure homogenous market condition. However, for EC it is observed from several empirical studies that culture dominantly interfere in EC quality perception, thus quality perception among developed and developing countries might be significantly different (Vehova, 2003, Shareef *et al.*, 2008). Also, EC purchase intention studies revealed that the price is a factor; however, quality perception plays a single most important role in purchase decision (Parasuraman *et al.*, 2005; Shareef *et al.*, 2008). These findings suggest the use of perceived quality of EC as the determining factor for selecting standardized or marketing mix strategy as the globalization approach for EC. Based on this theoretical findings, we propose to use several quality models of EC (like Devaraj *et al.*, 2002; Janda *et al.*, 2002; Loiacono *et al.*, 2002; Zhang & van Dran, 2002; Cai & Jun, 2003; Santos, 2003; Wolfinbarger & Gilly, 2003; Parasuraman *et al.*, 2005; Bauer *et al.*, 2006; Fassnacht *et al*, 2006; Kim *et al.*, 2006; Sebastianelli *et al.*, 2006) to capture quality perception of consumers of developing countries. These models are grounded on quality perception of consumers of developed countries. Therefore, if these models are used to capture the same effects, and observe substantial difference, we suggest implementing marketing mix strategy as the globalization approach for developed and developing countries. However, some scholars argue that cultural differences might be harmonized gradually (Bolton, 2000). Gradual convergence of cultural differences might develop harmony in quality perception of EC. So, future trend will ensure whether standardized globalization approach is a potential possibility for EC in future. As changes occur and there is a gradual convergence in quality perception by consumers across countries, the standardize globalization approach might succeed.

This chapter is designed to address a globalization strategy for B2C EC operation which is completely focused on external perspectives for selecting globalization strategy. There are numerous internal factors like firms' internal capacity, financial ability, availability of market and distribution channels, objective and vision etc. which are essential to determine a firm's ability to spread globally. These internal factors are mostly determining factors of globalization for specific E-retailer which have no effect on whether a globalization environment for EC prevails across the countries. But, the vision of this book chapter is to formulate and conceptualize overall globalization strategy for EC based on global technological, social, political, financial, and cultural aspects. Therefore, consideration of those external factors which affect overall global market can provide an integrative view of globalization approach. The propositions proposed in this study are fundamentally grounded on a digital divide between developed and developing countries. Considering the functional characteristics of B2C EC, major cultural differences between developed and developing countries related to quality perception of EC as explained in related literature, justify this globalization strategy. However, the many properties of market segmentation must also be noted. Even among European countries, quality perceptions of EC by consumers differ. However, again it is observed that these differences also lie between west and east Europe. The perceptions of quality dimensions of B2C EC by consumers are proposed in this study as one of the major parameters of a globalization strategy. The reason is that most of the research conducted in B2C EC in the last 10 years has suggested that successful operation of B2C EC among different countries primarily depends on perception of quality.

We have developed theoretical frameworks as the globalization strategy for B2C EC. Until now, hardly any scholarly research has been conducted and investigated to formulate globalization strategy for B2C EC. Therefore, these two theoretical frameworks could be considered as a future research direction for exploratory study. Measurement items of different constructs used in the propositions could be operationalized. To validate the propositions and to get deeper insights into the globalization of B2C EC, extensive empirical studies should be conducted among developing countries.

REFERENCES

Adam, L., & Wood, F. (1999). An Investigation of the Impact of Information and Communication Technologies in Sub-Saharan Africa. *Journal of Information Science, 25*(4), 307-318.

Alden, D. L., Steenkamp, J-B.E.M., & Batra, R. (1999). Brand Positioning through Advertising in Asia, North America, and Europe: The Role of Global Consumer Culture. *Journal of Marketing, 63*(1), 75-87.

Alden, D. L., Steenkamp, J. B. E. M., & Batra, R. (2006). Consumer Attitudes toward Marketplace Globalization: Structure, Antecedents and Consequences. *Proceedings of the 35th European Marketing Association Conference,* Athens, May 2006.

Anderson Consulting. (1999). E-commerce: what's All the Fuss. *Presentation, Anderson Consulting, 5*(Section 1).

Andersen, K. V., & Bjørn-Andersen, N. (2001). *Globalization and E-Commerce: Growth and Impacts in Denmark.* Center for Research on IT and Organizations University of California, Irvine.

Armstrong, A., & Hagel, J. (1996). The Real Value of On-line Communities. *Harvard Business Review, 74*(3), 134-141.

Balasubramanian, S., Konana, P., Menon, N. M. (2003). Customer Satisfaction in Virtual Environments: A Study of Online Investing. *Management Science, 49*(7), 871-889.

Baldwin, L. P., & Currie, W. L. (2000). Key Issues in Electronic Commerce in Today's Global Information Infrastructure. *Cognition, Technology & Work, 2*(1), 27-34.

Bauer, H. H., Falk, T., & Hammerschmidt, M. (2006). eTransQual: A Transaction Process-Based Approach for Capturing Service Quality in Online Shopping. *Journal of Business Research, 59*, 866-875.

Bell, D. (1973). *The Coming of Post-Industrial Society.* New York: Basic Books.

Berger, S., & Dore, R. (Ed.). (1996). *National Diversity and Global Capitalism.* Ithaca, NY: Cornell University Press.

Bhatnagar, S. (2002). E-government: Lessons from Implementation in Developing Countries. *Regional Development Dialogue, 24*, UNCRD, (Autumn Issue, 2002), 1-9.

Boyer, R. (1996). The Convergence Hypothesis Revisited: Globalization But Still the Century of Nations? In S. Berger and R. Dore (Ed.), *National Diversity and Global Capitalism* (pp. 29–59). Ithaca, NY: Cornell University Press.

Boyer, K. K., Hallowell, R., & Roth, A. V, (2002). E-Services: Operations Strategy—A Case Study and A Method for Analyzing Operational Benefits. *Journal of Operations Management, 20*(2), 175–188.

Castells, M. (1996). *The Rise of Network Society.* Oxford, UK: Blackwell.

Cavusgil, S. T. (2002). Extending the Reach of E-Business. *Marketing Management, 11*(2), 24-29.

Cai, S., & Jun, M. (2003). Internet Users' Perceptions of Online Service Quality: A Comparison of Online Buyers and Information Searches. *Managing Service Quality, 13*(6), 504-519.

Chen, S. C., & Dhillon, G. S. (2003). Interpreting Dimensions of Consumer Trust in E-commerce. *Information Technology and Management, 4*, 303-318.

Chiu, H. C., Hsieh, Y. C., Kao, C. Y. (2005). Website Quality and Customer's Behavioral Intention: An Exploratory Study of the Role of Information Asymmetry. *Total Quality Management, 16*(2), 185-197.

Collier, J. E., & Bienstock, C.C. (2006). Measuring Service Quality in E-Retailing. *Journal of Service Research, 8*(3), 260-275.

Cowles, D. (1989). Consumer Perceptions of Interactive Media. *Journal of Broadcasting and Electronic Media, 33*(Winter), 83-89.

Cowles, D. L., Crosby, L. A. (1990). Consumer Acceptance of Interactive Media in Service Marketing Encounters. *The Service Industries, 10*(July), 521-40.

Crane, D. (2002). Culture and Globalization. In D. Crane, N. Kawashima, & K. Kawasaki (Ed.), *Global Culture: Media, Arts, Policy and Globalization* (pp. 1–25). New York: Routledge.

Dabholkar, P. A. (1996). Consumer Evaluations of New Technology-Based Self-Service Options: An Investigation of Alternative Models of SQ. *International Journal of Research in Marketing, 13*(1), 29-51.

Dada, D. (2006). *The Failure of E-government in Developing Countries.* http://www.lse.ac.uk/collections/informationSystems/iSChannel/Dada_2006b.pdf. [Accessed: 2006].

Davis, F. (1989). Perceived Usefulness, Perceived Ease of Use and User Acceptance of Information Technology. *MIS Quarterly, 13*(3), 319-340.

Davis, F., Bagozzi, R. P., & Warshaw, P. R. (1989). User Acceptance of Computer Technology: A Comparison of Two Theoretical Models. *Management Science, 35*(8), 982-1003.

Devaraj, S., Fan, M., & Kohli, R. (2002). Antecedents of B2C Channel Satisfaction and Preference: Validating e-Commerce Metrics. *Information Systems Research, 13*(3), 316-333.

Eastlick, M. A. (1996). Consumer Intention to Adopt Interactive Teleshopping. Working paper, report No. 96-113 (August), *Marketing Science Institute*, Cambridge, MA.

Electronic Commerce Resource Center. (1996). http://www.sbpm.gwu.edu/research/centers/CASB/electronic.htm.

Fassnacht, M., & Koese, I. (2006). Quality of Electronic Services: Conceptualizing and Testing a Hierarchical Model. *Journal of Service Research, 9*(1), 19-37.

Gefen, D., Karahanna, E., & Straub, D. W. (2003). Trust and TAM in Online Shopping: An Integrated Model. *MIS Quarterly, 27*, 51-90.

Gibbs, J., Kraemer, K. L., & Dedrick, J. (2003). Environment and Policy Factors Shaping E-Commerce Diffusion: A Cross-Country Comparison. *The Information Society, 19*(1), 5-18.

Giddens, A. (1991). *Modernity and Self-identity.* Stanford, CA: Stanford University Press.

Gigler, B.-S. (2004). Including the Excluded - Can ICTs Empower Poor Communities?. *4th International Conference on the Capability Approach,* Italy.

Globerman, S., Roehl, T. W., & Standifird., S. (2001). Globalization and Electronic Commerce: Inferences from Retail Brokering. *Journal of International Business Studies, 32*(4), 749-768.

Gummesson, E. (1994). Making Relationship Marketing Operational. *International Journal of Service Industry Management, 5*(5), 5-20.

Hagel, J. III, & Arthur G. A. (1997). Net Gain: Expanding Markets through Virtual Communities. *Mckinsey Quarterly (winter),* (pp. 140–146).

Hannerz, U. (1990). Cosmopolitans and Locals in World Culture. *Theory, Culture and Society, 7*(2/3), 237–251.

Harris, R.W. (2005). Explaining the Success of Rural Asian Telecentres. In R. M. Davison, R. W. Harris, S. Qureshi, D. R. Vogel, & G-Jd. Vreede. (Eds.) *Information Systems in Developing Countries: Theory and Practice* (pp. 83-100), Hong Kong: City University of Hong Kong Press.

Heeks, R. (2002). Information Systems and Developing Countries: Failure, Success, and Local Improvisations. *The Information Society, 18*, 101–112.

Heeks, R. (2003). *Most eGovernment-for-Development Projects Fail: How Can Risks be Reduced?* iGovernment Working Paper Series, Paper no. 14.

Held, D., McGrew, A., Goldblatt, D., & Perraton, J. (1999). *Global, Transformations: Politics, Economics and Culture.* Stanford, CA: Stanford University Press.

Hermans, H. J. M., & Kempen, H. J. G. (1998). Moving Cultures. *American Psychologist, 53*(10), 1111–1120.

Hirst, P., & Thompson, G. (1996). *Globalization in Question: The International Economy and the Possibilities of Governance.* Cambridge: Polity Press.

Hofstede, G. (1994). Management Scientists are Human. *Management Science, 40*(1), 4-13.

Holt, D. B., Quelch, J. A., & Taylor, E. L. (2004). How global Brands Compete. *Harvard Business Review, 82*(9), 1–9.

Holton, R. (2000). Globalization's Cultural Consequences. *Annals of the American Academy of Political and Social Science, 570*(4), 140–152.

Janda, S., Trocchia, P. J., & Gwinner, K. P. (2002). Consumer Perceptions of Internet Retail Service Quality. *International Journal of Service Industry Management, 13*(5), 412-431.

Kim, M., Kim, Jung-Hwan, & Lennon, S. J. (2006). Online Service Attributes Available on Apparel Retail Web Site: An E-S-QUAL Approach. *Managing Service Quality, 16*(1), 51-77.

Kettler, H. F., & Benavides, E. (2002). *E-Business Globalization. Analyzing Foreign Countries for E-Commerce Opportunities.* www.hipermarketing.com/nuevo%204/columnas/efrain/ebus. pdf.

Koenig, W., & Wigand, R. T. (2004). Globalization and E-Commerce: Diffusion and Impacts of the Internet and E-Commerce in Germany. *Center for Research on Information Technology and Organizations,* University of California, Irvine

Kotler, P. (1973). Atmospherics as a Marketing Tool. *Journal of Retailing, 49*(4), 48-64.

Kraemer, K. L. (2001). *Globalization of E-Commerce.* Center for Research on IT and Organizations, University of California, Irvine. E-Business Center Director's Forum, Chicago.

Kraemer, K. L., Gibbs, J., & Dedrick, J. (2002). Impacts of Globalization on E-Commerce Adoption and Firm Performance: A Cross-Country Investigation. *Center for Research on IT and Organizations.* University of California, Irvine.

Krishna, S., & Madon, S. (2004). *The Digital Challenge: Information Technology in the Development Context (Voices in Development Management).* Ashgate Publishing Company, Brookfield, VT.

Kumar, V., Kumar, U., & Shareef, M. A. (2006). Implementation of Quality Management Practice in EC. *Proceedings of the Administrative Sciences Association of Canada Conference, 27,* 146-163. Banff, Calgary, Canada.

Kustin, R. A. (1994). A Special Theory of Globalization: A Review and Critical Evaluation of the Theoretical And Empirical Evidence. *Journal of Global Marketing, 7*(3), 79-102.

Levitt, T. (1983). The Globalization of Markets. *Harvard Business Review*, May_June, (pp. 92-103).

Li, J. (1994). Experience Effects and International Expansion: Strategies of Service MNCs in the Asia-Pacific Region. *Management International Review, 34*(3), 217-234.

Liu, B. S-C., Furrer O., & Sudharshan, D. (2001). The Relationships between Culture and Behavioral Intentions toward Services. *Journal of Service Research, 4*(2), 118-129.

Loiacono, E. T., Watson, R. T., & Goodhue, D. L. (2002). WEBQUAL: A Measure of Website Quality. *In K. Evans & L. Scheer (Eds.), Marketing educators' conference: Marketing theory and applications, 13*, 432–437.

Madon, S. (1997). Information-Based Global Economy and Socioeconomic Development: The Case of Bangalore. *Information Society, 13*(3), 227-244.

Madon, S. (2000). The Internet and Socio-Economic Development: Exploring the Interaction. *Information Technology & People, 13*(2), 85-101.

Mann, C. L., Eckert, S. E., & Knight, S. C. (2000). *Global Electronic Commerce: A Policy Primer.* Washington, DC: Institute for International Economics.

Meuter, M. L., Bitner, M. J., Ostrom, A. L., & Brown, S. W. (2001). Choosing Among Alternative Service Delivery Modes: An Investigation of Customer Trial of Self-Service Technologies. *Journal of Marketing, 69*(2), 61-83.

Nussbaum, M., & Sen, A. (Ed.) (1993). *The Quality of Life.* Oxford: Clarendon Press.

OECD, (1998). *The Economic and Social Impact of Electronic Commerce: Preliminary*

Findings and Research Agenda. http://www.oecd.org/dsti/sti/it/ec/index.htm.

Ohmae, K. (1990). *The Borderless World: Power and Strategy in the Interlinked Economy.* New York: Harper Perennial.

Ohmae, K. (1995). *The End of the Nation State.* New York: Free Press.

Ozsomer, A., & Simonin, B. L. (2004). Marketing Program Standardization: A Cross-Country Exploration. *International Journal of Research in Marketing, 21*(4), 397–414.

Papadopoulos, N., & Denis, J-E. (1988). Inventory, Taxonomy and Assessment of Methods for International Market Selection. *International Marketing Review* (Autumn), (pp. 38-51).

Papadopoulos, N. (1992). Trade Blocs and Marketing: Antecedents, Trends, and Implications. *Journal of Global Marketing, 5*(3), 1-29.

Parasuraman, A., Zeithaml, V. A., & Malhotra, A. (2005). E-S-QUAL A Multiple-Item Scale for Assessing Electronic Service Quality. *Journal of Service Research, 7*(3), 213-233.

Pohjola, M. (2002). The New Economy: Facts, Impacts and Policies. *Information Economics and Policy, 14*, 133-144.

Porter, M. E. (Ed.) (1986). *Competition in Global Industries*. Boston: Harvard Business School Press.

Ribbink D., Riel, A. C. R. V., Liljander, V., & Streukens, S. (2004). Comfort Your Online Customer: Quality, Trust and Loyalty on the Internet. *Managing Service Quality, 14*(6), 446-456.

Rogers, E. (1995). *Diffusion of Innovations*. The Free Press, New York, USA.

Rust, R. (2001). The Rise of E-Service. *Journal of Service Research*, 3 (4), 283-284.

Sahay, S. &. Avgerou, C. (2002). Introducing the Special Issue on Information and Communication Technologies in Developing Countries. *Information Society, 18*(2), 73-76.

Sein, M. & I. Ahmad. (2001). A Framework to Study the Impact of Information and Communication Technologies on Developing Countries: The Case of Cellular Phones in Bangladesh. *In BITWORLD 2001*. Cairo, Egypt.

Santos, J. (2003). E-Service Quality: A Model of Virtual Service Quality Dimensions. *Management Service Quality, 13*(3), 233-46.

Schaupp, L. C., & Bélanger, F. (2005). A Conjoint Analysis of Online Consumer Satisfaction. *Journal of Electronic Commerce Research, 6*(2), 95-111.

Sebastianelli, R., Tamimi, N., & Rajan, M. (2006). Perceived Quality Of Internet Retailers: Does Shopping Frequency And Product Type Make A Difference? *EABR & ETLC*, Siena, Italy.

Shareef, M. A., Kumar U., & Kumar, V. (2008). Role of Different EC Quality Factors on E-Purchase: A Developing Country Perspective, *Journal of Electronic Commerce Research, 9*(2), 92-113.

Sheth, J. N. (1986). Global Markets or Global Competition? *Journal of Consumer Marketing, 3*(spring), 9-11.

Steenkamp, J. -B. E. M., & Ter Hofstede, F. (2002). International Market Segmentation: Issues and Perspectives. *International Journal of Research in Marketing, 19*(3), 185–213.

Steinfield, C. & Whitten, P. (1999). Community Level Socio-Economic Impacts of Electronic Commerce. *Journal of Computer Mediated Communication, 5*(2), http://www.ascusc.org/jcmc/vol5/issue2/steinfield.html.

Stremersch, S., & Tellis, G. J. (2004). Understanding and Managing International Growth of New Products. *International Journal of Research in Marketing, 21*(4), 421–438.

Tiessen, J. H., Wright, R. W., & Turner, I. (2001). A Model of E-commerce Use by Internationalizing SMEs. *Journal of International Management, 7*, 211-233.

Tsikriktsis, N. (2002). Does Culture Influence Web Site Quality Expectations? An Empirical Study. *Journal of Service Research, 5*(2), 101-112.

UNCTAD. (2004). *United Nations Conference on Trade and Development Report.*

U.S. Census Bureau Report. (2007). U.S.

Van Everdingen, Y. M., Aghina, W. B., & Fok, D. (2005). Forecasting Cross Population Innovation Diffusion: A Bayesian Approach. *International Journal of Research in Marketing, 22*(3), 293–308.

Vehovar, V., (2003). Security Concern and On-Line Shopping. International study of the credibility of consumer information on the internet. http://www.ris.org/up-loadi/editor/ vehovarpaperconsumersinternational.doc. [Accessed 8-9 June 2003]

Wade, R. (1996). Globalization and its Limits: Reports of The Death of the National Economy are Greatly Exaggerated. In S. Berger & R. Dore (Ed.), *National Diversity and Global Capitalism* (pp. 60–88), Ithaca, NY: Cornell University Press.

Walsham, G. & Sahay, S. (2006). Research on Information Systems in Developing Countries: Current Landscape and Future Prospects. *Information Technology for Development, 12*(1), 7-24.

Wind, Y. & Douglas S. P. (1986). The Myth of Globalization. *Journal of Consumer Marketing, 3*(spring), 23-60.

Wolfinbarger, M. & Gilly, M. C. (2003). eTailQ: Dimensionalizing, Measuring, and Predicting etail Quality. *Journal of Retailing*, 79 (3), 183-98.

Wong, P.K. (2002). Globalization of American, European and Japanese Production Networks and the Growth of Singapore's Electronics Industry. *International Journal of Technology Management, 24(7/8), 843-869.*

World Bank. (2000). Electronic Commerce and Developing Countries. *In Global Economic Prospects 2001.* http://www.worldbank.org/prospects/gep2001/chapt4.pdf.

Yip, G. S. (2003). *Total Global Strategy II, Prentice Hall.* Upper Saddle River, New Jersey.

Zhan C. & Dubinsky, A. J. (2003). A Conceptual Model of Perceived Customer Value in E-Commerce: A Preliminary Investigation. *Psychology and Marketing,* 20(4), 323– 347.

Zhang, P., & von Dran, G. (2002). User Expectations and Rankings of Quality Factors in Different Website Domains. *International Journal of Electronic Commerce,* 6(2), 9-33.

Zwass, V. (1996). Electronic Commerce: Structures and Issues. *International Journal of Electronic Commerce,* 1(1), 3-23.

Chapter XI
Culturally Customizing International Web Sites

Nitish Singh
Saint Louis University, USA

Joseph P. Little
Saint Louis University, USA

ABSTRACT

As global e-commerce is expanding and the global online marketplace is becoming more lucrative for marketers, there is a surge in proliferation of international Web sites. However, most marketers equate their ability to tap the global online market by simply creating multilingual international Web sites. This chapter shows that effective international Web presence is not just about translating a Web site into local language. A truly localized Web site is one that is linguistically, technically and most importantly culturally customized to locale-specific requirements. This chapter provides insights into the importance and impact of Web site cultural customization on consumer perceptions of international Web sites.

11.1. INTRODUCTION

Global e-commerce is expanding rapidly and based on industry estimates several trillion dollars are being exchanged annually over the Web. The global online population is also increasing substantially. Jupiter Research (2008) estimates that by 2012 there will be 1.8 billion internet users world wide. The highest growth in internet usage is anticipated in countries like China, India, Russia and Brazil. According to Internet World Stats as of 2008, North America only accounts for 17.5 percent of global Internet users. Asia now has the largest number of internet users, accounting for almost 37 percent of the global online population, followed by Europe with 27 percent (Internet World Stats, 2008). Another interesting trend in global internet usage is that almost seventy percent of these users are now non-English speaking (Internet World Stats, 2008). Thus, besides English other languages like Chinese, Spanish, Japanese and French have significant online usage. In terms of e-commerce the U.S. may not be the predominant online market in future years to come. According to an e-marketer report, while U.S. retail commerce has grown 14.3 percent from 2007 to 2008, the sales growth is estimated to decline in the coming years (Grau, 2008a). By 2010 U.S. retail e-commerce will be about $182.5 billion (Grau, 2008a). On the other hand, European B2C e-commerce is expected to reach almost $234 billion by 2010 (Grau, 2006). According to e-marketer estimates by 2010 the British market share will fall to 44.5% as France and Germany ramp up their online sales. Asia will also see significant growth in B2C e-commerce with a 23.3 percent annual growth rate and eventually reaching almost $168.7 billion in 2011 (Grau, 2008b). Japan and South Korea currently lead the B2C e-commerce sales in Asia but by 2011 they will be overtaken by China and India (Grau, 2008b). From these numbers it is clear that e-commerce is now a truly global phenomenon.

To take advantage of the full potential of global e-commerce, companies need to tap diverse global markets and consider expanding online not only in developed countries but also the emerging economies of China, Brazil, India and others. A recent survey of multinationals by Petro, Muddyman, Prichard, Schweigerdt, and Singh (2007) found that, in terms of international expansion online, 71 percent of companies see Web site localization a crucial driver for successful expansion. The same study also reports that almost 70 percent of company executives see localization of Web sites crucial to acquiring international customers and even a larger percentage (76 percent) see localization important to achieving international customer satisfaction. Thus, to tap global online markets companies need to create localized international Web sites for specific locales and country markets. Some of the challenges to creating truly localized sites include:

1. Translating international sites into multiple languages and in some cases a single country may require multilingual content. For example, Canada companies will not only need to have an English site but also a French site to cater to the large French speaking population. In the U.S. several companies are now targeting Hispanics online by providing Web sites in Spanish. Similarly, in

countries like Switzerland, Belgium, and others with a significant multilingual population there is a need to develop multilingual sites to effectively tap the online market.

2. Furthermore, the translation should be linguistically correct and ensure translation, idiomatic, and conceptual equivalence of the translated text.

3. The style of the visual and graphics content would need to be adapted to the tastes and preferences of different local markets.

4. Modifying data fields, tables, forms, layout, colors, date and time formats, units of measurements and navigational elements may be required.

5. Making sure that the design of the user interface (UI) is flexible and neutral so that it can be leveraged for creation of future international Web sites without expending valuable resources.

6. Ensuring that the relevant character set is supported. For example, the Japanese use double byte characters, so if the program is built in western languages it must be made double byte compatible (e.g. using Unicode) so that the text can later be translated into Japanese. A fully internationalized product or Web site normally is double-byte or Unicode enabled.

7. International e-commerce readiness for multi-country transactions is crucial.

8. Enabling global logistics and import-export documentation is required to conduct e-business.

9. Finally, international Web sites will require modifying the cultural content of the site to be congruent to the local culture. This is crucial as culture prescribes broad guidelines for acceptable ways of behaving and acting in particular situations (Feather, 1990), and it influences how we interact and socialize with other members of the society (Rokeach, 1973).

Thus, several challenges exist for companies to establish effective international Web sites adept at reaching out and satisfying the tastes and preferences of international online consumers. Exploring all the issues relevant to creating an effective international Web presence is beyond the scope of this chapter, however an attempt is made to show the following:

1. The importance of culturally customizing international Web sites.
2. How Web sites of different countries depict local cultural values.
3. How online consumers respond to culturally adapted Web sites.

11.2. LOCALIZATION

Globalization, Internationalization, Localization and Translation (GILT) is commonly associated with the process required to create multilingual international Web sites.

Globalization: Globalization addresses all of the enterprise issues associated with making a company truly global. For the globalization of products and services this involves integrating all of the internal and external business functions with marketing, sales, and customer support in the world market (The Localization Industry Standards Association, 2008). From a more technical view point, Web globalization includes two complementary processes: Internationalization and Localization.

Internationalization: Internationalization is the process of generalizing a product so that it can handle multiple languages and cultural conventions without the need for redesign. In more technical terms, it is the process through which back-end technologies are used to create modular, extendible, and accessible global Web site templates that support front-end customization (Singh & Boughton, 2005). Internationalization takes place at the level of program design and Web document development.

Localization: Localization involves taking a product and making it linguistically and culturally appropriate to the target locale (country/region and language) where it will be used and sold. Web site localization is specifically the process of the front-end customization, whereby Web sites are adapted to meet the needs of a specific international target market (Singh & Boughton, 2005).

A whole industry has grown around helping companies internationalize and localize their international Web sites. This industry is called the Localization Industry and is comprised of companies offering translation, terminology management, localization project management, internationalization of applications and user interfaces, quality assurance and testing of the localized products, global content management and other related services in the context of Web globalization. However, most companies in the localization industry currently do not provide comprehensive cultural customization services as part of their offerings. Even among clients of the localization industry, which are normally companies wanting to develop international Web sites; there is a lack of awareness in terms of developing culturally customized international Web sites. This is because there is a wide spread perception that localization just involves translation and some basic modifications like currency conversions, time-date conversions, etc. A study by Singh and Boughton (2005) found that among a sample of almost 598 Fortune 500 global companies, less than half were highly localized and none were truly culturally customized. A more recent study by Petro et al. (2007) content analyzed 40 U.S. multinationals,

American Web sites and also their international Web sites for Germany and Spain. The results of the study found that only 3 percent of the sites were customizing graphics, colors, symbols and values to the local culture. Even more surprising is that the navigation of the international sites was not even at par with their U.S. English pages, with only 20 percent of company sites having navigational elements equivalent to the U.S. English pages.

Singh and Pereira (2005) define a culturally customized Web site as one that is completely congruent to the culture of a target locale. Such Web sites are culturally adapted at perceptual, behavioral and symbolic levels of cultural immersion. This means that culturally customizing Web sites entails in-depth understanding of target cultures and then adequately reflecting it when communicating over the Web. However, this high degree of cultural expertise is not readily available in the localization industry and people with this high level of cultural expertise demand a premium for their services. Moreover, currently very few universities (St. Louis University and California State University-Chico, USA) have created educational programs that provide comprehensive training to people in international e-business and cultural customization of Web sites. Thus, it is a combination of lack of awareness and lack of trained professionals that is causing companies to take a cookie cutter approach to creating international Web sites and not truly culturally customizing their sites.

Furthermore, there is also a lack of research in the area of localizing business Web sites and cultural customization of Web sites. Thus, there exists limited empirical evidence to show the impact of culturally customizing Web sites to different locales. However, in all fairness it must be said that international e-business and localization of Web sites has only started to grow in the past decade and it is still a relatively new field of investigation. It is possible that with future studies, books and academic or professional training a bridging of the knowledge gap in this new field of localization will occur. Currently, the Web site cultural customization framework proposed by Singh and Pereira (2005) is one of the few guiding frameworks available for Web marketers and localization professionals to use. Singh and Pereira (2005) base their Web site cultural customization framework on the cultural values proposed by Hofstede (1980) and Hall (1976). The framework of Singh and Pereira (2005), shows how cultural values such as individualism-collectivism, masculinity-femininity, power distance, uncertainty avoidance, and high and low context orientation can be depicted on the Web sites to make the Web sites culturally congruent to a culture high or low on the above mentioned cultural values. Such knowledge is beneficial for managers trying to understand a set of etic cultural values that can then be applied to create sites for different locales. In the remaining sections an attempt is made to show why cultural customization of

Web sites is important and how can businesses benefit from it.

11.3. IMPORTANCE OF WEB SITE CULTURAL CUSTOMIZATION

Some marketers equate culture to "soft" aspects of communication, seeing it as being of secondary importance to the conduct of international business. In the 1970's this perception of culture being of secondary importance, or not at all important, was pervasive among American multinationals. However, all of us are aware of various cultural blunders in advertising and communications that companies have made. Currently, most multinationals have started to recognize the importance of culture in advertising and marketing but when it comes to the Web the mentality is still "one size fits all." Marketers seem to forget that the Web is also a marketing communication medium and their Web site is just like an advertisement. Thus, it is important that we emphasize the importance of culture to marketers.

Culture has been defined as software of the mind (Hofstede, 1980) as it influences how we think, behave and interact with the society. In fact, culture is ingrained in our minds since birth. According to Bourdieu (1977), the knowledge acquired from everyday practices and experiences is stored in its most primitive form in "Habitus". Knowledge in form of Habitus is organized into schemas, or simplified mental structures, which are collections of elements that work together to process information (Strauss & Quinn, 1997). In other words, schemas are simple elements or conceptual structures, which serve as prototypes for underlying real world experiences (Casson, 1983; D'Andrade, 1992; Quinn & Holland, 1987). When a set of complex schemas become intersubjectively shared by a group of people, complex schemas then represent cultural models of a society (D'Andrade, 1987). Finally, these cultural models help individuals to learn culture and communicate it. Thus, culture is an important element that needs to be considered when communicating across different locales or nations. The marketing and international business literature is full of studies that have shown how culture impacts marketing communications (e.g., Albers-Miller & Gelb, 1996; Cho et al., 1999).

Mooij (1998) claims that advertising reflects a society's values and that effective advertising and marketing is inseparably linked to the underlying culture of the group to which it is targeted. It has been shown that advertising, which reflects local cultural values, is more powerful and persuasive than culturally insensitive advertising (Mueller, 1987; Zandpour *et al.,* 1994). Several researchers, therefore, have emphasized the use of country-specific cultural values appeal when developing international advertising campaigns and communication material (Albers-Miller & Gelb, 1996; Han & Shavitt, 1994). Studies have shown that Web site localization and cultural customization can lead to better navigation, usage, attitude toward the site and even higher purchase intentions on the site (Singh & Pereira, 2005). According to Luna, Peracchio, and de Juan (2002), culturally congruent Web content decreases cognitive effort to process information on the site, and represents an environment where demands are clearer, leading to easier navigation and a more favorable attitude toward the Web site. Research also confirms that online customers stay twice as long on Web sites that have been localized. Online business users are almost three times more likely to make purchases online when Web sites are localized (Singh & Pereira, 2005) and available to them in their local language (Singh, Furrer, & Ostinelli, 2004). A study by Ferranti (1999) found that more than 75 percent of Chinese and Koreans online shoppers prefer Web sites in Mandarin and Korean, respectively. Similarly, the French and Spanish have a strong preference for sites in their local language (Lynch, Kent, & Srinivasan, 2001). A survey by Forrester Research confirms that non-English speaking users stay twice as long on localized Web sites as they do on English-only Web sites, and business users are three times more likely to make purchases online when addressed in their local language (Singh & Pereira, 2005). More evidence for localization comes from a recent survey of 2,400 worldwide internet users, more than half of the sample buy only from Web sites that present information in their local language (DePalma, 2006).

Businesses expanding their e-business find understanding language and cultural expectations and building online trust as most challenging (Culnan & Armstrong, 1999; Jarvenpaa, Tractinsky, Saarinen, & Vitale, 1999; Singh & Pereira, 2005; Violino, 2001). The results from the above mentioned studies are not surprising in the light that Web sites, like any other communication medium, are culture-bound and culture has been shown in the literature to impact consumer behavior significantly (Clark, 1990). This cultural effect is so powerful, that Hall (1976) says that people cannot act or interact in any meaningful way except through the medium of culture. Thus, by ignoring the importance of culture Web marketers are also ignoring the lucrative global online consumer. Marketers still see Web as a culturally neutral medium and bask in the ignorance that a globally accepted Web style is emerging. They think all Web sites have a home page, a product page and a customer service page; so what is there to change and adapt? However, if they delved into the Web sites of different countries then they would realize how different the Web sites are in terms of how the information is communicated, how the graphics are being displayed, the importance given to various navigational elements, the style and rhetoric used to communicate locally and other features related to transactional safety, customer service, social networking, etc.

In fact, recent research is showing growing empirical evidence to suggest that the Web is not a culturally neutral medium, and Web sites of different countries are impregnated with cultural values unique to them (Cyr & Trevor-Smith, 2004;

Hermeking, 2005; Singh & Matsuo, 2004; Singh, Zhao, & Hu, 2003; 2005). Thus, the Web, like any advertising document, is to some extent a mirror or reflection of the culture of the country or locale. In the next section we will explore how Web sites of different countries differ in the depiction of cultural values and certain unique Web characteristics that need to be emphasized on Web sites of different countries.

11.4. DEPICTION OF CULTURE ON INTERNATIONAL WEB SITES

When doing e-business internationally it is important to consider the economic, political, legal, and socio-cultural environment of a country. The country-environment can have a significant impact on how e-business activities are carried out, how opportunities are leveraged, and how hurdles are overcome. For example, governments have been active in controlling and shaping the business environment and protecting national industries. With the emergence of e-commerce, however, governments are facing some new challenges such as being involved in the free flow of information, national security, the digital divide, convergence of media, content, communication technology, issues of the Internet and national sovereignty, regulating business conduct internationally over the Web, tax issues and also issues of laws governing e-transactions. Similarly, the legal environment also affects the conduct of international e-business. Most of the laws related to contracts, advertising, copyrights, domain names, information dissemination, etc. are nationally governed. Thus, companies need to check the local laws of the country before setting a Web site. Also, companies need to analyze the tax structure and subsidies available to them (for example, Value added tax for different goods differ across EU countries), exchange rate fluctuations, tariffs and customs, purchasing power parity of the country, internet penetration rates, telecommunications and logistics infrastructure, and impact of regional economic agreements on trade and e-commerce, etc.

So thus far it is outlined how economic, political, and legal issues may impact the conduct of global e-commerce. The socio-cultural environment also plays an important role in the conduct of global e-commerce, as Web sites from different countries are a reflection of the culture and the communication style prevalent in the country or locale. When designing international Web sites, the effects of the environment, culture, language and color can have profound influence on the appeal, usability, and performance of the Web site. They influence the spatial orientation of the content, text length, navigational modes, translation equivalence, Web site features, language dialects, graphics, and color usage. For example, in Arabic cultures pictures of women and animals are disliked and discouraged, while elaborate text in form of calligraphic style is acceptable and liked. Furthermore, the use of visual metaphors from religions, such as the cross, the crescent, or a star, as well as animal figures, taboo words, graphics of hand gestures, aesthetic codes, and forbidden foods may require detailed research to examine their appropriate uses in a specific country.

For example, in India a swastika as a religious symbol is extensively used, as it is seen as a sign of good luck and fertility. It is not uncommon to see the swastika on product labels, brands, packaging, Web sites and even in Indian advertisements. In fact, on the Web there is a Web site for a company named Swastika Industries www.swastikaindustries.com. It must be emphasized that in this new age of global Web access, even local businesses should be cautious using certain graphics or cultural markers on their Web sites. A Web site is literally, "born global" and thus visible to consumers all around the world. Our above example of Swastika Industries is relevant because in India, as mentioned, a swastika is a religious symbol, but across the world it has very negative connotations. In the past the Web site of Swastika Industries had the swastika symbols on it but the latest version of the site has removed such cultural markers.

Besides cultural symbols, other details, such as spatial orientation of Web sites, may differ depending on the culture and language. For example, many of the oriental scripts (Japanese, Korean, and Chinese) are justified and read vertically. On the other hand, Arabic is read from right to left, and English is read left to right. Thus, for an Arabic reader a left justified Web page might not be visually appealing. One of the company Web sites we found paying special attention to such local cultural issues is that of IKEA. The IKEA Web site is globally sensitive starting from its main landing page which happens to be its global gateway page. On this global gateway page of IKEA global online consumers can browse over 35 country specific Web sites that IKEA has created. On this global gateway page the IKEA Web site provides a link to the country Web site not only shown in English but also in the local language. Thus, if a consumer is non-English speaking they can still find their country Web site. More specifically, IKEA country specific Web sites seem to show a reflection of local cultural values and norms. For example, the IKEA Web site for Israel has more central spatial orientation compared to the IKEA Web site for Germany, which is more flowing from left to right. Similarly, the IKEA Kuwait site uses more country specific symbols like pictures of local models dressed in local dress. IKEA Germany has a virtual avatar "Anna" which looks more blonde compare to IKEA USA where "Anna" has brown hair.

In recent years there has been some research showing how country specific Web sites depict local cultural values. In the following paragraphs we review some of this research. One study in this area was a comparison of U.S. and Japanese Web sites to identify differences in depiction of cultural values between U.S. and Japanese Web sites.

Singh and Matsuo (2004) compared American and Japanese Web sites on five cultural dimensions namely individualism-collectivism, masculinity-femininity, power distance, uncertainty avoidance, and high and low context orientation. Their study found that Japanese Web sites significantly differ from the U.S. Web sites on several of the cultural category items. For example, Japanese society has been viewed as collectivist and group-oriented (Hofstede, 1980). Japanese people value the feeling of "amae", which means looking out for others in the group. This is reflected in the depiction of features like online clubs, family themes, and links to local companies. For example, the Web sites of Fujitsu, and Olympus prominently depicted features like camera clubs and news clubs. Japanese Web sites also showed prominence of clarity in gender roles as men dominated all the important positions in the company, and women held more customer service positions. In comparison to Japanese Web sites, the American Web sites were less collectivist, low on power distance, but were more geared toward low context orientation. Thus, American sites showed more of a hard sell approach using superlatives, and explicitly mentioning the rank and position of the company. American sites generally were more direct, emphasized rank and prestige of the company and had clearly laid out terms and conditions of Web site use (Singh & Matsuo, 2004).

Another study by Singh *et al.* (2005) analyzed the Web sites of China, India, Japan and U.S. to evaluate the depiction of national cultural values. Web sites of local Chinese, Indian, Japanese, and U.S. companies served as the sample for this study. Three main sources were used to generate the sample: 25 local Japanese and 26 local U.S. companies were selected from the Forbes list of top 500 U.S. and International companies at www.forbes.com. The sample of Indian (21) and Chinese (21) local companies was selected from the Yahoo! local Indian and Chinese Web directory. To control for industry effect only electronic and automotive companies were included in the sample. Thus, a total of 93 Web sites were used in the study. On average, 15-20 Web pages per Web site were content analyzed on 35 cultural categories. The results from Singh *et al.* (2005) study revealed that under collectivism dimension features like clubs, newsletters, family theme, and country-specific symbols are prominently depicted on local Chinese and Japanese Web sites. Under the individualism dimension the most common features found in highly individualist country Web sites were, product uniqueness and Web page personalization. High power distance societies like Japan and India prominently depicted features like Hierarchy information, pictures of important people, and a prominent vision statement. Masculinity on the Web sites was most prominently depicted via features like, clear gender roles and emphasis on product effectiveness. Japanese Web sites scoring highest on high contextuality prominently depicted features like a soft-sell approach, and liberal use of aesthetic drawings. One of the most striking features of the local Chinese Web sites was the recurrent images of the family theme. Similar findings have been reported in print and media advertising in China (Ji & McNeal, 2001; Tse, Belk & Zhou, 1996). Family is seen as the source of identity in the Chinese culture, and this is reflected in complex family terminology wherein there are separate words for older brother, younger sister, and maternal and paternal uncles. Chinese Web sites also showed high levels of power distance-oriented features, especially prominent were vision statements by the company heads, and "pride of ownership appeal." The importance of hierarchical relationships in Chinese society can be traced back to Confucius's five cardinal relations between sovereign and minister, father and son, husband and wife, old and young, and friends (Ji & McNeal, 2001). On the other hand the Indian Web sites seem to depict the highest levels of uncertainty-avoidance features. This could be attributed to religious factors in play in the Indian society. Hinduism, the main religion in India, advocates the philosophy that life is an illusion or "Maya" and the only pursuit worth considering is the quest for spiritual enlightenment. Intricately linked with this belief of "Maya" is the "law of karma", which basically emphasis that all events in the life are predetermined by our previous acts in this and our last life. That's why Indians seem to be less of risk-takers and believe more in destiny. For example, every act from childbirth to marriage in India is greatly influenced by astrology. Indian society is also a very hierarchical society, evidenced in a high power distance score and prominent depiction of power-distance oriented features. Hindus assume that people are born to a particular class or "caste" based on a natural law, and thus the society has the famous "caste-system" where in the society is divided into high class intellectuals, middle class traders and low class unskilled laborers. Even though, the class system is not officially practiced in India, it is deeply ingrained in the Indian psyche. For instance, most of the Indian Web sites prominently depicted the titles of the employees. Titles help to identify the rank of an employee in the organization, and the last name of a person reveals which part of India he or she is from and what caste he/she belongs to.

These studies provide evidence to international marketers and academics that instead of a "transnational Web style" with features, images and categories common across nations, a culturally unique Web style is emerging on the Web. Thus, marketers should be cautious when launching standardized or machine-translated Web sites for their global audience. Another online trend with companies is to develop regional Web sites for Europe, Asia-pacific, and the Americas, but targeting regional clusters does not translate into country-specific Web communication. The study by Singh *et al.* (2005) examining the Asian country sites of China, Japan and India shows that even within a geographic region (Asia), there is considerable variation in depiction of cultural values on the Web. For example, compared to Japanese and Chinese Web sites, Indian Web sites were significantly lower in depiction of collectivist-orientation with high context communication, while the

Chinese Web sites were low in depiction of masculinity compared to Japanese and Indian Web sites. Thus, grouping Japan, India, and China as eastern cultures with a predominant eastern cultural value orientation may be a mistake, instead each country's culture should be carefully studied before developing country-specific Web communication material.

11.5. IMPACT OF WEB SITE CULTURAL CUSTOMIZATION

Studies have shown that culture determines attitudinal preferences and that the attitude-behavior link is driven by the cultural assumptions of a society (Feather, 1995; Morris & Peng, 1994). For example, an experiment by Morris and Peng (1994) shows that Chinese and American students differ in their perception of social behavior. The American students are shown to rely on internal causes for social behavior, while Chinese students are shown to rely on external causes. This is because in America, or Western cultures, the belief is that the locus of control is internal to an individual, and behavior is a function of an individual's own actions, while in collectivist cultures like China, the locus of control is seen as external because people rely on group members to make decisions about them and for them (Mooij, 1998). Furthermore, Aaker and Maheswaran (1997) attribute attitudinal and behavioral differences between members of Western and Eastern cultures to individualist and collectivist cultural tendencies found in these respective cultures. It has also been shown that the power distance structure in a society affects people's attitudes toward service encounters (Furrer, Liu, & Sudharshan, 2000; Tsikriktsis, 2002). Furthermore, culture not only determines how we apprehend and assimilate the surrounding information but also guides our behaviors and actions (D'Andrade, 1992; McCracken, 1986). According to Pollay (1983), cultural values determine almost all kinds of behaviors and attitudes, ranging from purchasing to following a particular ideology. For example, motives for buying automobiles differ from culture to culture. Safety is an important motive behind the purchasing of cars in feminine cultures, while distinctive style is more valued in status conscious, high power distance societies (Mooij, 1998). The impact of culture on behavioral intentions is further documented in cross-cultural validation of Fishbein's Intention model by Lee and Green (1991). Thus, culture not only affects our attitudes and structures our subjective norms, but also serves as a motivational force guiding our product choices and purchase decisions.

In the academic literature new data is emerging showing how culture impacts attitudes and even purchase intentions online. Studies show that cultural customization of Web sites can lead to better attitude toward the site and higher purchase intentions on the Web site (Luna *et al.*, 2002; Simon, 2001; Singh *et al.*, 2004; Singh *et al.* 2006a,b; Tsikriktsis, 2002).

One such study by Singh *et al.* (2006b) provides empirical evidence as to whether local consumers prefer culturally adapted Web sites or standardized Web sites. This study shows that consumers from Germany, China, and India prefer Web sites adapted to their local culture, and that culture influences consumer beliefs, attitudes, and purchase intention on the Web. The study by Singh et al. (2006b) first attempts to measure the degree of cultural adaptation as reflected on U.S. companies' German, Chinese and Indian international Web sites. The study then ranks the Web sites, based on the degree of cultural adaptation depicted on them, into highly adapted Web sites and Web sites with little adaptation. The study explores whether German, Chinese and Indian consumers would find highly culturally adapted Web sites designed for their country to be more effective (in terms of presentation, navigation, purchase intention, and attitude toward the site) than Web sites that are not highly adapted to their respective cultures or standardized (home country) Web sites of American multinationals. The study used the theory of planned behavior as conceptual basis to show how subjective norms, attitudes, perceived behavioral control, and behavioral intention are influenced by cultural beliefs, and in turn shape consumer perceptions of Web site characteristics, attitude toward the site and purchase intention on the site. Results of this study show that among German, Chinese and Indian consumers, high cultural adaptation of Web site significantly impacted a favorable attitude and a higher intention to purchase online.

In another study Singh et al. (2004) investigated whether Italian, Indian, Dutch, Spanish, and Swiss online customers view an American company's "home" Web site (standardized English site) more favorably than a culturally customized Web site of this company for their respective country, or a local Web site of a company from their own home country. The results indicate that, in general (except Netherlands), customers have a more favorable attitude toward local Web Sites than to adapted or standardized Web Sites. This suggests that brands such as the Gap and Marks and Spencer, which offer a standardized, one size-fits-all Web site to cater to the needs of the global market, may not be following a sound strategy.

11.6. CONCLUSION

In conclusion an attempt is made in this chapter to show that localization does not stop with just translating the Web pages in local languages. Localization of Web sites also involves culturally customizing Web sites to meet locale specific cultural requirements. Miscommunications, in the international context, may occur when the message is perceived as culturally incongruent and fails to elicit the desired response from a target segment. When Web users are confronted with a different language (or second language), foreign signs and symbols, and non-local Web content that is culturally incongruent, it puts more cognitive stress on them, leading to diminished control over the interaction and loss of focus (Luna *et al.,* 2002). Thus, Web users from different countries prefer different Web site characteristics that meet their distinct needs in terms of navigation, security, product information, customer service, shopping tools, and other features (Fink & Laupase, 2000; Luna *et al.,* 2002; Tsikriktsis, 2002).

At times management might not see the direct impact of culturally customizing Web sites on their profits. But as technology is evolving there are means of tracking Web site traffic, Web usage behavior and other Web metrics to measure the impact of cultural customization. Moreover, in this chapter we have put forward empirical evidence from past studies that show the impact of Web site cultural customization on consumer attitudes and behavioral/purchase intention. In the marketing literature behavioral/purchase intention has been shown to be linked to actual consumer behavior. Thus, marketers must consider culture specific requirements when designing international Web sites.

REFERENCES

Aaker, J., & Mahaeswaran, D. (1997). The Effect of Cultural Orientation on Persuasion. *Journal of Consumer Research*, *24*(December), 315-328.

Albers-Miller, N., & Gelb, B. (1996). Business Advertising Appeals as Mirror of Cultural Dimensions: A Study of Eleven Countries. *Journal of Advertising*, *25*(Winter), 57-70.

Bourdieu, P. (1977). *Outline of Theory of Practice*. New York, NY: Cambridge University Press.

Casson, R. (1983). Schemata in Cognitive Anthropology. *Annual Review of Anthropology*, *12*, 429-462.

Cho, B., Kwon, U., Gentry, J., Jun, S., & Kropp, F. (1999). Cultural values reflected in theme and execution: A comparative study of U.S. and Korean television commercials. *Journal of Advertising, 28*(4), 59-74.

Clark, T. (1990). International Marketing and National Character: A Review and Proposal for an Integrative Theory. *Journal of Marketing, 54*(October), 66-79.

Culnan, M. J., & Armstrong, P. K. (1999). Information Privacy Concerns, Procedural Fairness and Impersonal Trust: An Empirical Investigation. *Organization Science, 10*, 104-115.

Cyr, D., & Trevor-Smith, H. (2004). Localization of Web Design: An empirical Comparison of German, Japanese and United Stats Web Site Characteristics. *Journal of the American Society for Information Science and Technology, 55*(13), 1199-1208.

D'Andrade, R. G. (1987). A folk Model of The Mind. In D. Holland & N. Quinn (Eds.), *Cultural Models in Language and Thought* (pp. 112-148). London: Cambridge University Press.

D'Andrade, R. G. (1992). Schemas and Motivation. In R. G. D'Andrade & C. Strauss (Eds.), *Human Motives and Cultural Models* (pp. 23-44). New York, NY: Cambridge University Press.

De Palma, D. (2006). *Does Language Matter? Can't Read, Won't Buy: Why Language Matters on Global Websites.* Retrieved July 28, 2007 http://www.commonsenseadvisory.com/research/reports_category.php?year=2006&id=0

Feather, N. T. (1990). Bridging the Gap between Values and Action. In E. Higgins & R. Sorrentino (Eds.), *Handbook of Motivation and Cognition* (pp. 151-192), 12, New York, NY: Guilford Press.

Feather, N. T. (1995). Values, Valences, and Choice. *Journal of Personality and Social Psychology, 68*, 1135–1151.

Ferranti, M. (1999). From global to local. *Infoworld, 21*(41), 36-37.

Fink, D. & Laupase R. (2000). Perceptions of Web Site Design Characteristics: A Malaysian/Australian Comparison. *Internet Research, 10*(1), 44-55.

Furrer, O., Liu B. S., & Sudharshan, D. (2000). The Relationships Between Culture and Service Quality Perceptions: Basis for Cross-Cultural Market Segmentation and Resource Allocation. *Journal of Service Research, 2*(4), 355-371.

Grau, J. (2006). Europe Retail E-Commerce: Spotlight on the UK, Germany and France. *Emarketer.com.* Retrieved July 28, 2007, from http://www.emarketer.com.

Grau, J. (2008a). US Retail E-Commerce: Slower But Still Steady Growth. *Emarketer.com.* Retrieved July 28, 2008, from http://www.emarketer.com.

Grau, J. (2008b). Asia-Pacific B2C E-Commerce: Focus on China and India. *Emarketer.com.* Retrieved July 28, 2008, from http://www.emarketer.com.

Hall, E. T. (1976). *Beyond Culture.* Garden City, NY: Doubleday & Company.

Han, S., & Shavitt, S. (1994). Persuasion and Culture: Advertising Appeals in Individualistic and Collectivistic Societies. *Journal of Experimental Social Psychology*, *30*(July), 8-18.

Hermeking, M. (2005). Culture and Internet Consumption: Contributions from Cross-Cultural Marketing and Advertising Research. *Journal of Computer Mediated Communication*, *11*(1). [Retrieved July 28, 2008], from http://jcmc.indiana.edu/vol11/issue1/hermeking.html.

Hofstede, G. (1980). *Culture's Consequences: International Differences in Work-related Values*. Beverly Hills, CA: Sage Publications.

Internet World Stats (2008). World Internet Users and Population Stats. *Internet World Stats*. Retrieved July 28, 2008, from http://www.internetworldstats.com/stats.htm.

Jarvenpaa, S. L., Tractinsky N., Saarinen, L., & Vitale, M. (1999). Consumer Trust in an Internet Store: Cross Cultural Validation. *Journal of Computer Mediated Communication, 5*(2). [Retrieved July 28, 2008], from http://jcmc.indiana.edu/vol5/issue2/jarvnpaa.html.

Ji, M. F. & McNeal J. U. (2001). How Chinese children's commercials differ from those of the United States: A content analysis. *Journal of Advertising, 30*(3), 80-92.

Jupiter Research (2008). *Jupiter Research*. [Retrieved July 28, 2008], from http://www.jupiterresearch.com/bin/item.pl/home/.

Lee, C. & Green, R. T. (1991). Cross-Cultural Examination of the Fishbein Behavioral Intention Model. *Journal of International Business Studies*, 2nd Quarter, (pp. 289-305).

Luna, D., Peracchio. L. A., & de Juan, M. D. (2002). Cross-Cultural and Cognitive aspects of Web Site Navigation. *Journal of the Academy of Marketing Science*, *30*(4), 397-410.

Lynch, P. D., Kent R. J., & Srinivasan S. S. (2001). The global Internet shopper: Evidence from shopping tasks in twelve countries. *Journal of Advertising Research*, (May/June), (pp. 15-23).

McCracken, G. (1986). Culture and Consumption: A Theoretical Account of the Structure and Movement of the Cultural Meaning of Consumer Goods. *Journal of Consumer Research*, *13*(June), 71-84.

Mooij, M. D. (1998). *Global Marketing and Advertising. Understanding Cultural Paradox*. Thousand Oaks, CA: Sage Publications.

Morris, M. W., & Peng, K. (1994). Culture and cause: American and Chinese attributions for social and physical events. *Journal of Personality and Social Psychology, 67*(6), 949-971.

Mueller, B. (1987). Reflections of Culture: An analysis of Japanese and American advertising appeals. *Journal of Advertising Research*, (June/July), (pp. 51-59).

Petro, B., Muddyman, G., Prichard, J., Schweigerdt, K., & Singh, N. (2007, January). *Strategic Role of Localization in MNE*. Paper presented at the meeting of the Applied Business Research Conference, Honolulu, HI.

Pollay, R.W. (1983). Measuring the cultural values manifest in advertising. In J. H. Leigh & C. R. Martin (Eds.), *Current Issues and Research in Advertising* (pp. 72-92). Ann Arbor: MI: University of Michigan Press.

Quinn, N., & Holland, D. (1987). Culture and Cognition. In D. Holland & N. Quinn (Eds.), *Cultural Models in Language and Thought* (pp. 3-40). London: Cambridge University Press.

Rokeach, M. (1973). *The Nature of Human Values*. New York, NY: Free Press.

Simon, S. J. (2001). The Impact of Culture and Gender on Web Sites: An Empirical Study. *Database for Advances in Information Systems, 32*(1), 18-37.

Singh N., Zhao H., & Hu, X. (2003). Cultural adaptation on the Web: A study of American companies' domestic and Chinese Websites. *Journal of Global Information Management, 11*(3), 63-81.

Singh, N., Furrer, O., & Ostinelli, M. (2004). To Localize or to Standardize On The Web: Empirical Evidence From Italy, India, Netherlands, Spain, And Switzerland. *Multinational Business Review, 12*(1), 69-88.

Singh, N., & Matsuo, H. (2004). Measuring Cultural Adaptation on the Web: A Study of U.S. and Japanese Websites. *Journal of Business Research, 57*(8), 864-872.

Singh, N., & Boughton, P. (2005). Measuring Web Site Globalization: A Cross-Sectional Country and Industry Level Analysis. *Journal of Web Site Promotion, 1*(3), 3-20.

Singh, N., & Pereira, A. (2005). *The Culturally Customized Web Site: Customizing Web Sites for the Global Marketplace*. Burlington, MA: Elsevier Butterworth-Heinemann.

Singh, N., Zhao, H., & Hu, X. (2005). Analyzing Cultural Information on Web Sites: A Cross-National Study of Web Site from China, India, Japan, And the U.S. *International Marketing Review, 22*(2), 129-146.

Singh, N., Fassott, G., Chao, M., & Hoffmann, J. (2006a). Understanding International Web Site Usage: A Cross-National Study of German, Brazilian, and Taiwanese Online Consumers. *International Marketing Review, 23*(1), 83-98.

Singh, N., Fassott, G., Zhao, H., & Boughton, P. D. (2006b). Cross-Cultural Analysis of German, Chinese and Indian Consumers' Perception of Web Site Adaptation. *Journal of Consumer Behavior, 5*(1), 56-68.

Strauss, C., & Quinn. N. (1997). *A Cognitive Theory of Cultural Meaning.* Cambridge: Cambridge University Press.

The Localization Industry Standards Association (2008). What is Globalization? *The Localization Industry Standards Association.* Retrieved July 28, 2008, from http://lisa.org/What-Is-Globalization.48.0.html.

Tse, D. K., Belk, R. W., & Zhou, N. (1989). Becoming a consumer society: A longitudinal and cross-cultural content analysis of print ads from Hong Kong, The People's republic of China, and Taiwan. *Journal of Consumer Research, 15*(March), (pp. 457-472).

Tsikriktsis, N. (2002). Does Culture Influence Website Quality Expectations? An Empirical Study. *Journal of Service Research, 5*(2), 101-112.

Violino, B. (2001). E-Business Lurches Abroad. *Internet Week, March 19th.* [Retrieved July 28, 2008], from http://www.internetweek.com.

Zandpour, F., & (A Team of 10 Researchers) (1994). Global reach and local touch: achieving cultural fitness in TV advertising. *Journal of Advertising Research, 34*(5), 35-63.

Chapter XII
A Cultural Perspective on Web Site Localization

Serkan Yalcin
Saint Louis University, USA

Ji Eun Park
Saint Louis University, USA

ABSTRACT

For the last two decades, companies have been increasingly operating in many foreign markets. Serving local consumers effectively and thus achieving success in individual foreign markets require both a solid understanding of local values and a reflection of this understanding on business activities in foreign markets that will facilitate serving local markets. Today, as the size of global E-Commerce is expanding, a Web site is an important medium of multinational companies in communicating with stakeholders. In this chapter, we will discuss from a cultural perspective how to create and manage Web sites that will enable multinational companies to successfully localize in their target markets. The localization model, a useful and comprehensive tool in Web site localization, indicates that effective Web sites must adopt the specific cultural characteristics for the local market beyond the simple content and the product/service localization. However, an analysis of some international (local) Web sites of the largest multinationals shows that although some multinationals localize their international Web sites well, many others are weak in reflecting even some key localization features let alone full localization in their local Web sites. Managers are advised to utilize the Web sites localization model to increase the effectiveness of their international Web sites.

12.1. INTRODUCTION

As the size of global e-commerce is expanding, the global online population is becoming more varied and Web sites are considered as important communication medium for marketers. The number of global internet users has been growing rapidly since 2000 along with increasing amount of e-commerce sales. The number of Internet users in the world is now about 1.4 billion people that represent about 20 percent of global populations (internetworldstats.com, 2008) and growing online transactions both for Business to Consumer (B2C) and Business to Business (B2B) are driven by easy computer access, increasing number of internet users, and the continuing trend of globalization across the world.

12.1.1. Recent Trends in E-Commerce

There are several indicators explaining diverse group of global online population. Recent estimates by Internet World Stats (2008) show that only 30 percent of all internet users are now English speaking (427 million). The rests 70 percent of non-English speaking online consumers are composed of Chinese (233 million, 16.6%), Spanish (122 million, 8.7%), Japanese (94 million, 6.7%), French (67 million, 4.8%), German (64 million, 4.5%), Arabic (60 million, 4.2%), Portuguese (58 million, 4.1%), and Korean (35 million, 2.5%) (Internet World Stats, 2008). Moreover, cultural values are very different across these countries. For example, Asian cultural values and languages like Chinese, Korean, and Japanese are very different from those of western countries (Hofstede, 1980), which makes challenging for Western multinational companies to localize the content of their Web sites according to Asian cultural expectations. Consequently, many companies have acknowledged that building an e-commerce Website to suit international target consumers is more complex than they expected (Sheldon and Strader, 2002). U.S. and European multinationals have had many challenges in localizing their operations for fast growing Asian online population due to unfamiliar business practices, intense competition (Grau, 2007) and different linguistic and cultural expectations.

These growing global online environments provide international marketers with an exceptional opportunity to reach their potential customers throughout the world through Websites. They provides companies with an efficient marketing tool by reducing advertising and communication costs as well as by enabling firms to get customer feedback easily. Therefore, a Website is an important global medium to communicate with consumers.

12.1.2. To Standardize or to Localize?

The debate over "to standardize or to localize" have received attention continuously in the field of international business (Levitt, 1983; Onkvisit, 1999). For the last two decades, companies have been increasingly operating in many foreign markets. Serving local consumers effectively and thus achieving success in individual foreign markets require both a solid understanding of local values and a reflection of this understanding on business activities in foreign markets that will facilitate serving local markets. On the other hand, the process of transformation of local features into global ones is important because as technology advances cultural differences will be minimized and homogenous and people throughout the world will be unified into a single society and function together. Thus, multinationals need to sell the same thing in the same way everywhere (Levitt, 1983).

This debate has been extended to study Web communications. There is an argument that the use of a standardized Web site and communication strategy is necessary due to the global integration and the emergence of transnational Web style that reduces the cost (Sackmary and Scalia, 1999). However, there are also considerable motives that show the use of localized Web communication strategies to be effective. First, there exist culturally diverse customers worldwide which provide multinationals with exceptional business opportunities. Recent studies have showed that Web sites from different countries have unique national and linguistic characteristics (for example, see Baack and Singh, 2007) and that online consumer behavior and internet usage patterns vary cross-culturally (for example, see Bin et al., 2003). Second, consumers prefer Web sites that are localized to their linguistic, cultural and other locale specific expectations (for example, see Cyr and Trevor-Smith 2004). This is evidenced by the fact that consumers display positive attitude and purchase intention when they utilize localized Web sites in their online purchases. In general, worldwide internet users prefer to buy products only from Web sites that present information in their local language. Researchers have also found that culturally sensitive Web content enhances usability, accessibility, and Web site interactivity (Barber and Badre, 1998; Fock, 2000; Simon, 2001). Therefore, Web site localization is an important element for multinationals in their operations in global markets to appeal to the culturally diverse customers.

This chapter discusses from a cultural perspective how to create and manage Web sites that will enable multinationals to successfully localize their operations to effectively communicate with their stakeholders in their local target markets.

The chapter mainly explains, among other things, a useful and comprehensive tool used in Web site localization to provide international marketers with insights into assessing and measuring their Web localization efforts. This chapter is organized as follows: the next part includes the explanation of the localization tool with its operational features on the Web site. Next, after examining the extant literature on Web site localization, we show some good and bad examples of Web site localization followed by a discussion of how this localization tool can be useful in creating culturally-sensitive Web sites and thus boosting the quantity and the quality of Web communications with local stakeholders. The conclusion and recommendations are in the last part of the chapter.

12.2. THE LOCALIZATION MODEL

This section presents international marketing professionals several ways to construct and utilize an effective tool in assessing and measuring their localization efforts in reaching their foreign target consumers.

12.2.1. Assessing and Measuring the Localization Efforts

According to the definition by Localization Industry Standards Association (LISA; www.lisa.org), localization is defined as "the process of adapting products and services (Web sites documents, manuals, and software application) in accordance to linguistic, cultural, technical, and other locale-specific requirements of the target market." Therefore, full Web localization is the process of adapting all aspects of a Web site to meet the linguistic, cultural, and other requirements of a specific target environment while Web internationalization simply aims at creating modular and culturally neutral Web templates. As we discussed in the previous section, Web localization is a necessary component in international business operations to reflect country-specific features and to include overseas subsidiaries and local partners for their local input (Globalsight.com, 2000). Several studies have classified Web sites from highly globalized Websites to highly localized Websites according to their degree of localization. Table 12.1 includes various studies categorizing Web sites with different steps.

The level of Web site localization can be measured by using elements such as language translation, navigation structure, use of appropriate colors and graphics, Web display formats, etc. (Cyr and Lew, 2003). Based on the studies mentioned above and the definition of localization by LISA, the quality of Web site localization can be also measured by assessing how simple contents such as translation depth, descriptions of all policies on Web sites are localized, how product/service

Table 12.1. Categorization of Web sites

Studies	Description	Number of Categorization Level
Global Sight Corporation (2000)	• **Centralized:** the Web operations are planned and managed centrally with minimal input from local offices • **Decentralized:** separate e-businesses are developed and maintained by each local office • **Distributed (Hybrid) model:** gives enough flexibility to support local requirements	3
IDC Corporation (2001)	• **Tin:** do not practice any form of localization • **Bronze:** Web sites display only basic level information about foreign operations and the localization effort is restricted to just plain translation of Web sites for different countries • **Silver:** company allows each branch office to develop its own version of Web site • **Gold:** subsidiary can localize the Web site using the global template	4
Tixier (2005)	• **Global:** not adapted for local requirement • **Local:** adapted to cultural, technical, and administrative specificities of the country • **Glocal:** the implementation of the constraints of globalization in accordance with the constraints of the local environment	3
Singh and Boughton (2002)	• **Standardized:** having the same Web content, in the same language, for both domestic and international users. • **Proactive:** standardized Web sites for both domestic and international customers. However, such Web sites have contact information about foreign subsidiaries or operations. • **Global:** not only have contact information but also some basic country level information describing the activities and operations in a country. • **Localized:** category exhibit some level of localization in form of country specific time, date, zip code, and number formats. • **Highly localized:** highly developed and sophisticated country specific Web sites. They differ from the localized Web sites in terms of easy navigation, greater extent of localization, and prominent display of international Web presence.	5

are customized for the specific local customers, and lastly how overall Web sites are reflecting specific cultural factors of individual foreign market. Fully-localized Web sites, the ones completely adequate for final users, include localization of an entire site in terms of language, product and service, and culture of a country. In order to accomplish this, localization starts with localizing contents including simple translation, contact information updates, etc. Then, companies need to reflect their localizing efforts in products and service on Web sites and finally must adapt the interactive experience to a specific local market in accordance with its culture. Culturally-customized Web sites beyond simply localizing the content and product/service indicate that customers generally feel more comfortable and also display more positive attitudes toward culturally-customized Web sites.

12.2.1. Web Localization

The explanation of the parts of the Web localization together with its operational-ization variables is as follows.

Content Localization: This localization deals with such localization issues as translation, the equivalency, relevancy, navigation, support and currency of the Web site when firms first start to localize. It provides a general understanding of how companies have localized the basic Web content according to the target market characteristics. The variables are derived from previous studies by Cyr and Lew (2003) and Singh and Boughton (2002).

Product/Service Localization: This localization examines the use of appropri-ate colors and graphics, Web page structure, and product and service unique to the characteristics of the target market. Recommendations by Singh and Pereira (2005) and Yunker (2006) are used to analyze these variables.

Cultural Customization: Cultural customization or localization, which is highly localized, is examined by assessing the content adaptation according to the local culture. Using the framework developed by Singh and Pereira (2005), cultural values in international Web marketing are identified in terms of collectivism, uncertainty avoidance, power distance, masculinity, and high context.

Companies differ in their degree to achieve fully-customization on the Web. Content localization is the first and thus the most achieved part of overall localiza-tion efforts by companies. Then, product/service localization is the second most achieved part followed by the least achieved part of the cultural customization. Table 12.2 displays the operational features of these three kinds of localizations.

12.3. A BRIEF LITERATURE REVIEW OF WEB SITE LOCALIZATION

The growth of e-commerce activity and increasing rate of internationalization activity by firms have made Web sites vital for business operations and this fact has urged marketing professionals and academics to search for ways to increase effectiveness of Web sites. One important part of these efforts has focused on creat-ing culturally-sensitive Web sites. The scholarship on this subject is in its infancy. The literature includes two analysis bases: domestic Web sites (the ones designed for a domestic market such as Ford's domestic (the U.S.) market www.ford.com) and international Web sites (the ones designed for individual international markets such as the Ford's Japanese market www.ford.co.jp). The literature indicates that companies generally create more culturally-sensitive Web sites for their domestic markets while in most cases they partially ignore to reflect indigenous cultural values in their Web sites designed for their international markets.

Full evidence for reflection of local values in domestic Web sites has been provided by Singh and Matsuo (2002), Singh *et al* (2003), Singh *et al* (2005a), and Burgman *et al* (2006). The evidence in this regard covers the U.S., Japanese, Chinese, India, German, British, and Greek domestic Web sites. In addition, Okazaki and Alonso (2002), Okazaki (2004), Singh et al (2005b), and Singh et al (2006) analyzed local cultural depictions in international Web sites of Japanese firms operating in the US and Spain, the U.S. firms operating in Germany, France, India, and China. Partial evidence regarding local cultural depiction in the American and Spanish international Web sites of Japanese firms has been found by Okazaki and Alonso (2002) and Okazaki (2004) whereas other partial evidence has been found by Singh *et al* (2005b) in German and French Web sites of the U.S. firms. Nevertheless, Singh *et al* (2006) also found full evidence for local cultural depiction in Indian and Chinese

Table 12.2. The variables used to operationalize Web site localization

Type of Localization	Operational Features
Content Localization	• Comparing translation depth of local Website with translation depth of foreign Website • Local customer support and contact • Availability of all policies • Navigational ease
Product/Service Localization	• Web page structure • Use of local models, graphics, colors • Unique products and services for the specific target market
Cultural Localization	**Collectivism:** Community relations, Clubs or chat, Newsletter, Family theme, Symbols & picture of national identity, Loyalty program, Links to local Web **Uncertainty avoidance:** Customer service, Guided navigation, Local stores, Local term, Free trials or downloads, Customer testimonials, Tradition theme Toll free no. **Power distance:** Hierarchy info, Picture of important people or CEO, Quality assurance & award, Vision statement, Pride of ownership, Proper titles **Masculinity:** Quizzes and Games, Realism theme, Product effectiveness, Clear Gender role **High context:** Politeness and indirectness, Soft sell approach, Aesthetics and images

Web sites of the US firms. The popular and widely-used cultural frameworks by Hall (1976) and Hofstede (1980) were utilized in these studies.

Based on the evidence from the major studies in the literature, it seems that companies do not fully take into consideration reflecting local values in their international Web sites as much as they do in their domestic Web sites. Various facts may explain this situation: ignorance of local culture, lack of cultural orientation, underestimation of the importance of local culture, disbelief in culture-Web connection. Whatever the reason is, lack of local cultural reflection may create problems in serving local markets.

12.4. EXAMPLES OF GOOD AND BAD PRACTICES IN WEB SITE LOCALIZATION

In this section, we will give examples of some good Web sites fully reflecting as well as some bad Web sites partially reflecting local cultural values mentioned in the preceding literature review section. These examples show what kinds of problems companies can have by not fully reflecting local values in their international Web sites. The localization model indicated that an effective Web site must adopt specific cultural characteristics as well as content and product/service factors for its Web localization.

Based on the localization model, the international (such as Turkish) Web sites of McDonald's, Coca-Cola, Peugeot, and Volvo are very good examples of the reflection of full localization on the Web. Local Turkish cultural characteristics can easily be seen from the very home page to other pages. Cultural characteristics such as family theme, symbols and pictures of national identity, links to local Web sites, tradition theme, local stores, and local terminology are successfully displayed with local colors, figures, and symbols throughout their Web sites. The language, perhaps the most important feature in Web site localization, of these Web sites are all Turkish; it is expected that the language is normally Turkish and nothing is special about it. However, as we will see in bad practices, many multinationals do not fully utilize the local language in their local Web sites. In addition, product and content localization can also be seen easily in these good Web sites. With respect to product/service localization, these multinational companies provided good examples of product/service localizations in terms of ingredient, shape, packaging, color, size. With respect to content, these multinationals provided detailed information regarding company hierarchy, CEOs, quality assurance and awards, vision statement, pride of ownership appeal, proper titles, good privacy statement, product/service, rank of prestige of the company, terms and conditions of purchase, and customer service.

Despite these good examples, many multinationals, even those included in the Fortune 500 list, have very poorly designed international Web sites. For example, when we visit the Ecolab's domestic (the US) Web site, we see a good site according to the localization model. However, its international (Turkish) Web site is very poorly designed and do not reflect localization at all. The Ecolab's and Unisys' Turkish local Web pages ignore even one of the most important localization features: local language. Much information given in these sites are not Turkish but English. Therefore, local Turkish companies and consumers need to know English to get information online, which is not appropriate. Or, we may say that these companies do ignore the effectiveness of Web. It is perhaps needless to indicate that unless used local language, international Web sites are nothing but waste of resources and we see those examples.

The lesson from these examples of good and bad practices on the Web is that multinationals are advised to monitor their international Web sites that are designed either by themselves or their local affiliates. Web sites are very effective and do not cost much to establish and manage. Ignorance of localization features can make a big difference on the part of local consumers and potential partners among many others.

12.5. THE LOCALIZATION MODEL: WHY AND HOW USEFUL?

The preceding section indicated that even the largest multinationals in the world do have flaws in their especially international Web sites. Without a comprehensive and effective tool, the efforts to excel in Web communications will have such flaws. The localization model or tool we described is useful because it is both comprehensive and effective. Using this tool, marketers can successfully design international Web sites rich in content and in product/service information as well as culturally sensitive enough. For example, both Ecolab and Unisys, and other companies small or big, domestic or multinational, can effectively improve their Web sites taking into these factors mentioned in this chapter consideration. In addition, multinationals are advised to collaborate with their affiliates in constructing their local Web sites so that both corporate and local values can best be reflected on the Web.

12.6. CONCLUSION AND IMPLICATIONS

Localization of Web sites to linguistic, cultural, technical, functional, and other local-specific requirements is now a necessary strategy to effectively tap international online markets. To enjoy the advantage by using Web site localization strategy, companies must culturally customize their Websites beyond localizing simply content and product and service. In this chapter, we explained a tool useful in designing and managing culturally sensitive Web sites. One key conclusion of this chapter is that although Web site design seems easy especially using advanced software and other technological tools, this is just the initial and elementary part of Web sites. Web sites are designed to serve the purpose of enabling effective marketing communication that include communication of corporate and product/service information, public relations, sales, etc. Without considering appropriate local cultural features and reflecting these on various parts of Web design, multinationals will have many flaws in their international Web sites as shown in the examples. Therefore, reflection of technological superiority in the Web design should be supported with the reflection of superiority in terms of cultural sensitivity and awareness.

This chapter has various implications on the practices of international market-ers, Web designers, online sales professionals, public relation professionals, and e-commerce consultants. First, this localization tool can be a useful diagnostic tool in assessing and measuring the quality of Web site localization; sheer number of hits may not be always an appropriate indicator of Web site and thus marketing commu-nication effectiveness on the Web. Using this tool, professionals can see flaws and missing points in their online communication designs. They then can improve or change Web communication structures and designs accordingly. Second, it is worth to ask "how can a company communicate with its local consumers without using the local language?" It cannot. Therefore, multinationals can at least pay attention to using the local language in their local Web sites; this is the primitive but important level of localization. In addition to local languages, multinational companies face other diverse cultural features in their international markets; however, they do ignore many of these cultural features. Therefore, companies should not be blinded by the superiority of their products/services or domestic success; international markets do differ and success in these markets partly and/or mostly depends on the solid understanding of local cultures and the reflection of these in all company opera-tions including the Web. Last, full localization is the highest level of localization and without paying a close attention to particular cultural values and their potential impacts on operations, such a complete localization cannot be achieved. Further-more, localized Web content may alleviate the liability of foreignness, especially in countries where nationalistic orientation is high. Thus, the strategy of Web site localization is particularly highly recommended if multinationals want to operate in countries with especially high nationalistic tendencies.

REFERENCES

Baack, D. W., & Singh, N. (2007). Culture and Web Communications. *The Journal of Business Research, 60*(3), 181-188.

Barber, W., & Badre, A. (1998). Culturability: The Merging of Culture and Usability. *Proceedings of the Fourth Conference on Human Factors and the Web*, Basking Ridge, New Jersey. http://www.research.att.com/conf/hfWeb

Bin, W., Chen, S., & Sun, S. Q. (2003). Cultural differences in e-commerce: a comparison between the US and China. *Journal of Global Information Management, 11*(2), 48-55.

Burgmann, I., Kitchen, P., & Williams, R. (2006). Does culture matter on the Web? *Marketing Intelligence & Planning, 24*(1), 62-76.

Cyr, D., & Lew, R. (2003). Emerging challenges in the software localization industry. *Thunderbird International Business Review, 45*(3), 337-358.

Cyr, D., & Trevor-Smith, H. (2004). Localization of Web design: An empirical comparison of German, Japanese, and United States Web site characteristics. *Journal of the American Society for Information Science and Technology, 55*(13), 1199-1208.

Fock, H. (2000). Cultural Influences on Marketing Communication on the World Wide Web. *A Paper Presented in Multiculural Marketing Conference*, Hong Kong, Sept.

Grau, J. (2007). Asia-Pacific B2C E-Commerce: China, Japan and South Korea. Emarketer report (February), www.emarketer.com

Hall, E. (1976). *Beyond Culture*. Doubleday & Company: Garden City, NY.

Hofstede, G. (1980). *Culture's Consequences: International Differences in Work-related Values*. Sage: Beverly Hills, CA.

Internetworldstats.com (2008). World Internet Users and Population Stats. http://internetworldstats.com/stats.htm

Levitt, T. (1983). The Globalization of Markets. *Harvard Business Review, 61*(3), 92-103.

Okazaki, S., & Alonso, J. (2002). A content analysis of multinationals' Web communication strategies: cross-cultural research framework and pre-testing: *Internet Research, 12*(5), 380-390.

Okazaki, S. (2004). Do multinational standardize or localize? The cross-cultural dimensionality of product-based Web sites. *Internet Research, 14*(1), 81-94.

Onkvisit, S. (1999). Standardized International Advertising: Some Research Issues and Implications. *Journal of Advertising Research, 39*(6), 19-24.

Sackmary, B., & L. M. Scalia (1999). Cultural Patterns of World Wide Web Business Sites: A Comparison of Mexican and U.S Companies. *Seventh Cross Cultural Research Conference Proceedings*, http://marketing.byu.edu/htmlpages/ccrs/proceedings99/sackmary.htm

Sheldon, L., & Strader, T. (2002). Managerial issues for expanding into international Web-based electronic commerce. *SAM Advanced Management Journal, 67*(3), 22-30.

Simon S. (2001). The impact of culture and gender on Websites: an empirical study. *The Database for Advances in Information Systems, 32*(1), 18-37.

Singh, N., & Boughton, P. (2002). Measuring Web site globalization: A cross-sectional country and industry level analysis. *American Marketing Association Conference Proceedings, 13*, 302-317.

Singh, N., Fassott, G., Zhao, H., & Boughton, P. (2006). Cross-cultural analysis of German, Chinese and Indian consumers' perception of Web site adaptation. *Journal of Consumer Behavior, 5*(1), 56-68.

Singh, N., Kumar, V., & Baack, D. (2005). Adaptation of cultural content: evidence from B2C e-commerce firms. *European Journal of Marketing, 39*(1/2), 71-86.

Singh, N. & Pereira, A. (2005). *The Culturally Customized Web Site: Customizing Web Sites for the Global Marketplace*. Elsevier Butterworth-Heinemann: Burlington, MA.

Singh, N., Zhao, J., & Hu, X. (2003). Cultural adaptation on the Web: a study of American companies' domestic and Chinese Websites". *Journal of Global Information Management, 11*(3), 63-80.

Singh, N., Zhao, H., & Hu, X. (2005). Analyzing the cultural content of Web sites: A cross-national comparison of China, India, Japan, and US. *International Marketing Review, 22*(2), 129-146.

Yunker, J. (2003). *The globalization report card*. www.bytelevel.com

Chapter XIII
Conclusion, Implications, and Future Trends

ABSTRACT

The explosive proliferation of Internet users has led to dramatic shifts in the methodology of conducting business and the business paradigms. Currently, business organizations can reach anywhere in the world quite substantially within virtually no time. Consequently, supply chain management among partners including customers is so dynamic that business organizations are considering their customers and partners just attached with them. This changed paradigm has left an innumerable scope for exploring global markets, especially for the Internet economy, for example., EC. EC presents enormous opportunities for businesses, consumers, and governments. Since the Internet is the main driving force of EC, and the proliferation of the Internet across countries is terrific, it is quite understandable that Internet economy might have an uncertain future.

13.1. INTRODUCTION

At this stage, we are tempted to comment that adoption, usage, proliferation, and possible barriers for globalization of B2C EC is a very topical and challenging issue, and understanding and exploring this issue demands extensive attention by its own merits. Globalization strategy of WTO addresses the issue of EC diffusion to create the universal level playing field as the first priority. Therefore, exploring the diffusion of ICT and EC throughout the world, especially in developing countries, the possible adoption criteria of customers, the plausible barriers for proliferation of ICT and EC, and the effects of related socio-economical and cultural issues on the international market is a wide and potential area to investigate and understand.

In this regard, we have addressed, analyzed, and discussed in this book the globalization strategy of EC, service quality and the quality management practice for global EC, the diffusion and adoption of ICT and EC, cultural diversity, the impact of proliferation of ICT on consumers of developing countries, different drivers and inhibitors of the proliferation of EC, the purpose of implementation of E-government (EG) and EC, and cultural adaptability of websites. Although, the previous twelve chapters of this book are independent and individually complete in terms of concepts, based on philosophical underpinnings, these chapters are rationally interconnected and ultimately provide a comprehensive view of EC diffusion and adoption. This book also develops a grounded theory on resistance against the proliferation of EC and the impact of the Internet economy on both developed and developing countries. This final chapter of the book is devoted to developing a comprehensive conclusion by summarizing the concepts, paradigms, and theoretical framework so far revealed in the scope of addressing the proliferation of EC in connection with global adoption, resistance, and cultural evolution. Then, we attempt to figure out the implications of the analyzed issues of EC and illustrate and guide future research efforts under the scope of our conceptualization. This chapter is divided into four sections to discuss the abovementioned objectives.

13.2. CONCLUSION

The first division of the book has two chapters to provide basic concepts and interrelated issues of EC. In this connection, this division, in the first chapter, has illustrated fundamental concepts of M-commerce, a subset of EC, and explained online government system, viz., EG, an extensive use of ICT in public administration.

The first two chapters of this book are designed to provide introductory concepts and aspects of EC to the readers. These two chapters explain the fundamentals of EC, its diffusion, proliferation, adoption, globalization, and the contemporary managerial issues related to EC. The related concepts of EC are also defined and elaborated in this scope. From different statistical analyses and reports, it is imperative that shedding deep light on the diffusion of EC and its possible consequences in terms of globalization is congruent to most topical issues.

Service quality paradigms and quality management practice for successful proliferation of EC are explained in details in the second division. Since consumers of developed and developing countries differ significantly in perceiving service quality of EC, quality management practice (QMP) is imperative for the globalization of EC. These issues have potential merits to be discussed in this scope and are addressed in this division. This division has two chapters.

Globalization of EC is certainly a function of global consumers' acceptance, use, and adoption of this phenomenon. Very rationally, consumers' perception of EC is a determining factor in this context. When we conjecture that EC is inherently global, therefore, global consumers' perception of service quality, grounded in cultural and social diversity, is a potential criterion to be addressed and analyzed. Chapter III of the book is designed to impart some general idea about expectation and performance of different service quality attributes for B2C EC as revealed by different researchers.

Expectation and perception are not homogeneous across customers of all countries. Over the past 40 years, several models have been developed to provide an approach for the comparative analysis of different cultures. Although each of the articles developed cultural models that employed somewhat different terminologies, the conceptual dimensions generated offer sufficient convergence to provide support for their universality. Over the past three decades, the validity of these findings has been confirmed in studies exploring consumer behavior, consumer risk perception, and decision-making. Although customers of EC are global, present trends of EC are focused only on the customers of developed countries. However, due to significant cultural, social, economical, and political diversity, consumers' expectations and perception of different service quality factors of EC also vary universally. To be specific, we can draw a bold demarcation line between developed and developing countries. Consequently adoption, barriers, and proliferation of EC are significantly affected by perception of service quality of EC by different segmented regions of the world market. It is also argued that the level of importance of different service quality factors might vary either highly significantly, or non-significantly, depending on the cultural, social, political, and economical characteristics of those segmented regions. Therefore, adoption, cultural barriers, and proliferation of EC globally have strong connections with the perception of service quality of EC.

Chapter IV is focused on conceptualizing QMP for EC. Since the Internet, the media of EC, is inherently global, retailers can sell and consumers can buy products through web pages from anywhere in the world. Consequently, global proliferation and global consumers' acceptance are important issues to be considered. Therefore, implementation of QMP in EC, which is an advanced step to ensure continuously global consumers' preferences for quality, is a potential subject from its own merit to be discussed in this aspect. This chapter has also focused on some related quality aspects of EC.

The first two chapters are integrated and incorporated in division 1 and the third and fourth chapters are included in division 2 of the book to present and portray EC as a global phenomenon and to illustrate discourses of service quality of EC in the global context. Consequently, the globalization aspects of EC - convergence and divergence of globalization based on consumers' perception, and quality requirements and practices - are formulated in these two divisions. Therefore, these divisions basically serve to provide the background paradigms of EC diffusion and possible reasons of barriers from global consumers' perception of quality.

Division 3 is comprised of the issues which translate and formulate core concepts of diffusion of EC, particularly focused on behavioral, social, cultural, technological, economical, organizational, and governmental aspects of developing countries. This division is enthusiastic in finding theoretical frameworks of diffusion and adoption paradigms. In this connection, possible barriers of proliferation of EC from developed to developing countries are identified in conjunction with the impact of ICT on the majority of the world's population who are living in rural areas of developing countries. The digital divide concept is thoroughly investigated in the light of implementing the purpose and strategy of EC and EG. This division is comprised of the following five chapters.

The success of technology acceptance and successive diffusion is heavily dependent on adoption capability, the way it is diffused in the private and public sectors, and the way it is adopted by the adopters. In Chapter V, we are primarily devoted to finding the impact of diffusion of ICT, the primary driving force of EC in the private sector and EG in the public sector. We then successively identified the stakeholders of EC diffusion and their roles in the extensive proliferation of EC in any country. From a theoretical background and the functional characteristics of EC diffusion, we postulate that diffusion of EC might significantly affect social, cultural, organizational, technological, economical, and political behavior. We also developed a framework of diffusion comprising some critical factors, namely government role, capability, and globalization policy; private organizations' capability; consumers' preferences; global E-organizations' mission; infrastructure; human development; and the market mechanism.

Based on the EC diffusion framework, in Chapter VI, we analyzed some cases of EC diffusion. Then we contrasted those factors evaluated from a theoretical perspective with the same of the actual status of those countries. Developed countries are in a good position to develop their capability in relation to diffusion of EC. North American, Western European, and some Asian countries show strength in this respect. However, some developing countries also exhibit bright promise concerning diffusion factors for an ICT-based Internet economy. These countries include India, Brazil, China, Mexico, South Africa, Singapore, Taiwan, South Korea, Malaysia, Thailand, Hong Kong etc. Nevertheless, most of the developing countries are really at a premature stage in light of the roles of different stakeholders of EC diffusion. We witnessed that the theoretical diffusion framework we developed in Chapter V can systematically reveal the actual status of any country in terms of diffusion of EC.

In Chapter VII, we aimed to provide a fundamental conceptual framework for adoption of EC by the consumers of developing countries. We explained adoption process and developed our theoretical framework for factors enabling adoption of EC among consumers of developing countries. The technology absorption capacity of consumers of developing countries is quite different from that of developed countries. Before funding and implementing ICT and extending business periphery from developed to developing countries, there is the challenging issue of identifying the generic and distinctive characteristics of consumers of developing countries in terms of adoption of EC and overall technology absorption capabilities. In this era of globalization, the answer to these issues, and thus the development of a framework regarding the plausible adoption criteria of EC for consumers of developing countries, is of utmost importance. This chapter has explored rigorously the behavioral, technological, social, governmental, cultural, and economical perspectives for adoption of B2C EC by consumers, especially of developing countries. The fundamental paradigms of this framework are grounded in the extensive review of literature and theories and concepts related to information systems, psychology, marketing, economics, sociology, and organizational behavior. The study identified some predictor variables for the adoption of B2C EC which might have an integrated effect on the adoption process.

Internet and E-business technologies are being adopted by both large and small businesses with a desire to reduce operational costs, improve management capabilities, increase transaction speeds, and provide access to the global market. Chapter VIII is designed to shed light on the nature of relevant factors affecting the acceptance of Internet and E-business technologies in Canada. A research framework was developed and nine hypotheses were formulated to test the relationships. Surveys were conducted, and responses were obtained from business owners, managers, and other relevant informants in the region. Statistical analyses reveal that organizational readiness, management support, and the perceived ease of use and usefulness are significant factors that influence the acceptance of Internet and E-business technologies in Atlantic Canada's SMEs. The study used TAM (technology acceptance model) as the basis of investigation. In the context of the research setting, the result may suggest that if a local SME has a clear understanding of Internet/E-business technologies and finds such systems easy to use, the SME would be in a better position to appreciate the usefulness of such technologies.

Chapter IX has placed its effort in the deep-rooted area of diffusion of EC by investigating the effect of ICT's driven economy on the majority of the population of the world who are living in the rural areas of developing countries. This chapter is designed to conceptualize the fundamental but undeniable causes of resistance for diffusion of the Internet economy. The theme arises from the great controversy of whether ICT-intense projects either on a public level or private level spur the digital divide and ultimately fail to get the desired result in developing countries. Different countries, especially developed countries, set so many citizen-centric purposes for promoting the Internet economy globally. At the same time, different countries, especially developing countries, often resist globalization and the Internet economy. The primary reason for resisting the Internet economy and thus globalization is the digital divide. A strong paradigm lies behind this argument that the Internet economy is basically nursing and enhancing the digital divide between the West and East internationally and between rich and poor citizens nationally. The WTO, United Nations, and other global organizations suggest that the Internet economy can bring equalization among countries internationally and among citizens nationally. To verify the claims, we described the purposes of promoting Internet economy like EC and EG and possible barriers against the proliferation of B2C EC and globalization. Then we investigated whether those purposes can be fulfilled by launching an ICT-based economy globally. More precisely, we aimed to investigate whether the majority of the world's population who are living in the rural areas of developing countries have the capability to adopt ICT and gain functional benefits from this. We propose two theoretical frameworks: an ad-hoc phase framework to identify separately the adoption capability of rural and urban populations and a post-hoc phase to identify the impact of implementing ICT on different private and public projects among the rural and urban populations separately.

Finally, division 4 with four chapters is engaged in developing a globalization strategy for B2C, EC acknowledging the fact that there might be significant differences, particularly between developed and developing countries in light of cultural, social, behavioral, logistical, legal, and financial aspects. The primary force of this conceptual framework of globalization strategy is theory driven. Therefore, by analyzing some country-context environments and multinational websites as examples, we attempted to justify our claims in suggesting a globalization strategy. This division also summarizes our findings, proposals, implications, and future guidelines.

In Chapter X, we conceptualize the issues, functional characteristics, and barriers of B2C EC related to globalization. Difference evidences suggest that successful globalization of EC demands a continuing understanding of changing global aspects, customer characteristics, and the fundamental paradigms that contribute to understand the strategic suitability of globalization for seamless movement of EC.

From this perspective, it is imperative that E-retailers who aim to capture the global market should identify the critical issues of globalization that are most concerned with their business pattern, and develop suitable and appropriate strategies to sustain, expand, and get a competitive advantage while adopting the opportunities of globalization. This chapter is designed to address a globalization strategy for B2C EC operation which is completely focused on external perspectives for selecting a globalization strategy. There are numerous internal factors such as firms' internal capacity, financial ability, availability of market and distribution channels, objective and vision etc, which are essential to determine a firm's ability to spread globally, are not the focus of this chapter. We strongly believe that consideration of those external factors, which affect the overall global market, can provide an integrative view of the globalization approach. The propositions proposed in this study are fundamentally grounded on the digital divide between developed and developing countries.

Our proposed paradigms can get strong support from the compelling findings of Chapters XI and XII. The continuing growth in global online markets necessitates companies to attract international consumers and motivate online transactions. Marketers are faced with a question of whether to culturally adapt their web sites or launch standardized global web sites. Chapter XI provides deep insight to reveal that instead of a "transnational web style" with features, images and categories common across nations, a culturally unique web style is emerging on the web. Thus, marketers should be cautious when launching standardized or machine-translated web sites for their global audience. The findings suggest that even though the Internet is global, consumers still interpret web content using the broad guidelines of their culture. This chapter shows that effective international web presence is not just about translating a web site into a local language. A truly localized web site is one that is linguistically, technically and most importantly culturally customized to locale-specific requirements. This chapter provides insights into the importance and impact of web site cultural customization on consumer perception of international web sites.

The aim of Chapter XII is to provide further paradigms of cultural influence on the globalization of EC, using the three-stage localization model, a useful and comprehensive tool in web site localization, as local consumers prefer culturally adapted web sites to standardized web sites. The study contributes to the existing literature by showing that global consumers prefer web sites adapted to their local culture, and that culture influences consumer beliefs, attitudes, and purchase intention on the web. The major marketing implication and contribution of this study is that it provides grounded theory indicating that effective web sites must adopt specific cultural characteristics for the local market beyond the simple content and the product/service localization.

13.3. MANAGERIAL IMPLICATIONS

This book provides a deep insight into the globalization of B2C EC and the minimization of the digital divide between developed and developing countries by detecting resistances and also facilitating factors for diffusion of B2C EC in developing countries. Therefore, for the practitioners who are searching for anticipated ways to extend their EC operations globally and the researchers who are engaged in conceptualizing EC diffusion criteria in developing countries, this book might have potential implications. Governments and ancillary organizations of developing countries will also be facilitated to identify and develop fundamental capabilities for expansion of EC in local markets by studying this book. This book also contributes to the knowledge of marketing, information technology, and electronic organization studies students.

We hope that this book contributes towards concept, theory, practice, and policy. The theoretical contribution of this book is that it identifies, addresses, organizes, and integrates the present situation of developing countries in terms of information technology, criteria of developing fundamental capabilities to accept and diffuse suitable technology, background of EC diffusion, and critical factors for proliferation of EC through proper globalization strategy. The book specifically develops theories in this scope to understand 1) background concepts and service quality of EC; 2) adoption, diffusion, and resistance of EC by global consumers and impact of proliferation of ICT in developing countries; and 3) globalization strategy of EC with special attention on technology acceptance, behavioral intention, and cultural aspects. It also focuses on cultural evolution with special consideration of the fundamental capabilities of developing countries focusing on the relation of technology acceptance, technology use, global paradigms, cultural aspects, and state policy. To develop concepts related to the impact of ICT and digital divide as a consequence of ICT proliferation in developing countries, precise description of EG is also included in this book.

From the above review of all the chapters and discussions, we can precisely draw some compelling conclusive remarks as managerial implications of the findings by interlinking the discourses of all the chapters of this book. These are:

1. The explosive diffusion of Internet users universally has led to dramatic shifts in the methodology of conducting business and also the business paradigms. This changed paradigm has left an innumerable scope for exploring global markets, especially for the Internet economy, viz., EC.

2. Therefore, exploring the diffusion of ICT and EC throughout the world, especially in developing countries, as well as possible adoption criteria of customers, plausible barriers for proliferation of ICT and EC, and the effects

of related socio-economical and cultural issues on the international market, is a wide potential area to theorize.

3. Globalization of EC is certainly a function of global consumers' acceptance, use, and adoption of this phenomenon. Consumers' perception of EC is a determining factor in this context. Very rationally, global consumers' perception of service quality, grounded in cultural and social diversity, is a potential criterion for EC diffusion.

4. Implementation of quality management principles and practice in EC context is a new theme which needs extensive research for sustainability and future proliferation. Quality is a potential indicator for global acceptance of EC.

5. However, the success of technology acceptance and successive diffusion is heavily dependent on the adoption capability, the way it is diffused in the private and public sectors, and the way it is adopted by the adopters.

6. Therefore, the diffusion of EC has multi-dimensional aspects, and the process of diffusion is controlled by the social, cultural, organizational, technological, economical, and political behavior of global consumers. So, the possibility and pattern of EC diffusion is country dependent. We cannot copy or transfer a successful diffusion model from developed countries to developing countries, since social, cultural, economical, technological, organizational, and political characteristics of developed and developing countries differ significantly.

7. Excluding the consumers, the strong stakeholder of EC diffusion globally, the government role and globalization policy, local private organizations, and international online organizations also play controlling roles in the diffusion of EC in the country context. When all the associated stakeholders of the market mechanism, demand side, supply side, and intermediary function favor adoption of EC, then only systematic diffusion of EC is possible and also feasible in a country context.

8. The countries that have shown high promise in adopting and diffusing Internet-based economy, like USA, Canada, UK, Singapore, Japan, EU countries etc, have strong profiles and supports from all the associated stakeholders of EC diffusion.

9. Organizational readiness, management support, and the perceived ease of use and usefulness are significant factors to influence the acceptance of Internet and E-business technologies in Canada.

10. The technology absorption capacity of consumers of developing countries is quite different from that of developed countries. Before funding and implementing ICT and extending business periphery from developed to developing countries, it is a challenging issue to identify the generic and distinctive characteristics of consumers of developing countries in terms of adoption of EC and overall technology absorption capabilities.

11. Awareness, availability of infrastructure, relative advantage, compatibility, website quality, information quality, multilingual options, and trust have positive relations while complexity has negative relations with adoption of EC by consumers of developing countries. Also, these constructs can measure the status of developing countries whether B2C EC could pursue consumers to use their systems.

12. Since the factors mentioned in the previous clause are mostly absent for the majority of consumers in developing countries, especially those who are living in rural areas, and/or they do not have that ability to adopt Internet economy, and/or they do not have the capability to perceive functional benefits from adoption of ICT, there is a great possibility that Internet economy, viz., EG on a public level and EC on a private level would spur a digital divide and ultimately fail to get the desired result in developing countries.

13. Therefore, the successful globalization of EC demands a continuing understanding of changing global aspects, customer characteristics, especially of developing countries, and the fundamental paradigms that contribute to understand the strategic suitability of globalization for seamless movement of EC.

14. Due to several barriers and constraints, EC functionally focuses primarily on local or regional markets. However, for the worldwide proliferation of the Internet, the main vehicle of B2C EC, EC has a great opportunity to spread throughout the world among the consumers of both developed and developing countries. Therefore, adoption of B2C EC by customers among developing countries can be considered as a crucial factor for proper globalization.

15. If developing countries have technological, social, political, and financial (tool) capabilities simultaneously to adopt EC, then E-retailers can extend their business periphery from developed countries to developing countries and adopt a globalization strategy. Otherwise the present status of regionalization is the appropriate solution for EC operation.

16. In several case studies it has been revealed that even though the Internet is global, consumers still interpret web content using the broad guidelines of their culture. Therefore, the evidences suggest to international marketers and academics that instead of a standard online system, a culturally unique web style is emerging on the web.

17. Therefore, the major obstacle for companies extending their EC globally is to understand the needs of global customers and overcome the cultural, social, and behavioral barriers on the web. This is because consumers prefer web sites adapted to their local culture, and that culture influences consumer beliefs, attitudes, and purchase intentions on the web.

13.4. FUTURE TRENDS

Some scholars argue that cultural differences might be harmonized gradually. Gradual convergence of cultural differences might develop harmony in quality perception of EC. And that harmony in social, behavioral, and cultural perception might ensure that a standardized globalization approach is a potential possibility for EC in future. As changes occur and there is a gradual convergence in quality perception by consumers across countries, the standardized globalization approach might succeed. Although consumers still prefer culturally congruent websites, the recent trend of unstoppable and a very high adoption rate of the Internet in developing countries can create an Internet-based single culture globally. Or, at least, the Internet has a strong influence on the synchronization of the global culture and making a bridge between eastern and western culture. This trend is pushing further to adopt a standard trend to accept standard EC operations globally.

There has also been an advancement in the diffusion of the global EC. The world has started to globalize over the past couple of decades, and due to the invention of the Internet and fall of communism, it has continued to globalize in an inevitable, irresistible movement. Different potential aspects have substantially contributed to this globalization. These factors include a stable market, political synchronization (emancipation of east Europe from a controlled market), rapid proliferation of the market economy, worldwide investment, economic advances in several developing countries, a supply chain of production and marketing, advances in telecommunication technologies and the Internet, increases in world travel, and the growth of global media.

Though a major percentage of on-line purchases are contributed by the developed countries – the U.S., Japan, UK, France, Germany, Canada, Italy, etc – and advanced developing countries – such as China, India, Brazil, Malaysia, South Korea, Taiwan, Singapore, and Thailand – other developing countries are also gradually entering the Internet-based market with significant promise. With the on-going efforts to build a global information infrastructure and a nationwide information infrastructure, developing countries are at the introductory stage of turbulent shifts in the information age. Within the past decade, the scenario has changed significantly in this context. This trend of different countries coming and joining in a single hub of ICT can create an enormous opportunity of EC to be globalized.

All the big companies are now considering pushing their markets throughout the world. However, in terms of cost of product and service, business operation, marketing, and other related issues, country-based market policy has been proven inefficient. As a result, international corporations are now very eager to adopt a consistent and uniform business policy which can sustain and prevail with competitive advantage throughout the world, viz., globalization.

The WTO and other global organizations are engaged and very much enthusiastic to liberalize the world market and create harmony among developed and developing countries in terms of rules and regulations prevailing to control the market, subsidies, duty, and tariffs. World globalization policy is continuously advocating a process of interdependence among states, and also interconnected and social relations are stretched. This trend is also a favorable condition for the diffusion of EC worldwide in future.

Due to the proliferation of the market economy, governments of most of the countries are also reforming their financial market with a favorable transaction policy. Banking systems have been revolutionalized within the past decade in both developed and developing countries. So many banks, even in developing countries have adopted online transaction systems. This revolutionary change might create favorable facilities for consumers, particularly of developing countries, for payment of global EC transactions.

Shipment and return of items is a possible barrier of EC to operate globally. However, lifting or gradual removal of other barriers can easily solve this problem by developing some regional distributing warehouses in some key locations.

So, we have identified several potential barriers for diffusion of EC globally. At the same time, we have evaluated the merits of those barriers to overcome. We find some reasons to be optimistic that the future trend of EC might have a stronghold in the world economy through capitalizing the benefits of massive globalization. However, the potential contribution of different stakeholders in this connection will ultimately determine the speed of globalization of EC.

However, we suggest that practitioners and researchers should put strong efforts into monitoring the market, behavioral, cultural, social, technological, financial, organizational, and government policy criteria, which have been revealed in this book as the potential aspects for diffusion of EC, to explicitly conceptualize the future trend of EC globalization.

About the Authors

Mahmud A. Shareef is currently a research associate, Ontario Research Network for Electronic Commerce (ORNEC), Ottawa, Canada. He is also a PhD candidate in Management of the Sprott School of Business, Carleton University, Ottawa, Canada. He received his graduate degree from both the Institute of Business Administration, University of Dhaka, Bangladesh in Business Administration and Carleton University, Ottawa, Canada in civil engineering. His research interest is focused on quality management of e-commerce and e-government. He has published more than 30 papers addressing adoption and quality issues of e-commerce and e-government in different refereed conference proceedings and international journals. He is the author of 2 book chapters in information technology handbook and has published 2 reputed books on quality management issues. He is an internationally recognized information technology (IT) consultant and has presented seminal papers in IT seminars. He was the recipient of more than 10 academic awards including 2 Best Research Paper Awards in the UK and Canada

Yogesh K. Dwivedi is a lecturer in Information Systems at the School of Business and Economics, Swansea University, Wales, UK. He obtained his PhD entitled, *Investigating consumer adoption, usage and impact of broadband: UK households*, and MSc in information systems from the School of Information Systems, Computing and Mathematics, Brunel University, UK. His doctoral research has been awarded the '*Highly Commended Award*' by the European Foundation for Management and Development (EFMD) and Emerald Group Publishing Ltd. His research focuses on the adoption and diffusion of information and communication technology (ICT) in organisations and society. As well as having presented at leading IS conferences such as *ECIS* and *AMCIS*, he has co-authored several papers which have appeared (or will be appearing) in international referred journals such as *Communications of the ACM, Information Systems Journal, European Journal of Information Systems, Information Systems Frontiers, Journal of Operational Research Society, Journal of Computer Information Systems, Industrial Management & Data Systems* and *Electronic Government, An International Journal*. He has authored a book on *Consumer Adoption and Use of Broadband* and also co-edited a *Handbook of Research on Global Diffusion of Broadband Data Transmission*. He is senior editor of *DATABASE for Advances in Information Systems,* assistant editor of *Transforming Government: People, Process and Policy* and member of the editorial board/review board of several journals including, *Journal of Enterprise Information Management, Journal of Computer Information Systems, Electronic Government, An International Journal* as well as being a guest/issue co-editor of the *DATABASE for Advances in Information Systems, Government Information Quarterly, Information Systems Frontiers, Journal of Enterprise Information Management, Journal of Electronic Commerce Research* and *Electronic Government*, an international journal. He is a member of the Association of Information Systems (AIS) and life member of the Global Institute of Flexible Systems Management, New Delhi.

Michael D. Williams is a professor in the School of Business and Economics at Swansea University in the UK. He holds a BSc from the CNAA, an MEd from the University of Cambridge, and a PhD from the University of Sheffield. He is a member of the British Computer Society and is registered as a chartered engineer. Prior to entering academia professor Williams spent twelve years developing and implementing ICT systems in both public and private sectors in a variety of domains including finance, telecommunications, manufacturing, and local government, and since entering academia, has acted as consultant for both public and private organizations. He is the author of numerous fully refereed and invited papers within the ICT domain, has editorial board membership of a number of academic journals, and has obtained external research funding from sources including the European Union, the Nuffield Foundation, and the Welsh Assembly Government.

Nitish Singh is assistant professor of international business at the Boeing Institute of International Business at Saint Louis University. Previously, he was a professor at California State University (CSU) Chico and headed the localization certification program there. His educational efforts in the field of localization have been supported by U.S. Department of Education, CSU, Google, HP, IBM, Microsoft and other companies. He is the co-author of *The Culturally Customized Web Site: Customizing Web Sites for the Global Marketplace*. Nitish holds a PhD in marketing and international business from Saint Louis University, an MBA from Pune University-India and an MA in marketing from University of Glamorgan, UK. He has been active in training and consulting in the field of localization for websites, international e-business strategy, doing business in China and India, and marketing to Hispanics online. Nitish is the recipient of research excellence awards from CSU and Saint Louis University and was named one of the top 10 reviewers for International Marketing Review. His research has appeared in the *Journal of International Business Studies*, *Journal of Business Research*, *Psychology & Marketing*, *International Marketing Review*, *Journal of Electronic Commerce Research*, *Thunderbird International Business Review*, *Journal of Advertising Research*, *Multinational Business Review*, *Journal of Consumer Behavior*, and others.

* * *

Princely Ifinedo is an assistant professor at the Shannon School of Business, Cape Breton University, Canada. He earned his PhD in information systems science from the University of Jyväskylä, Finland. He also holds an MBA in international management from Royal Holloway College, University of London, UK, a MSc in informatics from Tallinn University of Technology, Estonia and a BSc in mathematics/computer science from the University of Port-Harcourt, Nigeria. His current research interests include e-learning, e-business, e-government, ERP success measurement, social informatics, IT/business alignment, and the diffusion of IS/IT in transiting and developing economies. He has presented at various international IS conferences and his works have appeared in such journals as *Journal of Computer Information Systems*, *Enterprise Information Systems*, *Journal of Information Technology Management*, and *Journal of Global Information Technology Management*. Dr. Ifinedo has authored (and co-authored) 60 peer-reviewed papers. He is affiliated with AIS, ASAC, DSI, and ACM.

Joseph P. Little is a PhD student in international business and marketing at the John Cook School of Business, Saint Louis University. He received his MBA from Indiana University Southeast. His research interests include cross-cultural consumer behavior focusing on consumer animosity and consumer response to corporate social responsibility. Joseph has presented his research at the Academy of International Business and the American Marketing Association annual meetings.

Ji Eun Park was born and raised in In-cheon, Korea. After earning her Bachelor of Arts degree from Chung-Ang University, Korea, she pursued her MBA degree from Korea Development Institute of public policy and management in 2002. Since August 2006, Ji Eun has been actively involved in teaching and research at the John Cook School of Business at Saint Louis University. Her research interests have focused primarily on Website localization, corporate social responsibility, and animosity in an international context.

Mohini Singh is professor of Information Technology and Digital Business in the School of Business Information Technology at RMIT University in Australia. She is internationally recognised for her research and publications in the areas of information technology, e-business and e-government. Her track record includes research on e-business opportunities and challenges, e-business evaluation, B2B e-business issues, e-procurement, e-business intermediaries and e-government; outcomes of which have resulted in journal publications, book chapters and international conference proceedings. She is the principal editor of two highly regarded books on e-business and serves as a member on the editorial boards of several international journals. She has delivered key note addresses at international forums and presented her research on e-business to the Parliament of Victoria for policy development on telecommunications infrastructure for business in rural Victoria, by invitation. She is the program chair, for the forthcoming International Conference on E-Government 2008 - http://academic-conferences.org/iceg/iceg2008/iceg08-home.htm

Serkan Yalcin is a doctoral student at the John Cook School of Business, Saint Louis University (MO, USA). He has academic experience in different regions of the world such as Turkey, Republic of Georgia, Kyrgyzstan, and the U.S. His research interests include international marketing strategy, internationalization of brands, e-commerce, culture and localization, and cross-cultural consumer behavior. Some if his research appeared in such academic journals as *Multinational Business Review*, *Journal of Promotion Management*, and *Journal of Developmental Entrepreneurship*.

Index

A

Ad-hoc phase 205
adoption, perspectives and process 146
ARPANET - Advanced Research Projects
        Agency 11

B

B2C electronic-commerce, characteristics
        27
Bangladesh e-commerce 126
business-to-business (B2B) EC 20
business-to-business (B2B) transactions 2
business-to-consumer (B2C) EC 19
business-to-customer (B2C) transactions 2
business-to-government (B2G) EC 20

C

consciousness index 207
consumer-to-business (C2B) EC 20
consumer-to-consumer (C2C) EC 20
cultural diversity 55
cultural integration 197
customizing international Web sites
        251–268

D

Denmark e-commerce 112
developed countries, e-commerce 109,
        126
developing countries, e-commerce adop-
        tion 140–167
developing countries with ICT 119
diffusion impacts 84
diffusion of e-commerce 82
diffusion of e-commerce, critical factors
        90
diffusion of e-commerce, stakeholders 87
digital divide 201
Doha Development Agenda (DDA) 190

E

e-commerce (EC), introduction 1–8
e-commerce, classification 19
e-commerce, definition 18
e-commerce, global phenomenon 5
e-commerce, recent trends 270
e-commerce, relevant strategy 222–250
e-commerce adoption 29
e-commerce adoption in developing coun-
        tries 140–167

e-commerce diffusion 79–106
e-commerce diffusion in developed and
        developing countries 107–139
e-commerce service quality 41
e-government (EG) 9
e-government (EG), a subset 23
EC, quality concepts 68
EC adoption 55
EC adoption, literature review 143
EC adoption, theoretical framework 148
EC proliferation 55
EC service quality, models 44
electronic-commerce 15
electronic-government (EG) 187
electronic data interchange (EDI) 80

G

General Agreement of Tariffs and Trade
        (GATT) 110
General Agreement on Trade in Services
        (GATS) 110
Ghana e-commerce 130
global consumers, e-commerce 40–64
globalization 222–250, 227
globalization, cultural aspect and service
        quality perception 237
globalization, e-commerce 30
globalization, financial tool aspect 236
globalization, internationalization, local-
        ization and translation (GILT) 254
globalization, political aspect 235
globalization, technological and social
        aspect 233
globalization policy 109
globalization pursuit 198
globalization strategy 230
global quality management practice 65–78
government-to-business (G2B) EC 20
government-to-consumer (G2C) EC 20

H

human capital index 208

I

ICT impact 203
India e-commerce 120

Information Processing Techniques Office
        (IPTO) 11
internationalization 254
international Web sites, depiction of cul-
        ture 258
Internet, the evolution of 11
Internet economy, promoting 189
Internet economy, resistance 186

L

localization 254
localization model 272
localization model, how useful? 277

M

management issues 31
maritime Canada SMEs 168–185
measurement model, assessing 177
Mexico e-commerce 123

P

PLS (Partial Least Squares) 175
post-hoc phase 209
proliferation of Internet economy 186–221
proliferation of Internet economy, barriers
        195

Q

quality concepts for EC 68
quality management practice (QMP)
        65, 71, 283

R

regionalization 228
related concepts, defintion 227
resistance of Internet economy 186–221

S

self-service technology 70
service quality of e-commerce 40–64
small and medium enterprises (SMEs) 169
software quality matrix 69
standardize or to localize 271
structural equation modeling (SEM) 175
structural model, assessing 177

T

technology acceptance model (TAM) 171
technology index 208
total data quality management (TDQM)
      69
total quality management (TQM) 71
traditional service quality 43
transactional quality 71

U

uniform business globalization 198
USA e-commerce 115

V

virtual communal marketing 70

W

Web localization 274
Web site cultural customization 256
Web site cultural customization, impact
      262
Web site localization, cultural perspective
      269–280
Web site localization, good and bad prac-
      tices 276
wireless application protocol (WAP) 21
WTO 195